S0-AXJ-334

PSYCHOLOGISTS & THEIR THEORIES

for Students

PSYCHOLOGISTS & THEIR THEORIES
for Students

VOLUME 2: L-Z, Glossary, Index

Kristine Krapp, Editor

THOMSON
GALE

Detroit • New York • San Francisco • San Diego • New Haven, Conn. • Waterville, Maine • London • Munich

Psychologists and Their Theories for Students

Product Manager
Meggin Condino

Project Editor
Kristine Krapp

Editorial
Mark Springer

Indexing Services
Katherine Jensen

Rights and Aquisitions
Margaret Abendroth, Ann Taylor

Imaging and Multimedia
Robyn Young, Lezlie Light, Dan Newell

Product Design
Pamela A. Galbreath

Manufacturing
Evi Seoud, Lori Kessler

LIBRARY OF CONGRESS CATALOGING-IN-PUBLICATION DATA

Psychologists and their theories for students / Kristine Krapp, editor.
    p. cm.
      Includes bibliographical references and index.
      ISBN 0-7876-6543-6 (set : hardcover : alk. paper) —
      ISBN 0-7876-6544-4 (v. 1) —
      ISBN 0-7876-6545-2 (v. 2)
      1. Psychologists. 2. Psychology. I. Krapp, Kristine M.

BF109.A1P72 2004
150'.92'2—dc22
                                2004011589

Table of Contents

Introduction

Purpose of the book

The purpose of *Psychologists and Their Theories for Students* is to provide readers with in-depth information on major psychological theories, past and present, as well as the people who developed them. *Psychologists* explains each psychologist's theories in detail, then analyzes the historical context and critical reaction to the theories. Biographical information is also included. *Psychologists* is designed to meet the needs of high school and college students in the first two years of study.

Psychologists contains entries on 20 of the most frequently studied or most pertinent psychologists in history. Each entry is accompanied by sidebars containing information on related theories or other psychologists who were close to the subject of the entry, either through proximity or ideology. Photos and charts are included. Entries follow a standard structure and include a personal chronology, list of the subject's principal publications, sources, and bibliographic information on materials for a student's further exploration of the subject. The entries are accompanied by a historical overview of the science of psychology, chronology, glossary of terms used in the book, and a general index.

Selection criteria

Many individuals had input into the final content of *Psychologists*. A preliminary list of most-studied psychologists and theories was compiled from the suggestions of librarians who regularly receive requests from students for further information on psychologists studies in their classes. Another group of high school librarians and psychology teachers gave input on the list of entries and made suggestions for accompanying sidebars. Two academic advisers gave final approval on the list of topics and reviewed the content of every entry. Writers also gave input on the content of sidebars and complementary graphics.

How each entry is organized

Each entry, or chapter, in *Psychologists* focuses on one psychologist and his or her most important theories. Each entry heading lists the full name of the psychologist, birth and death dates, nationality, and occupation. The following elements are contained in each entry:

- **Brief overview:** An overview of the psychologist, his or her life, and introduction to the nature of his or her work.

- **Biography:** This section includes basic facts about the psychologist's life, including family background, education, positions held, and information on marriage and family.

- **Theories:** Detailed account of the psychologist's main theory(s). Each is broken down into sections on main points of the theory, explanations, and examples.

- **Historical context:** Analysis of the political, social, and scientific events in play during the psychologist's life, many of which may have influenced his or her career.

- **Critical response:** A summary of criticism of the theories, both during the psychologist's time and since. Related theories that other psychologists developed as a response to the main subject's theories are addressed here.

- **Theories in action:** A summary of how the theory is used in study or treatment. Sections on research and case studies are included. A final section explains the relevance of the psychologist's work to modern readers.

- **Sources:** Bibliographic citations of sources the writer used compile the entry.

- **Further readings:** Bibliographic citations of sources that readers, can go to for further information on the subject.

- **Sidebars:** Related topics are included in "Further analysis" sidebars. "Biography" sidebars are devoted to those psychologists close to the entry's subject.

Additional features

Psychologists further benefits readers with these features:

- Photos and charts within the entries give the reader more information on the topics being discussed.

- Lists of every psychologist's principal publications are included in the entries.

- A personal chronology in every psychologist's entry gives the important events in his or her life.

- A collective chronology of the psychologists' lives included in the frontmatter, in addition to selected world events, gives reader context for the psychologists' lives.

- A brief essay on the history of psychology gives the reader historical context and discusses major schools of psychological thought.

- A glossary of terms used in the book explains important concepts.

- A general index allows easy access to entry information.

We welcome your suggestions

The editor of *Psychologists and Theories for Students* welcomes your comments and suggestions. Please direct all correspondence to:

Editor, *Psychologists and Their Theories
 for Students*
Thomson Gale
27500 Drake Road
Farmington Hills, MI 48331-3535

Advisers

Three high school faculty members were consulted about the initial scope and nature of the book. Two university psychology professors finalized the entry list and review the entry content. The content review advisers include:

Bonnie Ruth Strickland, PhD: former President, American Psychological Association; Professor Emeritus of Psychology, University of Massachusetts, Amherst, Massachusetts.

William O'Donohue, PhD: Nicholas Cummings Professor of Organized Behavioral Healthcare Delivery, Department of Psychology, University of Nevada Reno, Reno, Nevada; adjunct faculty, University of Hawaii, Manoa; Distinguished Practitioner, National Academies of Practice.

High school scope advisers include:

Virginia Chaussee: Librarian, Compadre High School, Tempe, Arizona.

Charlie Jones: Library media specialist, Plymouth High School, Plymouth, Michigan.

Dana Serlin: Psychology teacher, North Farmington High School, Farmington Hills, Michigan.

Contributors

Linda Wasmer Andrews, MS: Science writer specializing in psychology, Albuquerque, New Mexico. Wrote entries on Albert Bandura, Alfred Binet, and Robert Yerkes.

Paula Ford-Martin, MA: Clinical and consumer medical writer, Wordcrafts, Warwick, Rhode Island. Wrote entries on Ivan Pavlov and Mary Ainsworth.

Rebecca Frey, PhD: Science and medical freelance writer, New Haven, Connecticut. Wrote entries on Aaron Beck, Carl Jung, Lawrence Kohlberg, and Kurt Lewin.

Gary Gilles, MA, LCPC: Psychologist and freelance writer, Chicago, Illinois. Wrote entries on Sigmund Freud and B.F. Skinner.

Clare Hanrahan, BS (Psychology): Author and researcher, CelticWordCraft, Asheville, North Carolina. Wrote entries on Kenneth Bancroft Clark and Jean Piaget.

Denise Schmutte, PhD (Clinical psychology): Freelance writer, Edmonds, Washington. Wrote entry on Abraham Maslow.

Joan Schonbeck, RN: Nurse and freelance writer, Marlborough, Massachusetts. Wrote entries on Karen Horney, Carl Rogers, and Max Wertheimer.

J.E. Spehar: Freelance biographer and science writer, Canton, Ohio. Wrote entries on George Kelly, Wilhelm Wundt, and Anne Anastasi.

Historical Overview

In a very real sense, psychology is probably as old as humanity. In fact, some scientists have argued that one of the defining characteristics of human beings is the ability to study the behavior of others, imagine oneself in their positions and make predictions about their future behavior based on these insights. Certainly, there is evidence that humans have done just that at least since the dawn of recorded history. Ancient writings from China, Egypt, India, Persia, and Greece all display an intense curiosity about the nature of thought, memory, emotion, sensation, and motivation.

The scientific study of psychology is a much more recent development, however. Many historians date the birth of modern psychology from the founding of the first experimental psychology laboratory by Wilhelm Wundt in 1879. As a science, then, psychology is still relatively young. Yet, over the course of little more than 120 years, it has managed to make a tremendous impact on both the academic world and society at large. Psychology has given rise to influential schools of thought ranging from psychoanalysis to behaviorism, and from Gestalt psychology to cognitive psychology.

Forerunners of psychology

Philosophical roots   Questions about mental life and human behavior have fascinated philosophers through the centuries. In seventeenth-century France, the great philosopher and mathematician René Descartes conceived of a system of true knowledge that was modeled on mathematics and supported by a philosophical approach called rationalism. This approach held that knowledge was derived from the use of reason and logic. Descartes' system was summed up in his famous pronouncement: "I think, therefore I am." Descartes also viewed the mind and body as two separate entities. The mind belonged to the spiritual sphere, while the body belonged to the physical world of science.

Descartes was an intellectual giant, but his was not the only voice of the day. Toward the end of the Renaissance period in Europe, some philosophers were starting to look at the world from a more science-based perspective. It was a heady time for science. In Italy, Galileo proposed a sun-centered theory of the solar system to replace the older earth-centered model. In England, Francis Bacon argued for use of the scientific method to solve problems, and William Harvey demonstrated that the heart was actually nothing more than a pump for circulating blood.

The stage was set for the rise of a philosophical approach called empiricism, which held that all factual knowledge came from experience. One of the founders of English empiricism was Thomas Hobbes, who, not coincidentally, served briefly as Bacon's secretary and numbered Galileo among his friends. Hobbes saw the world and everything in it as bodies in motion. For him, mental processes were merely the byproducts of motion inside the brain. In addition, Hobbes believed that all knowledge was derived through the senses. Although Hobbes' writings were sometimes incomplete or inconsistent, he succeeded in planting the seed of empiricism.

The approach soon blossomed into a more organized school of thought, thanks to John Locke, a seventeenth-century English philosopher. Locke believed that the mind at birth was like a blank slate, just waiting to be written upon by experience. Therefore, there were no innate ideas. Instead, all ideas came from two forms of experience: sensation, which referred to information received from the senses; and reflection, which referred to the mental processes involved in sifting through all that sensory information. Much later, Locke's influence could still be seen in behaviorism, a twentieth-century school of psychology that focused on conditioning and learning—in other words, experience—as the determining factors in behavior.

In addition, Locke introduced the term "association of ideas." In the eighteenth and nineteenth centuries, a group of British philosophers took up the term and applied it to a new theory called associationism. This theory started with the notion that knowledge is acquired through experience, but it then went a step further, attempting to explain how that knowledge is organized. Associationism held that the process involved the association of ideas within the mind. Proponents believed that the way these associations were formed could be described by fundamental laws.

Associationism reached its height in the work of British philosopher James Mill and his son, John Stuart Mill. James Mill believed that ideas were added together to form more complex ideas. However, there was a basic flaw with this philosophy: It required that consciousness be able to hold an implausibly large number of ideas, since even a not-too-complex idea such as "brick" would require a vast number of ever-simpler ideas to define it. To address this flaw, John Stuart Mill revised his father's position. He described a process called mental chemistry, by which complex ideas could be greater than the sum of the simpler ideas making them up. This concept was later echoed by Gestalt psychology. The younger Mill also was enthusiastic about the prospect of establishing a true science of human behavior, and his enthusiasm may have influenced Wundt, who founded his lab just six years after Mill's death.

Physiological roots   For centuries, as we have seen, philosophers had mused over the nature of the mind and its relationship to outward behavior. Yet their musings were pure speculation, since the technology to study the inner workings of the brain and nervous system was not yet available. In the nineteenth century, however, physiologists made great advances in the tools and techniques for studying the nervous system. These advances laid the groundwork for the development of a new discipline: psychophysics, or the study of the relationship between the physical properties of stimuli and the psychological impressions that those stimuli produce.

One of the scientific giants of the era was Hermann von Helmholtz, a German physicist. Helmholtz rejected the common idea that physiological and psychological processes in organisms needed to be explained in terms of mysterious forces or energies. Instead, he believed that the processes within a living thing could be explained by the same kinds of laws that applied to nonliving matter. Among other contributions, Helmholtz measured the speed of nerve impulses, conducted important research on sound perception, revised a theory of color vision, and invented the ophthalmoscope, an instrument used to examine the interior of the eyes. By achieving such impressive results, Helmholtz showed that the nervous system was indeed amenable to scientific study.

Around the same time, other scientists were making discoveries about the localization of specific functions in particular parts of the brain. For example, French neurologist Paul Broca came across a patient who apparently understood everything that was said to him, but who could only reply by saying "tan, tan." When the man died of an infection in 1861, Broca's autopsy revealed that there was a large lesion on the left side of the frontal lobe of his brain. Thus, this area of the brain, which became known as Broca's area, was identified as important for speech production. A little more than a decade later, German neurologist Carl Wernicke identified another area in the temporal lobe of the brain that was crucial for speech comprehension.

Still another pioneering figure was Ernst Weber, an anatomist and physiologist at the University of Leipzig in Germany. Weber studied the sense of touch by mapping what became known as the two-point threshhold. This was the smallest distance at which touching the skin at two different points was felt as two sensations rather than just one. Weber found that touch sensitivity varied for different parts of the body, with the tongue, for instance, being much more sensitive than the back.

One of Weber's younger colleagues at the University of Leipzig was Gustav Fechner. In 1860, Fechner published a book called *Elements of Psychophysics*, which was destined to become a classic. In the book, he described several methods of measuring responses to stimuli. The development of a practical research methodology paved the way for the first experimental studies in psychology.

Birth of a science

German beginnings German scientists—such as Hermann von Helmholtz, Ernst Heinrich Weber, and Gustav Theodor Fechner—had already developed many of the tools and techniques that would be needed if psychology were ever to stand on its own as a science. It is little wonder, then, that the first experimental psychology lab was established at the University of Leipzig. In this hotbed of scientific discovery, Wundt found fertile ground for his studies on topics such as attention, sensation, perception, and reaction time—the split-second needed for mental processing between the time when an event occurs and the time when the muscles start responding to it.

Wundt was trained in medicine and physiology, and he held professorships in philosophy. Yet, more than any of his predecessors, he not only melded these interests, but also expanded on them to create a brand-new science of psychology. In addition to actively pursuing research in his lab, he founded a journal and trained a steady stream of graduate students. He also wrote an influential two-volume book entitled *Principles of Physiological Psychology*.

American beginnings

The birth of psychology in Germany was closely watched in the United States. No one observed the developments with keener fascination than William James, an American scholar who went on to make his mark on both psychology and philosophy. Like Wundt, James had been trained in medicine and physiology, but his true calling lay elsewhere. In 1890, he published *Principles of Psychology*, a lengthy text that became an instant success and influenced generations to come. In this book, James argued the psychologists should base their studies not on isolated sensations, but on complete conscious experiences. Thus, he expanded the rather narrow borders of early German psychology to include a much wider range of mental processes.

Another towering figure of the same period was G. Stanley Hall. During his career, Hall racked up an impressive number of firsts. As a young man, he received the first U.S. doctoral degree in psychology. He earned the degree at Harvard University, where he studied with James. Afterward, Hall also studied for a time in Germany, where he was the first American student in Wundt's lab. Returning to the United States, Hall founded the *American Journal of Psychology*, the first English-language journal devoted exclusively to the new field. He also set up the first experimental psychology lab in the United States at Johns Hopkins University. Soon after, in 1889, he was named the

first president of Clark University in Worcester, Massachusetts, where he promptly established a world-class psychology department. The glory days at Clark were short-lived, since most of the outstanding faculty and students left a few years later over a dispute with the university and Hall. Yet Hall still had enough clout to become the driving force behind the founding of the American Psychological Association (APA), and it should come as no surprise that he served as that group's first president. Finally, Hall's last graduate student was also a notable first: Francis Sumner, the first African American student to earn a PhD in psychology in the United States.

It is perhaps less remembered that Hall was instrumental in giving the American public its first taste of Sigmund Freud's psychoanalysis. In 1909, Hall invited Freud to give a series of five lectures at a conference held at Clark. The lectures were well received by both fellow psychologists and the press. Hall also published Freud's lectures in the journal he edited, reaching an even wider audience. As an interesting sidelight, a second speaker at the same conference was a then-obscure psychologist who also went on to make a name for himself: Carl Jung.

Psychoanalysis

Freud's theory Modern psychology began as an experimental science. However, it was not long before a clinical offshoot of the new science appeared. Today, clinical practice is a very important part of the field. No figure looms larger in the history of clinical psychology than Freud. His method of psychoanalysis had an enormous impact, both on those who loved it and on those who hated it, some of whom reacted by offering up equally influential alternatives.

Freud was an Austrian physician whose ideas came out of his clinical experiences rather than a lab. When he first began presenting his ideas in the 1890s, they met with harsh criticism, in part because of his heavy emphasis on sexuality. By the early 1900s, however, he had attracted an international following. Freud theorized that there were three aspects of personality—id, ego, and superego—that existed at different levels of consciousness. He believed that instincts in general, and sexual instincts in particular, were at the heart of human behavior. He also thought that personality development proceeded through five stages: oral, anal, phallic, latency, and genital. Failure to successfully pass through the early stages in childhood could lead to emotional problems later in life.

Before Freud, there had been philosophical discussions of the differences among people. However, there was no psychological theory to explain exactly what made individuals who they were. As the first to advance such a theory, Freud opened the door to a host of other personality theorists who followed.

Psychoanalysis was not only a theory, however, but also a treatment approach. As such, it was the first true form of psychotherapy. Freud developed a therapeutic technique called free association, in which a patient was encouraged to say anything that came into his or her conscious mind without trying to censor the thoughts first. Freud also stressed the importance of dream interpretation for understanding a patient's mental life. In fact, many consider *The Interpretation of Dreams*, published in 1900, to be his most important book.

Neo-Freudian approaches Since Freud's day, a number of followers have attempted to pick up where he left off. Perhaps his most devoted disciple was his own daughter, Anna Freud. She became one of the leading figures in psychoanalysis after her father's death. Her major contribution was the detailed description of defense mechanisms, which are methods that the ego uses to defend itself when faced with conflicting demands from the id and superego.

Among Anna Freud's notable contemporaries was Karen Horney, a German-born psychoanalyst who moved to the United States in 1932. While Horney accepted many of Sigmund Freud's ideas, she criticized his views on the psychology of women. Freud had claimed that women felt inferior to men because of penis envy, and that this inevitably had a negative effect on their personality development. Horney disagreed strongly. She believed that, when women did lack self-esteem, it was due to their experiences living in a male-dominated culture rather than to their sexual anatomy.

One thing on which Freud and his followers all agreed was that the interactions between children and their parents played a critical role in molding the children's personalities. This led to research on how children form healthy emotional attachments. For example, Canadian psychologist Mary Ainsworth conducted studies in which she placed a mother and her infant in an unfamiliar room with toys. The mother would twice leave the room briefly and then return, and a researcher would observe the infant's reaction. Ainsworth noted that securely attached infants were distressed when their mothers left and comforted when their mothers returned. Other reactions signaled less healthy attachments.

Beyond psychoanalysis Psychoanalysis was just the start, of course. Numerous other theories of personality and schools of psychotherapy have emerged over the past century. Two early members of Freud's inner circle who eventually broke away to found their own analytic psychologies were Alfred Adler and Carl Jung.

Adler was an Austrian psychiatrist who joined Freud's discussion group in 1902. In 1911, however, he had left the fold to pursue his own theory of psychology. Called individual psychology, Adler's theory downplayed sexual instinct. Instead, it emphasized the importance of overcoming early feelings of inferiority. By focusing on the individual and the positive, goal-directed nature of humanity, Adler was a forerunner of the later movement known as humanistic psychology.

Jung was a Swiss psychiatrist who began an active correspondence with Freud in 1906. By 1913, however, the once-friendly relationship between the two men had turned into a bitter rift. Jung developed his own school of thought, which he called analytical psychology. Like Freud, he stressed the impact of unconscious ideas on behavior. However, Jung expanded this notion to include not only a personal unconscious, but also a collective unconscious—a deeper level of unconsciousness that he believed to contain emotionally charged symbols that were common to all peoples and had existed since the dawn of time.

In addition, Jung introduced a system for classifying personality types. He classified people based on their tendency toward an inward focus, called introversion, or an outward focus, called extroversion. In addition, Jung identified four functions of the mind: sensing, thinking, feeling, and intuiting. He believed that, while everyone used all four functions, people normally used one more than the others. Therefore, people could be grouped into categories based on their dominant mental function.

Legacy of psychoanalysis Freud was a rationalist in the tradition of Descartes, and he avoided experimental research. While this approach led to some brilliant insights, it also was a serious limitation. Some of Freud's specific concepts have not held up well to scientific study. Nevertheless, the psychoanalytic system as a whole has had an enduring and far-reaching impact on theory, therapy, and society in general. Terms such as id, ego, unconscious, Freudian slip, and Oedipus complex have become part of our everyday language.

In addition, modern versions of psychoanalysis continue to be used for treating mental illness. These modern therapies, often called psychodynamic therapies, all share a common focus on past experiences as an important cause of present problems. Using various techniques, therapists aim to help individuals gain insight into their emotional life, including influences from the past. Therapists also try to help people uncover their unconscious conflicts and understand how these conflicts may be affecting their current experiences.

Behaviorism

Animal learning   Adler and Jung devised alternatives to psychoanalysis, but their approaches still were based on the invisible and sometimes unconscious workings of the mind. From a scientific perspective, such approaches posed a big problem, since there was no objective way for scientists to validate the subjective thoughts and feelings that people reported having. In the early 1900s, the desire for greater objectivity led to the rise of behaviorism, a school of psychology that completely rejected the study of inner mental processes and focused instead on observable behaviors.

Like other schools of thought, behaviorism did not arise in a vacuum. Instead, it grew out of animal research on learning and conditioning. Early on, Wundt had written a book titled *Lectures on Human and Animal Psychology*, which helped establish animal research as a legitimate area of study for psychologists. By the turn of the twentieth century, animal research was a booming field. Around this time, William S. Small began using mazes to study lab rats, and Edward L. Thorndike tested the ability of cats to escape from puzzle boxes. Thanks to such creative experimental designs, a practical method for studying animal learning was rapidly developed.

One particularly prominent animal researcher was American psychologist Robert Yerkes. Although Yerkes later became known for his work with primates, he studied a wide range of species early in his career. In 1907, he published a book about the behavior, learning, and sensory capabilities of a particular type of mutant mouse. The next year, he coauthored a paper that presented the so-called Yerkes-Dodson Law, which originally related the strength of a stimulus to the speed of avoidance learning.

Meanwhile, a Russian physiologist named Ivan Pavlov had been studying the digestive process in dogs. He noticed that the dogs salivated when their keeper entered the room, apparently because they had come to associate the keeper's arrival with food. This led Pavlov to conduct his famous experiments on classical conditioning, the first form of learning to be studied experimentally. In classical conditioning, an association is formed by pairing a previously neutral stimulus (such as a bell) with an unconditioned stimulus (such as food) to produce an unconditioned response (such as salivation). Over time, the previously neutral stimulus becomes able to bring on the response all by itself.

Watson's theory   Yet another scientist who was drawn to the study of animal learning around this time was American psychologist John B. Watson. In early work, Watson studied matters such as the cues used by rats to learn their way through a maze. Unlike most psychologists before him, however, Watson completely rejected the study of inner mental processes, even in humans. Instead, he believed that the only way to turn psychology into a truly objective science was to focus strictly on observable behavior. In a 1913 paper, Watson laid out his ideas forcefully. It was the opening shot in what became the behaviorist revolution.

Watson argued that the proper goal of psychology was the prediction and control of behavior. He believed that the same principles of learning and conditioning that were being used in animal research could also be used to explain all of human personality and behavior. For example, he believed that most fears were the result of unfortunate conditioning experiences. In one famous study, he showed how fear could be instilled through classical conditioning. The study involved an 11-month-old boy called Little Albert. Before the study began, Albert showed no fear of a white rat, but he appeared frightened and started to cry when a loud sound was made. In the study, researchers showed Albert the rat. Whenever Albert reached for the rat, however, they made the scary sound. After the researchers repeated this procedure several times, Albert began to cry as soon as he saw the rat, even without the loud noise. Afterward, Albert also began avoiding other objects—such as a rabbit and a fur coat—that resembled the rat in some way. It seemed that his conditioned fear response had generalized from the original stimulus to other similar stimuli.

Locke had described the mind of a newborn infant as a blank slate. Watson took this idea quite literally. He once boasted that, given a dozen healthy infants and his own specific world in which to raise them, he could pick any child at random and train that child to become anything. In other words, Watson believed that people were entirely products of their environment. It was an extreme position, but one that had a lasting impact on psychology. For decades after Watson, students were taught that the definition of psychology was "the study of behavior."

Radical behaviorism   For half a century, behaviorism remained the dominant school of psychology in the United States. As had happened earlier with psychoanalysis, however, different factions soon developed within the ranks of the true believers. The most celebrated champion of behaviorism in the mid-twentieth century was B.F. Skinner. While Skinner was often controversial, he was also extremely influential. His approach, dubbed radical behaviorism, helped define the course of modern experimental psychology.

Skinner is perhaps best remembered for his discovery of what he called operant conditioning. This type of conditioning occurs when a behavior is shaped by its immediate consequences. If the consequences are positive, the behavior is more likely to occur again in the future, given the same environment. If the consequences are negative, the behavior is less likely to occur again. To study operant conditioning in animals, Skinner developed the Skinner box. This was a special box in which the rate of some behavior, such as pressing a bar, could be continuously recorded. Skinner found that an organism's behavior could be shaped by providing positive consequences for actions that came closer and closer to a desired behavior.

Legacy of behaviorism   Skinner envisioned a world in which behavioral techniques could be used to improve childrearing, education, and society as a whole. In his book *Walden Two*, he described a utopian community based on operant conditioning, in which government rewarded socially appropriate behavior, and life was trouble-free. Skinner actually designed both a special crib and a teaching machine based on behaviorist principles, but neither achieved commercial success. Nevertheless, his ideas are still widely used in education, business, and other settings where the aim is to encourage appropriate behavior using rewards.

Behaviorism also gave rise to a popular form of psychotherapy, known as behavior therapy or behavioral modification. This type of therapy is based on the assumption that maladaptive behavior is caused by faulty or inadequate learning. The aim of the therapy is to reduce or halt the unwanted behavior by rewarding more helpful responses.

Gestalt psychology

Three founders   While behaviorism was the dominant school of American psychology for much of the twentieth century, it was far from the only one. Gestalt psychology, founded in Germany and imported to the United States in the 1930s, offered an important alternative. This school of psychology dealt with organized wholes that could not be explained by breaking them down into their component parts. As such, it was opposed to behaviorism, which sought to reduce complex human experiences to simple behavioral explanations.

Three German psychologists are credited with founding Gestalt psychology: Max Wertheimer, Kurt Koffka, and Wolfgang Köhler. *Gestalt* is a German word that can be loosely translated as "a structured whole." The story goes that Gestalt psychology had its beginnings one day in 1910, as Wertheimer was taking a trip by train. Gazing out the train window, he was struck by the apparent movement of stationary objects, such as poles and buildings. Once back home, he began conducting experiments of apparent motion, which he called the phi phenomenon. His subjects were two younger colleagues, Koffka and Köhler. In 1912, Wertheimer published a paper about his experiments that is said to mark the official start of Gestalt psychology. Wertheimer and his two colleagues later moved to the United States to escape the Nazi regime.

Gestalt psychology flourished in the first half of the twentieth century. The three founders and their followers used Gestalt ideas to develop basic principles of perception, learning, and thinking. For example, the principle of proximity stated that elements that were close together in time or space would be seen as belonging together. The principle of similarity stated that similar elements would also be seen as going together in the mind. The principle of closure stated that, if there were gaps in an element, people would tend to mentally close those gaps to make the element complete.

Field theory   Other psychologists sought to apply Gestalt ideas to areas such as motivation, personality, and social relationships. Among those who wanted to broaden Gestalt psychology was Kurt Lewin, a Prussian-born psychologist who was educated in Germany. Lewin also immigrated to the United States in the 1930s.

Lewin soon developed his own theory, known as field theory, first published in 1935. It stood out from earlier approaches that had focused single-mindedly on either internal mental processes or external rewards and punishments. Instead, Lewin's theory stressed the interaction of the person and the environment. In this way, it anticipated some popular approaches of the late twentieth century, such as Bandura's social-cognitive theory.

One of Lewin's key concepts was life space, which consisted of all the influences acting on a person at any given time. These influences might include personal and biological facts (a memory, fatigue), physical events (an aroma, a room), and social facts (another person, being a member of a family). Lewin referred to the positive or negative features of objects in the life space as valences. In general, objects that met a need had a positive valence, while those that gave rise to frustration or fear had a negative valence. The concept of valences helped explain people's behavior in the face of interpersonal conflict. In an approach-avoidance conflict, for instance, people had to decide what to do when a goal had both positive and negative valence. Lewin believed that their decision would be based on which of the two forces—the one pulling them toward the goal or the one pushing them away—turned out to be more powerful.

Psychometrics

Intelligence testing   From its beginnings, psychology was grounded in basic lab research. However, it was not long before psychologists began seeking real-world applications for their research findings. After all, there was no better way to show psychology's value to society than by offering up practical solutions to vexing social problems. However, these practical applications often required classifying people into groups based on particular abilities, skills, or other characteristics. Such classification, in turn, required valid and reliable tests for measuring the characteristic in question. Thus was born the field of psychometrics, which involves the construction of psychological tests using statistical methods.

Intelligence testing, one very visible branch of psychometrics, began in France around the turn of the twentieth century. At that time, the French government enacted laws requiring that all children be given a public education. For the first time, mentally "subnormal" children—those who today might be called mentally retarded or developmentally disabled—were to be provided with special classes. However, this raised the question of how to identify those children who would benefit from special education. French psychologist Alfred Binet set out to solve the problem by devising a test for measuring mental abilities. In 1905, he introduced the Binet-Simon Scale, the world's first practical test of intelligence.

Binet's groundbreaking test soon attracted interest in the United States. When World War I arrived, an APA committee set out to devise a similar test that could be used by the U.S. Army to assess recruits. Yerkes, the noted animal researcher who had a side interest in intelligence testing, was APA president at the time. He headed up the committee, which eventually developed the first intelligence tests designed to be given in a group rather than individually. While the hastily thrown-together Army tests had many flaws, they introduced the idea of mass testing to the American public. Over the next several decades, standardized testing of vast numbers of people became common in schools and businesses nationwide.

Validity and reliability   Through the years, test development methods have become much more sophisticated. Statistical techniques have been developed for assessing a test's validity and reliability. Validity refers to the extent to which a test measures what it is supposed to measure. Reliability refers to the extent to which the measurements are consistent or repeatable over time. Several psychologists have played key roles in refining the methods that are currently used for testing the tests to make sure they meet acceptable standards.

One innovator in the field was American psychologist Anne Anastasi, whose contributions included work on test construction and the proper use of psychological tests. Anastasi also had a deep interest in the way that psychological development was affected by the environment and individual experience. This interest undoubtedly shaped her views on testing as well, making her especially sensitive to the role that culture played in test results. Today, test fairness and culture loading—the extent to which a test reflects the vocabulary, knowledge, and traditions of one culture more than another—are still subjects of lively debate.

Humanistic psychology

The Third Force   By the mid-twentieth century, many psychologists were growing disenchanted with behaviorism. They were looking for an alternative to what some saw as the bleak behaviorist view of humans as little more than two-legged lab rats. In addition, they were eager to study psychological health rather than focus on emotional maladjustment, the way psychoanalysis did. With behaviorism and psychoanalysis as the first two forces in American psychology, the time was ripe for what became known as the Third Force. This approach, also called humanistic psychology, focused more on positive rather than negative aspects of the self. It was also more concerned with present choices than past events. Among the central concerns of humanistic psychology were free will, the lifelong search for meaning, and each person's potential to achieve self-fulfillment.

At the forefront of this movement was American psychologist Abraham Maslow. He is best remembered for the hierarchy of needs that he proposed. This was often depicted as a pyramid, with the most basic needs on the bottom. These included physiological needs, such as food and water, and safety needs. Only after those needs had been satisfied was a person free to focus on the next level, which consisted of needs for belonging and love. Once those needs, in turn, had been met, a person could move on to addressing esteem needs, such as achievement and independence. Finally, after all of the lower needs had been met, a person could begin working on self-actualization, the feeling of fulfillment that comes from realizing one's potential.

Maslow believed that there was more to be gained by studying self-actualized individuals than by studying maladjusted people or nonhuman animals. This shift in focus opened the door to the psychological study of many subjects that had previously been considered off-limits, but that were clearly important aspects of the human experience. Such subjects included play, humor, love, aesthetics, personal values, and spiritual growth, among others.

Client-centered therapy   Carl Rogers was another member of the humanistic movement who helped change the face of American psychology. In the 1950s, he described a new therapeutic approach that he named client-centered therapy. This approach called for the therapist to show congruence, empathetic understanding, and unconditional positive regard. Congruence meant that the therapist would be honest and willing to express his or her true feelings. Empathetic understanding meant that the therapist would really listen to the client (not patient) and then share his or her understanding of what the client had communicated. Unconditional positive regard meant that the therapist would respect the client as an individual and accept whatever the client had to say.

The therapist's job, in short, was to create an atmosphere that was conducive to change. However, responsibility for the change itself rested squarely on the client. Rogers had great faith in people's ability to take control of their own lives. His ideas still affect the way that psychotherapy is conducted today.

Humanistic psychology gave rise to the human potential movement of the 1960s and 1970s. People were encouraged to get in touch with their inner selves and realize their potential through such activities as encounter groups, meditation, and communing with nature. At the time, these were considered fringe activities, more suitable to hippie communes than middle-class living rooms. Today, however, they have gone mainstream along with the notion that people should strive for self-knowledge and personal fulfillment.

Social psychology

Race and gender   Humanistic psychology placed individual fulfillment above all else. However, humans are also social creatures who are influenced by those around them. Social psychology, which looks at the way that individuals are affected by social trends and events, provided another valuable perspective on the human condition.

Social psychologists study a wide range of topics, including societal norms, group conflicts, obedience to authority, and social roles. In addition, they have made key contributions to the study of race and gender issues. Such issues came to the forefront of psychology after World War II. Even before that, however, American psychologist Kenneth Clark had conducted studies of racial identity and self-concept. In a famous study from the late 1930s, Clark and his wife found that African American preschoolers preferred white dolls to black ones. Clark went on to become the first African American president of the APA in 1971.

In the area of gender studies, social psychologist Sandra Bem has challenged widely held notions about what it means to be male or female. Bem is best known for the Bem Sex Role Inventory, a popular scale for measuring how well a person conforms to traditional sex-role stereotypes. Historically, masculinity and femininity were viewed as opposite poles on a single dimension. However, research in the 1970s showed that masculinity and femininity were actually two separate traits. Bem used her scale to classify individuals of either sex as high in masculinity only, high in femininity only, high in both traits, or low in both.

Social-cognitive theory   Another important topic in social psychology is observational learning, in which people learn to do something merely by watching others, without performing the behavior themselves or being directly rewarded for it. Pioneering work in this area was done by Canadian-born psychologist Albert Bandura of Stanford University. In the 1960s, Bandura conducted classic studies that looked at how observational learning affected aggressive behavior in children. A group of children were shown a film in which an adult punched, hammered, and kicked an inflatable doll, called a Bobo doll. These children were more likely to behave aggressively themselves when given a chance to play with the doll later. More than 40 years later, this research is still very relevant to the ongoing debate over violence in the media.

Bandura's Bobo doll experiments contained elements of both social psychology and learning theory. In the intervening years, Bandura has cast an even wider net in his research and theoretical interests. In the 1980s, he put forth a social-cognitive theory of human functioning that added elements of cognitive psychology, an approach that many consider to be the dominant school of psychology today. According to social-cognitive theory, human functioning results from the interplay of three forces: personal factors (such as thoughts, feelings, and physical states), the environment, and behavior. Cognition, or thought, plays a big role in people's ability to effectively manage their own responses to other people and the environment as a whole.

Cognitive psychology

Cognitive development Psychologists have long been fascinated by cognitive processes, such as thought, perception, memory, and attention. Many noted psychologists, including G. Stanley Hall and Kurt Koffka, theorized about the development of such processes in children. However, no name became more closely linked to the study of cognitive development than that of Swiss psychologist Jean Piaget.

In the 1930s, Piaget developed his stage theory of child development. Piaget believed that infants were born with simple cognitive structures, called schemas. As children matured, they built new schemas on the existing ones. Piaget also described two mental processes for dealing with new information: assimilation and accommodation. If a new experience fit the child's existing schemas, then it was assimilated, or taken into the mind. On the other hand, if the experience did not match existing schemas, the schemas were altered to accommodate the perceived reality.

Piaget believed that cognitive development passed through four stages: sensorimotor, preoperational, concrete operational, and formal operational. Later research has not always supported Piaget's descriptions of the stages in every specific detail. Nevertheless, Piaget's general concepts are still quite influential. It is now widely accepted that the mind of a young child differs from that of an older child or adult not only in the quantity of knowledge, but also in the quality of the thought processes.

While Piaget also wrote about the development of moral reasoning, it was American psychologist Lawrence Kohlberg who became the most influential figure in that field. According to Kohlberg's theory, there were three stages of moral development: preconventional, conventional, and postconventional. At the lowest stage, moral behavior was motivated by punishments or rewards. At the next stage, it was motivated by social rules. At the highest stage, however, people's moral behavior was guided by ethical principles that had become internalized.

Personal constructs Yet another take on the structure of the mind was offered by American psychologist George Kelly. In the 1950s, he put forth a personal construct theory, which stated that people construct their own theories about human behavior as they actively work to understand the world around them. As Kelly saw it, we are all personality theorists, developing a set of ideas for explaining and predicting our own behavior and that of other people.

Kelly's work foreshadowed some of the most important themes in modern cognitive and personality psychology. In recent decades, increasing attention has been paid to individual explanatory styles, or the habitual ways that people interpret the events in their lives. For example, some researchers have compared people with an optimistic explanatory style to those with a pessimistic one. In related research, Bandura has stressed the importance of self-efficacy beliefs, or people's beliefs about how capably they will be able to perform a specific behavior in a particular situation.

Cognitive therapy Cognitive theory has also produced a popular form of psychotherapy, known as cognitive therapy. Originally developed by American psychiatrist Aaron Beck in the 1960s to treat depression, it has since been applied to a wide range of emotional and behavioral problems. Among other things, cognitive therapy has been used to treat chronic stress, anxiety disorders, substance abuse, marital conflicts, and personality disorders.

The basic concept behind cognitive therapy is that people's feelings and behaviors are influenced by how they perceive situations. When people are in distress, their thoughts may be irrationally negative or otherwise distorted. Cognitive therapy aims to help people identify distorted thinking patterns and replace irrational thoughts with more rational ones. In practice, cognitive therapy is often combined with behavior therapy in what is called cognitive-behavioral therapy.

Now and then In the second half of the twentieth century, some cognitive researchers began using concepts from computer science to explain information processing inside the human brain. They soon discovered that the metaphor of the brain as computer could only be taken so far. It became apparent that there were fundamental differences between the inners workings of the human brain and those of computers. Nevertheless, the combination of cognitive psychology and computer science has led to some fruitful models for describing how information is processed within the brain.

In the twentieth-first century, cognitive psychology continues to evolve. Physiology is once again at the forefront of psychology, thanks to the development of sophisticated brain imaging technology that allows scientists to study the structure and function of the brain as never before. Such advanced technology is already providing fresh insights into age-old questions, such as how humans perceive sensory information, store information in memory, and use information to make decisions and solve problems. Such findings have recently given rise to a high-tech specialty known as cognitive neuroscience.

It is interesting to note that this technological specialty has a pedigree going all the way back to psychology's earliest days. Wundt and Wertheimer, among others, used what were then cutting-edge tech-niques to study mental processes such as perception, memory, and thought. It seems that the science of psychology keeps returning to the same traditional themes with the latest tools and techniques. The complexities of thought, feeling, and behavior will undoubtedly remain a never-ending source of fascina-tion and investigation.

Linda Wasmer Andrews, M.S.

Chronology

1832: Wilhelm Wundt born in Neckarau, Baden, Germany, outside of Leipzig, on August 16.

1849: Ivan Pavlov born in the village of Ryazan, Russia.

1852: Napoleon III founded the Second Empire in France.

1856: Sigismund Freud is born (changes his name to Sigmund at age 22).

1857: Alfred Binet born on July 8 in Nice, France.

1857: Louis Pasteur introduces his germ theory of fermentation.

1857: Wilhelm Wundt begins a seven-year position as lecturer in physiology at Heidelberg. During this time he serves as an assistant Hermann von Helmholtz.

1859: Charles Darwin presents his theory of evolution in *On the Origin of Species.*

1861–65: The Civil War is fought in the United States.

1864: Wilhelm Wundt appointed associate professor in physiology at University of Heidelberg.

1870–71: Prussia defeats France in the Franco-Prussian War. The Third Republic is founded in France.

1873: Sigmund Freud receives a summa cum laude award on graduation from the Gymnasium. He is already able to read in several languages.

1873–74: Wilhelm Wundt publishes first edition of *Principles of Psychology.*

1875: Carl Jung born in a country parsonage at Kesswil in Canton Thurgau, Switzerland.

1875: Wilhelm Wundt appointed one of two fellow professors at Leipzig University, focusing on practical-scientific theories.

1876: Robert Yerkes born on May 26 in Breadysville, Pennsylvania.

1876: Alexander Graham Bell patents the telephone.

1877: Sigmund Freud joins Brücke's laboratory.

1878: Alfred Binet receives a license in law, a career he chose not to pursue.

1879: Ivan Pavlov graduates from the Medical Academy; wins a gold medal in student competition.

1879: Wilhelm Wundt established the first laboratory for experimental psychology.

1880: Max Wertheimer born on April 15, 1880, in Prague.

1880: Alfred Binet publishes his first article, "On the Fusion of Similar Sensations."

1881: Sigmund Freud awarded a delayed doctor's degree in medicine.

1883–84: Wilhelm Wundt's laboratory receives official status at Leipzig as an institution of its department of philosophy.

1884: Francis Galton sets up a laboratory in London to measure individual differences in mental abilities.

1884: Sigmund Freud discovers the analgesic properties of cocaine.

1885: Karen Horney is born outside Hamburg, Germany.

1886: Alfred Binet publishes his first book, *The Psychology of Reasoning.*

1886: Sigmund Freud starts private practice.

1887: Sigmund Freud starts using hypnosis.

1890: Kurt Lewin born in Germany, now a part of Poland.

1890: James McKeen Cattell publishes a paper in which he coined the term "mental test."

1894: Alfred Binet receives a doctoral degree in natural science from the Sorbonne.

1895: Alfred Binet helps found the first French psychological journal.

1896: Sigmund Freud for the first time uses the term "psychoanalysis."

1896: Wilhelm Wundt dies in Groábothen, German, near Leipzig, August 31. His book, *Outlines of Psychology,* was published the same year.

1896: Alfred Binet publishes a paper outlining "individual psychology" with Victor Henri.

1896: Jean Piaget born in Neuchatel, Switzerland.

1897: Ivan Pavlov publishes "Lectures on the Work of the Main Digestive Glands."

1897: Sigmund Freud postulates Oedipus complex.

1898: Marie and Pierre Curie discovered the element radium.

1899: Alfred Binet began working with Théodore Simon.

1899: Sigmund Freud's *The Interpretation of Dreams* is published on November 4.

1900: After finishing medical school at the University of Basel, Carl Jung travels to Zurich to study psychiatry under Eugen Bleuler, a world-famous expert on schizophrenia.

1900: Gregor Mendel's basic laws of heredity, which went unnoticed when first set forth in the 1860s, are rediscovered.

1900–09: Carl Jung works as a psychiatric resident at the Burghölzli, a famous mental hospital in Zurich.

1900–20: Wilhelm Wundt's *Volkerpsychologie (Folk Psychology)* published in 10 volumes.

1901: Guglielmo Marconi sends the first long-wave radio signals across the Atlantic Ocean.

1902: Robert Yerkes receives a PhD in psychology from Harvard and begins teaching comparative psychology at Harvard.

1902: Sigmund Freud begins the Wednesday Psychological Society meetings at his home.

1902: Carl Rogers is born in Oak Park, Illinois.

1903: The Wright Brothers make the first successful airplane flight.

1904: Max Wertheimer receives his doctorate in philosophy at the University of Würzburg.

1904: Ivan Pavlov awarded the Nobel Prize in Physiology or Medicine.

1904: B.F. Skinner born March 20.

1905: George Alexander Kelly born on a farm near Perth, Kansas.

1905: Alfred Binet, along with Theodore Simon, introduces the first version of the Binet-Simon Scale.

1905: Albert Einstein publishes his special theory of relativity.

1906: Carl Jung publishes a book on schizophrenia that applies Sigmund Freud's psychoanalytic approach to the study of psychosis.

1906: Carl Jung starts his correspondence with Sigmund Freud.

1906: Jean Piaget publishes first article in local journal.

1908: Anne Anastasi born on December 19 in New York City.

1908: Robert Yerkes publishes the Yerkes-Dodson law, developed with John Dodson, which related the strength of a stimulus to the speed of avoidance learning.

1908: Abraham Maslow born in Manhattan.

1909: Publication of Sigmund Freud's *Analysis of a Phobia in a Five-Year-Old Boy (Little Hans).*

1909: Carl Jung travels with Sigmund Freud to the United States to give lectures at Clark University in Massachusetts.

1910: Max Wertheimer discovers the phi phenomenon on a train ride and published his groundbreaking paper "Experimental Studies of the Perception of Movement" two years later.

1910: Construction of Ivan Pavlov's "Towers of Silence" begins.

1911: Marie Curie wins her second Nobel Prize for her discovery and study of radium.

1911: Robert Yerkes founds the *Journal of Animal Behavior*, the first U.S. scientific journal devoted solely to animal behavior research.

1911: Alfred Binet makes the last revision of the Binet-Simon Scale. Dies on October 18.

1912: The ocean liner *Titanic* sinks after hitting an iceberg on her maiden voyage.

1913: Sigmund Freud publishes *Totem and Taboo*.

1913: Mary Salter (later Ainsworth) born in Glendale, Ohio.

1913: Carl Jung breaks with Sigmund Freud. Publishes *Psychology of the Unconscious,* the first account of his analytical psychology as an approach to therapy distinct from psychoanalysis.

1913–14: Carl Jung experiences a midlife crisis or period of psychological turmoil that resolves with the outbreak of World War I in July 1914.

1913–17: Robert Yerkes works half-time as a psychologist in the Psychopathic Department at Boston State Hospital.

1914: Kenneth Bancroft Clark born in Panama.

1914: Kurt Lewin volunteers to serve in World War I.

1914–18: World War I in Europe.

1915: Robert Yerkes introduces a point scale for measuring intelligence, developed with J. W. Bridges.

1916: Lewis Terman introduced the Stanford-Binet Intelligence Scales, a U.S. version of the Binet-Simon Scale that modified it substantially.

1917: The October Revolution occurs. The Bolsheviks take power, and Vladimir Lenin becomes new Soviet leader. The United States enters World War I.

1917: Kurt Lewin wounded in war.

1917: Robert Yerkes elected president of the American Psychological Association. Becomes a member of the National Research Council.

1917–18: Robert Yerkes chairs a committee that developed the U.S. Army Alpha and Beta intelligence tests during World War I.

1918: Jean Piaget receives PhD in Natural Sciences, University of Neuchatel. He works in Eugen Bleuler's psychiatric clinic at the University of Zurich and develops his technique of the clinical interview.

1919: Kenneth Bancroft Clark comes to America with mother and sister.

1919: Prohibition begins in the United States.

1919–24: Robert Yerkes works for the National Research Council.

1920: Women win the right to vote in the United States.

1920: Sigmund Freud publishes *Beyond the Pleasure Principle*.

1920: Wilhelm Wundt publishes autobiography entitled *Erlebtes und Erkanntes.*

1921: Sigmund Freud publishes *Group Psychology and the Analysis of the Ego.*

1921: Aaron Temkin Beck born in Providence, Rhode Island.

1921: Carl Jung publishes *Psychological Types,* a major work that secures his reputation as an original thinker.

1921: Jean Piaget appointed research director of the *Institut Jean-Jacques Rousseau* in Geneva, and publishes article in the *Archives de Psychologie* stating that logic is not innate but develops over time through interactive processes of self-regulation.

1923: Jean Piaget publishes *The Language and Thought of the Child.* Four more books follow, bringing him worldwide fame before the age of 30.

1923: Sigmund Freud diagnosed with cancer of the jaw. Publication of *The Ego and the Id.*

1924: The first Olympic Winter Games are played.

1924–44: Robert Yerkes holds a post as professor of psychobiology at Yale University.

1925: Jean Piaget begins the study of the intellectual development of his three children from infancy through their teenage years.

1925: Albert Bandura born on December 4, 1925, in Mundare, Alberta, Canada.

1925: Hitler publishes "Mein Kampf."

1926: Carl Brigham introduced the forerunner of the SAT.

1927: Lawrence Kohlberg born in Bronxville, New York.

1927: Ivan Pavlov publishes "Lectures on the Work of the Large Hemispheres of the Brain."

1928: Albert Einstein and Jean Piaget meet. Einstein suggests that Piaget study the origins in children of the notions of time and simultaneity.

1929: Stock market crash on Wall Street marks the beginning of the Great Depression.

1929: Robert Yerkes publishes *The Great Apes: A Study of Anthropoid Life*, coauthored with his wife, Ada Watterson Yerkes.

1929: Jean Piaget teaches the history of scientific thought at the University of Geneva until 1939. Begins 35-year tenure as director of the International Bureau of Education in Geneva.

1929–41: Robert Yerkes founds and directs the Yale Laboratories of Primate Biology, the first laboratory for nonhuman primate research in the United States.

1930: Anne Anastasi awarded a PhD from Columbia University. Hired as instructor of psychology at Barnard College.

1930: B.F. Skinner initiates research in reflexes.

1931: George Alexander Kelly receives his PhD from the University of Iowa.

1931–34: Abraham Maslow conducts primate research with Harry Harlow. Completes a masters thesis and doctoral dissertation on primate behavior.

1932: Karen Horney moves to United States.

1933: Kurt Lewin moves to United States to escape the rise of Hitler.

1933: Sigmund Freud has a letter exchange with Albert Einstein on the topic Why the War? The Nazis publicly burn Freud's work in Berlin.

1933: Adolf Hitler became dictator of Germany.

1934: Max Wertheimer arrives in New York and begins teaching at the "University in Exile" for the next 10 years.

1934: Kenneth Bancroft Clark earns his bachelor's degree from Howard University. Gains his master's the following year.

1934: Karen Horney takes teaching position at Washington-Baltimore Society for Psychoanalysis.

1935–37: Abraham Maslow completes postdoctoral fellowship at Columbia University. Research on sexuality and dominance in humans.

1936: Ivan Pavlov dies on February 27 after developing pneumonia at the age of 86.

1936: Karen Horney publishes *Feminine Psychology*.

1936: Jean Piaget publishes *The Origins of Intelligence in Children* based on his observations of his three children.

1937: Carl Jung invited by Yale University to deliver the Terry Lectures on psychology and religion.

1937: Anne Anastasi publishes her first major work, *Differential Psychology,* through Macmillan Publishing, New York.

1937–51: Abraham Maslow obtains a faculty position at Brooklyn College. Eventually reaches rank of associate professor.

1937–61: Carl Jung continues to practice medicine in Küssnacht, a suburb of Zurich, until his death in 1961.

1938: March 13th: Austria is annexed by Germany. Sigmund Freud's house and the headquarters of the Vienna Association of Psychoanalysis are searched. Anna Freud is arrested and interrogated by the Gestapo. In June, Freud and his family emigrate to Great Britain.

1938: B.F. Skinner's *The Behavior of Organisms* published.

1939: Mary Salter Ainsworth receives her PhD from the University of Toronto.

1939: Sigmund Freud dies. *Moses and Monotheism* is published.

1939: David Wechsler published the Wechsler Bellevue Scale, an adult-oriented intelligence test.

1939: Anne Anastasi appointed assistant professor of psychology and department chair, Queens College of the City University of New York.

1939–45: World War II in Europe.

1940: Jean Piaget appointed Chair of Experimental Psychology, University of Geneva (until 1971).

1940: Carl Rogers receives a full professorship at Ohio State University.

1941: The Japanese attack Pearl Harbor. The United States enters World War II.

1941–45: George Alexander Kelly serves during World War II as a Navy aviation psychologist, and teaches at the University of Maryland.

1942: B.F. Skinner awarded the Warren Medal by the Society of Experimental Psychologists.

1942: Jean Piaget lectures at the College of France during Nazi occupation. Lectures compiled into *The Psychology of Intelligence* published in 1963.

1942: Karen Horney publishes *Self-Analysis*.

1942: Mary D. Salter Ainsworth enters the Canadian Women's Army Corps.

1943: Max Wertheimer dies at his home after suffering a heart attack.

1944: Kurt Lewin invited to set up research institute at MIT.

1944: D-Day invasion occurs.

1945: United States drops the first atomic bombs. Liberation of the concentration camps in Europe.

1945: B.F. Skinner takes over the psychology department at the University of Indiana, where he developed the Teaching Machine and Aircrib.

1945: Mary D. Salter Ainsworth serves as Director of Women's Rehabilitation at Veteran Army Services Hospital.

1945: Carl Rogers joins faculty at the University of Chicago. Elected president of the American Psychological Association.

1945: Max Wertheimer publishes his only book, *Productive Thinking*.

1946: Aaron Temkin Beck graduates with a medical degree from Yale University.

1946: Mary D. Salter Ainsworth returns to University of Toronto to teach.

1946: George Alexander Kelly accepted the position as director of clinical programs for the school of psychology at the Ohio State University, following Carl Rogers.

1947: Kurt Lewin dies of heart attack.

1947: Anne Anastasi joins the faculty at Fordham University as associate professor, where she would be appointed to a full professorship in 1951.

1948: The state of Israel is founded and Gandhi is assassinated.

1948: B.F. Skinner's *Walden Two* published.

1949: NATO is established.

1949: David Wechsler introduced the Wechsler Intelligence Scale for Children.

1950: Kenneth Bancroft Clark publishes "Effect of Prejudice and Discrimination on Personality Development" for the Mid-Century White House Conference on Children and Youth.

1950: Mary D. Salter Ainsworth moves to London.

1950: Jean Piaget publishes his three volume book, *Introduction a l'epistemologie genetique*.

1951: Korean War breaks out. Aaron Temkin Beck takes a position at Valley Forge Field Hospital and treats soldiers with post-traumatic stress disorder.

1951–69: Abraham Maslow obtains a faculty position at Brandeis University. Serves as department chair until 1961.

1952: Polio vaccine is developed.

1952: Albert Bandura receives a PhD in clinical psychology from the University of Iowa.

1952: Karen Horney dies of stomach cancer at age 67.

1953: Albert Bandura takes a job as a psychology instructor at Stanford University.

1953: DNA is discovered.

1954: The publication of Abraham Maslow's *Motivation and Personality* brings national prominence.

1954: Mary Salter Ainsworth moves to Africa; starts Uganda mother-infant studies.

1954: *Brown v. Board of Education* uses Kenneth Bancroft Clark's studies as a basis for school desegregation.

1954: Anne Anastasi publishes *Psychological Testing,* Macmillan, New York.

1954: Aaron Temkin Beck joins the Department of Psychiatry of the University of Pennsylvania.

1955: Mary Salter Ainsworth hired as lecturer at Johns Hopkins in Baltimore.

1955: W. W. Norton & Company publishes George Alexander Kelly's groundbreaking, two-volume work, *The Psychology of Personal Constructs*.

1955: Jean Piaget's International Center for Genetic Epistemology opens at the University of Geneva.

1955: First edition of Kenneth Bancroft Clark's book *Prejudice and Your Child* published as Clark's first public scientific commentary.

1956: Fixed interval schedule of reinforcement described by B.F. Skinner.

1956: Robert Yerkes dies on February 3.

1957: The Soviet Union launches Sputnik, its first satellite, into Earth's orbit.

1958: Angelo Roncalli elected Pope; he takes the name John XXIII.

1958: Lawrence Kohlberg graduates from University of Chicago with a doctoral degree.

1959: Fidel Castro expels the dictator Fulgencio Batista and becomes premier of Cuba.

1959: Albert Bandura publishes his first book, *Adolescent Aggression*, with Richard Walters.

1959: Kenneth Bancroft Clark elected president of the Society for the Psychological Study of Social Issues.

1961: The first issue of *The Journal of Humanistic Psychology*, founded by Abraham Maslow, is published.

1961: Kenneth Bancroft Clark awarded the Spingarn Medal by the NAACP.

1961: The East German government builds the Berlin Wall. The Bay of Pigs Invasion occurs.

1962: Abraham Maslow publishes *Toward a Psychology of Being*.

1962: Mary D. Salter Ainsworth begins Baltimore replication study of mother-infant dyads.

1962–63: Abraham Maslow consults with Andy Kay at Non-Linear Systems.

1963: Albert Bandura publishes *Social Learning and Personality Development*, which summarized his research on observational learning and the Bobo doll experiments.

1963: President John F. Kennedy is assassinated while riding in a motorcade through Dallas.

1964: Carl Rogers elected "Humanist of the Year" by the American Humanist Association.

1964: Civil Rights Act passes in U.S. Congress.

1964: Albert Bandura becomes a full professor at Stanford.

1965: George Alexander Kelly begins research position at Brandeis University, where Abraham Maslow is also working at the time.

1965: Kenneth Bancroft Clark publishes *Dark Ghetto*.

1966: Abraham Maslow is elected president of the American Psychological Association.

1966: B.F. Skinner introduces the concept of critical period in reinforcing an event.

1966: Jean Piaget publishes *The Psychology of the Child* with Barbel Inhelder.

1967: Israelis fight the Six Days War.

1967: George Alexander Kelly dies on March 6.

1967: Mary Salter Ainsworth publishes *Infancy in Uganda*.

1968: Assassination of Martin Luther King, Jr.

1968: Lawrence Kohlberg becomes a full professor at Harvard University. Later founds the Center for Moral Devlopment and Education there.

1968: B.F. Skinner identifies the critical characteristics of programmed instruction.

1968: Robert Kennedy is assassinated.

1969: Lawrence Kohlberg studies moral development in an Israeli kibbutz.

1969: Jean Piaget awarded distinguished Scientific Contribution Award by the American Psychological Association. He is the first European to receive the award.

1969: The first human beings set foot on the Moon.

1970: Protesting students at Kent State University are shot.

1970: Carl Rogers' *On Encounter Groups* published. He would publish two more books before his death.

1970: Abraham Maslow dies of a heart attack at his home in Menlo Park, California.

1971: Lawrence Kohlberg coauthors "The Adolescent as Philosopher" with Carol Gilligan. Kohlberg also contracts a parasitic illness in Central America, which afflicts him for 16 years.

1971: Kenneth Bancroft Clark elected president of the American Psychological Association. Clark has been the only African American to serve in that capacity.

1971: B.F. Skinner publishes *Beyond Freedom and Dignity*.

1972: B.F. Skinner receives the Humanist of the Year Award by the American Humanist Association.

1972: Terrorists attack and kill athletes at the Munich Olympic games.

1973: Abortion is legalized in the United States.

1974: Kenneth Bancroft Clark publishes *Pathos of Power*.

1974: Albert Bandura serves as president of the American Psychological Association.

1974: Aaron Temkin Beck publishes *The Prediction of Suicide*.

1975: Mary Salter Ainsworth leaves Johns Hopkins for University of Virginia.

1975–95: Kenneth Bancroft Clark serves on the New York Board of Regents.

1976: North and South Viet Nam re-join.

1977: Albert Bandura publishes *Social Learning Theory*, which aroused interest in social learning and modeling.

1978: Mary D. Salter Ainsworth publishes *Patterns of Attachment*.

1979: Anne Anastasi named professor emeritus at Fordham.

1979: The Iranians under Khomeini take Americans as hostages.

1980: Jean Piaget dies at the age of 84 in Geneva, Switzerland.

1981: Sandra Day O'Connor becomes the first woman appointed to the United States Supreme Court.

1983: B.F. Skinner publishes *Enjoying Old Age*.

1984: The virus that causes AIDS is identified by two groups of scientists in France and the United States.

1984: Mary Salter Ainsworth retires from the University of Virginia as Professor Emeritus.

1985: Robert Sternberg presents his three-part theory of intelligence in *Beyond IQ*.

1986: The Challenger Space Shuttle explodes, killing all on board.

1986: Albert Bandura publishes *Social Foundations of Thought and Action: A Social Cognitive Theory*, which described his social-cognitive theory of human functioning.

1986: Carl Rogers travels to Russia to facilitate conflict resolution.

1987: Carl Rogers dies of heart attack.

1987: Lawrence Kohlberg commits suicide by drowning in Winthrop, Massachusetts.

1988: Aaron Temkin Beck publishes *Love is Never Enough*.

1990: B.F. Skinner dies on August 18.

1992: President George Bush of the United States and President Boris Yeltsin of Russia jointly declare an end to the Cold War.

1994: Kenneth Bancroft Clark receives the APA Award for Outstanding Lifetime Contribution to Psychology.

1997: Albert Bandura publishes *Self-Efficacy: The Exercise of Control*, which set forth his ideas about self-efficacy beliefs.

1998: Mary Salter Ainsworth receives APA Gold Medal Award for Life Achievement in the Science of Psychology.

1999: Mary Salter Ainsworth dies in Charlottesville, Virginia.

2000: Yassir Arafat launches the second Palestinian intifada (uprising) against Israel.

2001: Anne Anastasi dies on May 4.

2003: Space shuttle *Columbia* explodes on reentry, killing the seven astronauts on board.

2004: 50th anniversary of *Brown v. Board of Education*. Kenneth Bancroft Clark and Mamie Phipps-Clark awarded honorary degrees from Earlham College to mark their "historic contributions to the cause of equal rights for all Americans."

2004: Aaron Temkin Beck publishes *Cognitive Therapy of Personal Disorders,* second edition.

Kurt Lewin

1890–1947

GERMAN/AMERICAN SOCIAL PSYCHOLOGIST, EDUCATOR, RESEARCHER

UNIVERSITY OF BERLIN, Ph.D., 1916

BRIEF OVERVIEW

At the time of Kurt Lewin's death in February 1947, he was widely regarded as one of the outstanding psychologists of his generation. Edward Tolman, the colleague who delivered a tribute to Lewin at a meeting of the American Psychological Association (APA) later that year, thought that Lewin could be compared to Freud himself.

> Freud the clinician and Lewin the experimentalist—these are the two men whose names will stand before all others in the history of our psychological era. For it is their contrasting but complementary insights which first made psychology a science applicable to real human beings and to real human society.

One of many gifted scientists and teachers who fled Hitler's Germany for a new life in the United States, Lewin made significant contributions to so many different areas of psychology—child development, philosophy of science, psychology of prejudice, industrial psychology, organizational development, clinical psychology, personality structure, group process, leadership training, and others—that he has been called "the complete social scientist." As interested in applied psychology as he was in research, Lewin coined or popularized such terms and concepts as group dynamics, level of aspiration, sensitivity training, field theory, and action research. His colleagues also regretted that his sudden death had cut short the contribution he had hoped to make in the field that held together many of his other interests—the

Kurt Lewin. (Courtesy of the Library of Congress.)

comparative study of science, or in Lewin's native German, *vergleichende Wissenschaftslehre*.

In spite of the range, depth, and originality of Lewin's work, however, he received less recognition during his lifetime than many psychologists whose work proved less durable. He was never elected to the presidency of a major scholarly or professional organization, was bypassed for major awards and honors, and was never offered a tenured professorship in one of the more prestigious universities. Much of his career in the United States was spent in such unlikely departments as home economics and child welfare. Nevertheless many of his theories and concepts became so influential that their origin was forgotten. His saying "There is nothing so practical as a good theory" is often quoted even in the early 2000s without recognition of its source. Lewin's personal modesty—he rarely added his name as coauthor to his students' published papers—and his ability to stimulate the creativity of his students and colleagues also meant that his innovations in experimental method as well as theory did not attract the attention they deserved.

Lewin's most lasting contribution to psychology may well have been his social conscience. His teaching of evening classes for blue-collar workers during his graduate school years in Berlin, his concern for equal education for women, his action research projects

investigating anti-Semitism and racial prejudice—all of these inspired three generations of psychologists to undertake work that benefits the wider society as well as academic scholarship.

BIOGRAPHY

Childhood and early life

Kurt Lewin was born on September 9, 1890—what he himself called "the ninth nine of 90" in the small town of Mogilno, which is now part of Poland. At the time of Lewin's birth, however, it belonged to imperial Germany. His father, Leopold Lewin, ran a small general store on the ground floor of the family's home. The Lewins also owned a small farm a few miles outside Mogilno, where Kurt acquired a love of nature and enjoyed the freedom to explore the nearby fields and forests. He also had his own garden and became a skilled amateur mechanic.

Lewin's mother Recha was a warmhearted and energetic woman who reared her four children while she worked in the family store. Hertha, the firstborn child, was the only daughter. Kurt was the oldest of the three sons; his younger brothers were named Egon and Fritz. The family was close-knit and affectionate with one another. The Lewin family was not wealthy, but belonged to the financially secure middle class. Lewin's father served for a time as the president of the local synagogue.

In 1905, however, Lewin's family moved from Mogilno to Berlin because the parents wanted to give their children a better education than small-town schools could provide. Kurt was enrolled in the Kaiserin Augusta Gymnasium, a very selective high school that prepared students for university entrance. He was not regarded as an outstanding student until his last two years at the Gymnasium, when he began to study Greek philosophy and fell in love with it.

Lewin graduated from the Gymnasium in 1909 and entered the University of Freiburg, intending to study medicine and become a country doctor. He disliked the anatomy courses, however, and left Freiburg after one semester, transferring to the University of Munich. After completing one semester at Munich, Lewin transferred again—this time to the University of Berlin, where he remained until he completed his Ph.D. He took courses in philosophy instead of medicine, and found himself particularly attracted to the philosophy of science. One of Lewin's teachers suggested that he might find psychology interesting, and it was this suggestion that led to Lewin's work in the Psychological Institute of the University of Berlin. When the time came for Lewin to choose a director for his dissertation, he requested Carl Stumpf (1848–1936), who was the director of the university's Psychological Laboratory. Stumpf was a pioneer of the experimental method in psychology, which brought him into conflict with the reigning school of psychology in Germany in the 1890s. In addition to Stumpf, the other professor who made a deep impression on Lewin was Ernst Cassirer (1874–1945), who taught courses in philosophy of science. Lewin always admired Cassirer for encouraging him to push beyond the boundaries that limited the study of psychology at that time.

While in graduate school, Lewin became involved with socialist groups that advocated a democratic government for Germany as well as legal and professional equality for women. He formed a group of nine or 10 students who organized evening classes for working-class men and women in subjects ranging from arithmetic and reading skills to history and geography. The informal "school" continued to enroll more and more students each year until the outbreak of World War I.

World War I and early career

Although Lewin was not eager to go to war, he volunteered to serve in the Kaiser's army after World War I broke out in 1914. He had already completed the requirements for his doctorate, but the degree itself was not conferred until 1916. Lewin served throughout most of the war, working his way up to the rank of lieutenant. He was wounded in 1917 and hospitalized, but his younger brother Fritz was killed in action. While Lewin was recovering, he published his first journal article, "Kriegslandschaft" or "War Landscape," which was a preview of several of the concepts he developed in his later work, such as "life space," "boundary," and "zone." That same year, he married Maria Landsberg, a close friend of his best friend's wife. Maria taught English and German in a high school for girls.

The years between 1917 and 1921 were full of turmoil for German academics. In 1918, the Kaiser abdicated and fled to the Netherlands as the German army was defeated in France. Part of the Kaiser's former palace was used to house the University of Berlin, and the Psychological Institute was given several rooms to use for lectures and research. In 1921 Lewin was appointed a *Privatdozent* or university lecturer, but this position did not carry a salary; *Privatdozenten* were paid directly by their students. Lewin was well liked by his students, however, as he was much less formal than most European academics and encouraged his students to develop their own ideas. It was during this period also that Lewin began to add

PRINCIPAL PUBLICATIONS

- "Kriegslandschaft" [War Landscape]. *Zeitschrift für angewandte Psychologie* 12 (1917) 440–447.
- *Der Begriff der Genese in Physik, Biologie und Entwicklungsgeschichte* [The Concept of Origin in Physics, Biology, and the History of Evolution]. Berlin: Julius Springer Verlag, 1922.
- *A Dynamic Theory of Personality: Selected Papers of Kurt Lewin,* translated by Donald K. Adams and Karl E. Zener. New York: McGraw-Hill Book Company, 1935.
- *Principles of Topological Psychology.* New York: McGraw-Hill Book Company, 1936.
- *Resolving Social Conflicts: Selected Papers on Group Dynamics,* edited by Gertrud W. Lewin. New York: Harper and Row, Publishers, 1948.
- *Field Theory in Social Science: Selected Theoretical Papers,* edited by Dorwin Cartwright. New York: Harper and Brothers, 1951.

mathematical formulae and blackboard diagrams to his lectures. He taught courses in philosophy as well as psychology, and after 1924 began to supervise doctoral candidates as well. At a time when women were still not fully accepted in European universities, Lewin had an unusually large number of female doctoral candidates, many of them from the Soviet Union.

Lewin first came to the attention of British and American psychologists through J. F. Brown, an American who studied with him in Berlin. Brown published a paper on Lewin's methods in an English-language journal in 1929. Lewin had also been invited to give a lecture to the International Congress of Psychology, which met at Yale University in Connecticut in 1929. Lewin brought along a short film he had made of an 18-month-old child—his wife's niece—to illustrate some of his concepts. Even though he lectured in German, his ideas were so interesting that several American students came to Berlin in 1930 to work with him, and two of them translated several of his articles for republication in English. A collection of these translated articles was published in the United States in 1935 under the title *A Dynamic Theory of*

Personality. By that time Lewin had left Germany permanently.

Move to the United States

Lewin's work at the Psychological Institute came to an end when Hitler's rise to power led to riots that temporarily closed the University of Berlin. Lewin had been invited to Stanford University in California in 1932 as a visiting professor. When Hitler became chancellor of Germany in January 1933, Lewin realized that he and his family were no longer safe in their homeland because they were Jews. He resigned his professorship at the University of Berlin and returned to the United States in August 1933, when he was offered a two-year position at Cornell's School of Home Economics. When the Cornell appointment ran out in 1935, Lewin accepted a position at the Child Welfare Research Station at the University of Iowa, where he remained until 1944. Although Lewin was still struggling with learning English, he was again popular with students, gathering an informal weekly lunchtime meeting that the students nicknamed "the Hot-Air Club." He had a lively sense of humor and enjoyed telling jokes; in addition he never rejected students or colleagues for disagreeing with him. One of Lewin's colleagues later recalled,

> people could move out of Lewin's immediate circle even during his lifetime and still maintain ties with him and others in his circle. . . . I think Kurt was quite right in saying that he didn't want to develop a school of psychology; he was merely trying to develop a language for the representation of psychological phenomena.

While at Iowa, Lewin built a reputation as an outstanding experimental as well as theoretical psychologist. Some of the studies he undertook during this period are described under "Theories in action" below.

The fact that Lewin came to the United States from a very different academic as well as national culture gave him a fresh perspective on his new country. He was particularly interested in the question of different national characteristics. In 1936, he published an article still regarded as one of his finest—"Some Social Psychological Differences Between the United States and Germany," which appeared in the journal *Character and Personality*. Among other points, Lewin contrasted the degree of independence in American children and "the lack of servility of the young child toward adults or of the student toward his professor," with the behavior of their German counterparts. He also noted the relative openness of American adults compared to Germans. In view of Lewin's later work on social groups and group membership, it is interesting that he was determined to become an American—

which for him meant much more than formal citizenship, though he was certainly delighted when he became a citizen in 1940. He set about improving his English as quickly as he could, even though he never completely lost his German accent. When he noticed that his children were confused by the difference between the German pronunciation of their last name ("Luh-veen," with the accent on the second syllable) and the way their American teachers pronounced it ("Loo-in," with the accent on the first), Lewin asked his colleagues to pronounce his name the American way. His biographer tells of an incident at the World's Fair in New York in 1939, when dinner hour approached, both men were getting hungry, and the restaurants on the fairgrounds were already full. "'Let's have a couple of hot dogs,' Lewin said. 'That's what we Americans eat on Sunday evenings in the summer!' Five minutes later that's what we were doing."

Lewin brought his long-standing concern with social issues to bear on solving industrial problems during the late 1930s. Many of his first experiments with action research began during this period. The problems that Lewin and his colleagues tackled ranged from helping inexperienced factory workers raise their production levels, to training foremen and supervisors in leadership skills. One of Lewin's associates at Iowa, a psychologist named Alex Bavelas, set up a series of small-group studies at a factory in Virginia that ran from 1940 to 1947. These studies are described in more detail below. The experience that Lewin and his group had in teaching leadership skills was eventually put to use in later sensitivity training programs.

Wartime work

After the United States entered World War II in December 1941, psychologists as well as scholars in other fields were sought out by government officials to help solve problems related to the war effort, and to come up with better methods of measuring and analyzing results. Psychologists in particular were consulted about such questions as maintaining morale on the home front, improving leadership training in the military, and solving human relations issues in offices and factories in order to boost production. The Office of Naval Research (ONR) contacted Lewin and his group at Iowa to review research proposals and provide feedback on general ONR policy. In addition, Lewin advised the Office of Strategic Services (OSS) on psychological warfare. As of the 1980s, some of his contributions in this area were still considered classified information.

Lewin's wartime work involved frequent trips to Washington, which caused some tension with his colleagues in Iowa. In addition to disagreeing with his theories, some other faculty members resented his frequent absences from the campus, his smaller teaching load, and his growing reputation outside the academic community. Lewin also had growing doubts as to whether Iowa was the right place for carrying out some experiments that he wanted to do in the field of group dynamics, a subject that had captured his attention early in the war. He was convinced that psychologists needed to do more than simply look for explanations of people's behavior. In an article published in 1945, Lewin stated, "We must be equally concerned with discovering how people can change their ways so that they learn to behave better." These discoveries, however, depended on experimentation.

As Lewin became more committed to action research, he began to think about setting up a research institute associated with a university that would not be controlled by the university. After a possible job offer from the New School for Social Research in New York fell through, Lewin approached several foundations for funding for his proposed institute. He also thought about possible locations for it—he wanted it to be related to a university in a large city with a variety of community, racial, religious, and industrial problems that could serve as a laboratory for action research. In 1944, Lewin finally received an invitation to set up his institute at the Massachusetts Institute of Technology. It was called the Research Center for Group Dynamics. At the same time that Lewin was beginning to staff the new Center, he launched another new project, the Commission on Community Interrelations (CCI) for the American Jewish Congress (AJC). The purpose of the CCI was to investigate the roots of prejudice against Jews. Lewin expected that the research undertaken by the CCI would benefit all minority groups in the United States, not only Jews; as he put it in a letter to a well-known rabbi, "The fight of the Jews is a part of the fight of all minorities for democratic equality of rights and opportunities."

Lewin hoped to get the new Research Center at MIT ready by the fall of 1945, since the war had ended in August with the surrender of Japan. He had been able to attract additional funding from the National Institute of Mental Health, the Air Force, and the Rockefeller Foundation, which allowed him to enlarge the teaching staff. The Center supported six major areas of research: group productivity, communication, social perception, intergroup relations, group membership and individual adjustment, and leadership training. Within less than a year, students from many other countries as well as the United States were enrolling in courses at the new Center.

In spite of Lewin's busy schedule at the Center, he continued his involvement with the CCI, which had broadened its scope to include interracial problems as well as religious prejudice. He was also consulted about a project begun by the Connecticut State Interracial Commission to train leaders who could help resolve racial and religious tensions. Lewin designed a two-week workshop in 1946 to train 41 community leaders for the Connecticut program. This workshop led within months to the establishment of the National Training Laboratories, or NTL, in Bethel, Maine, in the summer of 1947. The technique of leadership training that Lewin pioneered in 1946 is considered by some psychologists to be "the most significant social invention of [the twentieth] century."

The many projects that Lewin took on during and after the war strained his health and energy. His friends urged him to slow down, but he insisted on keeping up his busy schedule. On February 11, 1947, Lewin went home for dinner and told his wife he felt ill. She called the family physician, who diagnosed a mild heart attack. Before the doctor could get Lewin to the hospital, however, he suffered a second attack and died. He was not yet 57 years old.

Marriages and family

Lewin's 1917 marriage to Maria Landsberg ended in divorce in 1927. The couple had had two children—a daughter, Agnes, born in 1919; and a son, Fritz, born in 1922. The marriage was strained by Lewin's work habits—he had an irregular work schedule in addition to being frequently away from home—and by Fritz's childhood illness. Fritz had been slow in learning to walk, and the family physician discovered at that time that he had been born with both hips dislocated. Two major operations were required, one on each hip joint, with a long recovery period in between. In addition, Agnes began to develop emotional problems related to the family's focus on her brother's health. Although both parents were devoted to the children, they could not agree on the best way to deal with these issues. Lewin moved out of the home, but continued to visit his children and former wife until they moved to Palestine when Hitler came to power.

In 1929 Lewin married Gertrud Weiss, whom he and Maria had known since 1921. They had two children—Miriam, born in 1931; and Daniel, born in 1933. Miriam became a clinical psychologist in her own right; among other publications, she wrote a handbook for student researchers in psychology as well as a historical account of psychologists' views of gender roles.

One of the tragedies of Lewin's last years was his inability to rescue his mother, who had remained in

Berlin after Lewin left Germany. After Hitler invaded Poland in September 1939, Lewin tried to bring his mother to the United States, but was unable to obtain a visa for her. Recha Lewin was sent to a concentration camp somewhere in Poland in 1943, where she died in 1944. Several of Lewin's friends believed that his personal sorrows contributed to his untimely death. He turned his private pain, however, into compassion for other victims of prejudice and discrimination, and he never lost his faith in a better future for all people.

THEORIES

Field theory and the structure of human personality

Main points   Lewin's theories in general are difficult for new psychology students for several reasons. One is that he coined a number of new terms and expressions, such as "life space" and "foreign hull." In addition to new terms, Lewin also used such familiar words as "locomotion," "fact," "event," and "tension" in unfamiliar ways. Lewin also borrowed mathematical and scientific terms, including "vector," "force," and "valence." As a result, Lewin's articles are not easy reading.

Lewin is well known in the history of psychology for his field theory. Field theory is a term that was originally developed by physicists in the 1870s to account for what happens when a number of different forces interact. The physicists began to refer to these collections of forces as energy fields. Lewin came to regard the human mind as a complex energy field containing tension systems in various states of equilibrium, or balance. He then defined human behavior as a change in the state of this energy field. Lewin begins with the life space, which includes all the possible facts that may influence a person's behavior at a given point in time. "Real-world" facts are important only to the extent that they are psychologically important to the individual. Lewin summarized his concept of behavior as a function of the life space in a mathematical formula: $B = f (LS)$. He also represented the life space by a drawing known as a Jordan curve, which is an irregular closed curved line resembling an egg or ellipse. The curve itself is the boundary that separates the person from the parts of the real world that are not psychologically significant to him or her. Inside the Jordan curve is a smaller circle containing a P, which represents the person. The circle is inside the ellipse but does not touch it. The area outside the circle but inside the ellipse is called the psychological environment. The total area inside the Jordan curve, including the circle, is called the life space. The area

outside the ellipse is called the foreign hull. Lewin invented the term "topological psychology" to describe these geometrical drawings, topology being the branch of geometry that deals with the properties of geometric figures that do not change when the figure is bent or stretched.

Lewin's diagram of the life space includes several subdivisions. The circle representing the person can be subdivided into two concentric circles. The inner circle represents what Lewin called the inner-personal region, and the outer ring is the perceptual-motor region. Similarly, the psychological environment surrounding the circle can be divided into regions, which represent possible intellectual, physical, or social activities. Lewin refers to the principal facts in the person's inner-personal region as needs, and the corresponding facts in the psychological environment as goals. Needs control the person's behavior and are satisfied when the person achieves his or her goals. Goals are related to needs by either a positive or negative attraction, which Lewin called a valence. To give an example of what Lewin meant by a valence, a warm sweater would have a positive valence for someone sitting motionless outside on a cold day, while the same sweater would have a negative valence for someone playing a fast game of tennis on an outdoor court in mid-July.

According to Lewin, people tend to move psychologically toward entities in their life space that have a strong positive valence, and away from those with a negative valence. He called these movements locomotions. Lewin did not use the word "locomotion" to refer primarily to a physical movement through space, but a movement through the psychological environment within a person's life space. Thus there are many different types of locomotions: a person might move toward an answer in solving a crossword puzzle, or move away from depressing thoughts by calling a friend, or move toward higher social status by joining a prestigious club. All of these psychological movements are locomotions as Lewin used the word. A locomotion in the life space might entail physical movement in the outside world—as when a hungry person decides to leave their house and go to a nearby restaurant—but the locomotion itself is the person's psychological movement toward food. Behavior to Lewin is always goal-directed, and therefore always involves locomotion toward or away from goals within the life space.

Locomotions through the life space, however, may be prevented by barriers. To Lewin, a barrier is anything that the person perceives as a block or resistance to locomotion toward a goal. An example of a barrier would be a person's fear of another family member's reaction to their choice of a movie for a family outing. Another type of barrier would be the obstacle posed to medical school admission by failing a college course in chemistry.

Explanation   Lewin's basic approach to questions of personality was derived from Gestalt psychology, which will be described more fully in a later section. The central point of Gestalt psychology for present purposes is that human perception is shaped by the total context of individual objects; that is, people perceive relationships among the various objects that they are looking at rather than the characteristics of each item by itself. Another way of putting the matter is that people do not perceive separate objects directly but rather impose an organizational pattern on them in their mind. Commonplace examples include the fact that people often "see" some kind of shape or pattern in cloud formations, or the way in which astronomers group individual stars into constellations. In contrast to behaviorist psychologists, who began with collecting masses of data and analyzing them from the bottom up, so to speak, Lewin and other Gestaltists began with the overall pattern or shape of a field, and then proceeded to study its smaller components. Lewin's field theory thus takes in everything in a person's life that is psychologically important to him or her, and organizes all the elements in that life—goals, needs, behavior, tensions, forces, etc.—into a single system of description and explanation. In addition, field theory holds that all the elements in the life space are interdependent and influence one another.

In addition to the influence of Gestalt psychology on Lewin's field theory, it is also important to understand that Lewin saw his drawings of egg-shaped curves and enclosed circles as more than just blackboard illustrations for teaching purposes; to him they were maps of reality itself. As Lewin's biographer expressed it, "The Jordan curve . . . is a conceptual representation of reality which can serve as a map to guide the psychologist." Other psychologists, however, disagreed with Lewin's own estimation of his topological psychology; their criticisms are discussed more fully below.

Examples   An example of Lewin's use of language as well as his way of diagramming his ideas is found in a 1946 article entitled "Behavior and Development as a Function of the Total Situation." Lewin's diagram represents a state of indecision, in this case a child who must choose between two goals, each with a positive valence. Perhaps the child has to choose between playing with friends and going to a movie with the rest of the family. Lewin maintains that "the person being in the process of making a decision usually alternates

between seeing himself in a future situation corresponding to the one and the other possibility." Two Jordan curves are used to diagram these hypothetical futures, with the decision identifying the overlapping region.

Tension systems and the dynamics of human personality

Main points   Lewin's field theory utilizes the concept of tension systems in order to explain human personality in action. In essence, a tension system is an energy system created by a need and released when the person achieves the goal related to that need. Lewin does not use the word "tension" in the sense of an undesirable stress or emotional strain; rather, he regarded tension as a desirable condition of readiness for action toward attaining a goal. He saw tension as increased by any barrier between the need and the goal. In addition to barriers, Lewin also related tensions to forces. Lewin distinguished three types of forces: driving forces, which arise from needs and cause locomotion toward a goal; restraining forces, which are associated with barriers; and induced forces, which are related to the wishes of other people in the person's life space. Lewin regarded forces as having both direction and strength, and represented them in his drawings as vectors (arrows), with the direction of the vector representing the direction of the force, and its length representing its intensity or strength. An inner-personal conflict results when the driving forces that affect a person come from different directions and are about equal in strength. The conflict may concern one negative and one positive goal, or two equally negative or equally positive goals.

Lewin maintained that tension tends to equalize itself by spreading from one region throughout a person's psychic system; he called the means of this equalization a process. Processes include such activities as thinking, remembering, perceiving, performing an action, and many others. Several different tension systems and processes may coexist simultaneously within a person and remain for various lengths of time. A simple example of what Lewin meant by process and the equalization of tension systems is a person who notices an itchy area between the shoulder blades at the same time that he is trying to balance his checkbook. The person may decide to interrupt his calculations in order to satisfy the need to scratch his upper back. After the tension in that part of his psychic system subsides, the person returns to his checkbook in order to fulfill his need to complete the interrupted task.

Lewin was not completely satisfied with the word "need" to explain increases in psychological tension. He used the word as a rough equivalent for "motive," "wish," or "urge." In Lewin's usage, a need is not limited to such physical conditions as hunger or thirst—it could include intentions (to finish a project), purposes (to get on the football team), or desires (to go for a walk outside on a nice day). Lewin never tried to reduce all human needs to one basic need as some psychologists did, although he did distinguish between needs derived from such bodily conditions as hunger, thirst, or feeling cold, and what he called quasi-needs, which include purposes and intentions. Lewin thought that quasi-needs are by far the more common type in everyday life.

Explanation   Lewin developed his concept of tension systems in part because he disagreed with the associationist explanation of human behavior. Associationist psychologists explained behavior as the end result of simple ideas derived from sense experience that became associated in the mind through repetition and conditioning. An associationist psychologist would regard doing any purposeful action as setting up a tendency to repeat the action. Lewin observed that there are many purposeful actions that people do not ordinarily repeat once they have achieved their goal. For example, a person who goes into the kitchen to pour themselves a cup of coffee does not automatically brew themselves another cup the next time they walk into the kitchen. On Lewin's account of the matter, the tension created by the person's desire for a cup of coffee is released by the act of going into the kitchen and filling their cup, which is why returning to the kitchen a few moments later to feed the cat or wash the dishes does not lead to making or pouring another cup of coffee. The psychic energy related to the first need has been released, and the other tension system(s) are now in the forefront of the person's attention.

Another important feature of Lewin's concept of tension systems is his emphasis on the here-and-now. He parted company with Freudian psychoanalysis in looking for long-term historical explanations of human behavior. Lewin argued instead for what he called the principle of contemporaneity in a person's life space, meaning that only present facts can influence present behavior. The facts of a person's infancy or childhood cannot affect adult behavior unless they have remained alive in some sense as the person matured. In one of his early articles entitled "On the Structure of the Mind," Lewin drew on his own experience as the basis for the principle of contemporaneity:

> Twenty-five years ago I awoke, happy that I did not have to go to school that day, I flew a kite . . . ate a great deal of dessert, and played in the garden . . . each single everyday experience of the past may somehow influence the present psychic life . . . *but . . . the influence is extremely small, approximately*

zero. . . . Behavior would not be changed or would change imperceptibly if a great many of our experiences did not occur or occurred in other ways.

Lewin thought that Freud and his followers failed to distinguish between historical and systematic problems in psychology, "more or less consciously preferr[ing] richness of content to logical strictness of theory. . . . In other words, psychoanalysis is a body of ideas, rather than a system of theories and concepts."

Examples   Lewin's theory of tension systems received its first experimental proof in a casual after-hours setting. During his years in Berlin, he would often go with his students to a nearby café, where they would sit for hours discussing their work over coffee and slices of cake. The waiters did not keep written notes of the customers' orders, but could easily give a correct account to each member of a group when the bills were called for, even though the group might have been in the café for two or three hours. Lewin began to think that the waiters' memories were kept sharp by a tension system building up that was not released until a group of customers called for their bills. The next time that the group visited the café, Lewin waited for about half an hour after his students had paid their bills, and asked the waiter to rewrite the group's check. The man was annoyed by Lewin's request and said "I don't know any longer what you people ordered. You paid your bill." This informal proof of Lewin's theory led to his student Bluma Zeigarnik's famous experiment and the naming of the so-called "Zeigarnik effect," namely, that people are better at remembering uncompleted than completed tasks.

Bluma Zeigarnik's discussion of task interruption and recall is now considered a classic. Her dissertation was published in 1927 in the *Psychologische Zeitung* (Journal of Psychology), which was sponsored by the University of Berlin. Lewin summarized her experiments in an article that appeared in English translation in 1935. Zeigarnik conducted a series of experiments between 1924 and 1926 involving 164 subjects, adults as well as children. She gave the subjects about 20 simple tasks, such as making a list of cities, answering riddles, counting backwards, stringing beads, and doing other paper-and-pencil exercises. In the first experiment, the subjects were allowed to complete half of their tasks, while the other half were interrupted before they had finished. After some time had elapsed, Zeigarnik asked her subjects to remember as many of the tasks as they could. She found that they remembered uncompleted tasks better than completed tasks by a ratio of 1.9 to 1. She also found that her subjects were more than three times more likely to list one of their unfinished tasks first than one that they had been allowed to finish without interruption.

Zeigarnik then decided to test the possibility that her subjects' memory was related to the surprise of being interrupted rather than the state of their tension systems. She ran a second experiment in which she interrupted her subjects in one-third of their assigned tasks, allowed them to finish another third without interruption, and interrupted them during the final third but then allowed them to complete the unfinished tasks. Zeigarnik's results showed that the memory of the subjects in the second and third groups was almost identical, which indicated that it was not the interruption by itself but leaving the task unfinished that was the critical factor. Zeigarnik had successfully demonstrated that memory is related to unreleased tension systems.

Action research

Main points   Lewin's interest in what he termed action research, or applied social psychology, began during his last years at Iowa. His role as a consultant in several factories with production problems also stimulated his work in this area. Action research as he defined it begins with an identifiable social problem—for example, racial prejudice in a specific neighborhood or small town. Lewin outlined the basic steps or phases in action research in his 1946 article "Action Research and Minority Problems." The first stage is defining the problem and "examin[ing] the idea carefully in the light of the means available." The second step involves fact-finding and forming an overall plan for reaching the goal, along with a first step toward the goal. Lewin notes that "Usually this planning has also somewhat modified the original idea." The second phase consists of "executing the first step of the overall plan," followed by a second round of "reconnaissance or fact-finding."

Lewin stated that the second phase of fact-finding served four important purposes:

- Evaluating the success of the first step, "whether what has been achieved is above or below expectation."

- Giving the planners a chance to learn and gather new insights.

- Helping to plan the next step.

- Providing a basis for changing the overall plan.

The third phase of action research consists of another cycle of planning, acting, and fact-finding. These steps are repeated as often as necessary until the goal has been reached. Lewin summarized the process: "Rational social management, therefore, proceeds in a spiral of steps each of which is composed of a circle of planning, action, and fact-finding about the result of the action."

Explanation   Lewin's concept of action research has two important features. The first is that Lewin thought of action research as a group activity rather than an individual undertaking, which is reflected in some of its other names: participatory research, collaborative inquiry, and contextual research. This emphasis on group involvement in action research is in part a reflection of Lewin's own personality. He enjoyed the companionship of others and preferred to work with them rather than being a "lone ranger" type of researcher. His friends described him as a cheerful, even playful person; as a man who delighted in telling jokes or inviting people to his home for dinner on short notice. On the last night of Lewin's life, he told a colleague named Ronald Lippitt that a person's competence should not be defined in terms of "going it alone." Lippitt recalled Lewin as saying:

> The American ideal of the 'self-made man' . . . was as tragic a picture as the initiative-destroying dependence on a benevolent despot. We all need continuous help from each other. This type of interdependence is the greatest challenge to the maturity of individual and group functioning.

In addition to the factor of Lewin's own personality, he emphasized teamwork in action research because his own interests had shifted in the late 1930s from the psychology of individuals to that of groups. After the early 1940s, Lewin published very little new work on personality theory; he was now interested in constructing a general theory of group processes—how groups set standards, select leaders, reach decisions, and similar issues.

The second feature is the relationship of action research to Lewin's strong commitment to egalitarianism and democracy. "Learning by doing" was one of philosopher and educator John Dewey's foremost principles of educational method, and Lewin incorporated Dewey's perspective into his own work. As will be evident in one of the case studies under "Theories in action," Lewin's involvement in studies of race relations and religious prejudice sparked a number of action research projects.

Examples   An early example of Lewin's action research took place in the 1940s, when he served on a wartime committee that investigated American tastes and habits in food consumption. While the government's chief concern was to maintain the health of the civilian population during a period of food rationing, rising expenses, and necessary shifts in the kinds of

Kurt Lewin in his classroom. (*Archives of the History of American Psychology—The University of Akron. Reproduced by permission.*)

foods available to the public, Lewin recognized that eating habits are only one specific part of a much larger question—namely, how are social changes brought about within groups and by groups? Lewin set up a series of experiments to test the ways in which different families in the Midwest and New England differed in the foods they chose, and which members of the family had the greatest influence on these decisions. One experiment concerned persuading housewives to purchase so-called variety meats (the internal organs, feet, and tails of butchered animals) instead of the more expensive rationed cuts of meat. Lewin discovered during this experiment that the wives determined food choices rather than their husbands, even though the women had said at the beginning of the study that their husbands made the decisions. Lewin concluded that the most effective way to promote greater use of variety meats on the home front was to convince the wives rather than the husbands that people could enjoy eating these less expensive meats.

One of Lewin's first community-related action research projects took place at the request of the CCI in 1946. It concerned an incident of religious prejudice in Coney Island, New York, in which a gang of four Italian Roman-Catholic boys had created a noisy disturbance during Yom Kippur services at a nearby synagogue. At the time of this incident, Lewin had only two assistants on his staff, but he quickly recruited a task force of psychologists that included Protestants and African Americans as well as Roman Catholics and Jews. All the members of the task force had been trained in human relations. The group's first action step was to stop a lawsuit against the four boys, who were then placed under the supervision of their parish priest and a group of Catholic Big Brothers. Lewin's group then made a survey of community attitudes, interviewing as many local people as they could. The researchers found that the boys were not angry at Jews in particular but felt angry and frustrated about life in general. The neighborhood as a whole felt that better housing, transportation, and recreational facilities would help ease tensions among the different racial and religious groups. The task force's findings were reported to the Mayor of New York, who earmarked some funds for the needed improvements. One member of the CCI staff was assigned to work closely with the four boys. A year later, CCI was able to report to the mayor that the gang members had virtually stopped their street fights and bullying of other people. The final measure of the project's success was that the gang members did not return to their former behavior even after CCI's consultancy ended.

Groups and change processes

Main points Lewin was interested in group processes for both theoretical and practical reasons. On the theoretical level, he thought that a solid body of knowledge, once collected, would allow him to form a general theory that would fit any group—marriages, nuclear and extended families, workplace groups, religious congregations, and community organizations. He understood group behavior as a function of both individual members and social contexts. From a historical perspective, Lewin was in the right place at the right time, as specialists in such fields as industrial management, group psychotherapy, and education were convinced by the mid-1940s that they needed to do more studies of group functioning. Lewin's first use of the term "group dynamics" appeared in a 1939 article called "Experiments in Social Space," in which he said that the purpose of his experiments was "to give insight into the underlying group dynamics."

Two key concepts regarding group process emerged from Lewin's field theory, namely interdependence of fate and task interdependence. As was mentioned in the preceding section, Lewin regarded interdependence in general as an essential feature of individual as well as group maturity. Interdependence of fate was a concept that Lewin used to explain the existence of groups that come into being "when people in [the group] realize that their fate depends on the fate of the group as a whole." Writing in 1946, Lewin described the Jews as an instance of this type of interdependence.

> It is not similarity or dissimilarity of individuals that constitutes a group, but interdependence of fate. . . . It is easy enough to see that the common fate of all Jews makes them a group in reality. . . . A person who has learned to see how much his own fate depends upon the fate of his entire group will be ready and even eager to take over a fair share of responsibility for its welfare.

Other examples of interdependence of fate would include groups of people engaged in dangerous activities, such as the members of mountain climbing expeditions or space shuttle crews.

Lewin recognized, however, that interdependence of fate by itself does not form strong bonds among the members of most groups. He regarded task interdependence as a stronger "glue" in keeping the members of a group together. Using the concept of tension systems from his field theory, Lewin argued that the tension within group members created by desires for a common goal resulted in interdependence in order to achieve the goal. He was not convinced by the psychoanalytical explanation of group activity as the result of aggressive drives in some individuals belonging to the group. Rather, Lewin concluded that groups provide a setting for their individual members' sense of identity and social reality. "The group a person is a part of, and the culture in which he lives, determine to a very high degree his behavior and character . . . [as well as] his personal style of living and the direction and productivity of his planning." In a later article, Lewin said, "What exists as 'reality' for the individual is, to a high degree, determined by what is socially accepted as reality. . . . 'Reality,' therefore, is not an absolute. It differs with the group to which the individual belongs."

Lewin's theoretical understanding of group dynamics had practical applications in terms of social change. As World War II drew to a close, psychologists as well as researchers in other fields were concerned about rebuilding the social as well as the economic structures of the defeated Axis powers. Lewin's understanding of group dynamics was directly relevant to such issues as reintroducing democratic values in Germany and Japan, and doing it in such a way that these nations would not return to dictatorial political systems. Lewin believed that the democratic government of the United States depended on a certain "social atmosphere" more than pure reason or logic, and that this social atmosphere had to be protected and maintained by each successive generation.

> The social climate in which a child lives is for the child as important as the air it breathes. . . . It seems to be 'natural' for people living in a thoroughly democratic tradition like that of the United States to believe that what is scientifically reasonable should finally become accepted everywhere. However, history shows . . . that the belief in reason as a social value is by no means universal, but is itself a result of a definite social atmosphere.

Lewin's research in group dynamics led him to conclude that social change must be brought about in and by groups rather than forced on people as individuals. One of his most famous psychological experiments involved two groups of schoolchildren who were asked to complete a task (making masks for a school play); one group in a democratic atmosphere and the other group directed by an autocratic adult. The results of the experiment convinced Lewin that democracy not only requires voluntary participation in groups, but is best learned through such participation. In "Cultural Reconstruction," an article that Lewin published in 1943, he observed:

> It is a fallacy to assume that people, if left alone, follow a democratic pattern in their group life. . . . In democracy, as in any culture, the individual acquires the cultural pattern by some type of "learning." Normally, such learning occurs by way of growing up in that culture.

Attempting to answer the question of reconstructing German culture after the war, Lewin proposed to focus on the country's teenagers, with that age group's typical enthusiasm and interest in group activities.

> The adolescent is at that age level which determines what the cultural pattern will be in the immediately following generation . . . transforming this very age level—which is full of enthusiasm and, in many respects, accustomed to cooperation—into cooperative groups for productive reconstruction in a radical democratic spirit might be one of the few chances for bringing about a change for democracy which promises permanency.

Explanation   One factor that helps to explain Lewin's conviction that groups are more significant than individuals in bringing about and maintaining social change is that he saw groups as the molds of individual character. In an important essay on "Conduct, Knowledge, and Acceptance of New Values" (1945), Lewin maintained that the processes by which an individual learns bad or deviant behavior are the same as those that shape normal behavior. "What counts is the effect upon the individual of the circumstances of his life, the influence of the group in which he has grown up."

Given this position, Lewin argued that reeducation in any society is essentially a process of cultural change. He saw this change as having three major aspects or levels:

• Changing people's cognitive structure.

• Changing their values. This transformation usually requires dealing with prejudices and stereotypes.

• Changing people's outward behavior. Lewin recognized that change on this level requires a change in a person's feelings about members of other groups as well as changes in their thinking.

Lewin observed, however, that "acceptance of the new set of values and beliefs cannot usually be brought about item by item." To bring about this three-fold change, the leaders of a society must establish what Lewin called an "in-group," which he defined as "a group in which the members feel belongingness." Lewin then postulated that

> the individual accepts the new system of values and beliefs by accepting belongingness to a group. . . . The chances for [successful] reeducation seem to be increased whenever a strong we-feeling is created. . . . It is basic for reeducation that this linkage between acceptance of new facts or values and acceptance of certain of certain groups or roles is very intimate and that the second frequently is a prerequisite for the first.

Examples   Lewin's work with organizational change and the first experimental T-groups is a good example of

his lasting influence on later psychologists as well as his work with group dynamics. He is often referred to as the "grandfather" of organizational change for the studies he conducted in the early 1940s, and for his insistence that any theory of change had to take into account not only the organization, but also the individuals in the organization and its surrounding environment. Lewin argued that none of these factors can be understood in isolation from the others. One of his most frequently quoted remarks has to do with changing organizations: "If you want truly to understand something, try to change it." Lewin outlined his basic model of the steps involved in organizational change in "Frontiers in Group Dynamics," a paper published in 1947. He drew on field theory to explain his three steps, which he called "unfreezing," "moving the group to a new level," and "refreezing," or making the changes permanent. Unfreezing refers to changing the force field within the organization. Lewin had pointed out that stability in any group is the result of a balance between driving forces (for change) and restraining forces (against change), all of which can be represented by diagrams and mathematical symbols. Trying to change an organization by adding more driving forces usually results in a counterforce that maintains the status quo. Lewin had the insight that it is generally easier to unfreeze an organization's internal balance by removing restraining forces than by adding driving forces.

Lewin's three-step model of organizational change—particularly the notion of unfreezing—became an important part of the training groups, or T groups, that grew out of his experimental work with the Connecticut State Interracial Commission in the summer of 1946. As was mentioned earlier, Lewin and three of his associates at MIT had been asked to conduct a two-week workshop for 41 community leaders in dealing with racial prejudice; including learning skills in dealing with people and more reliable ways to change social attitudes. The workshop was held on the campus of a teachers' college in New Britain, Connecticut. Some of the participants lived nearby and went home in the evenings, while others remained on the campus. Since the trainers held nightly sessions in which they discussed their observations of the trainees, the trainees who were staying at the college asked if they could attend these meetings. Most staff members were reluctant to allow the trainees to join the meetings, but Lewin saw no reason why they should not hear the observers discuss their behavior. The observers' feedback—a term that Lewin had borrowed from electrical engineering—was eye-opening to the trainees. The second development during the evening came when one of the female trainees disputed a staff member's observations about her behavior. Her disagreement led to a four-way conversation that involved the trainer, another observer, the trainee, and Lewin himself. The new data that emerged from this conversation as well as the open discussion of different opinions changed the format of the evening meetings. After that night the evening meetings became the most significant learning sessions of the workshop.

Although Lewin died before the first National Training Laboratory in Group Development was held in the summer of 1947, his theories formed the basis of the NTL's work, particularly its so-called laboratory method. The laboratory method was intended to provide "basic skills training," conducted in small discussion groups (usually 10 participants) with an observer who reported his observations to the group members from time to time. The skills had to do with becoming an effective "change agent." By 1949 the name of the basic skills training groups had been shortened to "T groups," which became the model for the encounter groups of the 1960s, sensitivity training groups in the 1970s, and team-building groups in the 1990s. In the process, however, Lewin's original vision of the laboratory as a setting for basic research in social dynamics was gradually deemphasized, and replaced with a focus on individual and personal growth. In the process, NTL also acquired a business rather than a research mindset, to the point where it has itself become a large business as of the early 2000s.

Lewin's influence was clearly evident, however, in what are still considered the four basic elements of T-group training:

- Unfreezing. Unfreezing refers to disconfirming or challenging a person's belief system in order to motivate them to change. T-group trainers try to create settings in which people's present values and beliefs are challenged.

- Feedback. As Lewin used the term, feedback refers to adjusting a process in light of accurate information about its results or effects. Feedback in T groups has been found to be most effective when it is based on here-and-now events and observations, and when the person receiving the feedback can check with other group members to test its accuracy.

- Participant observation. T-group participants are expected to participate in group sessions on an emotional as well as intellectual level. The trainers and observers in Lewin's original 1946 workshop modeled this combination of emotional involvement and analytic detachment.

- Teaching aids. Lewin's diagrams and mathematical models were eventually replaced by handouts and video clips, but the basic principle of reinforcing learning in T groups by visual means is derived from Lewin.

HISTORICAL CONTEXT

Gestalt psychology

The most important intellectual influence on Kurt Lewin was Gestalt psychology, a German school of thought that developed in the late nineteenth century in opposition to associationist and behaviorist views. Psychologists in both these groups broke down psychological events into separate parts and then proceeded to analyze the parts without reference to the whole. The Gestaltists insisted that psychological events had to be interpreted as integral wholes. The German philosopher Immanuel Kant (1724–1804) is regarded as a forerunner of Gestalt psychology. Kant argued in his *Critique of Pure Reason* (1781) that human perception by its nature organizes data received from the body's sense organs into unities or wholes that the person can understand. Although Max Wertheimer (1880–1943) is usually regarded as the founder of Gestalt psychology, the term "Gestalt" was first used by the philosopher Christian von Ehrenfels (1859–1932) in a paper on "form qualities" (*Gestalt Qualitaten* in German) in music.

The German word *Gestalt* does not have an exact English equivalent; it has been variously translated as "form," "shape," or "figure." German also has a verb form, *gestalten*, which can mean "to take shape" or "to assume a form." Wertheimer first began to use the term *Gestalt* when he heard von Ehrenfels' lecture about music. He observed that such terms as "major" or "minor" are characteristics of full chords or musical phrases rather than isolated notes. Later, in studying the phenomenon of apparent motion (in which two alternately flashing lights are perceived as one light moving back and forth), Wertheimer maintained that the apparent movement of the lights cannot be reduced to simpler physical stimuli. He defined what came to be called the Gestalt law of minimum principle—people do not perceive what actually exists in the external world as much as they tend to organize their sensory experiences in the simplest possible way. Wertheimer also formulated several laws of organization to explain how people organize sense experiences into simple and coherent wholes.

The five most important Gestalt laws are:

- Proximity. People perceive items that are close together in space as a group of items.

- Similarity. People perceive items that look alike as a group.

- Good form. What this law means is that human perceptions tend to become as clear and as fully developed as possible. For example, people will generally see a triangle with a small piece missing from one side as a complete triangle.

- Closure. People usually make their sensory experiences as complete as possible. This law is reflected in Lewin's theory of tension systems and the resolution of tensions.

- Figure and ground. This law refers to people's tendency to organize visual perceptions by distinguishing between a focus of attention (figure) and a background.

Anti-Semitism

Lewin's life was affected by anti-Semitism on the professional as well as the personal level. The close and affectionate bond that he had with his parents is reflected in the fact that they continued to support him financially as well as emotionally when he changed his course of study from medicine to philosophy of science and psychology. The reason that their approval was significant is that Lewin was risking his future employment by preparing for a university professorship. Although he would have had no difficulty in finding work as a country doctor, he faced the same strong discrimination against Jews in the German universities that Freud had confronted. Lewin's parents knew that his chances of obtaining a full professorship with a decent salary were very low; nevertheless they supported their son's decision.

After Lewin moved to the United States, he recognized that anti-Semitism existed in his new country, even though it was much less organized and murderous than the state-sanctioned anti-Semitism of Nazi Germany and Soviet Russia. Many American universities had admission quotas for Jewish students in the 1920s and 1930s, particularly at the graduate and professional school level. In addition, some of the most prestigious hotels in the United States openly identified themselves as "restricted," which meant that they did not accept Jewish guests. There is a striking scene in *Gentleman's Agreement*, a movie released in the year of Lewin's death, in which an undercover reporter pretending to be a Jew in order to do research on anti-Semitism finds that the exclusive resort where he has made a vacation reservation refuses to honor it.

Lewin understood that much of American anti-Semitism had to do with the aftermath of World War I and the Communist revolution in Russia. The Immigration Act of 1924, which sharply reduced the number of immigrants from Eastern Europe, shut the primary escape route for Jews from those countries trying to escape the anti-Semitic policies of Stalin and Hitler. In addition, the economic hardships resulting from the Great Depression of 1933 led many unemployed Americans to look for scapegoats for their anger. The Midwest, in which Lewin and his family had settled in 1935, was a relatively isolated part of the country with a small Jewish population, and many of Lewin's new neighbors did not question conspiracy theories regarding the role of "East Coast Jews" in controlling the United States' money supply. Lewin published several articles between 1935 and 1941 dealing with the effects of anti-Semitism on Jewish Americans, such as "Psycho-Sociological Problems of a Minority Group" (1935), "When Facing Danger" (1939), "Bringing Up the Jewish Child" (1940), and "Self-Hatred Among Jews" (1941).

The significance of Lewin's work in this area is threefold. First, the effects of cultural prejudice on individuals allowed him to explore both the connections and the differences between his social theories and Freudian psychoanalysis. Although Lewin disagreed with Freud's emphasis on childhood experiences and his neglect of social factors in emotional disorders, Lewin allowed that individual differences do influence a person's response to prejudice directed against him or her. In an article entitled "Personal Adjustment and Group Belongingness" (1941), Lewin observed, "It is clear that not all maladjustments of Jewish individuals stem from their being Jewish. Jewish maladjustment has the same source as that of non-Jews." Lewin went on to say, however, that "It would be difficult to find a maladjusted Jew for whom being Jewish has not influenced the type and degree of maladjustment." He attributed this effect to two factors, the first being the relative mildness of anti-Semitism in the United States. In Lewin's view, the relative openness of American society created a situation of "unclarity," in which a Jew could not be sure whether being rejected for a job or club membership resulted from personal failure or anti-Semitism. He or she therefore would not be able to decide whether to work on overcoming personal shortcomings or to work on changing the social environment. Lewin thought that the unclear situation would cause the person to become "disoriented." "In other words, this unclearness necessarily leads to a disorganized emotional behavior in the area of self-esteem which is so important for adjustment and personality development." Lewin concluded that emotional problems in individuals are often related to membership in a marginalized group, because the person must identify with the group to which they belong at the same time that he or she learns to judge that group by "the standards and values of the more privileged majority." "It is clear . . . that an individual cannot be well adjusted without being clearly adjusted to his own group, because the group is the ground on which the individual stands socially and without firm ground and clear orientation no one can act in an organized way."

The second significance is that Lewin's experience of anti-Semitism led him to extend his insights to the problems of other minority groups. As has already been mentioned, he regarded the struggle of Jewish citizens for equal rights as part of the struggle of all disadvantaged minorities. Many of Lewin's action research projects were undertaken with the desire to understand the nature of prejudice in order to create ways to overcome it. One major limitation of Lewin's work, however, is that he did not distinguish between discrimination against groups that can be clearly identified by external bodily features (race, sex, age, physical deformity, etc.) and groups that are less easily identified on the grounds of visual appearance (homosexuals, Jews and other religious minorities, people with prison records, etc.) It was left to such later researchers as Erving Goffman to study the differences among various forms of prejudice.

The third significance of Lewin's response to anti-Semitism is that it provided a model for other social scientists seeking to bring their research to bear on real-life social problems. Chris Argyris, who was influenced by Lewin's example even though he was not one of his students, has said:

> Lewin's work inspired me because it suggested a model that combined theory, empirical research, and relevance to reality. . . . Lewin had the skill to integrate scientific rigor with reality and for this reason became the first major model of social scientist-activist of the highest quality.

CRITICAL RESPONSE

Inadequate research

Lewin and his students were frequently criticized for publishing studies based on a relatively small number of subjects. Hoppe's study of aspiration, which is described below, used only 10 subjects, and the studies of leadership models and frustration in children, also described below, used only 20 and 30 subjects respectively. Lewin did not deny that studying a larger number of subjects would have improved the reliability of his findings, and added that "additional confirmation is always desirable." He also

pointed out that his own results had always stood up well when his studies were replicated by other researchers. But he mentioned on another occasion, "I do not expect ever to live down the misunderstandings created by my attack on some ways in which statistics have been used in psychology."

Misuse of concepts from mathematics and physics

Lewin's colleagues blamed his use of topology to illustrate his theories for the fact that his work was underestimated during his lifetime. When he published *Principles of Topological Psychology* in 1936, the book received a number of harsh reviews. Some reviewers maintained that Lewin's diagrams were distractions that led readers away from his theories to his mathematical representations of them. He replied in an article on "Formalization and Progress in Psychology" (1940) that his main interest was not "formalization or mathematization." The value of these tools for psychology "exists only in so far as they serve as a means to fruitful progress in its subject matter, and they should be applied . . . only when and where they help and do not hinder progress."

A related criticism of Lewin's use of topology and mathematical formulae is that they do not add any new insights to the behavior they supposedly explain. In addition, they cannot be used to predict a person's behavior before it occurs; rather, Lewin's diagrams are after-the-fact representations of his data. Lewin admitted that this line of criticism had some validity:

> It is true, however, that it is a clearer test of the adequacy of the theory if one can make predictions from it and prove these predictions experimentally. The reason for this difference seems to be that empirical data generally allow for quite a range of different interpretations and . . . therefore it is usually easy to invent a variety of theories covering them.

The diagram reproduced earlier as an example of Lewin's use of topology may also serve here to illustrate his critics' point. It is difficult to see what the mathematical formulae add to a verbal description of a situation of indecision. Moreover, the diagram has no predictive value. In order to indicate the child's decision, one of the two vectors would have to be measurably larger or longer than the other—which would imply that the outcome of the child's decision is already known to the psychologist drawing the diagram.

Inadequate attention to objective reality

Lewin's field theory was criticized from the early 1940s onward for its tendency to make the life space a closed psychological system without any clear

FURTHER ANALYSIS:
Group leadership models

Lewin's best-known series of experiments was conducted with Ronald Lippitt and Ralph White at the University of Iowa in the late 1930s. Known as the "Leadership and Group Life" study, it involved groups of children doing arts and crafts activities under different leadership styles. Lewin and his colleagues organized four groups of 10-year-old boys, with four adult leaders and a wide range of craft activities. All the boys in these studies were volunteers, and the groups were carefully matched for patterns of interpersonal relationships, intelligence, socioeconomic status, and a few other variables. The groups were led by an authoritarian leader, a democratic leader, or leader with laissez-faire style. Each group received a new leader every six weeks with a different leadership style. This second experiment lasted a total of five months.

The three leadership styles were described by Lewin and his colleagues as follows:

- Authoritarian: The leader determined all policy; dictated activity steps and techniques; dictated the work tasks and work companions of each member; remained aloof from group participation; was "friendly or impersonal rather than actively hostile."

- Democratic: The leader encouraged group discussions and decisions on all policies; suggested two or three alternative procedures for activities when asked for technical advice; allowed the group to decide on division of tasks and allowed members to choose their work partners; participated in group activities "without doing too much of the work."

- Laissez-faire: Leader allowed the group complete freedom, with no participation on his part. He supplied work materials but did not participate in work discussions or intervene in activities in any way.

The findings from both experiments were striking. Lewin summarized them in an article published in 1939:

- Autocratic groups. Boys in the autocratic groups tended to be either openly aggressive and rebellious or apathetic and submissive. Much of the aggression was directed at boys who became the group's scapegoats; none of it was directed at the autocratic leader. The submissive children, however, engaged in horseplay and wasting time when they were given a nonauthoritarian leader. The autocratic groups produced a larger quantity of masks than the democratic groups, but their masks were of lower quality.

- Democratic groups. These groups maintained high morale, with the boys behaving in a friendly manner toward the leader and one another. They were capable of working independently when the leader left the room. They produced fewer masks than the autocratic groups, but their work demonstrated more originality, and the masks were of higher quality. All but one of the 20 boys expressed a preference for the democratic groups at the end of the study; the one exception was the son of a military officer.

- Laissez-faire groups. These were the least productive groups, producing few masks, with those few of very low quality. These groups could not work by themselves when the leader was temporarily absent; they had a low level of group morale; the members could not cooperate among themselves; and they placed great demands on the leader. One striking finding was that some boys who had been in an authoritarian group became frightened and disturbed when they were given a laissez-faire leader.

Lewin was pleased with the outcome of the study in that it confirmed his convictions about the superiority of democratic systems of government. It also reinforced his belief that democracy must be reaffirmed anew in each generation, as he noticed that the change in the children's behavior from autocratic to democratic groups took longer than the reverse.

---

connection to the real world outside the person. Edward Tolman (1886–1959) argued that Lewin's field theory does not account for the ways in which the outside world produces changes in a person's life space or the

ways in which the life space changes the outside world. Tolman himself attempted to add to Lewin's field theory by proposing three types of psychological variables: dependent variables (the behaviors or actions of a person), independent variables (the person's age, sex, genetic makeup, and present physical functioning; conditions of drive arousal; and stimuli from the external environment); and intervening variables, which connect the dependent and independent variables. In other words, the intervening variables explain how a stimulus from the external world and a person's emotional and physical condition interact to produce behavior.

Tolman proposed four sets of intervening variables:

- Traits. These include an individual's basic temperament and intellectual capacity, and are influenced by heredity.

- Needs.

- Belief-value matrix. This concept is considered Tolman's most important addition to Lewin's field theory. What Tolman means by this term is the individual's thought categories, cognitive skills, beliefs, and values. The belief-value matrix allows a person to make distinctions among various needs as they are experienced, to evaluate them according to their importance, and to scan or analyze the external environment in order to satisfy them. Tolman also thought that the belief-value matrix includes the values shared by the person's community, thus providing a link between the individual and his or her society.

- The behavior space, which depends on the first three intervening variables plus the stimulus from the outside environment.

A somewhat different version of Tolman's criticism of Lewin was made by Floyd Allport in 1955. Allport argued that Lewin's field theory confuses physical realities (the outside world) and psychological realities (the life space) because Lewin used his terms ambiguously. For example, Lewin often speaks of locomotions as mental movements, but he also refers to some locomotions as physical movements. With regard to barriers, Lewin sometimes describes them as internal constraints on a person's behavior—such as fear of other people's reactions to an intended behavior—but in other instances he is clearly thinking of physical obstacles as barriers. For example, in the published article on the experiment with frustration and regression in children described below, Lewin repeatedly refers to the screen or partition used to frustrate the children in the second phase of the experiment as a "barrier." The central point of Allport's critique is that Lewin's field theory tempts the psychologist to mix and confuse external physical factors and internal psychological factors within the same field. Allport

maintained that the researcher must separate the two sets of factors conceptually in order to uncover the laws that govern their interactions.

Lewin's principle of contemporaneity

As has already been mentioned, Lewin defined his principle of contemporaneity in opposition to psychoanalytical explanations of a person's life history. As a result, some of his critics argued that he did not pay enough attention to the effects of the past on present behavior. Lewin replied that he did in fact include what he called the "psychological past" in the total field as part of the person's present "time perspective." He answered his critics in a 1943 article entitled "Defining the 'Field At a Given Time'."

> The psychological field which exists at a given time contains also the views of that individual about his future and past. . . . His views about his own past and that of the rest of the physical and social world are often incorrect but nevertheless constitute, in his life space, the "reality-level" of the past.

The question remains, however, as to whether Lewin's notion of the psychological past is an adequate account of memory. Researchers who have studied such mental disorders as post-traumatic stress disorder and dissociative identity disorder (formerly known as multiple personality disorder) would argue that Lewin's theory does not allow for the effects of traumatic experiences on human personality. Since the early 1980s, neurologists studying the formation of memory traces in the human brain have discovered that traumatic memories are formed in a very different way from normal memories. The types of childhood memories that Lewin listed on occasion as examples of the unimportance of the past in a person's present life space are all pleasant or neutral memories.

Traumatic memories are different, and are related to changes in the structure and function of the brain itself. Under normal circumstances, memories are formed when a person's senses register sights, sounds, and other sensory information, and pass on these data to an almond-shaped structure in the temporal lobe of the brain called the amygdala (which takes its name from the Greek word for "almond"). The amygdala is the part of the brain that attaches an emotional meaning to the data provided by the senses. A nearby part of the brain called the hippocampus organizes the information relayed through the amygdala and combines it with previous information from similar events. For example, if a person is trying on several different types of perfumes at a cosmetics counter, the hippocampus will organize this memory according to previously established memory patterns of pleasant smells, perfumes, shopping trips, the specific department store, etc. Under normal circumstances, the hippocampus is able to form memories efficiently according to the emotional significance assigned to them by the amygdala.

In traumatic situations, however, this system breaks down; the hippocampus is overwhelmed, shuts down, and cannot process the upsetting memory or combine it in any useful way with other memories. The result is that traumatic memories are not stored as unified wholes, but as bits and pieces of bodily sensations and sensory images that are not related to other events in the person's life or even localized in time. These memory fragments may resurface whenever the amygdala is triggered by anything in the present that is vaguely related to the original trauma. Such symptoms of post-traumatic stress as flashbacks, in which the person feels as if he or she is reexperiencing the sights, sounds, smells, or sensations of the traumatic event, represent a chaotic invasion of the present by the past that does not fit Lewin's notion of the psychological past as relevant to the present life space.

Lewin's concept of democracy and action research

Although one of Lewin's most famous studies is said to have proven the superiority of democratic leadership to other leadership models, Lewin has also been criticized for not having developed his notion of this type of leadership beyond a rough sketch. Some of Lewin's colleagues noted that he combined an elitist view of leadership with an element of control. Although Lewin maintained that democracy cannot be forced on individuals, he recognized the existence of "a kind of paradox." Speaking (in 1943) of the need to reconstruct the culture of Germany after the war, Lewin said:

> The democratic leader does not impose his goals on the group . . . the policy determination in democracy is done by the group as a whole. Still the democratic leader should "lead". . . . To instigate changes toward democracy a situation has to be created for a certain period where the leader is sufficiently in control to rule out influences he does not want and to manipulate the situation to a certain degree.

One of Lewin's associates at Iowa commented that Lewin's commitment to democracy reminded him of Freud's definition of reaction formation. "The autocratic way he insisted on democracy was a little spectacular. There was nothing to criticize—but one could not help noticing the fire and the emphasis." Ironically, Lewin was caricatured as often during his life as a "mere political propagandist" as he was criticized for an elitist view of leadership.

Some forms of action research that have evolved from Lewin's model since his death take issue with

certain aspects of his approach. In general, action research fell out of favor with academic psychologists during the 1960s because it was linked to left-wing political activism. In the 1970s, however, action research was reintroduced into schools of education and organizational development as a way of improving classroom practice. As of the early 2000s, Lewin's original model of action research has produced at least three major variations: traditional action research, which is most closely identified with Lewin's work and generally takes a conservative approach toward organizational power structures; radical action research, which takes a Marxist view of society and works to overcome power imbalances within organizational structures; and educational action research, which follows Dewey's belief that educators should involve themselves in community problem-solving at the local level. University-based action researchers in this third group often work with teachers in nearby primary and secondary schools.

Traditional action research based on Lewin's examples is sometimes referred to as technical action research because it focuses on improving the efficiency or effectiveness of an organization. It is usually started by a person or group of people who are considered experts or authority figures because of their greater experience or training. Technical action research is essentially product-directed even though it involves all the members of a working group. It is concerned with gathering information that confirms or refines existing theories, and that can also be used to predict future outcomes.

Even within the field of technical action research, however, contemporary practitioners take issue with Lewin on two points: First, modern researchers regard group decision-making as an important matter of principle, not just as a technique. In other words, it is not only a means to bring about social change, but also inspires participants to commit themselves to action. Some psychologists think that Lewin's spiral model has misled others into thinking that using the spiral as a rigid template constitutes "doing action research." Second, Lewin's critics object to his notion that action research is a way of "leading" participants to a more democratic form of life. Instead of action research serving as a recipe for creating a democracy, they maintain that it should be seen as a way to carry out democratic principles in a research setting.

Organizational change

Lewin's unfreezing-change-refreezing model of organizational change has also been criticized in recent years. One reason is that Lewin's model assumes that a static condition, or being frozen, is the normal condition of organizations. Second, the model assumes that managers are able to control or direct the processes of change within the organization. The increased pace of change in the business world over the past few decades has called that notion into question. Such recent researchers as David Nadler and his associates have argued that change in the current organizational environment takes two forms, continuous and discontinuous. Continuous change can be understood in terms of Lewin's model. It is the type of change represented by quality improvement programs and characterized by planned changes in performance as well as products. Discontinuous change, on the other hand, is caused by such external forces as disruptions in global markets, new technology, and rising expectations on the part of customers. It cannot be controlled by managers and frequently produces a sense of day-to-day chaos and disorder within businesses. As a result, people at all levels of these organizations need to learn and take action at the same time, as the speed of discontinuous change does not allow for the staff training programs and other relatively slow responses built into Lewin's freezing-change-refreezing model.

THEORIES IN ACTION

Research

Lewin's theoretical work gained him early recognition in Germany as well as in the United States because it stimulated a remarkable number of experiments. As two American commentators on Lewin's studies have stated:

> Few other theories of personality have been responsible for generating so much experimentation. Lewin himself, although he is known as a brilliant theoretician, was always a working scientist. He took the lead in formulating empirical tests of many of his basic hypotheses. . . . It is impossible to estimate the number of investigations that bear the imprint of Lewin's influence. . . . Whatever may be the fate of Lewin's theory in the years to come, the body of experimental work instigated by it constitutes an enduring contribution.

Lewin's early research into personality and motivation was revolutionary because these areas had been previously regarded as off-limits to psychologists; they were dealt with by the psychoanalysts, who in turn maintained that these issues could not be explored experimentally. Lewin and his graduate students at the University of Berlin showed instead that questions of personality and motivation could be studied in a laboratory. Second, Lewin thought that research in psychology should be guided by a systematic theory.

This approach distinguished him from earlier psychologists, who had usually performed laboratory experiments unrelated to one another and then broke down the data they collected into smaller categories. Lewin was convinced that the older technique led to oversimplified concepts of human behavior that did not fit observable facts.

Lewin's belief that research should proceed within the framework of a theory did not mean, however, that he concocted theories out of thin air and then looked for facts to fit them. Tamara Dembo, one of his first graduate students at Berlin, explained Lewin's approach as follows:

> He would say, "These are only the beginning concepts; we will have to find out more about them. We cannot do this [experiment] yet; this [other study] is possible to do," and so on . . . if you asked him, "How can one do this?" he would reply, "What's the problem? Let's first look at the problem and see whether any of this is possible." Those were the terms he thought in.

Another feature of Lewin's research that set him apart from his predecessors was the simplicity of the equipment he used for his experiments. Psychologists of the 1920s generally conducted their experiments with complicated machines and other expensive apparatus. Although Lewin enjoyed tinkering with and repairing laboratory equipment—he had a reputation at Berlin as one of the best repair technicians in the Psychological Institute—he used a minimum of equipment for his own work. The Berlin experiments that he conducted with his students were carried out with nothing more elaborate than pencils, papers, and simple games or tasks for the subjects to perform.

These experiments, which were conducted between 1926 and 1930 and published in the *Psychologische Zeitung*, have been described as "one of the most distinguished groups of empirical studies in the psychological literature." Lewin's analyses of the Berlin experiments were among the papers translated into English for publication in book form in 1935 as *A Dynamic Theory of Personality*. The students who carried out these studies for their doctoral dissertations included Bluma Zeigarnik, whose work on tension systems was described earlier, Tamara Dembo, Maria Ovsiankina, Vera Mahler, Sarah Sliosberg, Gita Birenbaum, Anitra Karsten, Sara Fajans, Sara Jucknat, Georg Schwarz, and Ferdinand Hoppe. It is noteworthy, given the prejudice against women in graduate education in both Europe and the United States in the late 1920s, that nine out of Lewin's first 11 students were women. The five major psychological categories that were investigated by Lewin and his students included recall of unfinished tasks; level of aspiration; substitution; satiation; and anger. These topics provided fertile ground for additional research after Lewin and several of his students emigrated to the United States.

Case studies

Level of aspiration
One of the topics that was investigated by Lewin's graduate students at the University of Berlin was level of aspiration, which refers to a person's behavior in regard to setting goals and working toward them. Ferdinand Hoppe performed the first experiments in this area in 1930. He worked with only 10 subjects, maintaining that a deeper investigation of a small number of cases would be more fruitful than a wide-ranging statistical study. Hoppe set out to measure the effect of success or failure on the subjects' level of aspiration. He offered his subjects a number of tasks ranging from throwing darts at a target to problems in arithmetic; all the tasks were offered with achievement levels ranging from "easy" to "difficult." Once a subject had established a baseline level of performance, Hoppe would ask what score he was aiming for on the next test. This goal then became the subject's level of aspiration. If the subject failed to meet the higher goal, he frequently regarded his previous score as a failure, even though he had considered it a success on the initial test. In many cases, the subject would set a lower goal for the third attempt.

Hoppe found that his subjects' experiences of success or failure were not related to any specific level of accomplishment, but were linked instead to a goal that measured whether their performances could be considered positive achievements. Hoppe then discovered that the subjects' level of aspiration changed according to their level of performance; if they experienced success at a task, they raised their level of aspiration for the next attempt. When they failed, they generally lowered their aspiration level or stopped doing the task. Hoppe did not find any instances in which a subject lowered his level of aspiration after a success or raised it after a failure.

Hoppe's study was one of the most important of the Berlin experiments in that it led to immediate practical as well as theoretical results. More than any of the other studies from this period of Lewin's career, Hoppe's work stimulated a flood of additional studies in the area of goal setting, particularly with regard to its applications in education. Lewin himself observed that

> The factors which determine the level of aspiration are of basic importance for learning. A child may permanently keep his level of aspiration too high or too low for his ability. Good students tend to keep their level of aspiration slightly above their past

achievements, whereas poor students tend to show excessively high or excessively low levels.

Action research in an industrial setting
In 1939, two years before the United States entered World War II, Lewin was asked to serve as a consultant to the Harwood Manufacturing Corporation, a new plant that had just opened in rural Virginia. The factory was having difficulty training 300 inexperienced apprentices who were eager to work but could not reach the output expected of apprentices doing similar work in plants in the industrialized Northeast. Lewin came to visit the plant that fall, beginning a relationship that lasted until his death in 1947. The Harwood managers were genuinely puzzled by their problems with the workers. On the one hand, the employees said that they liked their jobs, and they were paid much better than they had been as waitresses or domestic help; on the other, employee turnover was high. The supervisors had tried every method they knew to raise production, but nothing had worked.

Lewin began with a problem-solving session that drew on Hoppe's dissertation research on aspiration. Lewin deduced from his conversations with the workers that the production goals set by the company were so high in comparison with what the employees had been able to do so far that the goals had no reality for the workers; in other words, the difference was too great for them to try to meet the company's quotas. As a result, they did not feel any sense of failure in not meeting production goals. Lewin made three suggestions: first, the company should stop pressuring individual workers about quotas; second, the company should have the workers form small groups and then deal with the groups rather than with individual workers; third, the company should find a way to show the workers that the production quotas were realistic. The Harwood managers quickly put Lewin's proposals into action. To carry out Lewin's third suggestion, they brought in some experienced workers from a plant that was closing in a town about 40 miles from the Harwood factory. Within two weeks, the Harwood apprentices began to raise their output, as they saw that the experienced workers could easily reach the company's quota. They came to believe that they too could do what the experienced workers were doing.

Lewin made a number of visits to the Harwood factory, where he was well liked for his friendliness and sense of humor as well as his ideas. The workers enjoyed teasing Lewin about his initial problems understanding their heavy Southern drawl, and they were delighted when he began to use local slang expressions. In addition to visiting the plant himself,

Lewin suggested that Harwood hire Alex Bavelas from the University of Iowa to conduct some experiments on human factors in a factory setting. Bavelas carried out a number of studies between 1940 and 1947. One experiment involved the difference between discussion and decision-making in reinforcing people's motivation to raise production levels. Bavelas held informal meetings with two groups of high-producing workers at the Harwood plant. The first group discussed ways to increase its daily production and then voted on the issue of raising its daily production. The group decided to aim for 87 units per day instead of its current level of 75 within a five-day period. It met its goal and later raised the goal to 90 units, which it also achieved. The second group of workers met only to discuss ways to increase production but did not take a vote. Their production improved only slightly over the next few months. Looking at Bavelas' findings, Lewin maintained that they showed that motivation by itself is not enough to produce change. The link between motivation and change is provided by decisions, which often affect long- as well as short-term changes in actual behavior.

Another experiment that Bavelas performed at the Harwood factory under Lewin's supervision reflected Lewis' theory of force fields and his concepts of driving and restraining forces. Bavelas studied the use of pacing cards as a tool that the workers could use for self-management. They were to use the cards to set their own hourly pace as long as they kept at or above the plant's official quota. Lewin's force field theory predicted that a production worker's average output is almost stationary; therefore, one can raise production levels either by adding driving forces to push for higher output (in this case, pressure from management) or weakening the restraining forces that limit the worker's production. Bavelas found that the workers who were given pacing cards raised their average production from 67 units per day to 82 and remained at that level, whereas a control group of workers who were not given pacing cards did not raise their production level. In short, Bavelas' study showed that production is raised more effectively by weakening restraining forces than by putting workers under pressure that raises their stress levels and is ultimately counterproductive.

The Iowa frustration and regression studies
During Lewin's years as a researcher at the Child Welfare Research Station at the University of Iowa, he and his former student Tamara Dembo (who had also left Germany for the United States in the mid-1930s) conducted a series of experiments on the effects of frustration on young children. Dembo's

CHRONOLOGY

1890: Lewin born in Germany, now a part of Poland.

1914: Volunteers to serve in World War I.

1917: Wounded in war. Later marries first wife, Maria.

1927: Divorces first wife after son's illness strains family.

1929: Marries second wife, Gertrud.

1933: Moves to United States to escape the rise of Hitler.

1944: Invited to set up research institute at MIT.

1944: Lewin's mother dies in Nazi concentration camp.

1946: Pioneers leadership training.

1947: Dies of heart attack.

doctoral dissertation had involved the dynamics of anger and frustration. What she discovered during a series of 64 experiments with 27 different subjects confirmed Lewin's hypothesis that anger in a frustrating situation is a product of the subject's total life space at that point rather than of simple failure to reach a goal. Dembo's subjects reacted to the frustrating situations she created in one of three ways: they kept trying to complete the task she had set them, although in roundabout ways; they left the room where the experiment was being conducted; or they lashed out at Dembo verbally or even physically. The experiments that Lewin, Dembo, and a third colleague named Roger Barker conducted at Iowa were designed to take the study of anger and frustration to the next level, namely to discover the effects of frustration on children's intellectual creativity and behavior. Lewin and his colleagues reported on their findings in 1941 in the series of *University of Iowa Studies in Child Welfare*.

The researchers had hypothesized that frustrating the play activities of young children would lead to behavioral regression. Regression is a concept that was first used by Freud to describe a return from later to earlier stages of personality organization. For example, parents frequently note that a first-born child regresses to babyish behavior when a newborn arrives in the

BIOGRAPHY:

Fritz Heider

Fritz Heider (1896–1988) was a social psychologist best known for his book *The Psychology of Interpersonal Relations*, first published in 1958. Heider grew up in Vienna and received his Ph.D. from the University of Graz in Austria before coming to the Psychological Institute at the University of Berlin. There he met Kurt Lewin and formed a friendship with him that lasted until Lewin's death.

Heider left Germany for the United States in 1930 to accept a research position at the Clarke School for the Deaf in Northampton, Massachusetts. He fell in love with Grace Moore, a fellow researcher at Clarke, and married her in December 1930. The Heiders had three sons during their years in Northampton; they also provided Kurt and Gertrud Lewin with a place to stay during the Lewins' first months in the United States. In 1947 the Heiders left Massachusetts for Kansas, where Fritz had been appointed a full professor at the University of Kansas. He remained at Kansas until his retirement in the 1960s, although he continued to do research and work on the notebooks that he had kept throughout his career. The notebooks were published in six volumes shortly before his death in 1988. Heider was honored by the American Psychological Association in 1965, when he received the APA's Distinguished Scientific Contribution Award.

The two concepts most often associated with Heider's work are attribution theory and balance theory. Attribution theory is concerned with the ways in which people explain the causes of other people's behavior, and the reasons for their choice of explanations. Heider distinguished two types of attribution, external and internal. In external (or impersonal) attribution, an observer explains an event or action in terms of such impersonal forces as the weather or similar factors. For example, a baseball fan might interpret a player's falling down in the outfield as the result of heavy rain the night before creating a slippery playing surface. In internal, or personal, attribution, the observer explains behavior as caused by internal factors that make the other person responsible

for the behavior. In the case of the outfielder, the fan might attribute the fall to the player's intention (he meant to fall) as well as to his disposition (he's stupid, lazy, stays out too late the night before a game, etc.). What Heider means by a disposition is a "relatively unchanging underlying condition" that allows a person to "predict and control" events in the real world by referring "transient and variable behavior" to these unchanging conditions. Heider thought that people tend to overemphasize dispositions in judging the behavior of others and to discount any external factors involved; he called this tendency attributional bias.

Heider's balance theory, also known as P-O-X theory, is an attempt to explain the fact that people tend to seek balance (whether positive or negative) in their relationships. The letters refer to three points of a triangle formed by a person (P), another person (O), and an object (X). The triangle includes what Heider called relations of sentiment (liking or disliking) as well as unit relations (relationships to other people or objects). An example of balance theory would be a person (P) who has a friend (O) that he likes very much. O shows up for a get-together wearing the ugliest outfit (X) that P has ever seen. This situation creates an imbalance

Fritz Heider. (*Archives of the History of American Psychology—The University of Akron. Reproduced by permission.*)

between P's feelings for the friend (positive) and P's opinion of O's clothing (negative). Heider predicts that P will convince himself that his feelings about O's clothes are positive too—he might tell himself that "she has a unique sense of style" in order to restore balance. An example of negative balance would be P's dislike of a neighbor (O)'s dog (X) because P dislikes the dog's owner.

household, demanding to drink from a bottle again, crying and whining, refusing to take naps, etc. Psychiatrists studying shell-shocked veterans of World War I in the 1920s also observed that these emotionally damaged adults often regressed to attitudes and behaviors more characteristic of teenagers. In the Iowa study, Lewin, Dembo, and Barker collected a group of 30 children between two and six years of age. The first phase of this experiment did not involve frustrating the child, who was led alone into a room with play materials while the researcher sat at a desk and made notes. After the child had been playing for 30 minutes, the researcher opened a screen that had closed off half the room, revealing a set of new and exciting toys that the child was encouraged to enjoy. This part of the experiment was intended to create eventual frustration by setting up a desirable goal that the child could be prevented from reaching in the second phase.

After the child had become absorbed with the new toys, the researcher interrupted the play and led the child back to the first part of the room. The new play area was then sealed off with the screen and fastened with a padlock. The child could not reach the new toys even though he could still see them. This situation brought out two types of behaviors—playing with the old toys in the first part of the room and trying to reach the new toys behind the screen. The researchers compared the creativity of the children's play before and after frustration as well as their actual behavior. In the frustration phase of the experiment, the children spent an average of 35% of their time trying to get to the toys behind the barrier or to leave the room. The quality of their play with the old toys was much less creative and constructive than it had been during the first phase. In addition, the children's behavior regressed to a startling degree; some of the five-year-old children regressed to the behavior of three-year-olds, including thumbsucking and general restlessness. Some children even kicked, hit, or broke objects in the study room. Lewin and his colleagues found that the degree of intellectual regression in the children was directly correlated with the intensity of frustration. In addition, there was a marked change in the nature of the children's behavior toward the researcher during the frustration phase of the experiment—a 30% rise in hostile acts and a 34% drop in friendly actions.

In addition to the study that Lewin coauthored with Barker and Dembo, he published another paper in 1941 on "Regression, Retrogression, and Development," in which he proposed that the Iowa research and other studies of regression could serve to shed light on normal patterns of human development.

> Our knowledge of the factors determining [normal] development, its dynamics and laws, is extremely meager. Regression can be said to be a negative development. . . . Therefore, the indirect way of studying the dynamics of development by studying regression may prove to be fruitful for the whole theory.

Relevance to modern readers

Even though Lewin is usually classified as a social psychologist, he contributed to so many different areas within psychology that anyone interested in the field is likely to encounter his influence even when his name is not mentioned. The entire specialty of organizational management is indebted to Lewin's work, as well as technical action research and leadership training programs. Even people who have never studied psychology have been exposed to Lewin's theories if they have ever undergone sensitivity training in their workplace or have participated in team-building programs. Anyone who has been involved in encounter groups or similar programs associated with the human potential movement has also been affected indirectly by Lewin's ideas. Although Lewin's theory of personality has not been as influential over the long term as his work in group dynamics, his concept of tension systems and of human behavior as goal-oriented has stimulated countless research projects in the areas of motivation and aspiration—subjects that were once considered off-limits to scientific investigation. Lastly, anyone who studies psychology in the hope or expectation of making a difference in the world around them has Lewin as a forbearer and a model.

BIBLIOGRAPHY

Sources

Barker, Roger, Tamara Dembo, and Kurt Lewin. "Frustration and Regression." *University of Iowa Studies in Child Welfare* 18 (1941): 1–43.

Bavelas, Alex, and Kurt Lewin. "The Solution of a Chronic Conflict in a Factory." In *Proceedings of the Second Brief Psychotherapy Council.* Chicago: Institute for Psychoanalysis, 1944.

Bavelas, Alex, and Kurt Lewin. "Training in Democratic Leadership." *Journal of Abnormal and Social Psychology* 37 (1942): 115–19.

Darwin, John. *Action Research: Theory, Practice and Trade Union Involvement.* Sheffield Business School Working Paper No. 99/06. Sheffield, UK: Sheffield Business School, 1999.

Goffman, Erving. *Stigma: Notes on the Management of Spoiled Identity.* New York: Simon & Schuster, 1963.

Hall, Calvin S., and Gardner Lindzey. *Theories of Personality*, 2nd ed. New York: John Wiley & Sons, Inc., 1970.

Heider, Fritz. "Attitudes and Cognitive Organization." *Journal of Psychology* 21 (1946): 107–12.

Heider, Fritz. *The Psychology of Interpersonal Relations.* New York: John Wiley&Sons, Inc., 1958.

Lewin, Kurt. "Action Research and Minority Problems." *Journal of Social Issues* 2 (1946): 34–46.

Lewin, Kurt. "Behavior and Development as a Function of the Total Situation." In L. Carmichael, ed., *Manual of Child Psychology.* New York: John Wiley and Sons, 1946.

Lewin, Kurt. "Bringing Up the Jewish Child." *Menorah Journal* 28 (1940): 29–45.

Lewin, Kurt. "Constructs in Field Theory." *University of Iowa Studies in Child Welfare* 20 (1944): 1–29.

Lewin, Kurt. "Cultural Reconstruction." *Journal of Abnormal and Social Psychology* 38 (1943): 166–73.

Lewin, Kurt. "Defining the 'Field at a Given Time.'" *Psychological Review* 50 (1943): 292–310.

Lewin, Kurt. "Experiments in Social Space." *Harvard Educational Review* 9 (1939): 21–32.

Lewin, Kurt. "Forces Behind Food Habits and Methods of Change." *Bulletin of the National Research Council* 108 (1943): 35–65.

Lewin, Kurt. "Formalization and Progress in Psychology." *University of Iowa Studies in Child Welfare* 16 (1940): 7–42.

Lewin, Kurt. "Frontiers in Group Dynamics." *Human Relations* 1 (1947): 2–38.

Lewin, Kurt. "On the Structure of the Mind." *Vorsatz, Wille und Bedurfnis.* Berlin: Springer Verlag, 1926.

Lewin, Kurt. "Personal Adjustment and Group Belongingness." *Jewish Social Service Quarterly* 17 (1941): 362–66.

Lewin, Kurt. "Regression, Retrogression, and Development." *University of Iowa Studies in Child Welfare* 18 (1941): 1–43.

Lewin, Kurt. "Self-Hatred Among Jews." *Contemporary Jewish Record* 4 (1941): 219–32.

Lewin, Kurt. "Some Social-Psychological Differences Between the United States and Germany." *Character and Personality* 4 (1936): 265–93.

Lewin, Kurt. "When Facing Danger." *Jewish Frontier,* September 1939.

Lewin, Kurt, and Paul Grabbe. "Conduct, Knowledge, and Acceptance of New Values." *Journal of Social Issues* 1 (1945): 53–63.

Lewin, Kurt, Ronald Lippitt, and Ralph K. White. "Patterns of Aggressive Behavior in Experimentally Created 'Social Climates.'" *Journal of Social Psychology* 10 (1939): 271–99.

Lippitt, Ronald, and Kurt Lewin. "An Experimental Approach to the Study of Autocracy and Democracy: A Preliminary Note." *Sociometry* 1 (1938): 292–300.

Lippitt, Ronald, Ralph White, and Kurt Lewin. "Patterns of Aggressive Behavior in Experimentally Created Social Climates." *Journal of Social Psychology* 10 (1939): 271–99.

Marrow, Alfred J. *The Practical Theorist: The Life and Work of Kurt Lewin.* Annapolis, MD: BDR Learning Products, Inc., 1984.

Potter, Steve. "A Social History of the T-Group." *Nurturing Potential* 8 (2003). http://www.nurturingpotential.net/Issue8/T-Group.htm.

Rose, Kenneth H. "Leading Change: A Model by John Kotter." *ESI Horizons Newsletter* February 2002, 1–5.

Schein, Edgar H. *Kurt Lewin's Field Theory in the Field and in the Classroom. Notes Toward a Model of Managed Learning.* Society for Organizational Learning Working Paper 10.006. Cambridge, MA: Society for Organizational Learning, 1995. http://www.solonline.org/res/wp/10006.html.

Schwartz, Tony. "Nurturing the Human Potential." *What Really Matters: Searching for Wisdom in America.* New York: Bantam Books, 1996.

Shaw, Robert B., David A. Nadler, and Elise A. Walton. *Discontinuous Change: Leading Organizational Transformation.* San Francisco, CA: Jossey-Bass Publishers, 1994.

Smith, Mark K. "Kurt Lewin, Groups, Experiential Learning and Action Research." *Encyclopedia of Informal Education.* http://www.infed.org/thinkers/et-lewin.htm.

Stout, Martha, Ph.D. *the Myth of Sanity: Tales of Multiple Personality in Everyday Life.* New York: Penguin Putnam, Inc., 2001.

Further readings

Gold, Martin, ed. *The Complete Social Scientist: A Kurt Lewin Reader.* Washington, D.C.: American Psychological Association, 1999.

Lewin, Kurt. *Field Theory in Social Science: Selected Theoretical Papers,* edited by Dorwin Cartwright. New York: Harper and Brothers, 1951.

Lewin, Kurt. *Resolving Social Conflicts: Selected Papers on Group Dynamics,* edited by Gertrud W. Lewin. New York: Harper and Row Publishers, 1948.

Marrow, Alfred J. *The Practical Theorist: The Life and Work of Kurt Lewin.* Annapolis, MD: BDR Learning Products, Inc., 1984.

Smith, Mark K. "Kurt Lewin, Groups, Experiential Learning and Action Research." *Encyclopedia of Informal Education.* http://www.infed.org/thinkers/et-lewin.htm.

Abraham H. Maslow

BRIEF OVERVIEW

Abraham Maslow is one of the founding fathers of humanistic psychology, an approach to understanding behavior that developed in the middle part of the twentieth century. The humanistic approach is sometimes referred to as the "third force" in psychology, because it developed after both the psychoanalytic and behaviorist approaches were well established.

Maslow was an academic who spent most of his professional career teaching, conducting research, and developing his theories of behavior. Although he wrote an important text on abnormal psychology and provided informal counseling to some of his students, he never thought of himself as a psychotherapist, unlike many of the other contributors to the field of personality. He was much more focused on understanding healthy behavior than he was on treating mental disorders.

Maslow's theory centers on the role of motivation in personality. He was interested in explaining why people do the things that they do—the causes of their behavior. Drawing on research and theory from experimental psychology, anthropology, psychoanalysis, and other fields, Maslow's theory integrates a number of ideas into a comprehensive explanation of the forces that motivate people. Although he used animal behavior to understand some of the more basic motivational forces, Maslow was primarily interested in human behavior, and particularly in the behavior of healthy, high-functioning people.

1908–1970

AMERICAN PSYCHOLOGIST, AUTHOR

UNIVERSITY OF WISCONSIN, PhD, 1934

Abraham Maslow. *(UPI/Corbis–Bettmann. Reproduced by permission.)*

One of the key elements of Maslow's theory is the hierarchy of basic needs. Maslow recognized that there were a number of different motivating forces, or needs, that influenced human behavior, and he created the hierarchy of needs to understand how these different forces worked in relation to one another. For instance, if at some time a person were influenced by both a need for food and a need for safety and security, which of these two needs would have the greatest influence on the person's behavior? Maslow wanted to explain how a person would respond in such a situation, and also to understand how people came to be influenced by more complex, "higher" needs.

Another important element of Maslow's theory is the concept of self-actualization. This term, which he borrowed from neuropsychologist Kurt Goldstein, describes the tendency of humans to fulfill their potential, to become what they can become. Maslow felt that the need for self-actualization would emerge only after other needs had been reasonably satisfied, and he was particularly interested in people who were acting in response to this need. Maslow felt that it was important to understand this motivation, because he saw it as the key to making a better society.

In his later years, Maslow devoted much of his energy to finding ways to apply the principles of human

potential in a variety of fields. Maslow's theory is not a comprehensive personality theory; it says little about the process of development or about the origins of mental disorders. Despite these limitations, Maslow's theory, with its emphasis on healthy functioning, has had an important influence on counseling and other helping professions, on education, and in the business arena.

BIOGRAPHY

Abraham Maslow was born in 1908, the oldest of seven children. His father, Samuel Maslow, had immigrated to the United States from Russia and eventually settled in New York City, where he went to work repairing barrels. The family lived in Brooklyn during Abe's childhood, in working-class neighborhoods that were predominantly Jewish.

In later years Maslow would describe his childhood as rather unhappy. His parents' marriage was not a good one, and they divorced when Abe was a young adult. He was not close with his father, who spent relatively little time at home when Abe was a child. Abe's relationship with his mother was even worse. He later described her as selfish, ignorant, and hostile. Though he and his father grew closer in later years, he never reconciled with his mother and saw very little of her after he left home.

From an early age, Abe showed an aptitude for learning. He learned to read when he was five years old, and from then on he read constantly. Abe did well in school, and his academic achievement was a source of pride for his family. Although neither of his parents was school-educated, they placed a great deal of value on education, and they encouraged Abe to pursue his studies as a means toward a better life. Nonetheless, Abe's shyness and "bookish" interests made him feel different and separate from many of his peers.

Abe attended Boys High School in Brooklyn, a highly regarded school that served many of the working-class Jewish families in the area. Abe found the academically oriented atmosphere to be supportive and stimulating. Although he did not excel academically, he became involved in a number of clubs and activities. His social life was also helped by his relationship with his cousin, Will Maslow, who was more outgoing and athletically inclined than Abe. Abe and Will became close friends, and Will encouraged Abe to participate in sports and social activities.

When he was about 14 years old, Abe met his first cousin, Bertha Goodman, who had recently arrived from Russia. He was immediately attracted to her, and offered to help her learn English. Throughout his adolescence, Bertha was the only girl that he was comfortable talking to. They began dating and eventually talked about marriage.

Although he was sure he wanted to pursue some sort of academic career, Abe had trouble settling into a degree program once he entered college. He took courses at City College of New York and (for one semester) at Cornell University, but did not settle into a course of study. To please his father, he also briefly studied law at Brooklyn Law School, but left after only two months.

Maslow later credited a book he read for a philosophy course as one of the influences that led him to a career in psychology. The book, *Folkways*, by William Graham Sumner, proposed the idea that scientists and thinkers are the only ones who can lift society out of superstition and ignorance. Maslow was struck by this idea and decided to dedicate himself to scientific pursuits that would improve the lot of mankind.

Maslow eventually decided to transfer to the University of Wisconsin to finish his degree. He was attracted by the school's reputation for innovation and its liberal atmosphere. He initially planned to study philosophy, but again, his reading led him in another direction. At the suggestion of one of his former

PRINCIPAL PUBLICATIONS

- "Dominance-feeling, behavior and status." *Psychological Review* 44 (1937): 404–29.
- *Principles of Abnormal Psychology: The Dynamics of Psychic Illness (with B. Mittelmann).* New York: Harper and Brothers, 1941.
- "A theory of human motivation." *Psychological Review* 50 (1943): 370–96.
- "Problem-centering vs. means-centering in science." *Philosophy of Science* 13 (1946): 326–31.
- "Self-actualizing people: A study of psychological health." *Personality Symposia: Symposium #1 on Values* (1950): 11–34.
- *The S-I Test (A measure of psychological security-insecurity.* Palo Alto, CA: Consulting Psychologists Press, 1951.
- *Motivation and Personality.* New York: Harper and Row, 1954.
- *New Knowledge in Human Values (Editor).* New York: Harper and Row, 1959.
- "Eupsychia—The good society." *Journal of Humanistic Psychology* 1 (1961): 1–11.
- *Toward a Psychology of Being.* Princeton, NJ: Van Nostrand, 1962.
- *Religions, Values, and Peak Experiences.* Columbus, OH: Ohio State University Press, 1964.
- *Eupsychian Management: A Journal.* New York: Irwin-Dorsey, 1965.
- *The Psychology of Science: A Reconnaissance.* New York: Harper and Row, 1966.
- *The Farther Reaches of Human Nature.* New York: Viking Press, 1971.

philosophy professors, he read an essay by John B. Watson, the founder of American behaviorism. Watson's vision of transforming the world using principles of behaviorism was appealing to Maslow, and he decided to become a psychologist.

The atmosphere in the psychology department at the University of Wisconsin was exciting and stimulating for

Maslow. He felt that his instructors took a real interest in him and made him a part of the intellectual community, and he flourished in this atmosphere. He got excellent grades and completed his bachelor's degree within two years. He continued as a graduate student, earning a master's degree in 1931 and a doctorate in 1934.

Although he was very happy with his academic life at Wisconsin, Maslow found himself missing Bertha terribly, and he decided that he wanted to marry so that they could be together. Despite his parents' objections, Abe married Bertha in December of 1928, and the couple returned to Wisconsin together. The marriage was a great success. Later in life, Maslow would describe his marriage to Bertha as one of his best decisions and one of the great joys of his life. He and Bertha would remain devoted to one another and go on to raise two daughters.

About the time Maslow was ready to start work on his doctoral dissertation, he met Harry Harlow, who had been recently hired as an assistant professor in psychology. Dr. Harlow would later become famous for his classic studies of attachment and social behavior in monkeys. Harlow's interest in primate behavior attracted Maslow. Maslow became his research assistant, contributing to a number of studies on learning in primates. Maslow became interested in the relationship between social dominance and sexual behavior in monkeys, and he chose this as the topic for his doctoral dissertation. This was an area that had not been explored previously, and Maslow's work was considered groundbreaking. He published a number of well-received papers on the topic in the 1930s, and his work was respected as an important contribution to the understanding of primate behavior.

Maslow returned to New York in 1935, to complete a postdoctoral fellowship with Edward L. Thorndike at Columbia University. Thorndike was impressed by Maslow's intelligence, and he gave him free rein to pursue his own studies. Maslow embarked on a study of human dominance and sexuality, which extended some of the ideas from his primate research. He interviewed a number of people, mostly women, about their social behavior and about their sexual experiences. He developed the idea that dominance feeling (later renamed as self-esteem) had an important influence on sexual behavior and attitudes. He also developed a test of dominance feeling that was later published and widely used in various types of research. At the time very few researchers had studied human sexuality, which was still a somewhat taboo topic. Maslow's work was considered to be controversial and pioneering.

During this early part of his professional career, Maslow was fortunate to make the acquaintance of many of the day's leading thinkers in social science and psychoanalysis. Between 1935 and 1940 he attended various classes at the New School for Social Research in New York City, which was a haven to many important social scientists and psychoanalysts who had fled after Nazi domination of Europe. Maslow was greatly influenced by Gestalt psychologist Max Wertheimer, as well as psychoanalysts Alfred Adler, Karen Horney, and Erich Fromm.

Maslow also became interested in anthropology, and attended seminars at Columbia University, where he got to know Margaret Mead and Ruth Benedict, leading anthropologists of the time. Maslow's interest in anthropology led him to explore the role of cultural influences on behavior, and he wrote respected papers on this subject. He even spent a summer doing fieldwork among the Blackfoot Indians in Alberta, Canada.

After he returned from Canada, Maslow began work as a tutor in psychology at Brooklyn College, where he would remain for the next 14 years, rising eventually to the rank of associate professor. His position required a heavy teaching load, and he soon became a favorite of many students. He also engaged in informal counseling with a number of his students, who came to him with their personal problems. For many of these students, the lengthy and expensive process of psychoanalysis was not an option, and Maslow worked with them to find simpler, more cost-effective solutions to their problems.

Maslow taught courses in abnormal psychology, and within a few years he and a colleague, Bela Mittelmann, wrote a textbook on the subject, which was published in 1941. This book was innovative in devoting an entire chapter to discussing the normal personality, a topic that was rarely included in discussions of mental illness and abnormal behavior. Maslow's insistence that any discussion of abnormality should start from an understanding of normal behavior foreshadowed his later work and beliefs.

As World War II began, Maslow began to think about ways that psychology could contribute to worldwide efforts to achieve peace. He felt that understanding motivation would be an important step, and he set out to develop a comprehensive theory of human motivation. Maslow wanted to integrate many of the ideas he had developed through his studies in animal behavior, psychoanalysis, and anthropology, and he authored a series of papers that were eventually drawn together into his theory. His 1954 book, *Motivation and Personality*, presents his theory in detail.

One important aspect of Maslow's motivational work in the early 1940s was his focus on healthy, high-functioning people. Maslow felt that it was very important to understand people who were operating at the higher levels of motivation, who had been largely ignored by other researchers on human behavior. To accomplish this, he began to examine the lives of people who were functioning well, self-fulfilled, and essentially "good human beings," as he put it. He drew on descriptions of historical and public figures who seemed to meet his criteria, such as Thomas Jefferson and Eleanor Roosevelt, and he also studied people among his own acquaintances who seemed to function at this higher level of motivation. Despite difficulty in finding such people and finding a way to measure their behavior, he began to pull together a set of characteristics that described self-actualizing people.

Maslow's insistence on understanding high-functioning humans was something of a radical departure in the 1940s, and he did not publish his ideas at first. His first paper on self-actualized people did not appear until 1950, and then it was published in a new journal that was outside the mainstream of psychology. In a 1951 paper (co-authored with D. MacKinnon) he further developed his theory of personality and outlined a new approach to psychology that was based on a positive view of humanity and focused on growth and creativity. Although he would not use the term for another 10 years, the ideas in this paper represented the beginnings of humanistic psychology.

In 1951, Maslow was offered the new post of chairman of the psychology department at Brandeis University. He was given the opportunity to build the program any way he wished, and he went on to hire a number of gifted and innovative psychologists, many of whom had views that were quite divergent from his own. He proved to be a successful administrator, and he continued in this position at Brandeis for a number of years.

With the publication of *Motivation and Personality* in 1954, Maslow acquired a national reputation. His work was well-received and hailed as a very significant contribution to the field. His ideas were attractive to a number of social scientists who were interested in promoting values and using science to improve society, and these individuals eventually formed the humanistic psychology movement of the 1960s.

From the mid-1950s onward, Maslow's interests shifted further and further from empirical research and more in the direction of developing his theories of motivation and self-actualization. He became increasingly interested in higher needs, such as creativity and personal growth. He was also drawn to existential philosophy, and he began to see connections between his ideas on higher motivations and the ideas of existential thinkers. He wrote a number of papers and essays on the higher levels of motivation. In 1962, he published *Toward a Psychology of Being*, which was a collection of his papers on the subject. This book was extremely well-received, even becoming popular outside the field of psychology. Many of the ideas included in this book were adopted by the idealistic cultural movement of the 1960s, and Maslow became a reluctant "guru" of the movement.

Although he was an atheist, Maslow was increasingly drawn toward studying religious and mystical experiences. He saw a connection between his own observations about peak experiences and reports of religious or transcendental experiences. His thoughts in this area grew into *Religions, Values, and Peak-experiences*, which was published in 1964. This book became an important influence and was widely read in seminaries and programs that trained religious counselors.

Maslow's ideas attracted proponents from a number of other fields, and he began to apply the principles of humanistic psychology in fields such as education and business management. He was also stimulated by the ideas of business managers who had made progressive innovations in the workplace, and he became excited about the prospect of bettering the world by improving conditions for workers. He kept a journal of ideas, which was eventually published as the book *Eupsychian Management*. Despite its difficult title, this book on management philosophy has continued to influence the business world.

By the 1960s, Maslow was recognized as one of the leading thinkers in psychology. Along with Carl Rogers and Gordon Allport, he was considered to be a founder of the humanistic psychology movement, which exerted a growing influence on psychology into the next decade. He was also one of the founders of the *Journal of Humanistic Psychology*, which published its first issue in 1961.

Maslow was elected president of the American Psychological Association in 1966, a mark of the respect and esteem he received from his profession. During his tenure, he worked to remove barriers for black psychologists, seeing racial inequality as one of the great problems of his day. He continued to write about the many possible applications of humanistic psychology, and he was involved in a number of such projects when he suffered a severe heart attack in December of 1967. Although he recovered, he learned that he had a serious heart condition and would need prolonged rest in order to recover.

Maslow took a leave from his position at Brandeis University at the end of 1968 and accepted a fellowship

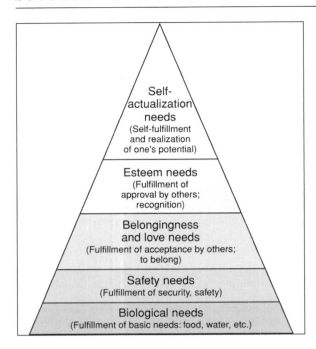

Maslow's hierarchy of needs. (Courtesy Thomson Gale.)

controlled by inborn physiological drives, particularly the sex drive, which governed all behavior at an unconscious level. Maslow disagreed with this viewpoint, suggesting that human behavior was influenced by a number of different needs, not all of which were physiologically based and not all of which were unconscious. He thought that most behavior was influenced by multiple needs interacting with one another.

To explain how different needs might interact, Maslow proposed a hierarchy of needs. According to his theory, the different needs could be arranged in order according to their ability to motivate the person. He referred to this ability to motivate as *pre-potency*. One need would be described as pre-potent over another if it was necessary for the first need to be satisfied before the second need could influence behavior. In his scheme of things, if a person were lacking both oxygen and food, the need for oxygen would be the most pre-potent need, because a person who is lacking oxygen would need to satisfy the need to breathe before he or she could be concerned with hunger. Maslow proposed a relatively large set of needs that could motivate human behavior, arranged in the order of their pre-potency.

with the Saga Administrative Corporation in Menlo Park, California. He was given the welcome opportunity to work on his writing and ideas without the pressures of teaching. He spent the next year and a half on several projects, including revisions of *Motivation and Personality* and *Religions, Values, and Peak-experiences*. He also pulled together a number of essays that would later be published as *The Farther Reaches of Human Nature*. On June 8, 1970, he suffered a massive heart attack and died at his home in Menlo Park.

Maslow was respected and loved by many people inside and outside the field of psychology. Although humanistic psychology does not enjoy the popularity that it had in the 1960s, Maslow's ideas continue to influence a number of fields, and he is remembered as one of the most important and innovative thinkers of the twentieth century.

THEORIES

Maslow's hierarchy of needs

Main points   Maslow thought that most behavior occurred in response to some kind of motivation, which was made up of the interplay among different needs, or drives. Previous (mostly psychoanalytic) theories of motivation had suggested that behavior was

Physiological needs   According to Maslow's theory, the most pre-potent needs are the physiological needs, such as the need for food or water. He suggested that there may be a very large number of such needs, many of which are governed by homeostatic mechanisms in the body. A homeostatic mechanism acts to keep the body in a fairly constant state, not allowing extremes in either direction, much the way a thermostat regulates the temperature in a house. Maslow pointed out the work of physiologists of his time who had discovered homeostatic mechanisms, and suggested that the body's need to maintain a steady level of certain substances would be the basis for many of the physiological needs and the motivated behavior necessary to satisfy these needs.

Maslow noted that if a particular physiological need were not satisfied, motivation to satisfy it would govern the person's behavior until the need was met. Thus a starving man would think about food, dream about food, and engage in behavior designed to get food. While the man might have other needs or wishes, his awareness would be dominated by his need for food.

According to Maslow's theory, a person must have his or her physiological needs reasonably well satisfied before he or she can respond to any other needs on the hierarchy. He noted, however, that most of the time people do have these needs satisfied, and thus the physiological needs recede into the background and other, "higher" needs emerge. Departing from other theories that had ascribed a greater importance to physiological needs, Maslow pointed out that the "emergency" conditions of extreme physiological need were not typical for most people, and thus these needs cannot explain most behavior.

Maslow also recognized that physiological needs can fluctuate over short time periods, as, for example, when a person's need for food varies over the course of a day depending on what they have eaten. He suggested that if the physiological needs were basically satisfied over time, then higher needs could come into play. In other words, it was not necessary for a need to be perfectly and completely satisfied in order for higher needs to be activated; it was only necessary that the need be satisfied relatively well. He also noted that a person might be able to tolerate chronic deprivation of some physiological needs at times, if they had previously experienced gratification of the need most of the time. So a person who had been well-fed for most of his or her life would be able to focus on some other need in a particular situation even though he or she was hungry.

Safety needs

Safety needs   Once the physiological needs are basically satisfied, the next set of needs to emerge involves safety and security. A person who is responding to these needs seeks protection from injury or attack and strives for order and predictability in the world. Maslow thought that the safety needs operated very much like physiological needs, although to a lesser degree. Thus if the person felt deprived of safety and security, he or she would focus on satisfying this need to the exclusion of other needs, living "almost for safety alone."

Maslow thought that safety needs could be understood well by studying infants and young children, who often express these needs very directly and clearly. Thus a young child becomes frantic when separated from his or her parents and reacts with fear when confronted with new and strange situations. Young children also have a great need for routine and predictability in their lives, and they become upset and anxious when their routine is disrupted. Maslow thought that most adults would try to hide their insecurities, so that the influence of safety needs would not be as obvious in adults.

Another illustration of the influence of safety needs comes from the behavior of neurotic individuals, who may devote a great deal of their energy to avoiding certain dangers, regardless of their actual risk. Maslow saw neurotic people as constantly afraid that a disaster was about to occur. In response to this fear, they would engage in rituals and other "magical" attempts to reduce their anxiety, or they would seek the protection of someone stronger.

According to Maslow's theory, safety needs are relatively less important for most healthy adults under normal circumstances. He thought society provided enough of a general sense of security that most people did not live in constant fear of disaster or attack. He noted that exceptional circumstances, such as wartime, could activate safety needs in people whose safety needs had previously been satisfied. Additionally, Maslow felt that ordinary behavior such as preferring a permanent job, buying insurance, and adhering to an organized religion could be understood, at least in part, as manifestations of the need for safety and security.

Love, affection, and belonging needs   Once the physiological and safety needs are reasonably satisfied, the next set of needs to emerge focuses on relationships with others. Maslow felt that people have a basic need for individual friendships and love, as well as for a sense of belonging to a group. Once a person feels basically secure and has basic physiological needs met, he or she will seek affection and belongingness. While he thought that sexuality was greatly influenced by the need for love and affection, Maslow pointed out that the need for love is not the same as the need for sex, which could be understood on a physiological basis.

Maslow noted that the need for love involved both giving and receiving love. In his later writings, he would distinguish two different types of love. One type, which he referred to as D-love (deprivation-love), is an essentially selfish need to give and receive affection from others. People experience this need strongly when they are lonely. In contrast, he also described B-love (being-love), which is a more unselfish desire for what is best for the loved one. People manifest B-love when they love and accept a person's failings and foibles rather than trying to change them. When he formulated the need hierarchy, Maslow seems to have been focused primarily on the need for D-love.

Maslow speculated that chronic failure to meet one's need for love would have serious implications for a person's mental health. Like many of the psychoanalytic theorists, he felt that severe psychopathology might be explained, at least in part, by a failure to meet a person's basic need for love and affection. Many of the person's symptoms could then be understood as attempts to deal with the confusion and anxiety that the lack of affection created. He also suggested that extremely aggressive or psychopathic behavior might occur in a person who has been chronically deprived of love.

Esteem needs   The next level of Maslow's need hierarchy involves the need for esteem, that is, positive regard and respect. Maslow distinguished two types of esteem needs, the need for self-esteem and the need for esteem from others. He noted that people who have reasonably satisfied their self-esteem needs feel confident and worthwhile, and also experience a sense of independence and freedom. In addition to this need, people also need to feel that other people respect and recognize them as worthwhile. Maslow pointed out that the respect and adulation of others must be earned; fame by itself, without merit, would not satisfy the person's need for esteem from others.

Maslow thought that self-esteem was related to feelings of dominance or powerfulness. In his early work with monkeys, he had observed that some monkeys assume dominance over others and that this seemed to come from the monkey's feeling that he "deserved" higher status. Maslow carried this idea into his understanding of self-esteem, which he equated with a sense of self-confidence and effectiveness.

Self-actualization   Once the physiological, safety, love, and esteem needs have been basically satisfied, the person tends to move into a new, higher level of motivation marked by the need for self-actualization. Maslow defined this need as the need to fulfill one's potential, to be what one *can* be. For example, a writer might experience the need for self-actualization as a motivation to create poetry, while a musician might experience it as a motivation to make music. Although he used artistic endeavors as examples, Maslow was quick to point out that self-actualization did not necessarily involve artistic creativity. He noted that an artist might create art based solely on inborn talent, without necessarily having satisfied all of his or her basic needs.

Maslow distinguished the need for self-actualization from the other needs by noting that the other needs, which he called basic needs, all involve deficiencies of some sort, such as hunger, anxiety, or loneliness. Satisfaction of these needs could be seen as attempts to make up for what is missing, or to move away from an uncomfortable state of deficiency. In contrast, the need for self-actualization does not involve moving away from a state of deficiency; instead, it involves moving toward a goal of fulfilling oneself.

Maslow made a particular study of people whom he thought were operating under the influence of the need for self-actualization. He saw the need for self-actualization as a characteristic of psychologically healthy, "good human beings," and he felt it was important to understand this motivation because of its implications for human growth and potential. Although he felt that very few people actually reach the level of self-actualization, he believed that most people would have the capacity for this state if they were able to adequately satisfy their more basic needs.

Through his studies of people he considered self-actualizers, Maslow came up with a list of characteristics for the self-actualizing personality. These included such traits as an accurate perception of reality, acceptance of self and others, spontaneity, independence, creativity, a non-hostile sense of humor, and a need for privacy. He noted that self-actualizers are often less restricted by cultural norms and expectations and therefore less inhibited. Although they are capable of forming close relationships, they tend to have relatively few friends, preferring a limited number of deeply rewarding relationships.

One of the most important characteristics Maslow noted was the tendency to have peak experiences. Peak experiences are instances of mystical insight and connectedness, when the person feels a heightened sense of awareness and awe. Such experiences are often growth promoting, as they seem to enable a person to look at his or her life in new ways and find new meaning in life. Maslow at first thought these experiences were relatively rare, but as he studied them further, he found evidence that ordinary people can also have such experiences, although they are experienced less often and less intensely than in self-actualizing persons.

Beyond self-actualization   Although self-actualization is often depicted as the endpoint in Maslow's hierarchy of needs, he did not think that new needs ceased to emerge once the person reached the level of self-actualization. Instead, he suggested that a whole new set of motivations would become important. These motivations, which he later referred to as B-values or *metamotivations*, have to do with growth and enhancement. The B-values have a universal and ultimate quality and include values such as truth, beauty, simplicity, and wholeness.

People who have reached this level of motivation find themselves striving for these ultimate values, which they experience as natural and inevitable. Maslow noted that these people often seem to dedicate themselves to a higher goal or vocation, something outside themselves which they find to be important and meaningful. Thus a self-actualizing person might be dedicated to bringing about world peace or fostering beauty in everyday life. This special vocation seems to embody many of the B-values that are important to a self-actualizing person, and such people often find it impossible to think of themselves as doing anything else. Maslow suggested that people who have satisfied all of the basic needs but do not find vocations outside of themselves would suffer from a kind of illness—a sense of pointlessness and emptiness. Thus it would be possible to have all of the basic needs satisfied and still fail to become a self-actualized person.

Other important features of the theory Although Maslow presented his theory of motivation as a hierarchy of needs, he noted that the order of the needs was not rigidly fixed, and he described a number of exceptions. For example, certain individuals might find self-esteem to be more pre-potent than love, and certain creative people might respond to the need to create without ever experiencing satisfaction of their basic needs.

Maslow was particularly struck by exceptions to the hierarchy in which people would sacrifice the satisfaction of their basic needs in order to meet certain ideals or values. For example, an artist might be willing to go hungry or sacrifice security in order to create art, or a humanitarian might choose a life of poverty in order to help others. He thought that these people must have experienced gratification of their basic needs in early life to the extent that they developed the strength to withstand great deprivation later on. He speculated that the most important time for satisfaction of the basic needs would be in the first two years of life.

Maslow also suggested another set of needs, which he referred to as the cognitive needs. These needs include motivations such as curiosity, the desire to know and understand, and the desire for meaning. He was somewhat unclear as to where these needs might fit into the need hierarchy; however, his later formulations of the theory seem to suggest that these needs may be aspects of the need for self-actualization.

Another important point regarding Maslow's theory is that complete satisfaction of a lower level of needs is not necessary in order for a higher need to emerge, and a person may be influenced by multiple needs at once. Maslow speculated that most people would experience partial satisfaction of each of their basic needs at any given time. He thought that as a person got closer to satisfaction of any given need, they would experience the next higher need on the hierarchy to a greater degree. He also noted that the influence of the needs could be unconscious as well as conscious, and he suggested that unconscious influences might be more important.

Finally, Maslow noted that motivation was only one of several influences on behavior. In particular, he

recognized that biological and cultural influences could have a strong impact on the person's behavior. He also recognized that circumstances in the immediate environment could have an impact on the way that motivations were experienced or acted upon.

Explanation

Maslow's theory sets out to explain how a person's behavior can be influenced by a variety of very different factors, ranging from physiological urges, such as hunger, to more abstract values, such as dedication to a social cause or love of beauty. He tried to arrange the various needs into an order that made sense based on observations of human behavior. One of the more important points about the theory is its explanation of how these vastly different influences could act together to influence a person in a given situation.

Maslow chose pre-potency, the ability to motivate, as the basis for organizing the needs into a hierarchy. In any given situation, a person could be influenced by a variety of needs, but the most pre-potent need is likely to have the greatest influence on his or her behavior. The hierarchy of needs is most evident when extreme cases are examined. For example, if a person is stranded in the desert all alone, he or she might experience both loneliness and extreme thirst. In that situation, the person is very likely to pay more attention to the problem of thirst than to the problem of loneliness. The physiological need for water, which is lower on the hierarchy than the need for love, would have the most influence on the person's thoughts, feelings, and behavior.

In circumstances that are less extreme, the relative influence of the different needs may be less obvious, and multiple needs may come into play at the same time. On an ordinary day when a person is not starving, terrified, or extremely lonely, he or she might be torn between two or more different motivations. For example, suppose that a high school student needs to decide whether to call a friend or work on a college application. The choice could be influenced by the need for love and acceptance, therefore influencing the person to call a friend. On the other hand, the need for safety and security might prompt the person to worry about his or her future, and thus work on the application. The need for esteem could also come into play, if getting accepted at a particular college were important to the person's pride and self-acceptance.

According to Maslow's theory, the person's past history of satisfaction would help to govern which of the needs was most influential at the time. If the person had a good history of positive relationships with others, the need for love might be less influential at that particular moment. Similarly, if the person had generally had his or her needs for safety and security met, the need for safety might not have as much influence. If both of these needs had been reasonably well-satisfied throughout the person's life, the need for esteem might have the most influence, leading the person to work on the application in order to achieve pride and self-satisfaction by getting into a good school.

The relationships among the needs are more subtle, and perhaps more variable, at higher levels of the hierarchy. In particular, the need for love and the need for esteem might be interchangeable at times. Some people seem to be willing to tolerate loneliness, as well as other discomforts, in order to do work that they can take pride in. Others are willing to sacrifice fame and the admiration of others in order to be with someone they love. The choices made by people who are operating at this level of need satisfaction might also be influenced by the beginnings of a need for self-actualization, as they start to feel a need to develop their talents and realize their potential.

In his early work on self-actualization, Maslow focused on people who seemed to be set apart from others by their self-actualizing tendencies. These "good human beings" seemed special and different from the average person, and self-actualization seemed like a goal that only a few people could aspire to. In his later writing, however, Maslow indicated that all people are born with a natural tendency toward self-actualization, although very few people are able to fully realize this goal. In certain circumstances, people who are usually influenced mainly by their basic needs can experience the need for self-actualization and respond to it.

The most likely time for an ordinary person to experience glimmers of the self-actualizing tendency is during a peak experience. Maslow found that many people can describe at least one time in their lives when they have had such an experience. These moments, marked by feelings of wonder and connectedness with the universe, can occur in many different circumstances. People have described peak experiences that occurred during vivid dreams, while contemplating natural beauty, during moments of personal crisis, or during surprisingly ordinary moments when the person has a sudden insight about himself or about the world. These experiences are powerful; people can remember them for years and often feel that the experience was life-changing.

Motivation, particularly human motivation, is a very complex phenomenon, and one important contribution of Maslow's theory is his attempt to make sense of that complexity. He realized that people can be motivated by a need to relieve discomfort, such as hunger, but also by a need to strive for something, such as fulfilling one's potential. Maslow's theory suggests a way that these very different types of motivation could work together to influence human behavior.

Examples

Maslow in the workplace   One good way to illustrate the hierarchy of needs is to examine the various types of motivation that could influence a person in the workplace. This example is particularly appropriate, because Maslow's theory has had considerable influence on business management and worker productivity.

At first glance, it may seem that people work because they have to in order to pay for things they need, such as shelter, food, transportation, and the like. However, when you examine the reasons why people choose one job over another, or why they choose to work longer hours or accept additional work responsibilities when they aren't required to do so, it becomes apparent that other motivations influence working behavior. Each of the five levels of Maslow's need hierarchy can offer a relevant motivation for working in a particular position or accepting particular job responsibilities.

At the most basic level of motivation, people work because they have to in order to survive. They must earn money in order to pay the rent, to buy food, to pay for clothing, and to purchase all the things they need to get along in the world. For people operating at this level of motivation, the pay they receive is the most important reason for working. This is probably the motivation behind working for many poor people, who have little or no choice whether they work or not. People who operate at this level often have little choice in the type of work that they do; they must take any job they can get in order to survive. This level corresponds to Maslow's most basic need level. Working helps to satisfy physiological survival needs.

At the next level, that of safety and security, people may choose a particular job because of the security it provides. A worker might prefer a job that promises to offer employment over the long term, rather than a higher paying job, because long-term employment helps to satisfy the person's need for security. People who respond in this way are likely to have their more basic physiological needs fairly well satisfied. They may still need to work for a living, but they aren't faced with starvation, and they can choose to look for a job that provides security. Security might also come in the form of job benefits, such as health insurance or a training program.

Some workers will stay in a job that they don't particularly like for many years, and this could be a reflection of their need for safety and security. This need can also explain why many workers are so upset by the phenomenon of "outsourcing," that is, having work done in countries where labor is cheaper. Outsourcing is seen as a threat to job security, and thus it concerns many workers, particularly those in manufacturing jobs.

Workers who have had their survival and safety needs met may respond next to the need for affection and belongingness. Many people form important relationships at work, and maintaining these relationships can be a reason for continuing in a particular position rather than moving on to another one. This may be true even though the other position offers higher pay or greater security. People who are near retirement age will sometimes continue to work when they no longer have to in order to maintain the relationships they make at work. In some employment settings, belonging to a particular working team can also satisfy the need for affection and belongingness, and it is not uncommon for employers to send workers to seminars and institutes that promise to improve teambuilding skills. And, as it turns out, high levels of teamwork can often enhance worker productivity and effectiveness.

If their needs for survival, security, and affection are met, workers may be influenced by the next level of motivation, the need for self-esteem and the esteem of others. At this level, doing a good job becomes an important motivating factor. Evidence of this level of motivation can be found in people who work longer hours than required in order to do a good job, or in people who take on harder job responsibilities when they aren't required to do so. People often take great pride in their work, and they may also seek the praise and approval of their supervisors and coworkers. Many people identify themselves in terms of their work, and they see it as an important aspect of their self-esteem. Workers who have been laid off through no fault of their own will often feel a blow to their self-esteem, seeing the layoff as a commentary on their ability or job performance.

Finally, if a person has been generally satisfied in all of the basic needs described above, he or she may be working in order to satisfy the need for self-actualization. At this level of motivation, we may be talking about a career or vocation rather than a job. The person may choose to work at something because they feel it is their destiny or calling, as when a person is inspired to enter the ministry, become an artist, or work for world peace. The compensation offered for a person working at this level may not be particularly good and the working conditions may not be particularly desirable; however, the person has had his or her more basic needs satisfied in the past and thus these concerns are unimportant. It is the work itself that motivates the person.

Maslow's hierarchy can explain the behavior of workers who operate at each of the different levels of motivation. Managers could use this understanding to enhance worker productivity, by arranging the work environment so that it offers satisfaction of the particular need that the worker is responding to. If most of the workers are working to meet survival or security needs, the manager should pay attention to salary and job security. On the other hand, if most of the workers are responding to belongingness needs, fostering teamwork in the work environment might be the most effective strategy. Managers also need to understand that many workers need to feel good about the work that they do and have input on how the work is done.

In reality most workers are responding to some combination of these needs at any given time. Survival and security needs may influence the worker's preferences regarding compensation and job security, while belongingness and esteem needs may determine the conditions that the worker prefers. And sometimes workers may respond out of a sense of mission or destiny. If the manager can understand these various needs and create a workplace that successfully addresses these needs, he or she may be able to improve the satisfaction as well as the effectiveness of the workers.

*A **self-actualizing person***   Another example illustrates Maslow's concept of the self-actualizing person. Some of Maslow's first ideas about self-actualizing persons grew out of his relationship with Max Wertheimer, a Gestalt psychologist who was one of Maslow's early teachers and mentors. Maslow was struck by Wertheimer's unique personality, and he went on to find similar traits in other people that he admired. These observations were the roots of his ideas regarding self-actualization.

Maslow noted Wertheimer's tremendous energy and enthusiasm for topics that were important to him, such as the nature of the human mind and questions of good and evil. Wertheimer was not afraid to show his enthusiasm, and seemed unconcerned about looking foolish or childlike. He particularly enjoyed children, and would play with his own children at his home during social gatherings for his colleagues. Wertheimer was generous with his time, and patient and respectful with his students. He particularly enjoyed music and art, and at a time when American science was supposedly too "hard nosed" for these topics, Wertheimer recognized the value in the arts and the merit of studying esthetic experiences. Maslow was also struck by Wertheimer's sense of humor. He enjoyed laughing and poking gentle fun at himself, but he never made other people the butt of his jokes, and seemed to find his humor in the human condition rather than in individual failings or foibles.

Maslow's list of characteristics of the self-actualizing person includes many traits that he found in Max Wertheimer, and later noted in other unique characters as well. Traits such as passion for a cause or idea, lack of concern for social conventions, appreciation of art, and a gentle sense of humor later became important aspects of Maslow's concept of self-actualization.

HISTORICAL CONTEXT

In the 1930s and 1940s, when Maslow began pulling together his ideas about motivation, the science of human behavior was dominated by two schools of thought: the behaviorist approach articulated by John Watson and the psychoanalytic approach originated by Sigmund Freud. Most of academic psychology was strongly experimental and behaviorist, adopting the position that only behavior that was objectively observable and measurable was appropriate for study. Much of the foundation for behaviorism had been studies of animal behavior, and very little attention was being paid to inner processes such as cognitions, emotions, or values. Behaviorists paid little attention to the question of motivation itself. They assumed that an animal was motivated to satisfy drives such as hunger or thirst and then focused on the environmental forces that shaped the way the animal responded to those drives. The behaviorist approach assumed that the same forces that governed animal behavior also governed human behavior.

The other main source of ideas about human behavior was the field of psychotherapy, which had its basis in clinical observations of people who were suffering from various mental and emotional disorders. Here the thinking of Sigmund Freud and his followers dominated the field. Although the psychoanalytic approach recognized that human emotions and thoughts are important, most psychoanalysts believed that the major influences on human behavior were instinctual and unconscious. As such, they could not be studied directly, and the main source of information about these influences was the record produced during sessions of psychoanalysis. Here the patient's behavior, language, dreams, and fantasies were thought to contain symbols of their unconscious motivations. Another key assumption of psychoanalysis was that normal human behavior could be inferred from studies of abnormal behavior.

Maslow was uniquely influenced by both of schools of thought. He was formally trained in experimental psychology at the University of Wisconsin, which had adopted a strongly experimental and behaviorist stance; his earliest professional work involved experimental studies of animal behavior. He was also exposed to the thinking of some of the leading psychoanalysts of his time, including Alfred Adler, Karen Horney, and Erich Fromm. He thus developed familiarity with the psychoanalytic approach and later tried to apply some aspects of the approach when counseling his students. He also underwent psychoanalysis himself and returned to it periodically throughout his life.

Finally, Maslow encountered yet another influence, which was not well-known in the United States at the time. This was the Gestalt psychology of Max Wertheimer and Kurt Koffka, who became familiar to Maslow early in his professional life. The Gestalt viewpoint recognized the importance of conscious human thoughts, feelings, and values, yet it also proposed that these things could be studied in a scientific manner.

One of Maslow's particular gifts was his ability to pull together ideas from these different schools of thought. He was also able to express his ideas clearly, and he had the courage to risk rejection by the mainstream of his profession. His work was an important departure from the thinking of his times, and it served as one of the sparks for the humanistic approach, which would become very influential during the middle years of the twentieth century.

Maslow was also influenced by the cultural and historical events of his time. He entered the field of psychology during a time of great optimism for the field and for the promise of science in general. The behaviorist John Watson had declared that it was possible to use the principles of behaviorism to shape human behavior in virtually any direction, and many people thought it would soon be possible to use this technology to solve problems such as crime, poverty, and ignorance. The early part of the twentieth century had also seen the rise of technological advances such as the telephone, radio, and the automobile, and it was not uncommon for people to expect that similar advances would soon eliminate many of the problems that had plagued mankind throughout history. Thus it was not unusual for the young Maslow to believe that he could use science for the betterment of humankind, and to choose to do so as a psychologist.

The darker developments of the early twentieth century also had an important influence on Maslow's thinking. He was personally acquainted with a number of people who had fled the horrors of Nazi Germany, and he was deeply troubled by the reality of human cruelty and oppression. He had been touched by anti-Semitism in his own life as well, and he understood the pain and confusion that such injustice could cause. Like most Americans, he was also deeply affected by the Japanese attack on Pearl Harbor. He was too old to serve in the armed forces by the time the war broke out, so instead he decided to devote his efforts to understanding the forces that could lead people to be violent and aggressive. He felt that one had to understand evil in order to find ways to eliminate it. His choice to study human motivation makes sense in this context—knowing why people do the things they do, both good and evil, was one of his key interests.

During the 1950s and 1960s, Maslow witnessed the rise of existential thought and the growth of interest in Eastern philosophies. His ideas about self-actualization seemed to fit well with these viewpoints, and he adopted a number of ideas from these schools of thought. The optimistic nature of his ideas and the attention he paid to mystical experiences were very attractive to young people, and he became something of a cult figure to the counterculture movement of the 1960s. He never abandoned his belief in science and his value for respectful discourse, however, and he openly rejected the behavioral excesses and the lack of discipline that he saw in many of his followers. He is remembered as a truly original thinker who was able to integrate many of the important ideas of his time.

CRITICAL RESPONSE

Reactions to Maslow's theory

Maslow's theory of motivation was a radical departure from the views of behavior that dominated psychology in the early twentieth century. He rejected the behaviorist notion that human behavior could be understood by studying animal behavior, and he also turned away from the psychoanalytic idea that normal behavior could be inferred from studies of abnormal behavior. He hesitated to publish some of his ideas at first because he knew they were very different from the mainstream views of his time.

Despite these concerns, Maslow actually found a receptive audience for his ideas. His 1943 paper, "A Theory of Human Motivation," met with relatively little interest at first, but over the next decade or so his work became increasingly influential, and "A Theory of Human Motivation" is now considered to be one of the classic works in psychology. Although experimental psychologists questioned whether Maslow's ideas could be proven by research, his theory had a lot of

appeal for contemporaries who worked in clinical settings. His developing ideas on self-actualization were particularly useful in this regard, and his work in this area was hailed as an important contribution to the growing field of counseling psychology. Carl Rogers, a founder of counseling psychology, praised Maslow's positive view of motivation and human growth. He thought this view was more appropriate for counseling healthy people than the prevailing psychoanalytic view, with its emphasis on neurosis and maladjustment.

After Maslow published *Motivation and Personality* in 1954, he was hailed as a leading thinker in the field of motivation. He was asked to present papers at important conferences, and he was able to publish a number of articles on his theory in leading professional journals. His ideas on motivation had implications for applied fields such as business management and education, and his work had an important influence in these areas. Maslow's theory of motivation was one of the key influences on Douglas McGregor, whose 1960 book, *The Human Side of Enterprise*, became a classic work on enlightened management practices. McGregor thought that managers needed to understand the motivations of workers in order to create a healthy and productive workplace, and he used Maslow's hierarchy of needs as the starting point for understanding workers' behavior and needs.

Despite continuing enthusiasm for Maslow's theory, a number of researchers were raising questions about the validity of his motivation hierarchy. It was difficult to validate many aspects of the theory with research. In particular, the middle levels of Maslow's hierarchy seemed to overlap, and the order he specified for emergence of different needs did not seem to hold true for all people. In 1969, Clayton Alderfer published an article in which he suggested a number of modifications to Maslow's theory. He proposed that Maslow's five levels of motivation could be reduced to three levels: Existence (referring to basic material needs such as food); Relatedness (referring to needs for relationships with others); and Growth (referring to needs for self-actualization and esteem). His theory is usually referred to as ERG theory, to signify the initials of the three needs he proposed. Alderfer's ERG theory suggested that more than one need could influence the person at the same time and also pointed out that different people could experience the needs in different order. Alderfer's modifications of Maslow's theory had some influence, particularly in the business management field; however, ERG theory never achieved the widespread popularity of Maslow's theory.

By the 1960s, Maslow's ideas had found their way into popular culture, where the concept of

BIOGRAPHY:

Viktor Frankl

Viktor Frankl (1905–1997) grew up in a Jewish community in Vienna. He studied medicine and neurology and became interested in psychoanalysis. He was becoming established as a psychiatrist and neurologist when the Nazis took over Austria in 1938. In his capacity as head of the neurological department of Rothschild Hospital, he shielded a number of psychotic patients from the Nazi policy of "mercy killing" of mentally ill patients. In 1942, shortly after his marriage, Frankl, his wife, his parents, and his brother were arrested and sent to concentration camps. Over the next three years, Frankl experienced the horrors of the camps but managed to survive, only to learn upon his liberation that all of his family members except his sister were dead.

Frankl would later write about his experiences in the camps in *Man's Search for Meaning*, a book that would sell millions of copies around the world. While in the camps, he had observed that the people who survived all had something to live for: reunion with a loved one, religious faith, or some important goal that they could focus on. He concluded that the survivors made it because they were able to find some meaning in the midst of pointless cruelty. He proposed that humans have an inborn drive to find meaning, and that this drive was the most basic source of human motivation. This was a radical departure from the classic psychoanalytic view that all motivation was based on pleasure seeking.

To describe his approach to psychotherapy, Frankl used the word logotherapy, which is based on the Greek word *logos*, or meaning. Thus his approach to psychotherapy was to help patients find meaning in their lives. Frankl proposed that people could develop a noogenic neurosis, or spiritual sickness, when they were frustrated in attempts to find meaning and therefore turn to behavior that was harmful or self-defeating. He offered logotherapy as a way to treat this neurosis. Frankl did not intend for his approach to replace psychotherapy for mental disorders; instead he thought it could complement more traditional psychotherapy in cases where spiritual issues were predominant.

Frankl is well-known for some of his unusual approaches to psychotherapy. Perhaps the most famous is paradoxical intention, or "prescribing the symptom." In this technique, a person would be asked to do the thing that they were avoiding. For instance, a person who was afraid of blushing in public might be told to try to blush on purpose. The absurdity of the request often helped break the vicious cycle of worrying and trying to avoid the unwanted behavior. Another strategy Frankl used was "de-reflection," which involved

Viktor Frankl. (Copyright Katharina Vesely. Reproduced by permission.)

shifting the patient's focus away from his or her problems and on to some more positive activity.

Frankl tried to bring a spiritual dimension into psychotherapy, and his ideas have considerable appeal in troubling times. *Man's Search for Meaning* continues to touch new readers, who find his thoughts on man's inner strength to be comforting and inspiring.

---

self-actualization and the notion of peak experiences were widely accepted. As his work became more philosophical and existential, it began to appeal to religious and spiritual leaders, as well as to members of the 1960s counterculture. His ideas on the higher reaches of self-actualization also fit well with the ideals of the encounter group movement of the late 1960s and early 1970s. A number of such groups experimented with ways to bring about self-actualization and higher consciousness, drawing upon Maslow's concepts of metamotivation and transpersonal psychology. Some proponents of Maslow's theory experimented with various forms of meditation as well as drug use in attempts to bring about self-actualization; however, Maslow cautioned against such practices. He thought that true self-actualization had to come from within the person, and artificial attempts to alter one's consciousness would not have much benefit in bringing about the higher need states.

As the enthusiasm for the human potential movement and the 1960s counterculture waned in the late 1970s and 1980s, interest in Maslow's theory waned as well. Critical reviews pointed out that few of Maslow's principles were actually supported by research. Maslow had outlined a large number of possible studies to validate his theory, but most of these studies were never done. Maslow became less and less interested in doing research himself as his career continued, and few others undertook the task. This may have been partly due to difficulties with defining and measuring key concepts in Maslow's theory. Also, many of those who were drawn to the theory came from outside the field of experimental psychology and had little interest in validating his propositions with research.

Although Maslow's theory of motivation is now generally considered to be outdated, it continues to have an influence in a number of fields. Introductory texts on counseling, management, education, and a variety of human service professions continue to include sections on the theory, perhaps because of its intuitive appeal. His ideas on management were even revived somewhat when *Maslow on Management* was published in 1999. This book, which is an updated edition of Maslow's 1965 book on management principles, generated new interest in his theory. Maslow's positive outlook and his enthusiasm for improving the human condition continue to inspire people who hope to work as effective leaders.

Maslow is still recognized as an important influence on counseling and psychotherapy. While the field of counseling psychology has moved beyond many of Maslow's ideas, a large number of clinical and counseling psychologists continue to identify themselves as humanistic in their orientation. Maslow's works are still read by students in these fields, and his books, particularly *Toward a Psychology of Being*, can be found in the libraries of many practicing counselors and psychotherapists. Maslow's insistence on studying healthy functioning is now seen as an obvious step toward understanding human behavior, and his thoughts on human potential and aspirations continue to inspire people in the helping professions.

Critical evaluation of the theory

Although Maslow's theory is intuitively appealing, it has several weaknesses that have never been resolved. In order for a theory of behavior to be useful, it has to meet certain logical criteria, and it also has to be supported by a body of well-designed research. Critics have pointed out that Maslow's theory falls short on these requirements.

Many of Maslow's important concepts are vague and poorly defined, and this makes it very difficult to do research on important aspects of the theory. In particular, Maslow's ideas about self-actualizing people are problematic. He seemed to use very subjective criteria to decide whether a person is self-actualizing, and some critics have suggested that Maslow's self-actualizing people were simply people that he admired. His list of historical figures who were self-actualizers includes artists, political leaders, philosophers, and scientists, but it is hard to see what else these people have in common besides success in their fields. Maslow also seemed to contradict himself in his writings about self-actualization. At times he seemed to describe it as a goal or end-point that healthy people aspire to, but at other times he seemed to be talking about self-actualization as a new kind of need itself, something that drives people. His reasoning about self-actualization also seems to be circular: healthy people are self-actualizing, and self-actualization is the ultimate sign of emotional health.

Another concept that seems to be poorly defined is the notion of need satisfaction. Maslow stated that people whose needs at one level are "basically satisfied" will begin to experience needs at the next level on the hierarchy, but he never indicated how "basic satisfaction" could be determined. His theory could not account very well for people who suffered from lifelong poverty and deprivation, yet managed to become great artists, thinkers, or humanitarians. The lives of these people might include very little evidence that their more basic needs were ever satisfied. Maslow hinted that the order in which the needs emerged could vary for different people, but he never explained how this could happen. He also stated that a person might respond to multiple needs at once and might be subject to influences other than the need hierarchy, but he never outlined how different needs would function simultaneously or interact with influences such as genetic inheritance or environmental conditions.

The concept of need itself is also problematic. Needs seem to be things that organisms require in order to function; however, people and animals often strive for things that they don't require at all. Curiosity and playfulness are examples, as are tendencies toward self-destructive behavior. One solution to this difficulty is to propose the existence of a very large number of needs, one for each observed behavior, but then the only way to prove that these needs exist is to show that organisms engage in behavior to satisfy each need— another example of circular reasoning. More recent theories of motivation have tended to move away from the concept of needs because of this problem.

Another problem with Maslow's theory is the lack of testability of many of its important concepts. In order for a theory to have scientific validity, it must be possible to test each of its key principles and disprove them. Principles that cannot be disproved are not really scientific; they fall into the realm of philosophy or faith instead. Many of Maslow's ideas about self-actualization are essentially non-testable. For example, Maslow seemed to imply that each person has a destiny that he or she will be driven to fulfill once the level of self-actualization is reached. This concept is very difficult to test because it is so elusive. How can we know what a person's destiny might be, except by examining what they become? The existence of something like destiny cannot be proved or disproved. It is essentially a matter of faith. A number of Maslow's later thoughts on self-actualization have a similar philosophical quality, which, while appealing, is not very amenable to scientific evaluation.

Other evaluators have criticized Maslow's theory on the grounds that it is culturally biased or elitist. They note that Maslow used very subjective criteria to define self-actualizing people. He chose examples from among famous people who were known to him through personal acquaintance or readings. Thus the members of his first group of self-actualizers were all Europeans or Americans, and nearly all were males. His choices reveal a decided bias toward Western values such as independence and self-determination. Maslow failed to allow for the fact that non-Westerners might have decidedly different values. He later recognized this limitation to some extent and proposed a broader cross-cultural examination of self-actualizing people, but he apparently never made such a study himself.

The charge of elitism is also difficult to answer. Maslow wanted to turn away from studying neurosis and abnormality and instead focus on understanding healthy people. But in his attempt to do so, he chose to look at the "best and the brightest" rather than at ordinary people who were functioning reasonably well. Thus very few people could meet his criteria for self-actualization. He studied hundreds of college students and only found one person that fit the description. Maslow's thinking may partly reflect the widespread psychoanalytic belief that most ordinary people suffered from some kind of neurosis, but it left little room for understanding healthy functioning in ordinary people.

Perhaps the most important criticism of Maslow's theory is the lack of research to support it. The ultimate test of a scientific theory is whether it is supported by carefully designed research, and Maslow's theory has not been very successful in meeting this test. As

mentioned earlier, problems of definition and testability make it difficult to evaluate many of his propositions. Even when researchers have been able to come up with concrete hypotheses to test, they have encountered methodological problems. Concepts such as self-actualization and need satisfaction are very difficult to measure objectively, and most studies have had to rely on self-reports by the participants. When asked about their own values and motivations, participants may not respond accurately for a number of reasons. They may try to present themselves in a favorable light rather than revealing their true feelings. They may also try to give responses that they think the researcher is looking for, or sometimes they may even try to deliberately mislead the researcher. Also, as Maslow speculated, important motivations may operate unconsciously, and the respondents may thus be unable to report their true motivations accurately. The lack of objective measures for many of Maslow's concepts has been an ongoing research problem.

The research that does exist has not provided a lot of support for Maslow's theory. In the early 1970s, Mahmoud Wahba and Lawrence Bridwell published a critical review of the research evaluating Maslow's theory and concluded that Maslow's propositions had received very little research support. They examined three different groups of studies. The first group was intended to determine whether motivations would actually group into five distinct levels, as predicted by Maslow's need hierarchy. These studies also investigated whether needs occurred in the order Maslow specified. The second group of studies investigated Maslow's proposal that unsatisfied basic needs would exert the strongest influence on behavior—in their words, the "deprivation/domination" proposition. Finally, they examined the "gratification/activation" proposition, that need satisfaction should decrease going up the need hierarchy, and that needs that were essentially satisfied would become less important, while needs at the next higher level of the hierarchy would become more important.

Wahba and Bridwell reported that research had failed to verify the existence of five distinct levels of motivation, as Maslow had proposed. A few studies suggested two independent levels and one suggested four, but no study validated all five levels. These studies also failed to show that self-actualization was a distinct type of motivation, and they did not support the order of the hierarchy that Maslow proposed.

With regard to the studies on the deprivation/domination hypothesis, Wahba and Bridwell concluded that there was partial support for Maslow's theory. In the case of self-actualization and autonomy needs, research participants had indicated that their least satisfied needs were the most important; however, they had not done so for security, social, or esteem needs. Wahba and Bridwell also noted that the positive findings for self-actualization and autonomy could be due to measurement problems rather than actual validity of the deprivation/domination hypothesis.

Finally, Wahba and Bridwell concluded that there was little or no support for the gratification/activation hypothesis. They noted that a few studies had generated limited support for this proposition, but they had significant methodological problems, which might have accounted for the positive results.

Wahba and Bridwell went on to conclude that Maslow's theory was largely unsupported by research; however, they did not suggest that the theory should be abandoned. Instead, they recommended improvements to measurement techniques and other aspects of research design, which might allow for better evaluation of Maslow's propositions. In particular, they noted that longitudinal research was necessary. Longitudinal research tracks the behavior of subjects over relatively long time periods, and looks for changes that occur with time. Since Maslow's theory proposed that motivations would change over time as different needs were satisfied, the appropriate way to test it would involve longitudinal research. This type of research is costly and difficult, however, and very few longitudinal studies have examined Maslow's propositions. The few existing studies have not shown strong support for the theory.

Since the mid-1970s, few investigators have shown interest in testing Maslow's theory. Influenced by reviews such as that of Wahba and Bridwell, many researchers have come to feel that the theory has been refuted by research. Despite this perception, studies on certain aspects of the theory continue to appear periodically, as researchers have continued to show interest in phenomena such as peak experiences and self-actualization.

Maslow's theory of motivation can be seen as an influential but flawed attempt to explain an important aspect of human behavior. Maslow's work helped to change the direction of psychology in the twentieth century, laying the groundwork for a new approach to understanding human behavior, which has come to be known as humanistic psychology. Although Maslow's theory is not widely accepted today, it has an important place in the history of psychology, and it continues to influence thinking about motivation in business management, education, and the helping professions.

THEORIES IN ACTION

Research

Maslow enthusiastically described a number of research ideas linked to his theory; however, the theory of motivation has not generated a large body of research. Unlike other personality theorists who were also psychotherapists, Maslow did not specify a treatment approach to go with his theory. Therefore, the theory did not generate a body of treatment studies, as would be common for theories that included a treatment component. Conceptual and methodological problems with the theory have also made it difficult to evaluate, and the philosophical nature of Maslow's theory has generated more speculation than actual data. Research on Maslow's propositions has been especially rare since the mid-1970s, when the body of research supporting the theory was critically reviewed and found lacking.

Although there is a general lack of interest in research on Maslow's principles, some areas continue to produce a few studies every year. In particular, the concepts of self-actualization and peak experience continue to intrigue researchers, and they are still finding new ways to investigate these phenomena.

One stream of research has focused on ways that different groups experience self-actualization. A number of scales to measure the tendency toward self-actualization have been developed over the years, including a scale specifically designed to measure self-actualization in children. Various groups have been compared on these scales, in attempts to understand how self-actualizing tendencies interact with gender, age, and other aspects of personality.

One interesting example involves the study of gifted students. Gifted students (i.e., those with high intelligence) have been compared to non-gifted students, on the assumption that gifted individuals should show stronger tendencies toward self-actualization. This is an interesting question that has implications for understanding the relationship between giftedness and creativity, which is an important aspect of self-actualization. Although creative people are often highly intelligent, not all intelligent people are unusually creative. It is also uncertain whether having unusual intellectual ability helps a person to reach the higher levels of Maslow's motivational hierarchy. At least one study has found that gifted students do show higher levels of self-actualization, but the relationship between intelligence and self-actualization is still not fully explained.

Men and women have also been compared on indices of self-actualization, with varying results. One issue is the way self-actualization is measured. If the indicator of self-actualization includes external signs of success such as career advancement, then men tend to show stronger tendencies toward self-actualization than women. However, as Maslow noted, self-actualization does not necessarily involve the external trappings of success, and a person who lives a relatively quiet life may still show self-actualizing tendencies. When self-actualization is defined in terms of inner values and aspirations, then women tend to show a tendency toward self-actualization that is as strong as, or stronger than, that shown by men. These studies highlight one of the recurring problems with research on Maslow's propositions—the difficulty of clearly defining important concepts.

Another set of studies has examined the tendency toward self-actualization in homeless people. According to Maslow's theory, these people should not show much tendency toward self-actualization, but the findings suggest that even people who are coping with extreme deprivation still experience some aspects of the self-actualizing tendency. These studies directly contradict Maslow's notion that satisfaction of the basic needs is necessary before one can experience self-actualization. The findings seem to fit better with Maslow's later thinking about self-actualization, in which he recognized that even ordinary people can show some self-actualizing tendencies.

Age differences in self-actualization have also been examined, on the assumption that self-actualizing tendencies should increase with age. The results of these studies have been variable, particularly in studies of children. Since children in general might be expected to show relatively limited tendencies toward self-actualization, it is not surprising that age increases are not easy to detect.

The phenomenon of the peak experience also continues to intrigue a few researchers. Studies of peak experiences have examined the way people with different backgrounds report such experiences. One study compared artists to non-artists, on the assumption that artists might be more prone to have peak experiences, but this was not found to be the case. Other studies have tried to determine how different cultural groups react to peak experiences. Evidence of peak experiences in childhood has also been explored. Studies in this area are often qualitative rather than quantitative, focusing on individual accounts of unique and mystical experiences. The significance of these experiences for individuals and the life-changing quality of such experiences are fairly well established.

One other study illustrates a novel application of Maslow's theory on an international level rather than an individual one. This unusual study applied the hierarchy to understanding changes in the quality of life in different countries as they became more developed. Looking at data for 88 countries gathered over a period of 35 years, the study used progress on Maslow's hierarchy as an indicator of improving quality of life. The results of the study confirmed the order that Maslow predicted for the emergence of different need states, but it did not confirm his prediction that satisfaction of one need would lead to less interest in meeting that need as other, higher needs emerged. Maslow would no doubt be pleased to see his theory applied in this unusual manner.

The limited body of current research on Maslow's principles reflects the general decline of interest in his theory. Nonetheless, the compelling concepts continue to attract new investigators, and Maslow's theory continues to generate a small body of ongoing research. The continuing interest in his theory is testimony to the intuitive appeal of his theory.

Case studies

Unlike other humanistic psychologists who were primarily psychotherapists, Maslow never specified a particular strategy for applying his ideas in therapy or counseling. Thus there is no "Maslovian psychotherapy" and no particular approach to handling the process of counseling. Maslow did provide informal counseling to some of his students, but he never really wrote in detail about the process of counseling or psychotherapy, and only limited accounts of his counseling experiences are available.

The most direct application of Maslow's ideas comes from the field of business management. Maslow was mainly focused on questions of motivation, which is a key issue for managers. In trying to maximize worker productivity, managers often struggle to understand the forces that motivate people, and Maslow's hierarchy offers one way to look at the interacting forces that drive human behavior.

Maslow's 1954 book, *Motivation and Personality*, had considerable influence on some business managers who were interested in using scientific principles to improve the workplace. One such manager was Andy Kay, an engineer who had started his own company to produce electronic instruments after World War II. Kay had read Maslow's book, as well as McGregor's *The Human Side of Enterprise*, and he used the ideas in these works as guidelines for creating a new approach to managing his company. At Kay's invitation, Maslow visited the company in 1962. He was very impressed by Kay's innovations, which sparked additional thinking of his own. Maslow's ideas grew into the book *Eupsychian Management*, and Kay's company, Non-Linear Systems, became a famous example of what Maslow liked to call "enlightened management."

One of the key elements of enlightened management was the notion that workers should be given more autonomy and control in the work environment. McGregor, who was strongly influenced by Maslow's theory of motivation, had proposed that most traditional business managers were operating under a set of flawed assumptions, which he called "Theory X." Under Theory X management, it was assumed that most workers were operating at the most basic levels of Maslow's need hierarchy, and thus they would be motivated primarily by wages and job security. Theory X managers would therefore pay little attention to relationships in the workplace or other aspects related to higher levels of motivation. In contrast, McGregor proposed "Theory Y," which assumed that most workers had their basic survival needs satisfied and were trying to satisfy higher needs in the workplace. Under Theory Y, the worker's need to belong to a team and to feel a sense of accomplishment in their work would be more important influences on their performance than more basic motivations.

Kay set out to apply Maslow's principles and McGregor's interpretation of them in a real-life experiment. In a rare display of managerial risk-taking, Kay reorganized his successful business to conform to Maslow's principles. Among Kay's most striking innovations was his reorganization of the production process. Drawing on Maslow and McGregor's ideas, Kay believed that workers had a need to see the results of their work, and not just to focus on one small aspect of the total process. He therefore dismantled the assembly lines in his plant and formed small teams of workers instead. After training team members in the entire production process, each team was made responsible for taking its share of several products through the complete assembly process. The team would build each instrument, inspect it, remedy any defects, and pack the product for shipping.

The workers at Non-Linear Systems were also given an unusually high level of control over other aspects of their work environment. Kay tried to foster the workers' sense of autonomy and teamwork, allowing them to take breaks according to team needs, and eliminating mechanisms for managerial control such as time clocks and hourly wages. Instead, workers were paid a flat salary (which was an increase over their hourly pay), and they were no longer subject to deductions from their pay for absences. Managers were no longer supposed to make all of the day-to-day decisions. Instead, they would serve in an advisory capacity, and the production teams would make their

CHRONOLOGY

1908: Born in Manhattan.

1930: Completes Bachelor of Arts degree at the University of Wisconsin.

1928: Marries Bertha Goodman.

1931–1934: Primate research with Harry Harlow. Completes a masters thesis and doctoral dissertation on primate behavior.

1935–1937: Postdoctoral fellowship at Columbia University. Research on sexuality and dominance in humans.

1937–1951: Faculty position at Brooklyn College. Eventually reaches rank of associate professor.

1938: Birth of daughter Ann.

1940: Birth of daughter Ellen.

1951–1969: Faculty position at Brandeis University. Serves as department chair until 1961.

1954: The publication of *Motivation and Personality* brings national prominence.

1961: The first issue of *The Journal of Humanistic Psychology*, founded by Maslow, is published.

1962: Publishes *Toward a Psychology of Being*.

1962–1963: Consults with Andy Kay at Non-Linear Systems.

1966: Is elected president of the American Psychological Association.

1970: Dies of a heart attack at his home in Menlo Park, California.

own decisions. Acting on McGregor's notion that record-keeping interfered with the workers' sense of self-control, much of the company's accounting system was also dismantled. Records were kept by the personnel, shipping, and purchasing departments, and their balances were reported to the company treasurer.

In the early years of the experiment, Kay was extremely enthusiastic about the changes. He reported that the workers were happier, productivity had improved, and customer complaints were reduced. The company's reputation for producing excellent

BIOGRAPHY:
Rollo May

Rollo May (1909–1994) was a clinical psychologist who is often identified as the founder of American existential psychotherapy. May earned his doctorate from Columbia University and spent his career doing psychotherapy and teaching at a number of distinguished institutions. He was greatly influenced by European existential philosophers, and he helped to introduce many of their concepts into American psychology. He was a prolific writer who produced several books on existential psychology and psychotherapy. Among the best known are *The Meaning of Anxiety*, *Love and Will*, and *The Cry for Myth*.

May's early interests included psychoanalysis and the problem of anxiety. In *The Meaning of Anxiety*, May disagreed with the popular view that most anxiety was neurotic, and that mental health would involve living without it. Noting that anxiety was a healthy response to threatening conditions, May proposed that the real goal of psychotherapy is to help clients face their anxieties and live creatively. This might mean increasing tension rather than reducing it.

May addressed himself to broad philosophical concepts and their place in psychotherapy. His book, *Love and Will*, focuses on the relationship between these two motivational forces. He defines love as a need to become one with another being, the source of many dreams or wishes. In contrast, will is the ability to take action, to "make wishes come true." Focusing too much on love leads a person to be infantile, lacking the self-discipline necessary to act on his or her wishes. In contrast, focusing too much on will leads a person

to be overly controlled and perfectionist. May thought that a person's goal in life should be to find a balance between these two forces.

Creativity is another important concept for May. He saw creativity as a manifestation of courage and commitment, and he thought that mental health would involve living creatively in the face of uncertainties. Psychotherapy involves making an authentic connection with the client and helping the person to discover a way to be creative in dealing with his or her reality. Freedom is another goal of psychotherapy. To be free, people must take responsibility for themselves and make informed choices in their lives.

May's last book was *The Cry for Myth*, in which he discussed the lack of values in twentieth-century life. May noted that people have a need to believe in something, and they have historically relied on religion to provide "guiding narratives" for their lives. With the deterioration of traditional values, people have been floundering and confused. May argues that we should be working to create new myths that help people find a sense of purpose and value in their lives.

Throughout his career, May worked to create an approach to psychotherapy that went beyond specific techniques. He thought of his approach primarily as an attitude toward therapy, in which the therapist would strive to form a connection with the client and help him or her live more fully. His ideas have helped to shape the humanistic view of personality and psychotherapy.

---

products was bolstered, and many observers believed that the experiment was a great success. In 1962, when Maslow visited Non-Linear Systems, he hailed it as an example of the positive application of his ideas. He also began to speculate about the ways that self-actualization could occur among business entrepreneurs, apparently using Kay as an example.

Non-Linear Systems continued the experiment in participative management until early 1965, when it abruptly returned to many of the pre-experiment conditions. Although the working teams continued to have responsibility for the entire production process,

managers resumed the job of supervising line employees, specific standards for work quality were reinstated, pay was tied to the amount of work done, and standard accounting practices were reinstated. The company had experienced falling profits, and it had laid off a number of workers in 1963 and 1964. Although production line workers were satisfied, managers had been unhappy with the experiment because they had no clearly defined responsibilities. Sales were falling as well. A later analysis determined that market forces were responsible for some of the falling profits, but the experiment was ultimately termed a failure.

This case study illustrates some of the ways that Maslow's theory could be applied in the workplace, and it also shows some of the problems with applying the theory. Although Maslow introduced some provocative and important ideas about motivation, his theory was not complete enough to explain the complexities of human behavior in the workplace. Competing forces that he had not accounted for in his theory turned out to be important, such as the managers' need to have a sense of purpose and the executives' need for accurate data to make business decisions. Maslow's theory also had nothing to say about the market forces that influenced Non-Linear Systems. His theory could not be applied in a vacuum, and perhaps the larger business world was not ready for some of his idealistic proposals.

Interestingly enough, Maslow himself had expressed concern that his ideas were being applied too quickly, without adequate testing to determine their validity. Although he was enthusiastic about the potential for applying his ideas, Maslow recognized that they were still very preliminary. He had hoped to generate a body of research to support his theory before applying it on a large scale.

Maslow's theory and Kay's application of it may seem rather naive to modern readers, but at the time they represented the cutting edge of a new approach to understanding human behavior. In the years since the experiment at Non-Linear Systems, other writers have proposed some of the same innovations, and participatory management has become a recognized management approach.

Relevance to modern readers

Abraham Maslow helped to introduce a new and positive dimension to our understanding of human behavior. He was one of the first psychologists to recognize that people can be motivated not just by a need to alleviate discomfort or make up for a deficiency, but also by higher purposes or goals as well. He created a legitimate scientific theory that took these higher goals into account, and his thinking helped to define the field of humanistic psychology. Humanistic psychologists can be found today in counseling centers, psychiatric clinics, hospitals, universities, and a number of other settings devoted to solving human problems or understanding human behavior.

Maslow's influence also continues in business management, education, and in many of the helping professions such as nursing, social work, and rehabilitation. A beginning student in any of these fields is very likely to read about Maslow's theory of motivation and use it as a framework for understanding the needs that can influence people in a variety of different

Rollo May. (Archive/Getty Photos. Reproduced by permission.)

situations. The simplicity of his needs hierarchy and its recognition of both deficiency needs and higher levels of motivation make Maslow's theory particularly attractive as a starting point. His work is a useful introduction to motivation for those who want to learn how to lead people or help them to grow and change.

The hopeful view of human behavior that Maslow offered still has a strong appeal, particularly for people who are drawn toward a more spiritual outlook on life. He recognized the value in exploring human virtues, such as altruism, creativity, and the love of beauty. He saw the great importance of those rare times in life when a person can see beyond their daily concerns and understand a higher truth about themselves and the world. Anyone who has had such a peak experience can appreciate his insights and observations about these moments.

Maslow's speculations about the best that humans are capable of can seem naive to modern readers, but many of his observations have an essential truth that has not been diminished by the passing years. He cautioned against cynicism and a lack of values, and he encouraged people to commit themselves to higher goals and to openly acknowledge the things that are important to them. He thought that this was the only way to achieve real growth. In an age marked by cynicism, alienation, and the specter of terrorism,

Maslow's positive view of human capabilities is both encouraging and inspiring.

BIBLIOGRAPHY

Sources

Bobic, M. P., and Davis, W. E. "A kind word for Theory X: Or why so many newfangled management techniques quickly fail." *Journal of Public Administration Research and Theory* 13 (2003): 239–65.

Boeree, C. G. *Personality Theories: Rollo May.* Shippensburg U. 1998 [cited March 28, 2004]. http://www.ship.edu/~cgboeree/may.html.

Boeree, C. G. *Personality Theories: Viktor Frankl.* Shippensburg U. 2002 [cited March 28, 2004].http://www.ship.edu/~cgboeree/frankl.html.

Burger, J. M. "The humanistic approach." *Personality,* 5th ed. Belmont, CA: Wadsworth, 2000.

Daniels, M. *Maslow's Concept of Self-Actualization* 2001 [cited March 25, 2004]. http://www.mdani.demon.co.uk/archive/MDMaslow.htm7.

Envision Software. *ERG Theory* [cited March 25, 2004]. http:// www.envisionsoftware.com/Articles/ERG_Theory.html.

Guest, D. "Motivation after Maslow." *Personnel Management* 8 (1976): 29.

Hagerty M. R. "Testing Maslow's hierarchy of needs: National quality-of-life across time." *Social Indicators Research* 46 (1999): 249–71.

Hall, E. G., and Hansen, J. "Self-actualizing men and women—a comparison study." *Roeper Review* 29 (1997): 22–28.

Hoffman, E. "The last interview of Abraham Maslow (conducted in 1968)." *Psychology Today* 25 (1992): 68–75.

Hoffman, E. "Peak experiences in childhood: An explanatory study." *Journal of Humanistic Psychology* 38 (1998): 109–21.

Hoffman, E. *The Right To Be Human: A Biography of Abraham Maslow.* Los Angeles: Jeremy P. Tarcher, Inc., 1988.

Lewis, J. D. "Scores on self-actualization for gifted junior high students." *Psychological Reports* 79 (1996): 59–65.

Lewis, J. D. "Self-actualization in gifted children." *Psychological Reports* 74 (1994): 767–72.

Lowen, J. "Viktor Frankl, the champion of humanness." *Free Inquiry* 21 (2000): 55.

Malone, E. L. "The Non-Linear Systems experiment in participative management." *Journal of Business* 48 (1975): 1–13.

Maslow, A. H. *Motivation and Personality,* 2nd ed. New York: Harper and Row, 1970.

Maslow, A. H. "A theory of human motivation." *Psychological Review* 50 (1943): 370–96.

Maslow, A. H. *Toward a psychology of being,* 2nd ed. New York: Van Nostrand Reinhold, 1968.

Pufal-Struzik, I. "Self-actualization and other personality dimensions as predictors of mental health of intellectually gifted students." *Roeper Review* 22 (1999): 44.

Rabinowitz, F. E., Good, G., & Cozad, L. "Rollo May: A man of meaning and myth." *Journal of Counseling and Development* 67 (1989): 436–41.

Robbins, B. D. *Rollo May.* [cited March 28, 2004]. http://www.mythosandlogos.com/May.html.

Sumerlin, J. R., and Bundrick, C. M. "Happiness and self-actualization under conditions of strain: A sample of homeless men." *Perceptual and Motor Skills* 90 (2000): 191–204.

Wahba, M. A., and Bridwell, L. G. "Maslow reconsidered: A review of research on the need hierarchy theory." In R. M. Steers and L. W. Porter, Eds. *Motivation and Work Behavior.* New York: McGraw-Hill, 1987.

Wilson, S. R., and Spencer, R. C. "Intense personal experiences: Subjective effects, interpretations, and after-effects." *Journal of Clinical Psychology* 46 (1990): 565–74.

Yeagle, E. H., Privette, G., and Dunham, F. "Highest happiness: An analysis of artists' peak experience." *Psychological Reports* 65 (1989): 523–31.

Further readings

Cain, D. J. *Humanistic Psychotherapies: Handbook of Research and Practice.* Washington, DC: American Psychological Association, 2002.

Frankl, V. *Man's Search for Meaning.* New York: Pocket Books, 1997.

Hoffman, E. *The Right to Be Human: The Biography of Abraham Maslow,* 2nd ed. New York: McGraw-Hill, 1999.

Journal of Humanistic Psychology. Beverly Hills, CA: Sage Publications.

Maslow, A. F. *Motivation and Personality,* 2nd ed. New York: Harper and Row, 1970.

Maslow, A. F. *Toward a Psychology of Being,* 2nd ed. New York: Van Nostrand Reinhold, 1968.

May, R. *The Discovery of Being: Writings in Existential Psychology.* New York: Norton, 1994.

Sneider, K. J., Bugental, J. F. T., and Pierson, J. F. *The Handbook of Humanistic Psychology: Leading Edges in Theory, Research, and Practice.* New York: Sage, 2002.

Ivan Petrovich Pavlov

BRIEF OVERVIEW

Although he won the Nobel Prize for his research on the physiology of the digestive system of dogs, Ivan Pavlov left his most lasting legacy in psychology. In a career that spanned nearly seven decades, Pavlov discovered the basic concepts behind associative learning in both animals and humans. His theory of conditioned reflexes, or "training" individuals to respond to a neutral stimulus, laid the groundwork for behavioral psychology and associative learning theory. In addition, his work on experimental neuroses, or behavioral and thought problems caused by conditioning techniques, explained the causes of some mental disorders and, more importantly, helped develop effective behavioral therapy methods.

Pavlov began to study conditioned reflexes after conducting research on the digestive system of dogs. He discovered that his laboratory dogs would salivate after hearing a sound or other sensory stimulus that they had learned to associate with food, even if no food was present. Pavlov conducted meticulous and extensive studies into this phenomenon. He also pioneered new laboratory techniques.

Influenced in part by British naturalist Charles Darwin, Pavlov theorized that conditioned reflexes served as a survival mechanism. He reasoned that animals must adapt quickly to changes in their environment in order to stay alive.

He also believed that his conditioning experiments could help him better understand both the physiology

1849–1936

RUSSIAN PHYSIOLOGIST, PSYCHOLOGY RESEARCHER

ST. PETERSBURG UNIVERSITY, 1875; IMPERIAL MEDICAL ACADEMY (A.K.A. MEDICAL-SURGICAL ACADEMY), MD, 1879

Ivan Pavlov. *(Hulton–Deutsch Collection/Corbis–Bettmann. Reproduced by permission.)*

and functioning of the brain. Pavlov believed that all nervous activity was based on the principals of excitation and inhibition. Individuals with strong and balanced excitatory and inhibitory responses were less likely to behave abnormally.

Throughout Pavlov's lifetime, his homeland of Russia experienced political and social upheaval. Because Pavlov worked and lived in the capital city of Saint Petersburg, he witnessed the changes firsthand. Pavlov spoke out frequently against the government, despite the fact that other protesters were being arrested and killed. It is a testament to his scientific prestige that he could openly criticize the Communist government while being financially subsidized by it.

BIOGRAPHY

Ivan Petrovich Pavlov was the eldest of 10 children born into a family with deep religious roots. His father, Petr Dmitrievich Pavlov, belonged to the sixth generation of Pavlov men appointed as local parish priests in the Eastern Orthodox Church. Ivan's mother, Varvara Ivanovna Pavlova, was a priest's daughter. With religion so deeply ingrained in both the family

lineage and in the culture of their native village of Ryazan, his parents expected Ivan to be one of the seventh generation of Pavlov priests.

Pavlov's mother suffered from headaches, hair loss, and various skin conditions during his childhood; her symptoms were termed a "nervous disorder." Pavlov's colleagues have speculated that her condition may have motivated Pavlov to study psychopathology, the neurological basis of neuroses and psychoses.

As a child, Ivan enjoyed spending time outdoors; he especially liked working in the family garden with his father. At the age of eight, Ivan suffered injuries after falling from a high fence. He was weakened from the experience and recovered slowly. Discouraged by his continued illness, his family sent him to recover at the nearby Saint Trinity's Monastery, which was overseen by Pavlov's godfather. Through a rigorous schedule of daily exercise, chores, and other activities, Ivan regained his health. He also discovered a love for reading that would be nurtured by his father's extensive library. Pavlov was schooled at home until the age of 11.

Ivan entered the Ryazan Theological School in 1860. Four years later, he graduated and began studying for the priesthood at the Ryazan Theological Seminary. He was an excellent student, and the discipline he had gained from his experience at the monastery helped him to adapt easily to the rigors of academic life.

But his passion for reading and learning, along with the social changes that were sweeping Russia under the regime of Tsar Alexander II, would soon call Ivan away from a life in the priesthood. Seminarians were allowed to read only books that agreed with Eastern Orthodox doctrine; Pavlov's insatiable appetite for the written word and his budding interest in science, however, led him to sneak frequently into the Ryazan library. Ivan started a *kruzhok,* or discussion group, with other seminary students to discuss previously banned books and political journals that the government had recently re-released to the public. Many of these were science books, as the government was attempting to strengthening Russia's research programs. Pavlov's contemporaries perceived the materialism of science as an alternative to the mysticism of the church, necessary to support Russia's progress (see "Historical context").

As Ivan approached his final year at seminary, he made a critical decision that would affect not only his relationship with his family but also the fields of physiology, learning theory, and psychology. Much to his father's dismay, Pavlov left the Ryazan Theological

Seminary to apply for entrance into St. Petersburg University. The university's faculty boasted many scientific luminaries and the campus was located next door to the prestigious Academy of Sciences. Pavlov began his studies there in 1870. He had difficulty coping with the demands of city and university life, however; before completing his first year of study, Ivan returned home suffering from nervous exhaustion. After the summer, however, Ivan returned to St. Petersburg accompanied by his younger brother Dmitry, who was entering the university's chemistry program.

Dmitry became Ivan's roommate and, although he was the younger of the two, he usually took care of Ivan. With his brother's support, Ivan began to flourish academically and socially. He joined a new kruzhok and chose a field of specialization—physiology.

Ivan's first mentor at St. Petersburg, physiologist Ilya Fadeevich Tsion, was well-known for his skilled surgical techniques in animal vivisection. Under his tutelage, Ivan won a gold medal for his work on the nerves of the pancreas.

In 1873, Tsion became the youngest-ever professor of physiology at the Imperial Medical Academy; he received the prestigious appointment at the age of 29. Tsion offered Ivan a lab assistant position, which Pavlov eagerly accepted. Tsion's tenure would be short-lived, however. His conservative social, religious, and political views caused controversy among his peers, who believed that everything could ultimately be explained through rigorous scientific experimentation. Moreover, Tsion thought physiologists could not study topics such as thought processes or emotions; his temperament alienated his colleagues, and he was a demanding teacher. Because Tsion was Jewish, he also faced anti-Semitism. Protests against his appointment reached their peak after Tsion flunked half of his sophomore physiology class. Both the Academy and St. Petersburg University were temporarily shut down as students demonstrated against the professor; eventually, the administration bowed to the pressure and removed Tsion from his post in 1874. Pavlov was devastated by the news.

After Tsion's departure, Pavlov went to work in the laboratory of Professor Ustimovich at the Veterinary Institute from 1876 through 1878. Instead of anesthetizing the dogs to insert a catheter that would be used to measure blood pressure, Pavlov first trained the animals to lie still. He then performed the procedure quickly and almost painlessly, without using anesthesia or causing stress to the dog.

Pavlov traveled to Breslau, Germany in 1877 to study the pancreas and digestive system. The following

PRINCIPAL PUBLICATIONS

- *Lectures on the Work of the Digestive Glands.* Translated by W.H. Thompson. 1897. Reprint, London: Griffin, 1902.

- *Lectures on Conditioned Reflexes: Twenty-Five Years of Objective Study of the Higher Nervous Activity of Animals.* Translated by W. Horsley Gantt. 1923. Reprint, New York: International, 1928.

- "Lectures on the Work of the Large Hemispheres of the Brain." (1827) *Experimental Psychology and Other Essays.* New York: Philosophical Library, 1957.

- *Psychopathology and Psychiatry.* Translated by S. Belsky and D. Myshene. New Brunswick, NJ: Transaction, 1994.

- *Conditioned Reflexes: An Investigation of the Physiological Activity of the Cerebral Cortex.* Translated and edited by G.V. Anrep, 1927. Reprint, Mineola, NY: Dover, 2003.

year, Professor Sergei P. Botkin hired Pavlov as his laboratory director. In addition to his career as a distinguished scientist, Botkin also served as personal physician to the tsar's wife. In Botkin's lab, Pavlov developed his theories of nervism—the idea that all physiological processes are somehow related to actions of the central nervous system.

In December of 1879, Pavlov graduated from the Medical-Surgical Academy, earning honors and a gold medal for his work on the circulatory system, and he was awarded a four-year postgraduate fellowship. That same year, Pavlov met a young teaching student and social activist, Serafima Vasil'evna Karchevskaia. As the school term ended, they began to write to each other; shortly after Serafima returned to St. Petersburg, they decided to marry. The wedding would not occur until 1881, however, after Ivan finished his doctoral work and Serafima had spent a year traveling and teaching the poor to read.

In Botkin's lab, Pavlov researched the cardiovascular system of dogs. His experiments led to his 1883 doctoral dissertation "The Centrifugal Nerves of the

Heart," in which he established that cardiac nerves played a part in regulating heart rhythm. Except for a two-year hiatus in Europe during 1884–86 to conduct research related to his fellowship, Pavlov directed Botkin's lab until 1890.

Pavlov's first child, Wirchik, was born in 1883 during a time of financial hardship. After the young family moved in with Serafima's sister in order to make ends meet, Wirchik became ill and died. Both parents were devastated by the loss; two years later, Serafima gave birth to a second son that the couple named Vladimir. Eventually, two more sons, Viktor (1892) and Vsevolod (1893), and a daughter, Vera (1890), joined the family. Unlike Ivan, who turned away from his father's profession, three of Pavlov's children would pursue careers in various scientific disciplines (the fourth studied law).

Pavlov finally received a teaching post in 1890, becoming chair of pharmacology at the Military-Medical Academy. Five years later, he would be appointed chair of physiology at the same institution, a position he would hold until 1925. He was happy to leave Botkin's lab, which he considered limiting due to its small size, poor equipment, and unsanitary conditions. Also in 1890, a wealthy cousin of the tsar decided to fund a new medical research facility. After his first choice for director refused the post, he appointed Pavlov to run the physiological department of the Imperial Institute of Experimental Medicine. Pavlov would remain in that position for 45 years until his death in 1936.

In 1893 the Institute received a generous donation from Swedish inventor and philanthropist Alfred Nobel. This additional funding allowed Pavlov to equip his laboratory to perform experiments on animals that were still conscious, the technique he had pioneered early in his career. The Institute also offered surgical and recovery suites for the lab animals, separate experimental areas, and sterile equipment.

Most of Pavlov's work at the Institute focused on the physiology of the digestive system, primarily investigating the interaction between the central nervous system and digestion. He liked to experiment on dogs, citing their low cost, accessibility, intellect, and the similarity of their digestive systems to those of humans. In 1897 Pavlov published his findings in a collection called "Lectures on the Work of the Main Digestive Glands," which earned him international acclaim.

Pavlov conducted feeding experiments on dogs that had received esophagotomies (a surgical procedures that severs the esophagus so that ingested food never reaches the stomach, a process known as sham feeding) and gastric fistulas (a hole in the stomach that contains a feeding tube). He found that dogs that were sham-fed produced more gastric juice and saliva than dogs that were fed through a fistula. This important result demonstrated that stimulating the nerves in the mouth was an essential part of the digestive process. Pavlov also discovered that dogs that were allowed to feed themselves digested their food better than dogs that had food placed directly into their mouths. Therefore, he showed that the psychological influence of appetite also influenced the digestion.

One of the greatest innovations Pavlov made in the field of physiology and animal experimentation was waiting until after his animals healed from surgery before testing his theories. His contemporaries performed vivisection on an anesthetized animal and then measured the physiological results immediately afterwards. By contrast, Pavlov performed vivisection and then waited for the dog to heal. He was the first scientist to recognize that the physiological stress of the vivisection procedure sometimes influenced the outcomes of an experiment.

A skilled surgeon, Pavlov also made great advances in vivisection techniques. For example, he developed a procedure known as "the isolated stomach" that created a separate small pouch, or second stomach, with all its nerve connections intact. The isolated stomach, which was accessible to researchers through a fistula in the abdominal wall of the dog, could be used to measure reactions to food via the amount of gastric juice it secreted, even though food never entered it.

At a conference in Madrid in 1903, Pavlov gave a lecture entitled "The Experimental Psychology and Psychopathology of Animals." This speech was his first public discussion of the theory of conditioned reflexes. The following year, at the age of 55, Pavlov was awarded the Nobel Prize in Physiology or Medicine for his research on the digestive system. He was the first physiologist, and the first Russian, to receive the prestigious award. While accepting the prize, Pavlov elaborated even further on the psychological theories he had first introduced at the Madrid congress. He asked:

> What now is the physiologist to do with the psychical phenomena? Disregarding them is impossible since in the action of the salivary glands, in which we are interested, they are closely connected with the purely physiological phenomena. If, nevertheless, the physiologist wants to study them, he finds himself faced with the question: How?

Pavlov would devote the rest of his career to delving into the interrelationship of the psychical (or psychological) with the physiological through studying conditioned and unconditioned reflexes. His findings in this area of research remain important nearly a century later.

Pavlov was awarded membership in the Russian Academy of Sciences in 1907. Between his work at the Institute of Experimental Medicine (IEM), the Medical-Military Academy, and the Physiological Laboratory at the Academy of Sciences, Pavlov had dozens of physiology students and medical doctors working under his direction. In fact, between 1891 and 1917, over 110 individuals passed through Pavlov's lab at the IEM alone.

To further refine his experiments, Pavlov designed a new laboratory facility that was completely soundproof. This lab also featured equipment that allowed him and his assistants to control every aspect of an experiment without coming into contact with their subjects, the dogs. Construction on the "Tower of Silence" was completed in 1913.

Pavlov's work suffered a setback over the next decade, as Russia experienced massive political and social upheaval with the outbreak of World War I, the Bolshevik uprising, the October Revolution, and the Russian civil war (see "Historical context"). Pavlov suffered personal losses as well; his eldest son Viktor died of typhus and his younger son Vsevelod, who had joined the White Army during the civil war, was forced to leave the country after its defeat. The Pavlov family was left nearly destitute, food was scarce, and lab work had ceased.

In the summer of 1920, Pavlov wrote a letter to the head of the Bolsheviks (later called the Communist Party), Vladimir Lenin. He explained his current circumstances and requested permission to leave the country to continue his work. In response to the threat of losing an important academic resource and national icon like Pavlov, Lenin responded decisively. He issued a government decree in January of 1921 that stated that "In view of Academician I. P. Pavlov's outstanding scientific services, which are of tremendous importance to the working people of the world," Pavlov would receive lifetime housing and rations for his family and full funding for publication of "a deluxe edition of the scientific work prepared by Academician Pavlov, summing up the results of his research over the past 20 years." In addition, Pavlov's flat and laboratory would be equipped with "every possible facility." Lenin also appointed a special commission devoted solely to ensuring that Pavlov's research could continue under "the best conditions."

The Communist Party continued to supply Pavlov with everything he needed for his research,

even though he openly criticized the government's religious persecution and political arrests. Pavlov frequently used his influence to free other scientists from imprisonment.

An act of nature in September 1924 paved the way for one of Pavlov's biggest discoveries in the emerging field of conditioning. Heavy rains caused the Neva River to swell beyond its banks, and floods swept the streets of St. Petersburg (by then renamed Leningrad). Pavlov's dogs had to be rescued from their kennels, and they swam to the nearby main laboratory building, where they were kept until the danger passed. Pavlov reported that "All this produced a very strong and obvious inhibition in all the animals, since there was no fighting or quarrelling among them whatever, otherwise a usual occurrence when the dogs are kept together." After the floodwaters had receded and experiments resumed, Pavlov and his colleagues discovered that the conditioned reflexes in some of the dogs had disappeared, apparently as a result of the trauma.

Pavlov soon theorized that traumatic experiences could also trigger psychoses and neuroses in humans. In *Conditioned Reflexes,* Pavlov stated that

> a development of a chronic pathological state of the hemispheres can occur from one or other of two causes: first a conflict between excitation and inhibition which the cortex finds itself unable to resolve; second the action of extremely powerful and unusual stimuli.

Pavlov had begun working with human psychiatric patients in 1890 as part of his investigative work on the actions of the cerebral cortex. In the 1920s, for his ongoing research into ways that the physiology of the brain and nervous system triggered mental illness, Pavlov attended seminars at Leningrad's Neuropsychiatric Hospital and the Balinskiy Psychiatric Hospital. Here, psychiatrists presented neurotic and psychotic patient case studies and Pavlov analyzed the patient's history, interviewed the patients, and recommended a course of treatment based on what he considered the cause of their neurosis or psychosis. Pavlov took a special interest in schizophrenia, which he likened to a "chronic hypnotic state." In the early 1930s, he studied dozens of schizophrenic patients at the psychiatric clinic of the Balinskiy Hospital.

At the youthful age of 80, Pavlov received a substantial grant from the Soviet government for a new laboratory: an entire dog village located on the outskirts of Leningrad. The Koltushi compound was fully outfitted for Pavlov's new line of research, known as eugenics. Eugenics was the science of improving the genetic stock of the human race by breeding out "inferior" qualities; it has since been discredited and is considered unethical today. The scientific theory dovetailed with the socialist ideals of the Soviets. Pavlov wanted to find a way to scientifically isolate the conditions necessary to create a dog with an ideal nervous temperament. He believed that the controlled environment of Koltushi would allow him and his staff to isolate the environmental and hereditary factors that determined the temperaments in the dogs he would raise there.

A big believer in brisk exercise, Pavlov remained more physically active than some men half his age and continued to work long days in his labs. (Besides winning the Nobel Prize as well as recognition from the Russian Academy of Sciences, he also received many other honors, including an honorary doctorate from Cambridge University, the Order of the Legion of Honour from the government of France, and honorary memberships in scores of medical societies.) In August of 1935, Pavlov helped to bring the Fifteenth International Physiological Congress, an esteemed gathering of physiologists from around the world, to the Soviet Union. Pavlov was honored by his fellow physiologists, and he was recognized as the preeminent leader in the field in an address by Scottish physiologist George Barger. Six months after the congress, Pavlov developed pneumonia. He died on February 27, 1936, and scientists from the Soviet Union and around the world mourned the passing of a scientific icon.

THEORIES

Even though his specialty was physiology, most experts consider Pavlov's contributions to psychology, specifically those related to conditioned reflexes, to be his greatest legacy.

Reflexes themselves were not a new concept. In his "Lectures on Conditioned Reflexes," Pavlov notes that the idea of man as a machine governed by complex nervous reflexes originated with French philosopher and mathematician René Descartes three centuries earlier. Several of Pavlov's contemporaries also had explored the reflexive properties of the nervous system. Pavlov's work, however, is based on the physiology of the brain, and therefore it is, as he puts it, a "purely objective investigation into the highest nervous activities."

Pavlov was particularly influenced by the work of his eminent Russian colleague Ivan Sechenov. Sechenov wrote *Reflexes of the Brain,* and he was considered one of the founders of objective (i.e., materialist-based)

psychology. Sechenov asserted that all mental processes, or "psychic phenomenon," were reflexive actions (or reactions) of the nervous system. In experiments with frogs, he was able to inhibit muscle reflexes by placing salt crystals on the animal's brain. Sechenov also suggested that reflexes might somehow be reshaped or changed, but he never tested his hypothesis in the lab. Pavlov used Sechenov's theory to experimentally demonstrate the phenomenon of classical conditioning.

Pavlov was the first to empirically demonstrate the existence of a "mind-body" connection; that is, to show that mental and emotional variables can have affect physical processes of the body. The learning theory that evolved from Pavlov's findings on conditioned reflexes became known as classical conditioning. Conditioning helps to explain the ways in which some people develop seemingly irrational fears and anxieties or associate certain smells and sounds with a specific place or situation. The theory even discusses why a dog barks and becomes agitated when the doorbell rings.

Through his work on the nervous system and cerebral cortex, Pavlov also was one of the first scientists to explore the role of personality and temperament in physiological reactions. Despite well-controlled conditions and precise measurements, not all dogs would react exactly the same to an identical stimulus, even when allowances were made for different physical characteristics. Furthermore, Pavlov discovered that certain temperament types were more prone to psychopathological conditions than others.

Pavlov conducted extensive experimentation that involved removing portions of the brains of dogs to establish that the cerebral cortex was related to reflexive reactions. He published his findings in his 1927 book entitled *Conditioned Reflexes: An Investigation of the Physiological Activity of the Cerebral Cortex.*

Pavlov believed that all of what was considered "psychic" phenomenon, which had previously been explained only in terms of abstract introspective processes such as psychoanalysis, could be explained through careful physiological experimentation. In his 1904 Nobel lecture, Pavlov stated the scope of his vision:

> Essentially only one thing in life interests us: our psychical constitution, the mechanism of which was and is wrapped in darkness. All human resources, art, religion, literature, philosophy and historical sciences, all of them join in bringing light in this darkness. But man has still another powerful resource: natural science with its strictly objective methods.

Ivan Pavlov (with beard) with his staff and research dog. (The Bettmann Archive. Reproduced by permission.)

Classical conditioning

Main points   Through Pavlov's work on the physiology of the digestive system, he discovered that digestive processes could be triggered even before food passed a dog's lips. Just showing food to a hungry dog could cause the animal to begin to salivate and secrete gastric juices. Why did these external factors cause these reactions, or reflexes? The dogs had previously learned through experience that the appearance of a bowl of kibble meant they would be eating shortly, so the sight of food cued their digestive systems to start up. This finding was Pavlov's first indication that what he called "psychic" influences (i.e., thoughts, emotional states, personality) could have a direct bearing on physiological processes.

Pavlov had already demonstrated that the taste of food in a dog's mouth stimulated the animal's oral nerves in such a way that salivation was triggered, an involuntary physiological reaction he called an unconditioned response. But Pavlov and his colleagues soon discovered that by repeatedly presenting a completely unrelated and neutral stimulus (e.g., the ringing of a bell, the click of a feeding device, or the beat of a metronome) to the feeding process, they could eventually trigger salivation in the dog with the neutral stimulus alone. Pavlov called this reaction a conditioned response, or reflex, and the process by which it was achieved was called conditioning.

Explanation   In his Nobel lecture, Pavlov explained his theory of unconditioned (or physiological) and conditioned (or psychic) reflexes:

> The difference between the two reflexes is firstly that our old physiological reflex is constant, unconditioned, while the new reflex continually fluctuates and, hence, is conditioned. . . in the conditioned reflex, however, those properties of the object act as stimuli that in themselves have no direct relation at all with the physiological role of the saliva.

In other words, conditioning involves pairing a neutral stimulus (or conditioned stimulus) with an unconditioned stimulus to create a conditioned response. Dogs that were exposed to a particular sound (the conditioned stimulus) each time they were given food (the unconditioned stimulus) eventually began to associate the bell with eating and would salivate at the sound of the bell. A conditioned reflex had been created in those dogs.

Does a conditioned reflex occur every time a neutral stimulus is presented with an unconditioned stimulus? No. Usually, the pairing must be repeated several times before conditioning takes hold; the number of repetitions depends upon the subject and the stimuli. A profound event or a very novel stimulus may require fewer pairings (also called trials). The conditioned response is dependent on the intensity of the stimulus itself.

BIOGRAPHY:

John Watson

An American psychologist who founded the field of psychology known as behaviorism, John Broadus Watson (1878–1958) believed that psychological study should be based on observable reflexes and behavior only instead of introspection of the subconscious mind.

Watson entered college at the age of 16, and received his Ph.D. from the University of Chicago in 1903 at the age of 24. His dissertation involved work with learning behaviors culled from maze experiments with white rats. In 1908 he joined Johns Hopkins University, where he was appointed a professor and made director of the psychological laboratory.

In 1913, Watson delivered a lecture at Columbia University (which was later published in *Psychological Review*) entitled "Psychology as the Behaviorist Views It." This work, which would become known as the "behaviorist manifesto" in later years, asserted that the only valid study of psychology was that of observable states and not of the introspection of "states of consciousness" that dominated the field at the time. This work was followed a year later by his text *Behaviorism: An Introduction to Comparative Psychology*, which built on Pavlov's conditioned reflexes and outlined Watson's stimulus-response theory of behavior.

Watson was elected president of the American Psychological Association in 1915 at the age of 36, making him the youngest person ever to hold that office. Around this time, his research focus shifted to infants and children. Watson believed that all human emotion was rooted in three reactions—fear, rage, and love—that were not innate but rather conditioned. Through a now infamous experiment with a white rat and an 11-month-old boy named "Little Albert," Watson conditioned the boy to be afraid of a white rat by banging on a metal bar loudly with a hammer and frightening him each time he reached for the animal. Albert quickly became fearful at the sight of the rat alone.

Later, he discovered that Albert subsequently transferred this fear-response reaction to another stimulus, also becoming afraid of a white rabbit with which he had previously played. This phenomenon of developing a conditioned response to a stimulus that is different from but similar to the original stimulus used in conditioning came to be known as generalization.

While at Johns Hopkins, Watson also did substantial consulting work for organizations as diverse as the Baltimore and Ohio Railroad and the Social Hygiene Board of the U.S. government. His distinguished career in academia came a sudden end in 1920 after a scandal involving an affair with a research assistant. Watson subsequently divorced his wife and married graduate student Rosalie Rayner, and he was asked to resign his professorship at Johns Hopkins.

By 1924, Watson had become a vice president at J. Walter Thompson, one of America's largest ad agencies, where he remained until 1935. Here he helped develop and refine a number of groundbreaking strategies that persist in the field today, including market research of the motivations behind consumer brand loyalty and testimonial advertising. Watson continued to write on behavioral psychology, making the field more accessible to the general public. He participated in applied psychology projects while working in the ad world; for example, he was one of the first proponents of personality testing for prospective employees in the corporate world.

Watson wrote a popular book entitled *Psychological Care of the Infant* (1928) that was based on his observational studies of infants and his theories of behavioral psychology. He believed that proper conditioning of the child was the key to forming healthy personality traits.

John Watson. (Copyright University of Akron. Reproduced by permission.)

In 1935, Watson left J. Walter Thompson to continue his advertising career at the William Esty Company, where he remained until his retirement in 1945. The APA awarded Watson a gold medal for his contributions to psychology in 1957. One year later, he passed away at the age of 80.

A unique or novel neutral stimulus is more likely to cause a conditioned response than a common one. For example, a woman who split up with her boyfriend while a certain song was playing on the radio may forever identify that particular tune with heartache. But if a telephone was also ringing at the same time, the less "novel" stimulus of a ringing phone would be less likely to trigger an emotional response in the future.

Finally, Pavlov believed that the neutral stimulus had to be contiguous (that is, occur at the same time or in close proximity to) the unconditioned stimulus in order for a conditioned response to develop. Later research has found that conditioning is most effective when the conditioned stimulus is presented just before the unconditioned stimulus, and when both stop at the same time.

Pavlov discovered that conditioned reflexes could be reversed if the neutral stimulus was presented enough times in the absence of the unconditioned stimulus. He explains the process, known as extinction, in the context of his study on salivating dogs and food: "On the other hand promptly active signals can lose their stimulating effect if repeated over a long period without bringing the object concerned into contact with the oral mucous membrane." Extinction would prove to be a useful psychological finding to treat phobias and other irrational fears.

Extinction of a behavior was not always permanent, however. Pavlov found that conditioned responses that were extinguished could spontaneously recur later (spontaneous recovery). One of Pavlov's dogs had been conditioned to salivate at the sound of a bell. Pavlov extinguished the reflex by repeatedly exposing the dog to the bell without the presence of food or feeding. Although the conditioned reflex was gone, Pavlov found that some time later, it suddenly reappeared when the dog was exposed to the sound of a bell. The response was weaker (less salivation), but it was still present.

Conditioned reflexes could also be temporarily interrupted if extra stimuli were introduced, either on purpose or unintentionally. In *Conditioned Reflexes,* Pavlov described how a co-worker would call him into their work area to demonstrate a dog's newly acquired conditioned reflex, only to have the dog fail to perform. The reason was Pavlov's presence itself; he was what he termed a temporary inhibitory stimulus; his presence triggered the dog's investigatory reflex and temporarily distracted it (what one might call a sense of curiosity, although Pavlov did not like to attribute human characteristics to his dogs).

Pavlov also developed the concept of higher-order conditioning, which involved pairing one neutral stimulus previously associated with a conditioned response with a second neutral stimulus. In higher-order, or second-order conditioning, a conditioned stimulus (A) is first paired with an unconditioned stimulus until a conditioned response is achieved. Then a second conditioned stimulus (B) is paired with the first conditioned stimulus (A). Even though the unconditioned stimulus is never presented with stimulus B, it is able to achieve a conditioned response simply by its association with the stimulus A.

Examples   Pavlov's drooling dogs are the most famous example of classical conditioning. A bell is rung immediately before or as food is served to a dog. With repetition, the dog eventually salivates at the sound of the bell only. Pavlov used a number of different neutral stimuli in his conditioning experiments, including the beat of a metronome, flashes of light, odors, and skin stimulation. When the bell was rung repeatedly without the presence of food (or feeding of the dogs), the conditioned response would eventually disappear.

Many dogs will also show a classically conditioned response to the sound of a doorbell. The dog knows that the sound of the bell means a visitor has arrived, because the sound of the bell has preceded a guest's presence many times before. So when the doorbell rings, the dog runs to the door, wags his tail, and perhaps even barks in response, even though he cannot see who or what is on the other side. In fact, even if the interior bell is located far from the front door, the dog will still run to the door because he knows from experience the visitor will appear here.

If someone plays ding-dong-ditch (rings the doorbell and runs away before the resident anwers the door) a few times, however, the dog may get a little less excited about the sound of the bell. And some dogs may also react to the sound of the phone, because they have generalized their conditioned response to the doorbell stimulus to apply to similar stimuli (in this case, all bells). For more on generalization, see "John Watson" sidebar.

The influence of classical conditioning is quite commonly seen in house pets. Any cat owner knows that the sound of a can opener will trigger a feline frenzy. Why? Because the owner has conditioned the cat to associate the sound of a can being opened with dinnertime.

For humans, conditioning can often be seen as phobias and irrational fears. Prior bad experiences associated with places, people, activities, or things can condition individuals to develop fearful or anxious reactions to neutral events or objects. For example:

- A man who was stuck in an elevator for 12 hours develops a fear of confined spaces.

- A child who is repeatedly dunked in the pool by a mean-spirited peer grows into an adult with a swimming phobia.

- A woman who was abused by her ex-husband when they lived in a small apartment over a music store is gripped by fear whenever she hears the sound of piano music.

Pavlov believed that the theory of classical conditioning could help eradicate neuroses and psychoses as well as explain their origins.

Temperament and psychiatric disorders

Main points   For Pavlov, temperament of both animals and humans is determined by the interplay of what he called excitatory and inhibitory responses. As the names suggest, excitation stimulates nervous reaction while inhibition suppresses it. Through his studies of the nervous system of dogs, Pavlov developed the theory that abnormalities in behavior and temperament occur when excitation and inhibition are either out of balance or when both processes are very weak. Dogs that had strong excitatory and inhibitory responses that were in equilibrium were the most easily disciplined; those dogs also responded the best to conditioning. Pavlov called their temperament type strong.

In those animals for which both excitation and inhibition were weak or were out of balance with each other, behavioral problems and neuroses were common. Pavlov found that these dogs were not able to deal appropriately with environmental stimuli. Pavlov called this type of dog inhibitable, or weak. An animal's ability to adapt quickly to a changing environment, called mobility, also influenced its temperament type.

Pavlov's theory of temperament types was rooted in the ancient concept made famous by the Greek physician Galen of four humors: choleric, melancholic, sanguine, and phlegmatic. The Greeks believed that the balance of the four humors (which corresponded to yellow bile, black bile, blood, and phlegm) determined an individual's personality type. The relative quantities of the humors created warm versus cool and dry versus moist (which were related to the elements of fire, air, earth, and water). A person with an excess of yellow bile was choleric (warm and dry—also easily excitable and hot-tempered), one with an abundance of black bile was melancholic

(cool and dry—also inhibited and pessimistic), someone with excess blood was sanguine (warm and moist—also confident and energetic), and finally, one with abundant phlegm was phlegmatic (cool and moist—also calm and hard-working). In Pavlov's system, the choleric temperament is analogous to the excitable type, the melancholic to the inhibitable type, and the phlegmatic and sanguine to the strong type.

Of course, Pavlov realized that the human personality was slightly more complex than the personalities of the dogs he studied. He believed human behavior was determined by three factors:

- environment

- second signal system (language)

- temperament (as determined by excitation and inhibition)

The first signal system is conditioned reflexes—instinctual behaviors learned through experience with one's environment. Pavlov also realized that, unlike his dogs, human beings also had a second set of signals at their disposal—language—or what Pavlov called "the signals of signals." In his view, personality was determined by which signal system was dominant in an individual. Those who reacted predominately to environmental stimuli rather than language were called artists, while those for whom language was a greater motivator were termed thinkers. Rarely, someone would have equal strength in both areas; Pavlov called these people "intermediate" types.

Personality types:

- artists = first signal system over second signal system

- thinkers = second signal system over first signal system

Furthermore, Pavlov believed that the different personality types were prone to certain psychological disorders based on their reaction to their environment. Thinking types were predisposed to obsessions and phobias, while artistic types leaned towards hysteria and outbursts. Whether or not these disorders manifested themselves depended on an individual's ability to cope with environmental stress or trauma.

Explanation   Pavlov found that neuroses could actually be induced in the lab in those animals with weak and unbalanced temperaments. Strong negative stimuli could cause experimental neuroses by overwhelming the animals' inhibitory or excitatory processes. Stimuli that were difficult to differentiate from previously introduced stimuli could also cause behavioral problems. Neurotic behaviors might be removed through counter-conditioning techniques or by extinction of the conditioned response. Pavlov also experimented with the use of bromide drugs to return dogs to a non-neurotic state.

Pavlov's physiological experiments on the brain function of his animal subjects also influenced his theories on personality and psychopathology. He held that the basic drives, emotions, and instinctual behavior, or unconditioned reflexes, were regulated in the subcortex area of the brain in both animals and human beings. Immediately above the subcortex, in the cerebral hemispheres, Pavlov believed could be found the "signal systems" that helped regulate temperament and subsequently behavior. He associated the first signal system (conditioned reflexes) with the cerebral hemispheres (excluding the frontal lobes) and the second signal system (language) with the frontal lobes.

In a 1932 work entitled "Essay on the Physiological Concept of the Symptomatology of Hysteria," Pavlov describes how the activity that takes place in each of these brain areas determines the temperament type of the individual:

> In the artist the activity of the cerebral hemispheres, while developing throughout their entire mass, least of all involves the frontal lobes and concentrates mainly in other parts; in the thinker, on the contrary, it is most intense in the frontal lobes.

Pavlov had a special research interest in schizophrenia, and he studied many patients with the disorder at the Leningrad Clinic. He theorized that schizophrenia was the result of both a weak temperament type and childhood trauma. Because of schizophrenics' weak inhibitory responses, the trauma overwhelms them and damages their nervous system.

Examples One of Pavlov's students, N. R. Shenger-Krestovnikova, was the first researcher to describe the role of sensory discrimination in producing neuroses. Shenger-Krestovnikova performed an experiment that conditioned a dog to salivate whenever it saw a light projection of a circle (that is, a visual image of a circle was paired with food). At the same time, the dog was conditioned to have an inhibitory response when it was presented with an ellipse (that is, the sight of an ellipse was followed by no food). Then Shenger-Krestovnikova gradually changed the shape of the ellipse to become more circular. Eventually, the dog could not discriminate the circle from the ellipse, and it lost all conditioned responses to both circles and ellipses. The dog also demonstrated behavioral problems, such as whining and struggling, when presented with the task. Pavlov believed that the neurotic behavior in the dog was produced by a clash between the

inhibition and excitation responses of its nervous system. Two stimuli that were once unique had become too similar for the dog to differentiate between; the result was an induced neurosis.

Pavlov and his associates also pioneered the use of negative or painful stimuli in experimental conditioning. Another Pavlov student, M.N. Eroféeva, used an electric shock as a stimulus before presenting food, thereby conditioning the dog to associate the shock with food (as evidenced by its salivary response) without reacting defensively (growling or barking). Initially, the shock was always applied to the same part of the dog's body. Later, when Eroféeva administered the shock to another part of the dog's body, the conditioned response disappeared and the dog acted defensively. This experiment proved to Pavlov and his colleagues that neurotic or maladaptive behavior—in this case, the loss of defensive reflexes when the subject was placed in a painful or dangerous situation—could be induced in the laboratory. Perhaps more importantly, this finding laid the groundwork for the concept that the conditioning of neurotic behavior could be reversed, a method known as counter-conditioning.

Hypnosis, sleep, and cortical inhibition

Main points Pavlov devoted considerable time to the study of sleep and hypnosis; he considered both states as forms of progressive "cortical inhibition" of the nervous system. Representing them as two points along a continuum, Pavlov portrayed sleep as complete, diffuse internal inhibition of the cortex and hypnosis as a "partial sleep" state.

According to Pavlov, certain conditioned reflexes, such as the salivation response, remained in his animal subjects during hypnosis, while other reflexes related to movement disappeared. Pavlov concluded that the reflexes that remained did so either because they were governed by the subcortex rather than the cortex, or because the state of hypnosis was light and did not significantly inhibit the cortex.

Explanation In Pavlov's lecture "Conditioned Reflexes: Pathological Disturbances of the Cortex," he discussed experiments in which a dog was hypnotized by applying a physical restraint or by placing the animal on its back. According to Pavlov,

> [t]he inhibitory influence of very strong stimuli can be regarded as a reflex of 'passive self-defense,' as, for instance, in the case of hypnosis. The immobility of the animal makes it less noticeable to the enemy, and thus abolishes or diminishes the aggressive reaction of the enemy.

Pavlov also described the use of "strong and unexpected stimuli" to induce hypnosis in cases of "hysteria" in man.

Strong stimuli were not the only triggers of a hypnotic response. Pavlov also described other "external stimuli which directly lead to inhibition of the cortical elements. These are of three kinds—monotonously reoccurring weak stimuli, very strong stimuli, and unusual stimuli." Repetitive, recurring conditioned stimuli gradually lulled dogs to sleep in several of Pavlov's experiments.

Pavlov believed hypnotic conditioning of humans was very similar to that of animals: According to Pavlov, "The classical method consisted in the performance of so-called 'passes'—weak, monotonously repeated tactile and visual stimuli, just as in our experiments upon animals." At present the more usual method consists in the repetition of some form of words, describing sleep, articulated in a flat and monotonous tone of voice. Such words are, of course, conditioned stimuli that have become associated with the state of sleep. In this manner any stimulus that has coincided several times with the development of sleep can now by itself initiate sleep or a hypnotic state. The mechanism is analogous to the inhibitory chain reflexes.

Pavlov also addressed the concept of hypnotic suggestion in terms of conditioned response. He theorized that because language is a excitatory stimulus,

> [t]he command of the hypnotist, in correspondence with the general law, concentrates the excitation in the cortex of the subject (which is in a condition of partial inhibition) in some definite narrow region, at the same time intensifying (by negative induction) the inhibition in the rest of the cortex and so abolishing all competing effects of contemporary stimuli and of traces left by previously received ones. This accounts for the large and practically insurmountable influence of suggestion as a stimulus during hypnosis as well as shortly after it.

In other words, suggestion works because a) it is a novel stimulus and b) language, as Pavlov's "second signal," dominates and overrides all other competing stimuli.

Examples The concept of hypnotic inhibition as a reaction to a new and overwhelming stimulus was described in Pavlov's description of an experimental dog that was brought to a large lecture hall filled with people for a demonstration of the animal's conditioned reflexes. Because of the new location and the large audience, the dog became almost catatonic, and while it exhibited a digestive reflex when a conditioned stimulus was presented, it refused to take the food that was presented. A short time later, it fell asleep in its stand. Pavlov explained that the conditioned reflex remained because the dog was in a hypnotic state due to the unfamiliar stimulus of the lecture hall. After a time, the animal's diffuse inhibition had spread throughout the cortex and subcortex, triggering sleep.

Pavlov also related the story of a dog that was left in its stand (or experimental harness) for hours at a time between experiments. Eventually, the dog would shift into a hypnotic or pre-sleep stage immediately upon entering the experimentation room, and it would fall asleep within ten minutes if the experiment was not begun. It had been conditioned to associate the monotony of the room with the inhibited sleep state.

HISTORICAL CONTEXT

Russia during Pavlov's lifetime was in constant turmoil. He lived through the reigns of four tsars, a world and civil war, a revolution, and two socialist governments. When Pavlov was born in 1849, Russian society was on the cusp of significant change. Since medieval times, Russia had been bound by a rigid class structure: many poor serfs ruled by a few wealthy, land-owning aristocrats, all of whom were subject to a supreme ruler called the tsar.

Tsar Nicholas I ruled Russia from 1825 to 1855. Near the end of his reign, his army suffered a devastating defeat in the Crimean War, eventually surrendering to France and England in 1856. Nicholas' son and successor, Alexander II, had to bear the burden of his father's failures. In order to return Russia to international prominence, Alexander initiated the Great Reforms, which included rapid industrialization, infrastructure improvements, and removal of censorship restrictions. Most importantly, Alexander II also became a great patron scientific research. For young students such as Pavlov, this abandonment of state-sanctioned censorship and support of science was very exciting.

In order to ensure the success of his reforms, the tsar decided to abolish serfdom. In 1861, he granted freedom to the approximately 50 million Russian serfs, much to the chagrin of the landed nobility. With greater Russian freedoms and relaxed censorship, public discussion of a wide range of issues became commonplace. Journals were published that covered virtually every aspect of Russian life. The availability of these journals, and books such as Charles Darwin's *On the Origin of Species* and G.H. Lewes *Practical Physiology,* inspired Pavlov's interest in science.

A failed 1879 assassination attempt caused Alexander to roll back many of the reforms he had instituted during the previous two decades. Alexander appointed six military governor-generals to enforce a stringent censorship system. He banned controversial books throughout Russia, and arrested and imprisoned many critics of the government.

The renewed repression intensified revolutionary opposition to Alexander's government. A second assassination attempt succeeded in 1881, and the new tsar, Alexander III, vowed to stamp out all revolutionary activities and regain governmental control. He reduced access to education, established 'land captains' to beat the peasantry for committing minor offenses, and exiled or executed members of revolutionary groups. Even with this dramatic shift in public policy, however, Russian industrialization grew at a faster rate than that of any other European nation during the 1890s.

Despite the booming economy, however, working and living conditions in the urban areas were deplorable. Newlyweds Ivan and Serafima Pavlov suffered from these difficulties; one of Pavlov's biographers reported that the couple once found their infant son covered in lice. Ivan's later appointment to the Institute of Experimental Medicine, however, would improve their lifestyle considerably.

After the death of Alexander III in 1894, the last tsar of Russia assumed the throne: Nicholas II. Famine became commonplace and discontent rose throughout the nation. Once again, revolutionary groups began to grow in size and strength.

One such group, the Social Democrats, formed in 1898 to foster a revolution by the Russian working class. In 1903, this organization split into two opposing factions: the Mensheviks and the Bolsheviks. The Mensheviks, led by George Plekhanov, believed that all Russians should be eligible for membership and that all members should be given a voice in the party policy. The Bolsheviks, led by Vladimir Lenin, believed that the party should contain only a few highly dedicated and intelligent revolutionaries. This group would conceive and implement all legislation on behalf of the people. The Bolsheviks wanted to overthrow the tsar and establish the working class (the proletariat) as the ruling class of Russia, completely eliminating the nobility (the bourgeois).

Despite the rise of revolutionary groups, Nicholas II did nothing to alleviate the social and economic burdens facing his nation The situation continued to deteriorate until a major strike was called in St. Petersburg in July 1914. Within days however, on August 1, 1914, World War I broke out. A new wave of patriotic support postponed revolutionary activity for a while.

The Russian army that entered World War I was pathetic. Starvation, military ineptitude, and tremendous loss of life in the world war sparked the final Russian revolution in March 1917. Nicholas II was forced to abdicate and a provisional government was established, led by Aleksandr Kerensky. Kerensky's government disappointed most members of the proletariat, mainly because of it did not enact genuine land reforms or withdraw from the war.

The Russian scientific community, however, was primarily pleased with the political changes. Under the tsar, the development of new institutions and acquisition of funding had been slow and difficult. Not only had the Kerensky government promised additional support for scientific research, it had also appointed several leading scholars to commissions that were designed to expand Russia's academic and scientific scope.

Over the the next eight months, many revolutionary organizations and anarchists attempted to overthrow Kerensky. Then, on November 7, 1917, the great October Revolution erupted. (The Russians used a different calendar than the rest of the world, and so they were a few days behind.) Led by Bolshevik leader Vladimir Lenin, the rapid coup d'etat overthrew the Kerensky government and immediately led to several dramatic reforms.

Following the October Revolution, the Russian Academy of Sciences (of which Pavlov was a member) met to discuss their options in dealing with the new Bolshevik government. Most academy members were disappointed that the advances that the Kerensky government had promised would never materialize. They also did not trust the Bolsheviks' political motivations. Nevertheless, the general assembly of the academy decided to enter into negotiations with the Bolsheviks. Pavlov was one of only two academy members who voted against the proposal, advocating a boycott of the Bolsheviks instead.

On the evening of July 16, 1918, several Bolsheviks stormed the house where the tsar and his family were being held and executed them all.

As did most Russians, Pavlov and his family found life during wartime difficult. The Bolsheviks searched Pavlov's home several times between 1918 and 1920, and he and his son were even arrested for a brief period. Scientific experimentation ground to a halt as supplies and food became scarce and many of Pavlov's colleagues and students left university to fight in the war.

By 1922, the Bolsheviks had solidified their control over the new Soviet Union. In part because of the Russian Academy of Science's swift acceptance of the Bolshevik government, the Academy's doors remained open. The Bolsheviks, believing that a strong science program was essential to building the socialist state, generously funded research and established prestigious awards, such as the Lenin Prize, for individual scientific achievements.

Yet the relationship between the government and science faced some challenges, especially in Pavlov's case. In 1931 the state planning committee ordered the Academy members to compile detailed work plans. Many members, objected, however, citing concerns such as practicality (scientific discoveries could not always be held to a deadline) and productivity (a predetermined agenda could hamper theoretical exploration). Pavlov simply refused to comply. Pavlov also strongly opposed many other government initiatives, including the Politburo's insistence in 1927 that the Academy should elect communist members. Pavlov and others argued that membership should be determined by scientific merit only and not political affiliation. The fact that he could defy the authorities with so little repercussion proved his esteemed position and reputation within the Bolshevik government.

Moreover, the Soviets greatly valued Pavlov's scientific theories on conditioning. They dovetailed nicely with the government's concept of humans as mechanistic—biological machines that could be understood and controlled through science. In addition, the the Soviet military employed knowledge gained from Pavlov's experimental work on neuroses and the physiological mechanisms underlying hypnosis.

CRITICAL RESPONSE

Pavlov's work on conditioned reflexes earned him international scientific recognition and great prestige in his homeland; as Russia's only Nobel Prize-winning scientist in a field, physiology, that was highly regarded by the Communist government, he was considered a national treasure. But as a physiologist working in the realm of psychology, he faced some unique challenges within the scientific community. Ironically, however, Pavlov's psychological theories have stood the test of time more readily than have his physiological theories of brain function.

In *Conditioned Reflexes,* Pavlov discussed "the close connection between physiology and psychology," something he recognized that many psychologists in Russia and America did not acknowledge or appreciate:

> I am convinced that an important stage in the development of human thought is approaching, a stage when the physiological and the psychological, the objective and the subjective, will really merge, when the painful contradiction between our mind and our body and their contraposition will either actually be solved or disappear in a natural way.

Of course, advances in neurological research and imaging have provided a much clearer understanding of the workings of the frontal lobes and other sections of the brain about which Pavlov theorized. He was correct in his assessment that the subcortex region of the brain regulated autonomic and instinctual functioning. Later re-searchers have found that conditioning of some subcortical functions may also be possible.

While Pavlov was partially right in his supposition that the frontal lobes were involved in processing language (the "second signal"), researchers now know that the temporal lobes are primarily responsible for language recognition (left temporal lobe) and speech (right temporal lobe).

Among his contemporaries, Polish researcher Jerzy Konorski criticized certain aspects of Pavlov's physiological work. Konorski was actually a student in Pavlov's lab from 1931 to 1933. He had a strong research interest in the concept of association and the relationship between stimuli and responses. But Konorski found Pavlov's concepts of diffuse inhibitions and theoretical waves of cortical excitation and inhibition centers speculative and inconsistent with his knowledge of neuron theory. Yet the Polish scientist was respectful of Pavlov's contributions to conditioning theory, and he dedicated his 1948 book, *Conditioned Reflexes and Neuron Organization,* in part to Pavlov.

In 1937 Konorski published a paper with S. Miller to present their ideas on classical versus instrumental conditioning to the growing behaviorism movement in America. They had trained a dog to lift its foot in response to a cue in order to receive a food reward. Konorski and Miller explain that "[i]n conditioned reflexes of the first type, the reaction is effected by organs innervated through the central or autonomic nervous system, while, in conditioned reflexes of the second type, the effector can probably be only a striate muscle." In other words, the conditioning was formed through the conscious actions of the dog itself, not through external stimuli triggering a reflex, as Pavlov had surmised. Konorski also developed the idea of avoidance conditioning in later works.

Some additional concepts about the interrelationship between stimuli in conditioning that have been

BIOGRAPHY:

Clark Hull and Kenneth Spence

Clark L. Hull (1884–1952) and Kenneth Wartinbee Spence (1907–67) met at Yale University, where Hull was a professor of psychology and Spence was a graduate student and research assistant in the primate lab of Robert Yerkes. Hull and Spence shared an interest in experimental psychology, researching maze learning in the rat. Although the two men jointly authored only one published paper, they created one of the most influential learning and conditioning theories of their time—the Spence-Hull theory.

The Spence-Hull theory attempted to quantify the way behavior was learned by using a mathematical equation, or model. It also elaborated on the concept of conditioned and unconditioned motivation in behavior formation. Environmental cues can condition motivation; strong environmental events, such as an electric shock, are an unconditioned source of behavioral drive.

Both Hull and Spence were considered part of the neobehaviorist movement, along with their contemporaries B.F. Skinner and Edward Tolman. Neobehaviorism was founded on Pavlovian conditioning, but the field also explored the role of motivation and environment in forming behavior. Hull, Spence, and others developed complex associative learning theories that were typically tested on laboratory animals.

The concept of drive reduction theory as an essential part of learning was developed by Hull. Drive reduction theory held that behavior was motivated by basic drives, or instinctual needs, such as hunger and sexual desires. When an individual responded to those drives (for example, by obtaining and eating food to satisfy hunger), the drives were reduced. This reduction in basic drives consequently served as a form of reinforcement for the behavior that fulfilled them. This was tied to Hull's idea of "habit strength," that the reinforced behavior would be self-perpetuating as long as the drive was satiated by the behavior. Both habit and drive strength elicit what Hull calls "reaction potential," or the likelihood that a response or behavior will occur again. Hull combined all of his ideas into a series of complex mathematical theorems and formulas designed to explain behavior.

Hull wrote *Principles of Behavior* in 1943, in which he stated that the strength of a fear response corresponds directly with the level of negative reinforcement. He also discussed ways by which negative reinforcements increase fear and anxiety. For example, repeatedly avoiding an anxiety-provoking situation, such as public speaking, can actually heighten the anxiety response.

Clark Hull earned his Ph.D. from the University of Wisconsin in 1918 after doing undergraduate work at the University of Michigan. Hull joined Yale's Institute of Human Relations in 1929, and was elected president of the American Psychological Association in 1936. He also did extensive research into both psychometric testing and the field of hypnosis, publishing *Aptitude Testing* (1929) and *Hypnosis and Suggestibility* (1933). Hull remained at Yale until his death in 1952.

Beyond his association with Hull, Spence is best known for his theory of discrimination learning, published in the *Psychological Review* in 1936. The theory explained how animals choose, or discriminate, between two or more stimuli that are presented at the same time, selecting the one that produces a reward.

Kenneth Spence received his Ph.D. from Yale in 1933. He was awarded a four-year fellowship to the Yale

Clark Hull. (Archives of the History of American Psychology. Reproduced by permission.)

Laboratories of Primate Biology at Orange Park, Florida. In 1938, he took a faculty position at the State University of Iowa, where he taught for over two decades. In 1956, Spence received the Distinguished Scientific Contribution Award from the American Psychological Association. He moved to the University of Texas in 1964, and three years later he succumbed to cancer at the age of 59.

developed and refined since Pavlov's original work include:

- Cue competition. The interplay of two conditioned stimuli presented simultaneously with an unconditioned stimulus.

- Blocking effect. Initial conditioning to stimulus A alone prevents or minimizes conditioning to stimulus B when A and B are presented together. This idea is rooted in Pavlov's concept of overshadowing, which said that if stimulus A is stronger or more novel than stimulus B, even if both are presented simultaneously, stimulus B will create minimal conditioning (that is, A will overshadow B).

- Differential conditioning. The concept that an animal can learn to discriminate between two different but similar stimuli if one is presented with some sort of reinforcement.

At the start of the twentieth century, Pavlov's ideas on conditioning and stories of his laboratory investigations began to spread beyond Russia. First came Pavlov's Nobel Prize; in 1906, he gave a lecture in the United Kingdom at Charing Cross Hospital on "The scientific investigation of the psychical faculties or processes in the higher animals" that was published in the noted American journal *Science*. Researchers Robert Yerkes and Sergius Morgulis also published a review of Pavlov's lab work that was printed in *The Psychological Bulletin* in 1909.

But it was the publication of G. Anrep's English translation of Pavlov's lectures on conditioned reflexes that really brought Pavlov's theories on conditioning to the attention of American scientists. His work had a significant impact on learning theorists and the fledgling psychological field of behaviorism, attracting the attention of behavioral psychologists such as B.F. Skinner.

Although he built on Pavlov's work in conditioned reflexes and acknowledged the Russian scientist's major contributions to the field, American behavioral psychologist B.F. Skinner (1904–90) diverged from Pavlov's theories on two fronts. First, he did not believe that Pavlov could accurately determine the physiologic structure and nature of the nervous system simply by examining the behavior of his experimental subjects. In other words, he believed that physiology and behaviorism were completely separate areas of study that could not be extrapolated from each other. Secondly, Skinner was more interested in behavior as a reaction to environment, where choice and consequences reinforce behavior.

Skinner went on to delve deeper into the concepts of operant conditioning outlined by Konorski and Miller in their earlier work. He explained the differences between the two approaches: "In the Pavlovian experiment, however, a reinforcer is paired with a stimulus; whereas operant behavior is contingent upon a response." Reinforcers in an operant conditioning experiment only appear when the subject has made the correct behavioral "choice." The well-known "Skinner box" provided an environment for lab animals to learn how to receive food by pressing a lever. Within the box, different simultaneous stimuli (e.g., light and dark, sounds) provided additional operant stimuli. Skinner used different forms of positive and negative reinforcement to shape an animal's behavioral choices.

Beyond behaviorism, Russian psychologist and learning theorist Lev Vygotsky applied Pavlov's conditioning theory to the process of language development, or "second signaling" system. Vygotsky hypothesized that children acquired language through imitation and interaction with adults. Eventually, a child's internal concept or picture of what a word symbolizes becomes her conditioned stimulus for language.

The neuropsychologist Alexander Luria, a student of Vygotsky's, used the concept of "semantic conditioning" to establish a conditioned reflex to a word and then investigated whether words that were similar in structure or sound would elicit the same reflex. For Luria, internal conceptualizations of words (that is, "inner speech") were temporary mental associations that were flexible and therefore easily modified and revised with experience. This theory was in contrast to the rigid mental associations formed by conditioning in animals that Pavlov had inferred.

During the summer of 1950, the Russian Academy of Sciences the Academy of Medical Sciences held a joint session and issued a directive to their members that Pavlov's scientific principles should guide all future research work. This edict significantly limited research freedom, and several scientists were removed from their posts and publicly denounced for espousing non-Pavlovian theories. Among those discredited were Russian physiologist I.S. Beritov, who had disagreed with Pavlov's concept of inhibition in the forming of conditioned reflexes, instead surmising that reflexes resulted from spontaneous electrical activity in the brain. Also removed from his position as director of the Institute of Physiology of the Academy of Medical Sciences was Pyotr K. Anokhin, a former student of Pavlov's who had attempted to refine his theory of the reflex arc of the conditioned reflex. This display of political muscle and restriction of scientific autonomy would have greatly distressed Pavlov himself, had he been alive to witness it, and it significantly hampered Russian research initiatives.

THEORIES IN ACTION

Pavlov's rigorous scientific method, innovative experimentation techniques, and aseptic (sanitary) laboratory environment revolutionized the way animal research was performed; many of his methods remain in widespread use today. Pavlovian conditioning continues to be a methodological and conceptual foundation for psychological research and learning theory—the benchmark by which behavioral animal experiments are designed.

Behavioral therapy, which emerged in the 1950s, also owes a tremendous debt to Pavlov's theories of conditioning. The concept of conditioning gave psychologists a way to uncover the etiology, or causes, behind certain phobias and neuroses. Pavlov's theories on experimental neuroses have also laid the foundation for modern behavioral-based treatment of psychiatric disorders such as panic and anxiety disorders and phobias. Behavioral therapy is based on the concept of replacing undesirable or maladaptive conditioned responses (such as irrational fear) with a positive and appropriate conditioned response (such as relaxation). Gradually, the positive response should replace or extinguish the maladaptive one. Cognitive-behavioral therapy (CBT), an offshoot of behavioral therapy, also uses behavioral techniques supplemented by an increased awareness of the causes behind the maladaptive behavior.

The behavioral-based treatment method of systematic desensitization—the process of eliminating fear or anxiety by gradual and constant exposure to the source of fear—is rooted in Pavlov's findings that learned conditioned behaviors could also be extinguished, or unlearned. The technique was developed by psychiatrist Joseph Wolpe in the 1950s. Relaxation exercises are usually used as part of systematic desensitization techniques to further eliminate feelings of anxiety by introducing a substitute conditioned stimulus to associate with the source of the fear. For example, someone who is afraid of the water can overcome the fear by gradual exposure to a pool coupled with deep muscle relaxation techniques. Each time the person enters the pool and does not experience something terrible, the learned association between water and bad feelings is eroded.

Aversive therapy is another offshoot of Pavlovian theory. It involves pairing a highly negative stimulus with a harmful stimulus to eliminate a maladaptive behavior. Aversive therapy is used frequently in the treatment of alcoholism. One form of aversive therapy is the use of disulfarim (Antabuse), a drug that triggers extreme nausea and vomiting when combined with alcohol. In a technique called "taste aversion therapy," an individual may be put through several sessions at which they are given the drug and then given alcohol to smell and drink, making them ill. More frequently, the drug is prescribed to individuals that are newly recovering alcoholics as a prophylactic to prevent relapse.

Stimulus control therapy (SCT), commonly used in treating sleep disorders, is also based in classical conditioning theory and is a form of counter-conditioning. This treatment is based on the idea that insomnia is actually a self-perpetuating learned response that is caused by an individual's association of their bedroom with sleeplessness and anxiety. In SCT, the sleep environment is carefully controlled—the individual is instructed to leave the room for a period of time when they are unable to sleep, to have a fixed waking time each day, and to avoid any activities in the bedroom that aren't related to sleep or sex.

Research

Modern learning theory continues to build on Pavlovian conditioning. Researchers have developed models of associative learning that examine the relationship between multiple conditioned stimuli. Pavlov's theories of personality also have influenced later behaviorists. German-born psychologist and statistical researcher Hans Eysenck built on Pavlov's idea that excitation and inhibition activity determines temperament. Eysenck theorized that personality is predetermined by both genetics and by the physiological balance of cortical arousal and depression. Eysenk's "dimensions" of temperament were neuroticism and introversion-extroversion (the latter being his interpretation of inhibition and excitation). Later, he also added psychoticism to his theory. Neuroticism was determined by the level of activity in an individual's sympathetic (or autonomic) nervous system; neurotic behaviors, such as anxiety or panic attacks, were caused by hyperactivity of this area of the brain.

The Pavlov Department of Physiology at the Institute of Experimental Medicine continues his research tradition, conducting animal and human studies in the department's three laboratories. For example, in the Laboratory of Psychophysiology of Emotion, researchers investigate anxiety, depression,

CHRONOLOGY

1849: Born in the village of Ryazan, Russia.

1870: Leaves the seminary to enroll at St. Petersburg University

1875: Begins physiology studies at the Medical Academy

1879: Graduates from the Academy; wins a gold medal in student competition.

1881: Marries Serafima Vasil'evna Karchevskaia, a teacher.

1897: Publishes "Lectures on the Work of the Main Digestive Glands."

1904: Awarded the Nobel Prize in Physiology or Medicine.

1910: Construction of "Towers of Silence" begins.

1917: The October Revolution occurs; the Bolsheviks take power and Vladimir Lenin becomes new Soviet leader.

1921: Lenin issues special decree giving Pavlov full funding and supplies for his research and living expenses.

1927: Publishes "Lectures on the Work of the Large Hemispheres of the Brain."

1929: Construction of Pavlov's research facilities at Koltushi begins.

1936: Dies on February 27 after developing pneumonia at the age of 86.

and other emotional disorders. Victor Klimenko, the department's director since 1995, reports that:

> Nowadays the phenomenon of reinforcement is the central point in different theories of emotions and behavior. Main principles of forming conditioned reflexes—a specially directed control of emotional state—are employed by staff during investigations of purposeful activity of dolphins in free behavior.

At the Institute's Clinical Laboratory of Neurodynamic Correction of Psycho-Neurological Pathology, researchers study how conditioned reflexes cause childhood behavior, and how deficits in

emotional reinforcement and environmental feedback can trigger neurological problems. At the Laboratory of Neurobiology of Integrative Brain Function, scientists continue to map the complex interrelationships and functions of the brain through both the analysis of conditioned reflexes and behavior and via research on biochemical regulation of the brain.

Case studies

A fear of dentists is a common phobia that often is conditioned by societal messages but also may be rooted in other experiences. A 2002 case report in the *Journal of Clinical Psychology* described a 39-year-old woman ("Carly") who had a phobia of dental work that started at the age of eight, when a dentist slapped her after she tried to get out of the chair during a procedure. She had avoided dentists ever since; consequently, she had to have half of her teeth surgically removed due to neglect. Clearly, this traumatic childhood experience had conditioned her anxious response to the dentist's office. Carly received a deconditioning therapy known as Eye Movement Desensitization and Reprocessing (EMDR), which couples a stimulus, such as eye movement or finger tapping, to redirect attention from the anxiety-provoking stimulus (in this case, the dentist) and remove any negative associations. At the end of the treatment period, Carly reported significantly less anxiety, and she was able to proceed with dental treatment.

Two case studies reported in *Virtual Environments in Clinical Psychology and Neuroscience* described a unique treatment approach of systematic desensitization—the use of virtual reality simulations (called virtual reality therapy, or VRT). The first was a 32-year-old woman who underwent eight 30-minute sessions of VRT that simulated the experience of flying over an urban area. Her anxiety level, which was high at the initiation of VRT, was gradually reduced and had declined significantly enough to allow her to undertake "real-world" long-distance flights by the end of her therapy. The second subject, a 42-year-old man, underwent five sessions of VRT. Although he experienced emotional anxiety and physical symptoms (such as sweaty palms) at the start of each session, the researchers reported that subjective and objective measures of his anxiety level would decrease significantly as the session progressed. At the end of the treatment, the subject was able to fly with minimal anxiety.

Conditioning is also used to eliminate behaviors or habits considered undesirable for health reasons. Behavioral and cognitive-behavioral techniques are frequently used in smoking cessation programs. Other less dangerous but unwelcome habits, such as nail-biting, can also be extinguished through these techniques. A study in *Psychological Reports* describes a 32-year-old woman that underwent systematic desensitization in order to eliminate her nail-biting habit. During the 28-day study, she completed interviews and self-reporting questionnaires that uncovered the triggers of anxiety that caused the nail-biting behavior. Through techniques of muscle relaxation and meditation, she learned to replace the negative behavior with positive stress-reduction techniques when faced with anxiety.

The ways in which behaviors are conditioned in infancy and even before birth continue to be a rich source of study for psychologists. Animal studies, in particular, frequently use conditioning techniques to explore how prenatal and neonatal environments affect development. A 2004 study in the journal *Developmental Psychobiology* reported on a classical conditioning experiment with a chimpanzee fetus. The chimp fetus was exposed to a combination of vibro-acoustic (that is, sound vibration) stimulation and two specific tones of different frequencies. Tone A was always followed by the VAS (the unconditioned stimulus), while tone B was never followed by the VAS. After birth, when the tones were presented to the chimp, it could differentiate between the two, and it responded more excitedly to tone A.

Relevance to modern readers

Pavlov's influence is so far-reaching because conditioning forms an integral part of people's lives. Learning through association—either consciously or unconsciously—is part of the essence of humanity. Behaviors and attitudes are shaped by a person's life experiences, or conditioning. A man's ongoing preference for a suit that he was wearing when he landed his last job, a woman's aversion to a food that made her extremely ill in the past, a boy's fear of wasps as a result of a previous bee-sting—all of these are common examples of the ways in which conditioning, reinforcement, generalization, and aversion affect common aspects of everyday life.

An example of conditioning in modern society is popular advertising. The creative forces behind print and broadcast advertising know that associating a product with popularity, beauty, money, and love can make the public identify that product with those desirable traits (even when it has nothing to do with them). Young people should drink a certain soda because a beautiful pop star does, kids should wear a designer's clothes because the coolest kids do, and moms should serve the best brand of rice because it means they love

their families. Fear may also be invoked and associated with brand identity; without the "right" insurance protection, car, stockbroker, or health plan, families will be left penniless. In short, brands become attractive not simply because they represent inherently good products, but because they become associated with some other appealing characteristic.

BIBLIOGRAPHY

Sources

Boakes, Robert. "The Impact of Pavlov on the Psychology of Learning in English-Speaking Countries." *The Spanish Journal of Psychology* 6, no. 2 (November 2003): 93–98.

Catania, A. Charles and V. Laties. "Pavlov and Skinner: Two Lives in Science." *Journal of the Experimental Analysis of Behavior* 72, no. 3 (1999): 455–61.

David-Fox, Michael and György Péteri, eds. *Academia in Upheaval: Origins, Transfers, and Transformations of the Communist Academic Regime in Russia and East Central Europe.* Westport, CT: Bergin & Garvey, 2000.

De Jongh, A. et al. "Efficacy of Eye Movement Desenstization and Reprocessing in the Treatment of Specific Phobias: Four Single-Case Studies on Dental Phobias." *Journal of Clinical Psychology* 58, no. 12 (2002): 1489–503.

Kawai, N. et al. "Associative Learning and Memory in a Chimpanzee Fetus: Learning and Long-Lasting Memory Before Birth." *Developmental Psychobiology* 44, no. 2 (March 2004): 116–22.

Klimenko, Victor and J.P. Golikov. "The Pavlov Department of Physiology: A Scientific History." *The Spanish Journal of Psychology* 6, no. 2 (November 2003): 112–20.

Kreshel, Peggy. "John B. Watson at J. Walter Thompson: The Legitimization of 'Science' in Advertising." *Journal of Advertising* 19 (1990).

Lenin, V.I. "Concerning the Conditions Ensuring the Research Work of Academician I.P. Pavlov and his Associates." *Lenin's Collected Works* Vol. 32. Moscow: Progress Publishers, 1965. *Marxist Internet Archive* Eds. Robert Cymbala and David Walters. [cited April 10, 2004]. http://www.marxists.org/archive/lenin/works/1921/jan/24.htm.

Mackintosh, Nicholas. "Pavlov and Associationism." *The Spanish Journal of Psychology* 6, no. 2 (November 2003): 177–84.

McClanahan, T.M. "Operant Learning (R-S) Principles Applied to Nail-Biting." *Psychological Reports* 77, no. 2 (October 1995): 507–14.

North, Max M. et al. "Virtual Reality Therapy: An Effective Treatment for Phobias." In *Virtual Environments in Clinical Psychology and Neuroscience.* Amsterdam, Netherlands: IOS Press, 1998.

Pavlov, Ivan P. *Conditioned Reflexes.* Mineola, NY: Dover, 2003.

Pavlov, Ivan P. *Psychopathology and Psychiatry*. New Brunswick, NJ: Transaction, 1994.

Plaud, Joseph. "Pavlov and the Foundation of Behavior Therapy." *The Spanish Journal of Psychology* 6, no. 2 (November 2003): 147–54.

Ruiz, Gabriel et al. "Pavlov in America: A Heterodox Approach to the Study of his Influence." *The Spanish Journal of Psychology* 6, no. 2 (November 2003): 99–111.

Smith, Gerald. "Pavlov and Integrative Physiology." *American Journal of Physiology—Regulatory, Integrative, and Comparative Physiology* 279, no. 3 (September 2000): 743–55.

Spence, Kenneth W. *Behavior Theory and Learning, Selected Papers*. Englewood Cliffs, NJ: Prentice-Hall, 1960.

Todes, Daniel. *Pavlov's Physiology Factory: Experiment, Interpretation, Laboratory, Enterprise* Baltimore, MD: Johns Hopkins University Press, 2001.

Viru, A. "Early contributions of Russian stress and exercise physiologists." *Journal of Applied Physiology* 92, no. 4 (April 2002): 1378–82.

Further readings

Nobel e-Museum. "The Nobel Prize in Physiology or Medicine 1904." The Nobel Foundation. [cited April 10, 2004]. http://www.nobel.se/medicine/laureates/1904/index.html.

Todes, Daniel. *Ivan Pavlov: Exploring the Animal Machine.* New York: Oxford University Press, 2000.

Windholz, George. "Ivan P. Pavlov: An Overview of His Life and Psychological Work." *American Psychologist* 52, no. 9 (1997): 941–46.

Wolpe, Joseph, and Joseph J. Plaud. "Pavlov's Contributions to Behavior Therapy: The Obvious and the Not So Obvious." *American Psychologist* 52, no. 9 (1997): 966–72.

Jean Piaget

BRIEF OVERVIEW

The Swiss psychologist and epistemologist Jean Piaget (1896–1980) developed his theory of genetic epistemology throughout a nearly 60-year career as a professor and experimental researcher. He first began his scientific investigations as a young biologist immersed in the study of mollusks. Before he was 30 years of age, he was world renowned for his explorations of the cognitive development of children. Piaget is credited with foundational contributions to the emerging disciplines of child psychology, educational psychology, and cognitive development theory. Piaget's empirical studies of infants, children, and adolescents provided insight into the nature of knowledge and how it is acquired. He took children's thinking seriously and respected them as the architects of their own intellectual development.

Jean Piaget was the only son of Arthur Piaget, a professor of medieval studies at the University of Neuchatel, and Rebecca Jackson. He spent his childhood and adolescence in Switzerland in the region near Lake Neuchatel. He was trained as a zoologist, receiving his Ph.D. from the University of Neuchatel in 1918. His early fascination with and competence in the biological sciences, particularly the study of mollusks, continued throughout his lifetime. Piaget moved to Paris in 1919 for postdoctoral studies.

The turning point in his academic life came through his work with French school children, in which he administered and standardized British intelligence

1896–1980

SWISS GENETIC EPISTEMOLOGIST, PSYCHOLOGIST

UNIVERSITE DE NEUCHATEL, B.A., 1915, Ph.D., 1918; POSTDOCTORAL STUDY AT UNIVERSITY OF ZURICH, UNIVERSITY OF PARIS, AND THE SORBONNE

Jean Piaget. (Copyright Bettmann/Corbis. Reproduced by permission.)

tests as a research associate at the Simon-Binet experimental psychology laboratory. During the course of his work with intelligence testing, Piaget decided that the important issue to explore was not whether children gave the right answers to the IQ test, but rather, how they gave the wrong answers and what the patterns of the children's responses revealed about their developing capacities for reasoning.

In 1921, Piaget returned to Switzerland, where he made his home until his death. He was appointed Research Director of the Institut Jean-Jacques Rousseau in Geneva in 1921 and that same year published his first article on the psychology of intelligence. Piaget was known as *le patron* (the boss) by his graduate students and research associates. His early work studying the reasoning of elementary school children became the basis of his first five books on child psychology and marked the beginning of his international fame as a revolutionary thinker in the area of childhood cognitive development.

Piaget used the term genetic epistemology to define his disciplined investigation into how knowledge develops within the human being and the means by which the developing mind moves through distinct stages toward maturation. At the heart of Piaget's biological theories of development is his emphasis on the human being's ability to adapt to the world through

the dual processes of assimilation and accommodation, modifying one's mental schemes to allow room for new information.

Piaget's child-centered research and respectful observations of infants and children led him to the discovery that children think in qualitatively different ways than adults as they progress through four distinct and universal stages of development.

• Sensorimotor stage (birth to about two years): Infants rely on their senses to understand the world around them.

• Preoperational stage (about two to seven years): Pre-school children develop an increased capacity for symbolic thinking and the use of language and images.

• Concrete-operational stage (about seven to 11 years): Children think logically and begin to see the world from others' perspective.

• Formal operational stage (age 11 to adult): Hypothetical and abstract reasoning with systematic problem solving and abstract thinking.

Piaget's consuming interest was in the discovery of the universal mechanisms that underlie how knowledge is acquired. He understood this as a process governed by genetic factors and environmental experiences, with the environment playing an increasingly more important role as the individual matures. Piaget respected the developing child as an active agent in the construction of knowledge through trial and error experimentation. Even the fundamental ideas of space, time, relation and causality, he observed, are subject to this process. The child's earliest years, he believed, laid the foundation for the rational and moral adult personality, with increasingly complex intellectual processes building on the successful passage through earlier, more primitive stages of development. Piaget did not consider the fourth stage of formal operations as a final one. He believed there was no fixed limit to the possibilities of human development.

Throughout a brilliant research career that spanned more than 60 years, Piaget refined his structural and holistic methodology for observing, describing, and evaluating the stages of human cognitive development from the point of view of the child. His pioneering research and prolific publications on the nature of thought and the development of intelligence assured Piaget's place as a major influence in the scientific thinking of the twentieth century. The ingenuity of his approach to the study of children's ways of thinking continues to inform and influence the fields of epistemology, education, and developmental and child psychology.

Piaget continually changed his thinking as new possibilities occurred to him. His impressive list of publications include over 60 books, professional papers, book chapters, and articles in scientific journals. He received over 30 honorary degrees and awards from universities throughout the world. In 1955 Piaget created the International Center for Genetic Epistemology and served as its director for the remainder of his life. He died in Geneva, Switzerland, on September 16, 1980. His genuine respect for and appreciation of the mind of the child and his prodigious research accomplishments continue to inspire and challenge scholars and researchers worldwide.

BIOGRAPHY

Child prodigy

Jean Piaget was born in Neuchatel, Switzerland, August 9, 1896, the first of three children of Arthur Piaget and Rebecca Jackson. The Piaget family lived in a quiet French-speaking region near Lake Neuchatel, in the cradle of the Swiss Alps in an area of Switzerland noted for its vineyards and watch making.

Jean was a child prodigy. His father, a professor of medieval literature at Neuchatel University, nurtured his son's innovative and inquisitive mind and encouraged young Jean in the systematic pursuit of answers to his many queries about the natural world.

Jean's mother was a strict Calvinist, adhering to a system of biblical interpretation focused on the supreme sovereignty of God and the fallen nature of humans. She was politically active and concerned with the social causes of the day. By some accounts Rebecca Piaget was a troubled woman, seriously challenged with mental illness. She encouraged her son to attend religious instruction, but young Piaget soon lost interest in what he considered "childish" religious arguments. Piaget began his study of various philosophies in an effort to find his way through the inconsistencies he perceived between the religious instruction he received at church and his own observations of the natural world. At the suggestion of his godfather, the Swiss scholar Samuel Cornut, Piaget began his study of philosophy. He was especially touched by the French writer Henri Bergson's 1907 book, *Creative Evolution.* Piaget said the book "stirred him almost to ecstasy."

He told interviewer Elizabeth Hall much later in his professional life:

> Suddenly the problem of knowledge appeared to me in a new light. I became convinced, very quickly, that most of the problems in philosophy were problems of knowledge, and that most problems of knowledge

were problems of biology. You see, the problem of knowledge is the problem of the relation between the subject and the object, how the subject knows the object. If you translate this into biological terms, it is a problem of the organism's adapting to its environment. I decided to consecrate my life to this biological explanation of knowledge.

Jean grew into a serious young man, disciplined and determined in his pursuit of knowledge. He chafed within the strictures and routines of his early schooling and became bored and restless in the classroom. His early interest in the scientific study of nature led him to membership in a local biology club while a student at Neuchatel Latin high school. When he was only a boy of 10, Jean published a paper in the club's *Journal of Natural History of Neuchatel* describing his observations of an albino sparrow. Jean took his work quite seriously. He sought and gained access to the university library where he could explore more books and journals to further his studies.

In later years, Piaget described his youthful home life as being not particularly happy. As a young student he spent most of his time away from the difficulties at home, immersing himself in study and seeking to solve the mysteries of nature. He was intrigued with the study of fossils, bird life, and even with the invention of a steam engine car. He read constantly in the fields of philosophy, psychology, and natural sciences, a habit he sustained throughout his life.

During high school, Jean's remarkable scholastic accomplishments continued to bring him to the notice of his teachers and others in the field of natural sciences. He became a leader in the Friends of Nature Club, sponsored by professors at the University of Neuchatel, and he prepared and read papers on natural science at the club meetings. He became an assistant to Paul Godet, the director of the Neuchatel Museum of Natural History. He worked there for four years as an apprentice, helping to classify the museum's considerable collection of mollusks. As compensation Piaget received numerous rare mollusk specimens to add to his personal collection. He began to publish a series of scientific papers on the mollusks, particularly the *Limnaea* species, a Swiss lake snail.

When he was 16, Piaget's scholarly work drew the attention of the board of directors of the Museum of Natural History in Geneva. He was offered the prestigious post of curator of a mollusk exhibit at the museum. The admirers of his scholarship were unaware that Jean was still a high school student when they honored his work with an offer of employment. By the time of his high school graduation, Jean Piaget had become a well-known malacologist throughout Europe with 20 scientific papers published in professional

PRINCIPAL PUBLICATIONS

- *Le Langue et la pensee chez l'enfant.* Paris: Delachaux and Niestle, 1923. Published in English as *The Language and Thought of the Child.* Trans. by Marjorie Worden. New York: Harcourt, Brace, 1926, 3rd revised edition, Humanities 1959, reprinted, 1971.

- *Le Jugement et le raisonnement chez l'enfant.* Paris: Delachaux & Niestle, 1924, 5th edition, 1963. Published in English as *The Judgement and Reasoning in the Child.* Trans. by Marjorie Worden. New York: Harcourt, Brace, 1928, published as *The Judgment and Reason in the Child.* 1929, reprinted, Littlefield, 1976.

- *Le Representation du monde chez l'enfant.* Paris: Delachaux and Niestle, 1926. Published in English as *The Child's Conception of the World.* Trans. by Jean Tomlinson and Andrew Tomlinson. New York: Harcourt, Brace, 1929, reprinted, Littlefield, 1976.

- *La Causalite physique chez l'enfant.* Paris: Delachaux & Niestle, 1927. Published in English as *The Child's Conception of Physical Causality* Trans. by Marjorie Worden Gabain. New York: Harcourt, Brace, 1930.

- *La Naissance de l'intelligence chez l'enfant.* Paris: Delachaux and Niestle, 1936, 5th edition, 1966. Published in English as *The Origins of Intelligence in Children.* Trans. by Margaret Cook. New York: International Universities Press, 1952. Published in English as *The Origin of Intelligence in the Child.* London: Routledge & Kegan Paul, 1953, Norton, 1963.

- *La Formation du symbole chez l'enfant: Imitation jeu et reve, image et rpresentation.* Paris: Delachaux and Niestle, 1945, 2nd edition, 1959. Published in English as *Play, Dreams, and Imitation in Childhood.* Trans. by Gattegno and Hodgson. New York: W. W. Norton & Co., 1951, reprinted, Peter Smith, 1988.

- With Barbel Inhelder. *La Psychologie de l'enfant* Presses universitaires de France, 1966, 6th edition, 1975. Published in English as *The Psychology of the Child.* Trans. by Helen Weaver. New York: Basic Books, 1969.

- *L'Epistemologie genetique.* Presses universitaires de France, 1970. Published in English as *The Principles of Genetic Epistemology.* Trans. by Wolfe Mays. New York: Basic Books, 1972.

- *L'Equilibration des structures cognitives: probleme central du developpement.* Presses universitaires de France, 1975. Published in English as *The Development of Thought: Equilibration of Cognitive Structures.* Trans by Arnold Rosin. New York: Viking, 1977.

---

journals. Such early success with his study of clams and snails gave young Piaget a firm basis for the continued development of his scientific approach to the study of nature. He sustained his interest in mollusks throughout his life.

In 1918, at the age of 21, Jean Piaget graduated with a doctorate in natural sciences from the University of Neuchatel. That same year he published his first book, *Recherche*, meaning "the search" or "searching," an autobiographical novel dealing with the conflict between science and religion. In this book Piaget first explored the idea of equilibrium, a concept that he understood as an ideal balance between parts and the whole, both within an individual and within society.

Piaget published his doctoral thesis on the classification of mollusks. During the intense periods of academic exploration and focus throughout his university years, Piaget's physical health suffered. He was forced to take a year off from his studies and retreated to the mountains to recuperate. This rest period in the Swiss Alps became a yearly habit throughout his life, providing him with critical time for reflection and rest. Piaget valued his relationship with the natural world as a necessary ingredient in a balanced life.

Early career
Piaget enrolled for a semester of postdoctoral study at the University of Zurich in Switzerland. While in

Zurich he also worked in Eugen Bleuler's psychiatric clinic. His curiosity about psychological issues, due in part to his mother's poor mental health, led him to the study of the psychoanalytical theories of Sigmund Freud and the analytical psychology of the Swiss psychoanalyst Carl Gustav Jung. Piaget attended many of Jung's lectures, and he was particularly interested in Jung's emphasis on the human psyche's drive toward balance and wholeness, and on the individual's significance as the agent of his or her own maturation and individuation. During these years Piaget was reading psychology only in French and was not exposed to the contemporary writings of Max Wertheimer and Wolfgang Kohler, the Gestalt psychologists. He later told an interviewer that had he come across the Gestalt writings when he was 18 he might himself have become a Gestalt psychologist.

In 1919 Piaget moved to Paris, where he studied logic and abnormal psychology and lectured in psychology and philosophy at the Sorbonne. He found work as a research associate in the Simon-Binet experimental psychology laboratory. There Piaget worked with Theophile Simon in administering intelligence tests to French children at the *École de la rue de la Grange-aux Belles* a school for boys. Piaget's task was to standardize the French version of British psychologist Cyril Burt's intelligence test, noting what kind of errors children made as they answered a series of questions. Though he was not particularly challenged by the work of test administration and never completed the task of standardizing the test, in the process of his work he began to realize the qualitative differences in how children and adults think.

Piaget's work with these young children (ages five to eight years), was a turning point in his career, leading to his lifelong study of the origins, nature, and development of intelligence. Piaget believed this research into how children think was an essential source of information about the nature of knowledge itself. He was intrigued with the answers the children gave, even if those answers were considered wrong by the standards of the intelligence test he administered. It was the patterns of their responses that caught his attention. Children of the same age, he found, invariably came up with the same wrong answer to the test questions. Piaget began to explore the thinking processes of the children, making use of a technique of clinical interviewing he had learned during his work at Eugen Bleuler's psychiatric clinic in Paris. He was fascinated with the processes of children's reasoning and the unique psychological mechanisms at work as they construct, apply, and adapt their own theories of the world in a trial and error process leading to the acquisition of practical intelligence.

Piaget came to believe that children of all ages are interactive agents in their personal intellectual development. His experience with testing these French children led him to develop his own experimental working philosophy of how knowledge grows, which later evolved into his systematic theories of cognitive development known as genetic epistemology.

In 1921 Piaget published a paper in the *Archives de Psychologie*. In the paper, he claimed that logic is not an innate characteristic but is developed over time through interactive processes of self-regulation. Piaget believed that this adaptive process is common to all living things. He discounted the prevailing doctrines of innate ideas and environmental determinism. His published work drew the attention of other researchers and scholars, and at the age of 25, Jean Piaget was offered the position of research psychologist at the Jean-Jacques Rousseau Institute in Geneva (now *Institut des Sciences de l'Education* at the University of Geneva). The Institute was highly regarded for its programs of educational research. There Piaget studied children's language and reasoning processes, and began writing in earnest. He later became co-director of the Institute and produced five more books during his five-year tenure there.

Marriage and family life

Piaget married psychologist Valentine Chatenay in 1923. Piaget's young wife had been one of his first graduate students at the Jean-Jacques Rousseau Institute in Geneva where Piaget worked. She soon became his research associate in the observation and detailed study and analysis of the behavior of their three children: Jacqueline, Lucienne, and Laurent. The young couple documented the intellectual development of their children from infancy throughout their childhood years. They listened to their children, watched them at play, and played with them, respecting how their cognitive processes differed from an adult's. They attempted to describe and evaluate the point of view of their developing children and to gain insight into how knowledge is acquired. They recorded the children's words and actions, without criticism, as they observed the unique thought processes and underlying logic that the children revealed.

The painstaking observation of Piaget's own three children prior to their acquisition of language led to his development of the theories of sensorimotor intelligence and publication of three books detailing his observations. Piaget respected children as active agents in their personal intellectual development. His early publications provided a coherent account of human development in the first year of life.

In photographs taken throughout his adult life, Piaget is often shown wearing his characteristic beret, with an engaging smile and horn-rimmed glasses framing his twinkling eyes. He was a tall man who always seemed to have a pipe in hand. In later years, his snow-white hair added to his distinctive appearance. Piaget was a somewhat eccentric and tireless worker fully absorbed in his academic pursuits. He was kind and possessed of enormous charisma, but by some accounts was remote and obsessed with his work.

"Fundamentally I am a worrier whom only work can relieve," Piaget said. He was an early riser, customarily beginning his day at 4 AM. His desk was said to be piled high with stacks of books and papers organized in a way only he could decipher. He spent four hours each day composing new material writing with pen and paper. In addition, he supervised the work of graduate students, taught classes, attended meetings, continued with his empirical research, and fulfilled the multiple obligations of his employment at the university. Even his leisure time was spent in productive ways. He combined exercise with transportation and often rode his bicycle to work. In the afternoons he took long walks as he puzzled out the complex theories that consumed his intellectual life. But Piaget the naturalist was never completely consumed with his intellectual pursuits.

> It is true I am sociable and like to teach or to take part in meetings of all kinds, but I feel a compelling need for solitude and contact with nature. . . .As soon as vacation time comes, I withdraw to the mountains in the wild regions of the Valais and write for weeks on end. . . .It is this dissociation between myself as a social being and as a "man of nature" which has enabled me to surmount a permanent fund of anxiety and transform it into a need for working.

Return to Switzerland and international acclaim

Piaget returned to his home in Switzerland in 1925 to work at his alma mater, Neuchatel University, where he was to occupy academic chairs as professor of psychology, sociology, and the history of sciences during a five-year tenure. In 1928, Piaget had the good chance to meet Albert Einstein who, Piaget said, "impressed me profoundly, because he took an interest in everything." Einstein recognized the genius in Piaget's insights and work. He suggested to Piaget that he should study the notions of time in children, and in particular the notions of simultaneity. Piaget, before the age of 30, had become the most well-known psychologist in the French-speaking world.

In 1929 Piaget taught the history of scientific thought at the University of Geneva. He remained there until 1939. During this time Piaget and his associates studied children from four to 12 years of age researching the development of logical thinking in childhood and adolescence, particularly with regard to concepts of speed, quantity, number, geometry, space, time, and movement. It was also during this period that Piaget began major collaborative research with other psychologists. He collaborated with Professor Barbel Inhelder, an experimental child psychologist at the University of Geneva. Together they wrote *The Child's Construction of Physical Quantities. Conservation and Atomism*, published in 1942, and *The Growth of Logical Thinking from Childhood to Adolescence*, published in 1955, and began a collaborative relationship that lasted 40 years. Piaget also worked with Alina Szeminsa on several books. Piaget was influential in bringing the work of women psychologists into more prominence in the field of experimental psychology, which was dominated by male theoreticians.

During the years of World War II, Piaget's work was not easily available outside of Switzerland. His ideas, though well accepted in Europe, were not often heard in American universities, where the behaviorist theories of human development dominated. None of his books was translated into English for the nearly 20 years between 1932 and 1950. In 1942 he lectured at the College of France during the time of the Nazi occupation. These lectures were compiled into his book, *The Psychology of Intelligence*, published in 1963.

Piaget served for 35 years (1929–67) as director of the International Bureau of Education in Geneva, working in collaboration with the United Nations Educational, Scientific and Cultural Organization (UNESCO), and in 1932 he became director of the Institute of Educational Sciences at the University of Geneva. He continued in that capacity until 1971, when he was named Emeritus Professor at the University of Geneva, a position he held until his death in 1980.

Throughout his long career Piaget won numerous awards and gained international acclaim. He received the Distinguished Scientific Contribution Award by the American Psychological Association in 1969. He was the first European to receive the award that honored him for his "revolutionary perspective on the nature of human knowledge and biological intelligence." In 1972 Piaget was awarded the *Praemium Erasmianum* (known in English as the Erasmus Prize), from The Netherlands. This prestigious award was established to "honour persons or institutions that have made an exceptionally important contribution to European culture, society or social science."

Piaget edited numerous scientific journals; received honorary degrees from over 30 universities, including Cambridge and Harvard; and held memberships in more

Jean Piaget. *(Copyright Farrell Grehan/Corbis. Reproduced by permission.)*

than 20 academic societies. In 1955 he founded the International Center for Genetic Epistemology at the University of Geneva, and in 1956 he persuaded the Rockefeller Foundation to provide financial assistance for his interdisciplinary work there. He continued his active association with UNESCO as a member of its Executive Board, as director of the International Bureau of Education (IBE), and for a short time as Assistant Director-General for Education.

Jean Piaget has been called a foundational thinker. He remained intellectually active, continuing with his research and publishing, until his death in Geneva at

the age of 84 on September 17, 1980. More than 3,000 people gathered at his funeral in Geneva to honor his life and work, according to obituary reports of the day. Piaget was buried with his wife, Valentine, in a gravesite marked with a cairn of simple stones. They rest together in the *Cimetiere des Plainpalais*, on the *Rue de Rois*, a cemetery reserved for Geneva's most distinguished departed.

Piaget's theories of cognitive development have had a major impact in the fields of education, sociology, and developmental and child psychology. He is a founder of the scientific discipline he called genetic epistemology, the term he used to describe his academic pursuit of the origin and nature of knowledge. His pioneering theories and the enormous respect he held for the thinking processes of children have distinguished Jean Piaget as one of the most significant psychologists of the twentieth century.

THEORIES

Genetic epistemology

Piaget developed his theory of genetic epistemology throughout 60 years of focused work as an experimental psychologist and interdisciplinary theoretician. He was concerned with the fundamental question of the nature and origin of knowledge. His own thinking on the subject was constantly changing. Sometimes in the course of writing a book, one scholar has observed, "Piaget had different ideas when it came time to write the conclusion than he had when he wrote the introduction." He wrote in French about abstract ideas using technical terminology, and this has made his books challenging to read and interpret. Fortunately there are many good translations of his works available, and scholarly writing help students navigate the complexities of Piaget's comprehensive theories of cognitive development.

Piaget was prolific. He authored, collaborated with others, or edited more than 60 books, or book chapters. He published frequently in professional journals and produced a large quantity of lecture notes and research papers. The Jean Piaget Archives Foundation in Geneva is a repository for his collected works. Piaget's writings have been translated in 24 languages, extending his influence and thinking throughout the world. Piaget's research career extended from the 1920s to the 1980s. He published his first article on the psychology of intelligence in 1921, and was still at work developing new theoretical ideas at the time of his death in 1980.

First principle: To take psychology seriously

Main points The first principle of genetic epistemology is "to take psychology seriously," Piaget said in the 1968 Woodbridge Lectures at Columbia University. By this he meant "when a question of psychological fact arises, psychological research should be consulted instead of trying to invent a solution through private speculation." Piaget considered his work that of an empirical scientist. The fundamental hypothesis that he investigated throughout the course of his career is what he called "the parallelism between the progress made in the logical and rational organization of knowledge and the corresponding formative

psychological processes." Piaget's empirical studies of infants, children, and adolescents were the best way he found to study the development of logical knowledge, mathematical knowledge, physical knowledge, and the nature of knowledge itself.

Piaget attempted to understand the evolution of knowledge in all human beings through the study of the individual. As a biologist, Piaget's approach follows directly from a neo-Darwinian emphasis on evolution via small, gradually accumulated changes, an idea which is now a subject of some debate within the discipline of developmental biology. Piaget sought to demonstrate the continuity between biological intelligence, manifesting in plants and lower animals, and human knowledge developing throughout the lifetime of the individual. Intelligence develops through a slow process of self regulation informed by environmental interactions that lead to internal reconstruction. This ability to adapt, he believed, is the common link between all living things, and it forms the basis of the biological theory of knowledge that he called genetic epistemology.

Piaget was interested in general mechanisms, intelligence, and cognitive functions, not in what makes one individual different from another. He believed that his theory of genetic epistemology was the legitimate psychological study of species behavior as opposed to the study of the individual as in more conventional understandings of psychology.

Robert L. Campbell, of the Department of Psychology at Clemson University, has identified four main points in Piaget's theory:

- Knowledge has a biological function, and arises out of action.

- Knowledge is basically "operative." It is about change and transformation.

- Knowledge consists of cognitive structures.

- Development proceeds by the assimilation of the environment to these structures, and the accommodation of these structures to the environment.

Piaget asserts that it is organization and adaptation, two processes he considers to be basic invariants of functioning, that provide the continuity between biology in general and intelligence in particular. Through the process of adaptation, the organism evolves and adjusts to its environment. For every adaptive act there is an underlying organized system of relationships or totalities. Any act of biological intelligence, from the exploratory movements of early infancy to the complex and abstract judgment of an adult, is always in relationship to an organized structure of the whole of which a single action is only a part.

Piaget defined intelligence as an adaptation. Mental life, he said is an accommodation to the environment. Adaptation involves the process of fitting new information into one's existing knowledge base through a dual process of assimilation and accommodation, altering the ideas (or what Piaget called schemes) one has constructed to make room for new information. Piaget asserted that learning is not passive; it is a process of dynamic discovery.

Piaget wrote about this cognitive evolution in his book *The Construction of Reality in the Child.*

> These global transformations of the objects of perception, and of the very intelligence which makes them, gradually denote the existence of a sort of law of evolution which can be phrased as follows: assimilation and accommodation proceed from a state of chaotic undifferentiation to a state of differentiation with correlative coordination.

Schemes are the "cognitive mental maps" that are the building blocks of intelligence. Development, then, involves a predictable and sequential series of assimilation and accommodation. Knowledge develops continually, with the invention and construction of reality emerging from active participation in the world. In Piaget's view, the basis of all human knowledge is experience, activity, and practice.

Another important concept in Piaget's theory is equilibrium, a balance between a person's internal ideas and their perceptions of the outside world. It is a state in which allows all information a place in the cognitive structure. Piaget defined it "a harmony between internal organization and external experience."

According to Piaget, the dual concepts of assimilation and accommodation are "the two poles of an interaction between the organism and the environment, which is the condition for all biological and intellectual operation." An individual takes in new ideas through assimilation, then makes room among his or her schemes for the new idea through accommodation. The result is a new level of awareness or understanding that is qualitatively different from the one preceding assimilation.

Equilibration is the unification of ideas that creates cognitive growth. Equilibration can be understood as a kind of thermostat acting to restore equilibrium between the dual processes of assimilation and accommodation. It is the means whereby the individual regains balance by acting, physically or mentally, on an environmental stimulus in order to understand it within the framework of one's existing mental schemes. With equilibration the individual is returned to a state of balance, though now she has spiraled to a higher level of understanding.

For the genetic epistemologist, Piaget wrote,

> knowledge results from continuous construction, since in each act of understanding, some degree of invention is involved; in development, the passage from one stage to the next is always characterized by the formation of new structures which did not exist before, either in the external world on in the subject's mind.

Piaget outlined four conditions that determine cognitive growth.

- maturation of the nervous system
- social interactions
- experiences based on interactions with the physical environment
- equilibration

Cognitive development is a dynamic adaptation to the environment that incorporates both nature and nurture. It follows a gradual and predictable sequence for all individuals throughout all stages. Piaget believed that each individual "is the product of interaction between heredity and environment. It is virtually impossible to draw a clear line between innate and acquired behavior patterns."

Cognitive structures are the central concept in Piaget's theory. The development of intelligence is a flexible and mobile process. Each developmental stage contains many detailed structural forms or schemes that mark developmental progress. Increasingly complex intellectual processes are built on the foundations of these earlier stages of development. Progression through the stages takes place in a continuous sequence, with each new level of understanding arising out of the preceding one. Much as a spiral, each level encompasses and integrates in a higher form the achievements of the prior stage. Each stage involves a qualitative advance.

The patterns of physical or mental action correspond to distinct and universal stages of development. Children think with logic that is consistent with the developmental stage to which they have progressed, and this development occurs at a different pace for each individual. A child cannot undertake certain tasks until he or she is psychologically mature enough to do so. Piaget demonstrated that children's thinking does not develop smoothly. At some junctures it seems to speed up, taking off into completely new areas. Such transitional points mark the movement from one stage of development to the next. The ages of transition from one stage to the next will vary, and none can be skipped. Once a developmental stage has been reached, the individual cannot go backwards (excepting instances of mental or physical trauma). No stage is lost once the skills have been achieved.

COMMUNICATION MILESTONES

Age	Milestone
0–12 months	• Responds to speech by looking at the speaker; responds differently to aspects of speakers voice (such as friendly or angry, male or female). • Turns head in direction of sound. • Responds with gestures to greetings such as "hi," "bye-bye," and "up" when these words are accompanied by appropriate gestures by speaker. • Stops ongoing activity when told "no," when speaker uses appropriate gesture and tone. • May say two or three words by around 12 months of age, although probably not clearly. • Repeats some vowel and consonant sounds (babbles) when alone or spoken to; attempts to imitate sounds.
12–24 months	• Responds correctly when asked "where?" • Understands prepositions *on, in,* and *under;* and understands simple phrases (such as "Get the ball.") • Says 8–10 words by around age 18 months; by age two, vocabulary will include 20–50 words, mostly describing people, common objects, and events (such as "more" and "all gone"). • Uses single word plus a gesture to ask for objects. • Refers to self by name; uses "my" or "mine."
24–36 months	• Points to pictures of common objects when they are named. • Can identify objects when told their use. • Understands questions with "what" and "where" and negatives "no." "not," "can't," and don't." • Responds to simple directions. • Selects and looks at picture books; enjoys listening to simple stories, and asks for them to be read aloud again. • Joins two vocabulary words together to make a phrase. • Can say first and last name. • Shows frustration at not being understood.
36–48 months	• Begins to understand time concepts, such as "today," "later," "tomorrow," and "yesterday." • Understands comparisons, such as "big" and "bigger." • Forms sentences with three or more words. • Speech is understandable to most strangers, but some sound errors may persists (such as "t" sound for "k" sound).
48–60 months	• By 48 months, has a vocabulary of over 200 words. • Follows two or three unrelated commands in proper order. • Understands sequencing of events, for example, "First we have to go to the grocery store, and then we can go to the playground." • Ask questions using "when," "how," and why." Talks about causes for things using "because."

(Courtesy Thomson Gale.)

Scholars of Piaget disagree on the number of distinct stages of cognitive development. Some view the stage of concrete operations as one stage subdivided into the preoperational and concrete operational phases. Each of Piaget's stages has many levels and subdivisions that mark a child's progress. The important point is not if there are three or four distinct stages, but rather, an understanding of the sequence of skills acquired in the process of intellectual development.

Piaget's stages of cognitive development
Sensorimotor stage (birth to two years) It is in this very first stage of development, according to Piaget, that "the most fundamental and the most rapid changes take place." The newborn infant is primarily a bundle of reflex actions interacting with the environment in an active and practical manner. Sucking and grasping are the first of these primary instinctive tendencies. Sucking is a most practical behavior needed for obtaining nourishment. With practice, the infant's sucking

skills will improve. The newborn is thinking with her body and experimenting with her own stimulus. She is the center of her own universe. At this early stage the infant does not connect sensations and stimulus to anything outside of herself. Her world is one that is first to be sucked, then looked at and listened to, and then, as coordination develops, something to be manipulated.

The infant experiments with what Piaget called repetitive circular reactions She performs an action, is interested in the result, and repeats the same action again. Gradually, at about the age of four months, the infant begins to explore the immediate environment beyond her own body with secondary circular reactions. These reactions incorporate an item or stimulus from the environment, such as a squeeze toy that squeaks, a rattle, or other baby toy. As the infant handles and manipulates objects and acquires more complex motor skills, she begins to recognize herself as the agent of the action. Then, through trial and error, the infant will begin to add purpose to her movements. She comes to understand that squeezing a certain toy will result in a squeaky sound, or batting a hanging mobile over a crib may cause it to move, or pulling mother's hair will cause a grimace on the mother's face.

Piaget considered the addition of purpose to the infant's physical actions as the beginning of intelligence. Each progressive skill the developing infant acquires is known as a scheme. Schemes are "sensory motor intelligence in action," Piaget said. A scheme is above all an instrument of assimilation that ties actions together. But still, at this early stage, an object that is out of sight remains out of mind. It has simply ceased to exist in the infant's world.

One of the central development tasks of these first two years of life is the acquisition of an understanding of the concept Piaget called object permanence. This involves the ability to form a mental representation of an object that will enable the child to realize that the object still exists, even if it is out of view. It is generally not before nine months of age that the baby can understand the concept of object permanence. One clue indicating acquisition of this skill is the characteristic high-chair game where the child delights in dropping objects from the tray to the floor and then repeating the action, over and over, after the item is returned by the caregiver. "Peek-a-boo" is also a favorite game at this stage of development. The child now understands that a face can disappear and will reappear. It is not lost forever. She may also begin to display the distressing emotions of separation anxiety. The child now realizes that the person that is out of sight still exists, and she may become quite distressed and cry continuously in an effort to bring back the missing caregiver. She has learned that

crying sometimes brings a desired result. The little scientist has by trial and error learned a key developmental task for this first stage in a lifetime of learning.

After the child's first birthday, she will begin to employ tertiary circular reactions. The child is now experimenting with constantly varying her interactions with items in the external environment. First she may use an object to hit another object and observe the reaction. Then with the same tool, may strike a different surface to get a different sound or reaction. She may learn, after some trial and error, to manipulate an object a certain way to fit it through an opening. This is an exciting period of active experimentation and interactive play that is critical to developing an understanding of how things behave outside oneself in the external environment.

Another concept particular to this first stage of cognitive development is object constancy. This is acquired at about one and one half years of age, when the baby comes to understand that an object will continue to be itself no matter what its position or the perspective from which the infant is viewing it. As the child approaches the transition from this first developmental stage to the next, she will also acquire the ability to imitate another person's action. This imitation grows increasingly sophisticated. As the child grows she learns to more quickly copy sounds, gestures, and expressions without as much trial and error. Then, close to the end of her second year, she reaches the stage of symbolic imitation and is able to incorporate a pretend object into her imitative play.

Preoperational stage (two to seven years) Operations is Piaget's term for thought. By this Piaget means the actions that take place in the mind rather than in the physical environment. Children in the preoperations stage of development have the advantage of their emergent language skills. Piaget noted that preoperational children have the ability to reconstruct past actions in the form of narration and to anticipate future actions through verbal representations. They can name or label objects and understand that these objects can be classified and grouped. Such grouping at this stage is by a single feature only. For instance, the child will place all the green blocks together regardless of their shape, or will group all the square blocks together regardless of their color.

Piaget delineated the preoperational years into the preconceptual period (ages two to four years) when the child first begins to use language and employ mental images, and the perceptual or intuitive period (ages four to seven years), where the child's level of reasoning is still symbolic and based on subjective intuition and appearances, rather than on objective logic or reasoning. At this stage the child believes that events happening simultaneously also have a cause-effect relationship. Everything is connected in the child's view of how the world works.

Thinking and perception in children younger than age seven is limited in many ways. They have not yet developed a full understanding of cause and effect relationships, but they have developed a high level of curiosity. This is when the child seems to always be asking "why?" They are beginning to seek logical explanations for the events that occur in the world around them.

The notion of animism, that inanimate objects are alive with attributes of consciousness and will, is evident in the child's thinking in this preoperational stage, as is the notion of artificialism, that human beings have made the natural world of mountains, lakes, trees, the moon and the sun.

Preoperational children understand the world in egocentric ways. They form their ideas of the world from their own direct experience, and from their own limited point of view. The child simply cannot understand how someone else's point of view might be different from his own, and is unable to coordinate how he sees the world with another person's perspective. Piaget considered the egocentrism of the preoperational child "as the main obstacle to the coordination of viewpoints and to cooperation." He stressed the importance of peer interaction as a means of freeing the child from the constraints of egocentrism.

A delightful aspect of the behavior of a preoperational child is the ability to engage in creative play. With this new skill of mental imagery, the progression to higher levels of thought can be seen in the child's increasing ability to represent reality through pretend play activity. The child can now pretend that a box is a table, a line of chairs is a train, and a leaf is a plate, for instance. Such imaginative play reaches a new level of abstractness when the child begins to encode experience as words. There is consistent correlation between pretend play and cognitive development and between pretend play and language development at the ages of two or three years.

With the egocentric thinking typical at this stage, children's play remains their own, even when they are playing together. This is known as parallel play. The child is aware, and even welcomes the company, of other children, but those children are not a necessary part of his particular game. A child's imagination and creativity is enhanced through play, which is a valuable component of cognitive, social, and emotional development.

Preoperational children have a clear understanding of the past and the future. They can remember a past experience and the emotions that accompanied that experience and are also able to anticipate a future event, and to anticipate possible outcomes.

Concrete operations stage (seven to 11 years) Children at this stage have developed the ability to perform mental operations, what Piaget called "interiorized action." Operations cause the child to decenter; that is, the child can now consider several attributes of an object or person at once rather than limiting concentration to a single attribute.

Mental operations such as the concepts of conservation of number, length, area, weight, and volume have been accomplished through the child's own manipulation and observation of concrete objects. Conservation means that the child has come to realize that certain attributes of an object or set of objects will remain constant even when they are made to look different. The various aspects of conservation develop sequentially throughout this stage in response to the child's continued observations and interactions with the world around her. Conservation of liquid volume, where the child can recognize a liquid is of the same quantity regardless of the shape of the glass it may be poured into, may not develop until as late as the age of twelve.

During this concrete operations stage, the child acquires the ability to think back, a concept known as reversibility. A child who has developed reversibility can literally retrace their mental and physical steps, for instance, to find an object that has been left behind. Children in the concrete operations stage can also successfully complete arithmetic operations, adding, subtracting, multiplying, and other forms of abstract thinking. Other concrete operational skills developed during this period include the classification of objects, telling time, and aligning objects systematically according to size.

However, at this stage children will continue to take life literally, so the use of satire or language metaphor is lost on them. A child at the stage of concrete operations can logically organize her experiences and understand the world from another person's perspective, but continues to live in the moment.

Formal operations (11 years to adult) Individuals who reach this stage of development now have the capacity for logical and abstract thinking and hypothetical, theoretical reasoning. They are capable of using logic to solve complex problems and can investigate a problem in a careful and systematic fashion, considering all factors that could affect an outcome. Not all children who grow into adulthood reach this stage of formal operations. Research has shown that this level of abstract thinking and theoretical reasoning may be reached by as few as 35% of adults. And not all persons who have acquired these skills of abstract thinking and hypothetical reasoning will operate from that level at all times.

The formal operations stage is characterized by an orderliness of thinking and a mastery of logical thought that allows for a more flexible kind of mental experimentation. The adolescent or young adult at this stage has learned to see the implications of his own thinking and that of others. He has constructed a value system and possesses a sense of moral judgment. In Piaget's view there are no additional mental strucures that will emerge in the individual. Development at this stage is a deepening of understanding.

Methodology

Piaget's empirical research took many forms throughout his career, depending on what aspect of cognitive development he was studying at the time. He employed techniques of careful, naturalistic observation of the child's spontaneous behavior. Sometimes this observation was without intervention; other times he introduced some form of verbal or motor stimulus to elicit a response. He attempted to follow the child's thought as he observed. Piaget and his coworkers then added experimental tasks for the child to complete. These tasks were designed in response to an idea or intuition that occurred to the observer as they followed the child's line of thought and observed behaviors. The tasks were intended to elicit pertinent and interpretable behavior that would further describe and explain the variety of intellectual structures children possess at distinct levels of development.

Piaget's earliest research began with French school boys, ages five to eight years, at the *École de la rue de la Grange-aux Belles* in Paris. He attempted through careful and respectful questioning to elicit information that would further reveal the workings of the curious minds of these children who first intrigued him with their patterns of wrong answers to the IQ tests he was hired to administer to them. He made systematic and detailed records of his findings as he watched and interacted with the children at play.

Piaget asked questions of the children in order to decipher the type of thinking they might be using. He called his experimental technique "the clinical method," which became his method of choice in working with children. Piaget's clinical method was similar to the diagnostic and therapeutic interviews

and informal exploration he learned while working in Bleuler's psychiatric clinic in France.

The willingness Piaget showed to engage his young research subjects at their own level often brought him to his knees where he observed and engaged with them in play. With children in the preoperational stage he explored how they think about the system of rules that pass from older children to younger ones, informing their play. He played marbles with the young boys, asking questions such as, "What do you mean by rules?" and "Where do the rules come from?" and "Who makes them up?" He sought to understand the emerging sense of morality inherent in the rules by which the children played the simple game.

When Piaget returned to Switzerland to become a research psychologist at the Jean-Jacques Rousseau Institute in Geneva in 1921, he continued to observe school children and began to articulate his ideas about how children develop reasoning, language, and morality in his first series of books, including *The Language and Thought of the Child*, published in 1923, and *The Judgment and Reasoning in the Child*, published in 1924. The books brought his preliminary and revolutionary research to the attention of the world's scientific community. At this point in his career, Piaget's investigations focused on how children develop reasoning skills and the mechanisms they employ as they satisfy their curiosity and gain new knowledge.

In 1925, Piaget, together with his wife, Valentine, also a research psychologist, began the painstaking observations and detailed recording of the cognitive development of their three children, a son and two daughters, from infancy through their teenage years. The couple documented the results of their careful observations of the children. Piaget published five new books about child psychology from these studies, including the 1936 publication *The Origins of Intelligence in Children*.

Piaget developed research methods to serve his intent to get "to the heart of the child's cognitive structure and describe it as it really is," according to John Flavell, writing about Piaget's rationale in his book, *The Developmental Psychology of Jean Piaget*.

"One simply must adopt a technique, whatever its hazards and difficulties, which permits the child to move on his own intellectually, to display the cognitive orientation which is natural to him at that period in his development," Flavell wrote, explaining the rationale of Piaget's early methodology. Piaget also understood some of the dangers and difficulties in his clinical method, as he is quoted in Flavell's book:

> The good experimenter must, in fact, unite two often incompatible qualities; he must know how to observe, that is to say, to let the child talk freely, without ever checking or side-tracking his utterance, and at the same time he must constantly be alert for something definitive; at every moment he must have some working hypothesis, some theory, true or false, which he is seeking to check.

As his studies in genetic epistemology continued, Piaget tried to adapt his methodology to the special problems involved in using children as subjects in perceptual experiments. Piaget employed what he and his coworkers called the clinical concentric method. In this method, according to Flavell, the experimenter presents a series of stimuli of different values and requires the subject to judge each of these stimuli with respect to some standard stimulus (greater than, less than, or equal to the standard). Piaget developed techniques to discover and demonstrate the cognitive abilities and developmental markers at each stage of the child's intellectual growth.

Examples

Three mountains task   To explore the egocentric way of thinking so typical in the preoperational stage, Piaget used what he called the three mountains task. He positioned children in front of a three dimensional model of a mountain range, then seated himself to the side. He then presented the child with a set of four photographs of the mountains as displayed in the papier-mâché model and asked them to pick out the view of the mountains that they believed the professor could see from his seat. Consistently, children in the preoperations stage will choose the picture depicting the view from their own perspective and not that of Piaget. Children who have progressed into the concrete operations stage will consistently choose the photograph taken from the experimenter's point of view.

Conservation studies   Piaget tested for the concept of conservation of liquid volume with differently shaped glasses. He poured equal amounts of liquid into glasses of a different height and width. The child in the preoperational stage, who still relies on perceptual information rather than logic to form their opinions, will consistently insist that the liquid in a thin, tall glass holds more than an equal amount of liquid poured into a wide, shallow bowl. A child demonstrates a grasp of the concept of conservation of liquid when they can recognize that both vessels, regardless of shape, hold the same amount of liquid. This skill is developed in the concrete operations stage.

Piaget tested for the concept of conservation of number with coins. He placed two sets of coins on a table in parallel lines. Each line contained the same number of coins, but in one line Piaget spread the coins farther apart than in the other. When asked which line contained the most coins, children younger than seven years old consistently choose the line in which the coins are spread farther apart. They will persist in this belief, despite being shown, by stacking the coins, that each set contains an equal number. A child demonstrates a grasp of the concept of conservation of number when they can recognize that each line of coins contains an equal number, no matter how they are arranged.

Piaget used clay to demonstrate two concepts, that of conservation of substance and reversibility, two developmental tasks of the concrete operational stage. In this experiment he first obtains the child's agreement that two balls of soft clay are of equal size. Then he rolled one ball of clay into a long cylinder or sausage-like shape. Placing the two masses of clay side by side, the ball shape alongside the cylinder shape, he asks the child again if they are of equal quantity. If the child has acquired the skill of conservation of substance, she can now answer correctly what she could not grasp earlier. She now comprehends that the substance is conserved regardless of the changes in shape it may undergo. This recognition also is evidence of the child's grasp of the concept of reversibility. She has acquired the skill to follow in her mind the changing form and shape of the clay and can then think back to that same clay when it was a round ball and recognize it has having the same quantity.

Questions and answers   Piaget posed simple questions in his clinical interview style to determine if a child had passed beyond the stage of seeing all objects as animate, or alive, a concept called animism. He questioned children in the preoperational stage to determine their perceptions of the aliveness of objects. He wanted to determine the types of objects the child would our would not classify as alive.

"Does the sun know it gives light?" he asked, or "When I pull off this button will it feel it?" The children's answers varied throughout the developmental stage. The number and type of objects they endowed with consciousness declined with the age of the child and the increased experience with the outside world.

Piaget questioned adolescents to determine if they had made the transition from the concrete operational stage to the stage of formal operations with its capacity for hypothetical deductive reasoning. He asked why a pendulum swings faster or slower.

Individuals who have achieved the formal operations stage will test the pendulum by systematic variations of one factor at a time, holding the others as a constant, to determine each factor's effect on the pendulum's motion. Adolescents who have not yet reached the formal operations stage will vary more than one factor as they struggle to find a solution to the question, making an accurate conclusion unlikely.

Through his interactive observations and empirical research, Piaget demonstrated that the developing intellect of the child is self-motivated and energized by the need to satisfy curiosity. To Piaget, thought is a process in continual transformation and reorganization. Children construct their own knowledge, Piaget said, through their action in, and on, the world. Like Maria Montessori, whom Piaget studied, Piaget believed that when children are allowed to act on the environment, performing the tasks themselves rather than merely being told how things work, they are better able to construct a more comprehensive scheme as their thinking evolves from the concrete to the abstract.

Philosophy: The constructivist's vision

"I am a constructivist." Piaget wrote. "I think that knowledge is a matter of constant, new construction, by its interaction with reality and that it is not preformed. There is a continuous creativity." As a constructivist, part of the philosophical school of structuralism, Piaget understood learning as an active process in which new ideas or concepts are constructed based on current or past knowledge. The individual selects and transforms information, constructs hypotheses, and makes decisions, relying on a cognitive structure that provides meaning and organization to the experiences. For Piaget, constructivism means that an individual always and only learns through constructing. He maintained that biological maturation provides the range of potential for cognitive growth, but developing the ability to perform operations requires an active, supportive environment and social interactions that encourage children to construct their own knowledge. Piaget also understood that there is no beginning and no end to the construction of knowledge. The individual is continuously acquiring and modifying skills.

Michael J. Mahoney, writing on the Constructivism site on the World Wide Web has outlined five basic themes that are found throughout the diversity of theories that express constructivism. These are active agency, order, self, social-symbolic relatedness, and lifespan development.

"Jean Piaget developed a model of cognitive development in which balance was central. Piaget described knowing as a quest for a dynamic balance between what is familiar and what is novel," Mahoney writes, "We organize our worlds by organizing ourselves. This theme of developmental self organization pervades constructive views of human experience."

The methods of constructivism that Piaget advanced in his theories of genetic epistemology continue to inform and challenge educational technology today. Though Piaget did not see himself as an educator, he did have some advice for teachers. He told interviewer Richard Evans that he hoped his work would influence teachers to begin "educating for an experimental frame of mind." It is important, he said, that teachers present children with materials and situations and occasions that allow them to move forward. "It is not a matter of just allowing children to do anything. It is a matter of presenting to the child situations which offer new problems, problems that follow on from one another. You need a mixture of direction and freedom."

HISTORICAL CONTEXT

Twentieth-century psychological theories

Piaget's professional life spanned a tumultuous six decades of the mid twentieth century, during a time of rapid growth and development in the scientific disciplines. Piaget read widely in the fields of philosophy and psychology. He was influenced in his reading by the ideas of Immanuel Kant (1724–1804), whose concept of categories was a precedent for later psychological theories using terms such as "constructs" and "schemes." He was also influenced by Henri Bergson (1859–1941), whose book *Creative Evolution* changed Piaget's thinking about the nature of life. Other philosophers and thinkers in the nineteenth century also influenced Piaget's thinking, including Charles Darwin, John Dewey, Emil Durkheim, and James Mark Baldwin, from whom Piaget borrowed the phrase genetic epistemology to describe his theory of the acquisition of knowledge.

Piaget was fortunate to meet many of the influential European psychologists of his day. He studied with Carl Jung, shared the podium with Sigmund Freud at the 1922 Congress of Psychoanalysis in Berlin, had conversations with Albert Einstein, worked as a research associate at the Simon-Binet laboratory in Paris, knew Maria Montessori, and met

Robert Oppenheimer and the Gestalt psychologists Max Wertheimer and Wolfgang Köhler.

Much of the seminal writing of the era, particularly that of the early Gestalt thinkers and the constructivist theories of the Russian psychologist Lev Vygotsky, was unavailable to Piaget early in his career because of language barriers. His own later work was not made available in translation in the United States until well after World War II. Not one of his books was translated into English between 1932 and 1950. This was due, in part, to the prevailing influences of the behavioral psychologists in the United States, whose stimulus-response views Piaget did not embrace. France was under German occupation during parts of World War II, and this further restricted the free flow of ideas within the global scientific community. During the occupation of France in 1942, Piaget lectured at the College of France. He later remarked that his invitation to lecture during the German occupation enabled him to bring to his French colleagues, "testimony of the unshakable affection of their friends from the outside."

Piaget shared the point of view of the constructivists, and, with some differences in approach, engaged in the study of cognitive development in ways similar to John Dewey, Lev Vygotsky, Jerome Bruner, Maria Montessori, and others. These psychologists believed that children actively construct knowledge and that this construction happens within a social context. Piaget also felt a kinship in his work with the theories of Edward Tolman (1886–1959), whose work attempted a synthesis of Gestalt psychology and behaviorism, and with other Gestalt psychologists and their ideas regarding the "totalities" of cognitive structure.

The dramatic shift in psychology from behaviorism to cognitivism that began in the early part of the twentieth century was greatly influenced by the work of one of Piaget's American contemporaries, Jerome Bruner. Bruner was instrumental in bringing Piaget to the United States at a time when psychologists and educators were losing confidence in the field of behaviorism, which had dominated American educational psychology for decades. Behaviorism was starting to be viewed as far too limited with its reduction of learning to a reactive stimulus-response relationship. Piaget had a different view of learning than behaviorist B.F. Skinner. To Piaget, learning is first of all an active process, one that is linked to specific stages of development and includes both external and internal, self-regulating reinforcements.

Piaget traveled to the United States on numerous occasions to lecture on his theories and to accept honorary degrees from prestigious universities. After World War II his books were finally translated and available to American scholars, further encouraging the growth of the emerging science of cognitive development that increasingly attracted students and psychologists to his Geneva research laboratories. Piaget was a man whose time had come.

CRITICAL RESPONSE

Contributions and shortcomings

Extensive criticisms of Piaget's work have been voiced in the scientific community throughout the 60 years that he labored to develop and articulate his theory of genetic epistemology and in the decades since his death in 1980. Despite the shortcomings that many critics point out in Piaget's work, few have disputed the considerable contributions of his theory to scientific thought, or his role as one of the most influential research psychologists of the twentieth century. Piaget is respected, even by his critics, for transforming how we think about children. His foundational work continues to influence educational theory throughout the world. Piaget's work has been characterized as the starting point for many different strands of theoretical investigation in the area of education and developmental psychology.

General criticisms of Piaget's theory include:

- complexity of his writing style
- flawed methodology
- qualitative rather than quantitative interpretation of findings
- rigidity of developmental stages
- failure to consider variables of culture, race, gender, etc.
- lack of longitudinal or life-span studies
- underestimation of the intelligence of young children
- the fact that not everyone in every culture reaches the formal operations stage
- possibility of development beyond formal operations

Piaget's theoretical writings total as many as 120,000 pages, according to Jacques Voneche, Professor of Child and Adolescent Psychology at

The University of Geneva and Director of Jean Piaget Archives. Piaget wrote in an abstract way, according to Professor John Flavell, who provided the first English language summary of Piaget's theory in his definitive book *The Developmental Psychology of Jean Piaget*. Most of Piaget's publications were from largely unedited materials, delivered to the printer in handwritten drafts. This extensive body of writing is difficult to assimilate, in part because of the complexities of his writing style. He uses complicated sentence structures and introduces new terms and concepts, while redefining the meaning of other familiar terms. According to N. R. Carlson and W. Buskist, writing in the 1997 edition of *Psychology: the Science of Behavior*, "One criticism leveled at Piaget is that he did not always define his terms operationally. Consequently, it is difficult for others to interpret the significance of his generalizations."

Piaget's original work is in French and not all translations interpret his concepts consistently. Professor Flavell used the term "opaqueness" with regard to Piaget's writing. The lack of clarity, or "communicative inadequacy," as Flavell called it, has created a barrier to the understanding of this important body of work. Flavell believes that this is a most unfortunate handicap in a cognitive theory that contributed so significantly to a revolution of thought in twentieth century psychology.

Much of the early research with regard to Piaget's theories reported in Flavell's 1963 book was concerned with replication and validation of his theories. Piaget left a lot of room for concern with what Flavell called a "habitual failure to give a clear and full account of precisely what he did in the experiment." Still another criticism is with regard to Piaget's analysis of his data. He did not provide a sufficient quantitative evaluation of his findings. Without statistical analysis of the results, the findings are difficult to interpret or compare with other studies. Subsequent researchers, uncertain about the empirical basis for his experimental conclusions, focused on replication and validation, rather than on elaboration of the work that Piaget began. Piaget "simply did not conduct and report his research in such a way as to make a very convincing case," Flavell explained. Nonetheless, these early researchers, for the most part, were able to validate most of the essentials of Piaget's conclusions.

Flavell's criticism, and that of others, extends to Piaget's theoretical conclusions, particularly with regard to the stages of cognitive development. Flavell contends that Piaget has "attributed too much

system and structure to the child's thought." He proposes theoretical changes that reflect a "somewhat looser clustering of operations." Flavell believed such an adjustment to Piaget's stage structure might free it from what he called its "rigidity and maladaptability."

Annette Karmiloff-Smith, professor of neurocognitive development at the Institute of Child Health in London began her career as a member of the International Centre for Genetic Epistemology run by Jean Piaget. From 1972 to 1980 she worked on normal cognitive development across various areas of cognition, publishing several research papers with Barbel Inhelder. Professor Karmiloff-Smith has recently criticized Piaget's stage theory of cognitive development, which she considers "almost obsolete." Speaking on a BBC radio interview in 2003, she commented, "there are more structures to the brain than Piaget ever imagined."

Another major criticism of Piaget concerns the empirical aspects of his work. Many believe that his research methodology was flawed. Piaget relied on observation, the clinical interview, and the administration of certain tasks at each developmental stage to formulate his theory. In this way he hoped to discover and delineate the characteristic behaviors and perceptions that determine cognitive growth. The unstructured clinical interview style that Piaget favored, using a question and answer format to elicit information about the child's thinking, has been criticized by many who study his work. British researcher J. G. Wallace believed that the "ambiguity of verbal response" may have been used by Piaget "to derive support for his preconception."

Other critics have expressed concern with the limited samples Piaget used to develop his broad assertions about the progress of all children. Critics also point to Piaget's lack of cross-cultural subjects in his investigations, and the fact that he did not consider other variables of social factor, such as personality, race, gender, and nationality, nor did his investigations follow individuals throughout their lifespan. Piaget's first five books were largely based on detailed observations of his own three children from infancy through their teen years. Though Piaget considered these books as only preliminary, they were widely read and brought him early fame. Young researchers from throughout the world came to work with him in his Geneva laboratory.

Lev Vygotsky

One of the earliest and by some accounts best of Piaget's critics was the Russian scientist Lev

Stages in the Development of the Personality

Stage	Age (Years)							
	1	2	3	4	5	6	7	8
VIII								INTEGRITY vs. DESPAIR
VII							GENERATIVITY vs. STAGNATION	
VI						INTIMACY vs. ISOLATION		
V	Temporal Perspective vs. Time Confusion	Self-Certainty vs. Self-Consciousness	Role Experimentation vs. Role Fixation	Apprenticeship vs. Work Paralysis	IDENTITY vs. IDENTITY CONFUSION	Sexual Polarization vs. Bisexual Confusion	Leader- and Followership vs. Authority Confusion	Ideological Commitment vs. Confusion of Values
IV				INDUSTRY vs. INFERIORITY	Task Identification vs. Sense of Futility			
III			INITIATIVE vs. GUILT		Anticipation of Roles vs. Role Inhibition			
II		AUTONOMY vs. SHAME, DOUBT			Will to be Oneself vs. Self-Doubt			
I	TRUST vs. MISTRUST				Mutual Recognition vs. Autistic Isolation			

SOURCE: Table from Erikson, Erik H. "The Life Cycle: Epigenesis of Identity," *Identity: Youth and Crisis*, W. W. Norton: New York, 1968, 94.

Erik Erikson's stages of personality development. (Courtesy Thomson Gale.)

Vygotsky. He was born in 1896, the same year as Piaget, and like Piaget became prominent while still a young man. Unlike Piaget, Vygotsky died early, of tuberculosis at the age of 34. Vygotsky was a linguist and educator interested in the origins and mechanisms of knowledge. In the 10 years prior to his death, Vygotsky set down a comprehensive theory of cognitive development, providing many alternatives to Piaget's work. Though Vygotsky had access to Piaget's writings, the language barrier kept Piaget from reading Vygotsky's criticisms until decades after the Soviet researcher died.

There are many similarities in the two men's views. Piaget pointed to biological development as the process that impels movement from one stage to the next. Vygotsky agreed that individuals pass through distinct stages of development, but stressed the importance of historical and cultural forces on the individuals' ability to reach or move through each developmental stage. This cultural context of learning is an important element in Vygotsky's theory. Like Piaget, he understood that experience with physical objects is a necessary element in cognitive growth, but Vygotsky also noted the important part played by the use of tools. Both theorists recognized the child as an active agent who constructs his own reality, but Vygotsky was an educator who understood learning as a cooperative venture of both teacher and child. Learning, to Vygotsky, is co-constructed. He put forth the concept of a "zone of proximal development," the gap existing between the limit of what a child can learn acting alone and the extent to which a child can learn with the help of an adult or other more capable peers.

As a linguist Vygotsky considered language as the basis for cognitive development. He paid particular attention to the role of gestures in language acquisition. Like Piaget, Vygotsky rejected the mechanistic theories of behaviorism. He believed that it was language that helps human beings break the stimulus-response cycle and gain control over their environment. The child's earliest attempts at speech, often indecipherable to adults, nonetheless assists the developing child with memory, problem solving, and even in making plans for the future. Piaget viewed the child's self-talk as primarily an indication of the cognitive limitation he called "egocentric." Vygotsky, on the other hand, believed that such child's talk reflects the formation of a plan that would modify the child's subsequent behaviors.

Discovery learning at any stage

Jerome Bruner, a Harvard professor and Director of the Center for Cognitive Studies, developed a stage theory of cognitive growth that differs from Piaget with regard to the impact of environmental and experiential factors on the developing child. Bruner's theories were influenced by Vygotsky, particularly with regard to his emphasis on the importance of the social and political environment. Bruner understood that the process of constructing knowledge of the world is not accomplished in isolation. He emphasizes the importance of the social context within which learning takes place. Bruner helped to define the concept of discovery learning, defined by J. Ormrod as "an approach to instruction thorough which students interact with their environment by exploring and manipulating objects, wrestling with questions and controversies, or performing experiments."

Bruner's sociocognitive stage theory of learning is based on the child's reciprocal interaction with the teacher. He has departed from Piaget's idea of developmental readiness for learning with the hypothesis "that any subject can be taught effectively in some intellectually honest form to any child at any stage of development."

Making "human sense"

Margaret Donaldson of Edinburgh University put forth yet another criticism of Piaget's method, claiming the he used unfamiliar concepts and objects to test the cognitive development of the children he worked with, and that this led to the misinterpretation of their cognitive skill levels. The tasks proposed to the child and the language used to describe them need to make "human

sense," she said. Donaldson, a child development psychologist, visited Piaget's research center in Geneva where she attended seminars and observed actual testing. She has criticized what she described as "contrived experimental work," that provides the experimenter with only one view of the child. Donaldson and others tested Piaget's theories on preschool children and concluded that the reason these children were unable to perform Piaget's tasks successfully was primarily due to their difficulties understanding the questions being asked of them, rather than a lack of logical skills or the cognitive limitations of what Piaget called "egocentric" behavior. Donaldson took issue with Piaget's findings, particularly with regard to his three mountains task, in her 1978 book *Children's Minds*. When the researcher uses more familiar items and language, children may perform beyond Piaget's stages. Young children are capable of much more than Piaget ever gave them credit, she contends. There is now a significant theoretical work that suggests children perform beyond Piaget's levels when using more familiar testing tools.

Out of sight, not out of mind

Renee Baillargeon, professor of psychology at the University of Illinois at Urbana-Champaign, has tested Piaget's concept of object permanence, the out of sight, out of mind perception that Piaget considered a cognitive limitation of the early sensorimotor stage. In a 1997 study Baillargeon and others demonstrated that infants as young as three and one half months of age can remember a toy (a Mr. Potato Head) after it has been hidden from sight.

In two later experiments published in 2003, Baillargeon and others tested four-month-old infants in what she termed "violation of expectation," or VOE tasks.

> The infants still gave evidence that they could represent and reason about hidden objects: they were surprised, as indicated by greater attention, when a wide object became fully hidden behind a narrow occluder (Experiment 1) or inside a narrow container (Experiment 2).

Unlike previous tests, in these experiments the infants were not first given "habituation or familiarization trials," but only a single test trial. Baillargeon's research provides additional support for the conclusion in her previous studies that "young infants possess expectations about hidden objects." Her experiments have shown that very young infants already are learning concepts of object permanence relative to visible and hidden objects before Piaget believed they were developmentally able to do so.

Spatial learning

Janellen Huttenlocher, a professor of Psychology at the University of Chicago, and the 2002 recipient of the G. Stanley Hall Award for Distinguished Contribution to Developmental Psychology, is a leading researcher on spatial learning. Her studies have shown that children acquire an understanding of spatial information much earlier than Piaget proposed. Infants as young as six months, she said, are able to use the inborn ability of dead reckoning skills to understand the location of objects around them. By the time they reach their first birthday, children can comprehend distance enough to locate hidden objects. Huttenlocher suggests that growth in spatial understanding develops through a combination of the child's innate abilities, a process of trial and error interaction with the environment, and the child's cultural environment. She suggests an "interactionist" approach to spatial development that will incorporate and integrate the insights of Piaget, who believed infants develop knowledge of space through trial and error experience; the nativists' approach that holds that the basic intelligence of spatial understanding is innate; and Vygotsky's emphasis on the cultural transmission of spatial skills.

Huttenlocher is investigating how teachers can influence the development of the intellectual skill of spatial understanding, and with other researchers is using computer games to investigate students' navigational skills and their ability to perform "mental rotation" tasks. She is also developing computer software to help students sketch maps as a way of further developing a spatially mature intellect.

A higher law

Children define morality individually, according to Piaget, and this occurs in the process of their struggles to arrive at fair solutions. He theorized that the way children learn respect for rules is by playing rule-bound games. Mary Elizabeth Murray, of the Department of Psychology at the University of Illinois at Chicago, acknowledged that "Jean Piaget is among the first psychologists whose work remains directly relevant to contemporary theories of moral development."

Lawrence Kohlberg (1927–1987) studied with Jean Piaget. He did most of his later research at Harvard University, where he worked to modify and elaborate on Piaget's work, particularly with regard to the issues of moral development. Kohlberg extended the development of moral judgment beyond the ages studied by Piaget, according to psychologist Mary Murray, "and laid the groundwork for the current debate within psychology on moral development." He determined that the process of attaining moral maturity was a longer and more gradual one than Piaget first theorized.

Kohlberg investigated 84 schoolboys in a longitudinal study that followed the boys development over a period of 20 years. Kohlberg concluded that an even more advanced stage of cognitive development, beyond Piaget's formal operations stage, may be reached by some adolescents. In this advanced stage, the individual will perceive the rule of law as valid only if it serves a purpose greater than oneself or those in one's circle of care. For a law to be obeyed it must also serve universal moral or religious values. Kohlberg found that only 5% of the student population he studied had attained this stage of moral understanding.

Kohlberg's six stages of moral development include:

- Stage one: The punishment and obedience orientation. The physical consequences of action determine its goodness or badness regardless of the human meaning or value of these consequences.

- Stage two: The instrumental relativist orientation. Right action consists of what instrumentally satisfies one's own needs and occasionally the needs of others.

- Stage three: The interpersonal concordance or "good boy-nice girl" orientation. Good behavior is what pleases or helps others and is approved by them.

- Stage four: The "law and order" orientation. The individual is oriented toward authority, fixed rules, and the maintenance of the social order.

- Stage five: The social-contract legalistic orientation (generally with utilitarian overtones). Right action tends to be defined in terms of general individual rights and standards that have been critically examined and agreed upon by the whole society.

- Stage six: The universal ethical-principle orientation. Right is defined by the decision of conscience in accord with self-chosen ethical principles that appeal to logical comprehensiveness, universality, and consistency.

Carol Gilligan, writing in her 1982 book *In A Different Voice*, criticizes both Piaget and Kohlberg's work in the area of moral development as being biased against girls and women. She is concerned with Piaget's "bias that leads him to equate male development with child development," particularly in his studies of childhood games, and with Kohlberg's bias in studying only boys in his longitudinal investigations of moral development leading to his six-stage theory.

Piaget observed that young girls play differently from boys. Boys are more concerned with rules, and girls with relationships, Gilligan says. If the study of moral development would begin from the lives of women, Gilligan writes, the moral problems would be characterized as those "arising from conflicting responsibilities rather than from competing rights." Such moral questions would require for solution "a mode of thinking that is contextual and narrative rather than formal and abstract."

In contrast to Gilligan's views, Mary Elizabeth Murray contends that "the preponderance of evidence is that both males and females reason based on justice and care."

Many thousands of studies

One of the marks of a good theory is in the amount of research it stimulates, and within this criteria, Piaget's theory is truly great. Many thousands of research studies throughout the world have been published in scientific journals regarding Jean Piaget's theories of genetic epistemology. In 1974 an eight-volume set of compilation and commentary referenced over 3,500 studies. In the 30 years since those volumes appeared, Piagetian research has continued, particularly in the area of the application and utility of genetic epistemology to the fields of early childhood education, including the acquisition of morality. A vast body of research has arisen to test Piaget's theories and confirm or refute his claims.

The beginning student of Piaget has a daunting task in assimilating the complex theory of genetic epistemology. It is an additional challenge to distinguish the most relevant studies from among the thousands that have been done, and to find those investigators whose critical work will either validate, refute, or extend Piaget's findings in a way that will further the understanding of the origin and nature of knowledge, and not confound the search.

THEORIES IN ACTION

In a 1970 interview with Elizabeth Hall in *Psychology Today*, Jean Piaget addressed the question of the practical applications of his theory of genetic epistemology.

> The danger to psychologists lies in practical applications. Too often psychologists make practical applications before they know what they are applying. We must always keep a place for fundamental research and beware of practical applications when we do not know the foundation of our theories.

Piaget's caution is well taken. Since the late 1950s, when his writings were translated for readers in the United States, his influential ideas have been applied widely and survived extensive criticism. Piaget's theory of genetic epistemology changed the educational philosophy of the mid-twentieth century by providing a scientific basis for understanding how learning happens. His comprehensive theory remains vital today.

Decades after his death, Piaget's revolutionary insights and innovative theories continue to stimulate volumes of research and academic discussion published in scientific journals throughout the world. His interdisciplinary approach to the discovery of the nature and origin of knowledge informs numerous fields of scientific thought today, from educational psychology and learning theory to computer technology and artificial intelligence. Parents, educators, child-care workers, pediatricians, child psychologists, and software designers all benefit from the work of Piaget and his many collaborators.

In the classroom

Piaget's influence has been extensive in the field of education, particularly in the areas of teaching practice and curriculum design. Piaget never considered himself to be an educator and had little to say regarding the practice of education. Nonetheless, this Swiss innovator's many insights into how children learn have been studied and applied throughout the educational system. Piaget helped educators understand the importance of novelty and active participation in learning, as well as the value of collaborative learning in a sensory rich environment. Piaget's theory offers an understanding of students' developmental readiness and insight into ways a teacher can facilitate a child's growth to more complex cognitive levels. Both are vital components to developing a child-centered, child-directed curriculum. Piaget's findings about the distinctions between concrete and abstract thinking, and the general ages at which these skills predominate, has had tremendous influence on when and how science and mathematics are presented to children.

Teachers who understand Piaget know that the very young student learns through trial and error and needs access to a diversity of objects for manipulation. As the child becomes older and has progressed into the concrete-operational stage, a teacher influenced by Piaget's theories will know to present the child with problems of classification, ordering, location, and conservation. Teachers facilitate cognitive development by providing activities that engage learners, challenge their existing beliefs, and stimulate adaptation to new levels of understanding. Teachers applying Piaget's insights will make the learning environment interesting with support for exploratory activity and peer interactions, and keep the focus on projects that require solutions to real-life, practical problems.

Jean Piaget believed in the power of knowledge and the importance of children learning to think for themselves, as architects of their own destinies.

> If we desire to form individuals capable of inventive thought and of helping the society of tomorrow to achieve progress, then it is clear that an education which is an active discovery of reality is superior to one that consists merely in providing the young with ready-made wills to will with and ready-made truths to know with.

Research Marie Anne Suizzo, writing in the journal *Child Development* in 2000, cited a 1996 study by researchers Robbie Case and Yukari Okamoto that explored the cross-cultural attainment of Piaget's formal operations stage of abstract reasoning. They administered Piagetian tasks to determine the developmental stage of individuals tested and concluded that "children, and even adults who live in societies where the base ten number system is not in use, or where formal schooling is not available to all, do not usually attain the level of formal operational thought normally reached by adults in industrial societies."

Teachers who understand Piaget's work are aware that direct instruction may fail if it is not appropriate to the stage of the child's cognitive capacity, and that not all persons will attain Piaget's stage of formal operations.

Cyberspace

Educators have realized that for students to be successful in the twenty-first century, they need to acquire the skills to become lifelong learners. Lifelong learning is a concept with which Piaget would have been comfortable, though he may not have anticipated the tremendous advances in technology that are bringing a revolution to how students acquire information and interact with the world.

"Twenty-first century children can access more information at greater speed than any generation in history," says Wilborn Hampton, an editor at the *New York Times*, writing about children, television, and the Internet. He cautions that teachers and parents must teach this "fledgling generation of the cyberspace age to look beyond the first answer they get." His caution, like Piaget's regarding the application of his theories, is worth remembering in this age of artificial intelligence and worldwide connectivity through the Internet. The Internet is a goldmine of information and resources on virtually any topic imaginable. Specialized search engines assist in computer-assisted learning and retrieval of information, and the interactive multimedia encyclopedias and CD-ROM technology can provide a rich and stimulating learning experience with opportunity for both collaborative and individual learning. Tools such as word processors, spreadsheets, databases, and drawing programs enable a student to publish the results of their explorations, reaching beyond the classroom to a potentially vast number of learners with whom they can share and discuss their discoveries.

Computer-supported collaborative learning and the Internet have extended Piaget's ideas of lifelong learning in ways even this creative genius many never have imagined. "ThinkQuest," is an international competition where student teams engage in collaborative, project-based learning to create educational websites. The winning entries received from students throughout the world form the ThinkQuest online library. Computer programs such as "Cybrid" CDs add the expert help of cyberspace teachers and experts who are available at the click of a mouse.

One of Piaget's collaborators, Jean Papret, now a professor of education and media technology at the MIT Media Laboratory, called Piaget a "towering figure and a major theorist of how the mind works." Speaking at a symposium on computers in education at MIT in 2002, Papert said, "the essence of Piaget was how much learning occurs without being planned or organized by teachers or schools." Papret has focused his study on how individuals learn to learn. His interest has been in the tools, media, and context of learning. Papret shares Piaget's view that the child actively constructs knowledge by interaction with her world, and he has taken his understanding of cognitive development into the realm of artificial intelligence. Papret says he started out in the field of artificial intelligence with the questions, "Can we make a machine to rival human intelligence? Can we make a machine so we can understand intelligence in general?"

Papret is a constructionist, who shares Piaget's constructivist view, but adds the insight that learning is enhanced in a context where the learner finds a way to share those ideas with the wider community. Papret believes that it is important to make ideas tangible, to shape and sharpen them by making them public in some way. He studied how knowledge is formed, transformed, processed, and expressed through different media. Papret was involved in early research into artificial intelligence. Now, he says, "I see my contribution as helping to birth a perspective on learning: not 'education' or 'school,' but a field that is bigger and essentially different from anything that has existed."

A scientific society formed in 1979, the American Association for Artificial Intelligence (AAAI), is "devoted to advancing the scientific understanding of the mechanisms underlying thought and intelligent behavior and their embodiment in machines." This seems to echo Piaget's genetic epistemology with a quest for what might be called mechanistic epistemology. The study of artificial intelligence seems to be asking some the same questions Piaget posed to children.

David Wood, writing in his book, *How Children Think and Learn* notes that "Communication between man and machine and skillful control of complex systems demands designs that do not overtax or exceed people's abilities to attend to, monitor, and react to the behavior of the system under control." He sees the necessity for application of cognitive development principles to systems design. "Any system that provides too much critical information at any one moment or which leaves the human operator with too little time to interpret and react to it makes inhuman demands and cannot be controlled."

Case study
Piaget recognized the importance of play, and the necessity for children to handle and explore objects to find out how they work. Play is the fundamental way children construct their theories about how the world works.Over the years since Piaget's innovative research with children, toys have changed. In the 1980s computer toys that dramatically altered the way children play began to appear on the market.

Sherry Turkle, a professor in the program in science, technology, and society at MIT, has studied the relationship between children and their electronic pets and computer toys over three generations. She has observed in her studies the emergence of a new consciousness among children who play with computer toys. "Cyborg consciousness," Turkle says, is "a tendency to see computer systems as 'sort of' alive, to fluidly cycle through various explanatory concepts, and to willingly transgress boundaries."

In her early research Turkle observed that "children described the life-like status of machines in terms of cognitive capacities (the toys could 'know' things, 'solve' puzzles)." But in her research with a later generation of computer toys, the Virtual pets and digital dolls of the 1990s, Turkle sees a blurring of boundaries with what children consider to be alive. These toys require an interaction that necessitates some form of nurturance from the child. When children play with these new computerized toys, Turkle's observations show, they seek a feeling of mutual recognition. They want to know how to make the toy happy. The furry and cuddly electronic pets, called Furbies, "add the dimensions of human-like conversation and tender companionship to the mix," Turkle says. The children consider Furbies as "sort of alive." This belief, Turkle says, "reflects their emotional attachments to the toys and their fantasies that the Furby might be emotionally attached to them."

These children of the computer age will, perhaps, construct quite a different reality than the Paris school boys who Piaget first sat down with to observe their simple game of marbles. Watching children at play led him to an understanding of how children's rules of fair play relate to the development of a moral consciousness. Researchers are just beginning to ask how these new interactive toys, embedded with artificial intelligence and feigned affection, will affect the psychological processes of twenty-first century children and the evolution of their world view.

Moral and ethical applications
Piaget's work with children led him to investigate the realm of moral reasoning. His initial work has inspired other researchers to pursue the questions of moral and ethical judgement with Piagetian theory as a starting point.

Research In a 2000 study titled "Older isn't wiser in moral reasoning," reported in *Science News*, psychologists Lakshmi Raman and Gerald Winder of Ohio State University tested Piaget's findings on the evolution of moral reasoning, particularly with regard to the

CHRONOLOGY

1896: Jean Piaget born in Neuchatel, Switzerland.

1906: Publishes first article in local journal.

1918: Receives Ph.D. in Natural Sciences, University of Neuchatel, as Zoologist; He attends the University of Zurich for postgraduate studies. He works in Eugen Bleuler's psychiatric clinic and develops his technique of the clinical interview.

1919: Works as research associate in Simon-Binet experimental psychology laboratory administering British IQ tests to Paris school boys.

1921: Appointed research director of the *Institut Jean-Jacques Rousseau* in Geneva, and publishes article in the *Archives de Psychologie* stating that logic is not innate but develops over time through interactive processes of self-regulation.

1923: Marries psychologist and former student Valentine Chatenay and publishes *The Language and Thought of the Child*. Four more books follow bringing him worldwide fame before the age of 30.

1925: Returns to Neuchatel University. Daughter Jacqueline is born and the Piaget's begin the study of the intellectual development of their three children from infancy through their teenage years.

1928: Albert Einstein and Piaget meet. Einstein suggests that Piaget study the origins in children of the notions of time and simultaneity.

1929: Teaches the history of scientific thought at the University of Geneva until 1939. Begins thirty-five year tenure as director of the International Bureau of Education in Geneva.

1936: Publishes *The Origins of Intelligence in Children* based on his observations of his three children.

1940: Appointed Chair of Experimental Psychology, University of Geneva (until 1971).

1942: Lectures at the College of France during Nazi occupation. Lectures complied into *The Psychology of Intelligence* published in 1963.

1950: Publishes his three volume book, *Introduction a l'Epistemologie Genetique*.

1955: Jean Piaget's International Center for Genetic Epistemology opens at the University of Geneva.

1966: Piaget publishes *The Psychology of the Child* with Barbel Inhelder.

1969: Piaget is awarded distinguished Scientific Contribution Award by the American Psychological Association. He is the first European to receive the award.

1980: Jean Piaget dies at the age of 84 in Geneva, Switzerland.

---

idea of immanent, or inherent, justice, the "what goes around, comes around," notion. In their cross-cultural study the researchers presented the students with the story of a robber who contracts a mysterious deadly disease. They asked the students if they believed that the reason the robber became ill was because he was bad. They posed the question to sixth grade students and college students in both the United States and India. The results surprised them. Contrary to what Piaget's theory would suggest, it was the college students who agreed most often that the robber became ill because he was bad, an expression of the idea of immanent justice that, according to Piaget's findings, they should have long ago outgrown. The

researchers concluded that even though the sixth grade children may understand the biological basis of illness, over time they will become socialized into acceptance of the "irrational idea of immanent justice."

In 1988, authors Iordanis Kavathatzopoulos and Georgios Rigas published a study in the journal of *Educational and Psychological Measurement* in which they sought to describe how individual politicians solve moral problems. They used Piaget's theory as a frame for development of a measurement device they called the Ethical Competence Questionnaire-Political (ECQ-P), composed of real-life ethical dilemmas from the political arena.

Stage	Approximate Ages	Characteristics and Accomplishments
Sensorimotor stage	Birth to two years	Reflexive, instinctive behaviors as center of own universe Repetitive circular reactions coordinated into purposeful motions Manipulation of objects and recognition of self as agent of action in world outside self Object permanence: recognition that objects exist when out of sight Object constancy: recognition that an object remains the same despite perspective or conditions
Preoperational stage	Four to seven years	Language skills emerge with ability to use symbols to label objects and people Memory and imagination improve with creative parellel play Non-logical reasoning, subjective intuition, and judgement by appearance Logical explanations sought; frequent "why?" questions Egocentric thinking only Consciousness and will are given to inanimate objects Single-focus thinking; only one aspect of subject seen at a time Incorrect generalizations from single experiences Literal thinking; taking words at exact meaning Ability to reconstruct past actions and anticipate future actions
Concrete operational stage	Seven to 11 years	Logical and systematic manipulation of symbols for problem solving Ability to consider several attributes of a subject at once Well-organized, coordinated structure of thought Conservation of number, length, mass, area, and volume Ability to group subjects into different classes Growing awareness of outside world
Formal operations stage	Eleven years to adult	Logical and abstract thinking Hypothetical reasoning Systematic problem solving Flexible mental experimentation Sees implications of own and others' thinking Has developed value system and moral judgement

"The ECQ-P is an attempt to assess ethical function independent of moral, ideological, and political content," the researchers explained. The questionnaire focused solely on cognitive processes. According to the researchers, Politicians, as well as every decision maker, need a capacity to cope with moral conflicts that arise in their ordinary activities; that is, they need high ethical competence. This competence means that the individual must have:

- "high ethical awareness, the ability to anticipate ethical problems in real life and to perceive them in time

- the cognitive skill to analyze and solve them in an optimal way

- the capability to discuss and handle moral problems at group and organization levels and, together with significant others, formulate ethical principles and guidelines

- the power to argue convincingly for preferred actions or decisions made

- the strength to implement controversial decisions"

According to the authors, the results of the study demonstrated "that it is possible to construct a Piagetian paper-and-pencil questionnaire for the assessment of ethical autonomy in the domain of politics that can produce reliable results." Such research builds on Piaget's earliest work expressed in his 1932 book, *The Moral Judgment of the Child,* and sheds further light on the importance of moral consciousness development as an adaptive cognitive mechanism.

LeoNora M. Chen and Younghee Kim, writing in the *Roeper Review* in 1999, have articulated the value of Piaget's work to provide further understanding of the gifted child. Though Piaget was primarily concerned with universal child development, they note, his work is a useful foundation to the study of the gifted child. According to Chen and Kim, research in the late 1960s and middle 1980s demonstrated that gifted children move more quickly through each of Piaget's development stages. The intellectually gifted child, like the high-powered computer systems of today, is a pattern seeker. The gifted child moves toward construction of general principles that apply to all circumstances based on feedback from a few encounters. They grasp the big picture more readily than less intellectually gifted children.

Piaget concluded in *The Psychology of the Child,*

Child psychology enables us to follow their step-by-step evolution, not in the abstract, but in the lived and living dialectic of subjects who are faced, in each generation, with endlessly recurring problems and who sometimes arrive at solutions that are slightly better than those of previous generations.

BIBLIOGRAPHY

Sources

Atherton, J. S. 2003. "Learning and Teaching: Piaget's developmental psychology." [cited March 20, 2004] http://ww.dmu.ac.uk/~jamesa/learning/piaget.htm.

Bacon, Jonathan. "Application of theory in the construction of learning materials." [cited March 20, 2004] http://www.jonobacon.org/writing/.

Boeree, Dr. C. George. "Personality Theories: Erik Erikson." [cited March 27, 2004] http://www.ship.edu/cgboeree/erikson.html.

Bransford, John D., et al., eds. *How People Learn: Brain, Mind, Experience, and School.* Washington, D.C.: National Academy Press, 1999.

Campbell, Robert L. "Jean Piaget's Genetic Epistemology: Appreciation and Critique," Two lectures presented at the Institute of Objectivist Studies Summer Seminar, Charlottesville, VA, July 7 and 8, 1997, Rev. April 25, 2002. [cited March 4, 2004] http://hubcap.clemson.edu/campber/piaget.html.

Chapman, M. *Constructive evolution: Origins and development of Piaget's thought.* Cambridge University Press, 1988.

Cohen, LeoNora M. and Younghee M. Kim. "Piaget's Equilibration Theory and the Young Gifted Child: A Balancing Act." *Roeper Review* 21, no. 3 (Feb 1999): 201.

Conway, Judith. "Educational Technology's Effect on Models of Instruction." (May 1997) [cited March 25, 2004] http://copland.udel.edu/ jconway/EDST666.htm.

Cousins, Donald, Ph.D. "Jean Piaget, Neuchatel, Switzerland." *European Traces of the History of Psychology* [cited March 20, 2004). http://www.ric.edu/dcousins/europsych/.

Dawson, M. and David A. Medler, eds. "Piaget's Stage Theory of Development." *The University of Alberta's Cognitive Science Dictionary* [cited March 4, 2004] http://www.psych.ualberta.ca/mike/Pearl_Street/Dictionary/dictionary.html.

Donaldson, Margaret. *Children's Minds.* Fontana Press, 1978.

Evans, Richard L. *Jean Piaget: The Man and His Ideas.* Translated by Eleanor Duckworth. New York: E. P. Dutton& Co., Inc., 1973.

Flavell, John H. *The Developmental Psychology of Jean Piaget.* New York: D. Van Nostrand Company, Inc. 1963.

Gallagher, Jeanette McCarthy, and D. Kim Reid. *The Learning Theory of Piaget and Inhelder.* Monterey, CA: Brooks/Cole Pub. Co., 1981.

Grant, Ted and Alan Woods. "Reason in Revolt: Marxism and Modern Science. The Genesis of Mind, Vygotsky and Piaget." *In Defense of Marxism.* [cited March 24, 2004] http://www.marxist.com/rircontents.asp.

Guinard, Mavis. "Piaget: the man who listened to children." *Swiss WORLD* 1 (Feb-March 1997): 21.

Hall, Elizabeth. "A Conversation with Jean Piaget and Barbel Inhelder." *Psychology Today* 3 (1970): 25–32, 54–56. [cited March 20, 2004] http://www.abrae.com.br/entrevistas/entr_pia.htm.

Hampton, Wilborn. "Fast and Loose: Television and the Internet offer kids instant information, but how much of it should they trust?" *Riverbank Review of books for young readers* (Spring 2003): 19–21.

Harms, William. "Huttenlocher to continue spatial learning research with funding from NSF," *The University of Chicago Chronicle* 20, no. 5 (Nov. 16, 2000).

Huitt, W. and J. Hummel. "Cognitive Development." *Educational Psychology Interactive.* [cited March 4, 2004] http://chiron.valdosta.edu/whuitt/col/cogsys/piaget.html.

Jean Piaget Society. Society for the Study of Knowledge and Development. "Resources for Students." [cited March 4, 2004] http://www.piaget.org/students.html.

Kappa Delta Pi: International Honor Society in Education. The Laureate Chapter. "Jean Piaget (1974)". [cited March 17, 2004] http://www.kdp.org/resources_laureate.asp?B=245.

Kohlberg, Lawrence. "Stages of Moral Development," with comments by Charles Kramer. [cited March 31, 2004] http://www.xenodochy.org/ex/lists/moraldev.html.

Lee, K. *Childhood Cognitive Development: The essential readings.* Malden, Mass. Blackwell, 2000.

Mahoney, Michael J. "What is Constructivism and Why is it Growing?" *Constructivism Site* http://www.construtivism123.com/What_Is/What_is_constructivism.htm.

Mark, Ruth. "Biography of Jean Piaget." *Pagewise, Inc.* [cited March 18, 2004] http://ndnd.essortment.com/jeanpiagetbiog_rhhh.html.

McGriff, Steve. J. "ISD Knowledge Base-Cognitivism." [cited March 28, 2004] http://www.personal.psu.edu/faculty/s/j/sjm256/portfolio/kbase/Theories & Models/Cognitivism/cognitivis.

Meins, Elizabeth. "Lecture 5: Piaget." Psychology Department, University of Durham. [cited March 28, 2004] http://psychology.dur.ac.uk/elizabeth.meins/lect2.htm.

Modgil, Sohan and Celia Modgil. *Piagetian Research: Compilation and Commentary, Vol. 1.* Windsor: NFER; Atlantic Highlands, NJ : distributed in the USA by Humanities Press, 1976.

Mooney, Carol Garhart. *Theories of Childhood: an Introduction to Dewey, Montessori, Erickson, Piaget and Vygotsky.* St. Paul, MN: Red Leaf Press, 2000.

"Papert misses 'Big Ideas' of the good old days in AI," *MIT News* July 10, 2002. [cited April 2, 2004] http://web.mit.edu/newsoffice/nr/2002/papert.html.

Papert, Seymour. "Child Psychologist Jean Piaget: He found the secrets of human learning and knowledge hidden behind the cute and seemingly illogical notions of children." *Time* 153, no. 12 (March 29, 1999): 104.

Papert, Seymour. "My passion is learning: doing it, thinking about it, promoting it." *MIT Media Lab: Papert Momentum* [cited April 2, 2004] http://momentum.media.mit.edu/papert.html.

"Piaget Describes Stages of Cognitive Development, 1923–1952" *A Science Odyssey: People and Discoveries.* [cited March 4, 2004] http://www.pbs.org/wgbh/aso/databank/entries/dh23pi.html.

Piaget, Jean. *Genetic Epistemology.* Trans. by Eleanor Duckworth. New York: Columbia University Press, 1970.

Piaget, Jean. "The Elaboration of the Universe. The Construction of Reality in the Child," *Philosophy Archive* Routledge and Kegan Paul.: 1955. http://www.marxists.org.

Piaget, Jean. and Barbel Inhelder. *The Psychology of the Child.* Trans. Helen Weaver. New York: Basic Books, Inc., 1969.

"Piaget—Just the Basics Please." *Florida Gulf Coast University.* Learning Principles, Module 7. [cited March 18, 2004] http://ruby.fgcu.edu/courses/80337/6215m7a.htm.

Pulaski, Mary Ann Spencer. *Understanding Piaget: An Introduction to Children's Cognitive Development.* New York: Harper and Row Publishers, Inc. 1980.

Putwain, David. "Early learning: The 1967 Plowden Report heralded what was to become the first of many significant changes in the education of primary school children." *Psychology Review* 9 (November 2002): 2–5.

Raman, Lakshmi, and Gerald A. Winer. "Older isn't Wiser in Moral Reasoning," *Science News* 158, no. 8(Aug. 19, 2000): 120.

"Resources for Students," *Jean Piaget Society: Society for the Study of Knowledge and Development.* [cited March 4, 2004] http://www.piaget.org.

Rowe, Donald. "Chomsky and Piaget: Assimilation and Accommodation." [cited March 29, 2004] University of Western Australia: 1997. http://www.physics.usyd.edu.au/drowe/research/theoretical/language.html.

Schumaker, Richard. "A Foundational Thinker." *UNESCO Courier* (Nov. 1996): 48.

Singer, Dorothy G., and Tracey A. Revenson. *A Piaget Primer, How A Child Thinks.* New York: Plume, 1996. Rev. ed. International Universities Press, 1997.

Smith, Les. "A Short Biography of Jean Piaget," *Jean Piaget Society,* 2002. [cited March 4, 2004] http://www.piaget.org.

Smith, M.K. "Jerome S. Bruner and the process of education." *The Encyclopedia of Informal Education.* January 23, 2004. [cited March http://www.infed.org/thinkers/bruner.htm.

Suizzo, Marie-Anne. "The Social-Emotional and Cultural Contexts of Cognitive Development: Neo-Piagetian Perspectives." *Child Development* 71, no. 4 (July 2000): 846.

Thurber, Christopher A. "I Am. Therefore, I think: explanations of cognitive development." *Camping Magazine* 76, no. 4 (July–August 2003): 36.

Turkle, Sherry. "Cuddling Up to Cyborg Babies." *The UNESCO Courier* September 2000 [cited March 18, 2004] http://www.unesco.org/courier/2000_09/uk/connex.htm.

Wolfgang, Edelstein and Eberhard, Schroeder. "House or Pandora's Box? The Treatment of Variability in Post-Piagetian Research." *Child Development* 71, no. 4 (July 2000): 840.

Wood, David. *How Children Think and Learn.* Oxford: Basil Blackwell, Inc., 1998.

Wozniak, Robert H. "Classics in Psychology. James Mark Baldwin: Mental Development in the Child and the Race." *Thoemmes Continuum.* [cited March 28, 2004] http://www.thoemmes.com/psych/baldwin1.htm.

Further readings

Chapman, M. *Constructive Evolution: Origins and Development of Piaget's Thought.* Cambridge University Press, 1988.

DeLisi, R. and Golbeck, S. "Implications of Piagetian theory for peer learning," (3-37). In A. O'Donnell & A. King (Eds.) *Cognitive Perspectives on Peer Learning.* Mahwah, NJ: Lawrence Erlbaum Associates, 1999.

Evans, Richard L. *Jean Piaget: The Man and His Ideas.* Trans. by Eleanor Duckworth. New York: E. P. Dutton and Co., Inc., 1973.

Flavell, John H. *The Developmental Psychology of Jean Piaget.* Princeton, NJ : D. Van Nostrand Co., 1963.

Furth, Hans G. and Harry Wachs. *Thinking Goes to School: Piaget's Theory in Practice.* New York: Oxford University Press, 1974.

Gallagher, Jeanette McCarthy, and D. Kim Reid. *The Learning Theory of Piaget and Inhelder.* Monterey, CA: Brooks/Cole Pub. Co., 1981.

Gruber, H. E., and J. Vonèche. *The Essential Piaget.* Northvale, NJ: Aronson, 1995.

Jean Piaget Society. Society for the Study of Knowledge and Development. "Resources for Students." http://www.piaget.org/students.html.

Lee, K. *Childhood Cognitive Development: The Essential Readings.* Malden, MA: Blackwell, 2000.

Meadows, S. *The Child as Thinker: The Development and Acquisition of Cognition in Childhood.* London; New York: Routledge, 1993.

Mooney, Carol Garhart, *Theories of Childhood: an Introduction to Dewey, Montessori, Erickson, Piaget and Vygotsky.* St. Paul, MN: Red Leaf Press, 2000.

Palmer, J. A., ed. *Fifty Modern Thinkers on Education. From Piaget to the Present.* London; New York: Routledge, 2001.

Piaget, J. *Genetic epistemology.* Trans. by Eleanor Duckworth. New York: Columbia University Press, 1970.

Piaget, J. (1952). "Jean Piaget (Autobiography)". In *A History of Psychology in Autobiography*, Vol. 4 (pp. 237–256). Edit. by E.G. Boring. Englewood Cliffs, NJ: Prentice Hall; 1974.

Piaget, J., and Inhelder, B. *The Psychology of the Child.* New York: Basic Books, 1969. (Original work published 1966).

Singer, Dorothy G. and Tracey A. *A Piaget Primer: How a Child Thinks.* Revenson Madison, CT: International Universities Press, 1997.

Wood, D. *How Children Think and Learn.* Oxford: Blackwells, 1998.

Carl Ransom Rogers

1902–1987

AMERICAN PSYCHOLOGIST, PROFESSOR

COLUMBIA UNIVERSITY, Ph.D., 1931

BRIEF OVERVIEW

> Experience is, for me, the highest authority. The touchstone of validity is my own experience. No other person's ideas, and none of my own ideas, are as authoritative as my experience. . . . Neither the Bible nor the prophets—neither Freud nor research—neither the revelations of God nor man— can take precedence over my own direct experience.

These words, from Carl Rogers's classic book *On Becoming a Person,* probably best describe Rogers's contributions to the study of psychology. Neither the Bible, from which his mother had taught him, nor the Freudian tenets so popular among his colleagues could make Rogers conform to the prevalent views of his time. He stubbornly refused to follow the perceptions of others. Rogers relied solely on his own personal experience rather than on dogma.

Carl Rogers practiced psychotherapy his way for over 50 years. He never earned the adoration of those considered the intelligentsia, either in the United States or the rest of the world, as did Sigmund Freud and other luminaries of the twentieth-century mental health movement. Yet in the introduction to *The Carl Rogers Reader,* a biography that was published posthumously in 1989, authors Howard Kirschenbaum and Valerie Henderson note that Rogers was "the most influential psychotherapist in American history." Five years before Rogers's death, a 1982 study published in the journal *American Psychologist* ranked the ten most influential psychotherapists. Carl Rogers was rated as number one.

Carl Rogers. (Copyright Roger Rossmeyer/Corbis. Reproduced by permission.)

One of Rogers's techniques, the therapist reflecting back said the patient's statement by rephrasing it and asking the person "How do YOU feel about that?" has become almost a caricature of contemporary psychotherapy. Indeed, comedian Bob Newhart, who grew up in Rogers's hometown of Oak Park, Illinois, caricatured Rogers's style of therapy in his highly successful television sitcom, "The Bob Newhart Show." But much of what Rogers contributed to psychotherapeutic theory is both remarkably simple and refreshingly optimistic. Rogers trusted people to want, and to work toward, good mental health and stability.

Yet Rogers introduced a multitude of revolutionary concepts to psychotherapy. His terminology, developed during half a century of research, helped to change mental health treatment forever. Rogers pioneered the notion that the people he saw were not "patients" who were "sick" in a medical sense, but rather "clients," people seeking help with problems of living. Today, that change in labeling from "patients" to "clients" is embraced by nearly all psychotherapists. Rogers not only perceived human beings as being primarily competent and striving toward good health, but he also viewed human ills such as insanity, criminal behaviors, and war as aberrations, anomalies

superimposed upon a basic, commonly held desire for good.

Everything in Rogers's scheme starts from one life-force, a power that Rogers calls the "actualizing tendency." This life-force also exists outside the human psyche, according to Rogers. The actualizing tendency is present in all forms of life—trees that grow out of the sides of rocky cliffs, violets that push their way up through cracks in a concrete sidewalk, and men and women who struggle against the odds to do good things or create great accomplishments such as timeless works of art. This actualizing tendency is even active in the ecosystems of the world. Rogers found this life-force in the forests he roamed and in the cornfields he worked in as a youth.

Rather than identifying persons as "sick" or fundamentally flawed from childhood as the Freudians did, Rogers was interested in how he and other mental health professionals could recognize the health in people. Mentally robust people, in Rogers's view, exist in the here and now, free of defense mechanisms that would make it difficult for them to accept reality as it is. Called "the quiet revolutionary," Rogers went where no mental health professional had been before. His 1942 innovation of the tape-recording of psychotherapeutic interviews was far ahead of his time, but this method has now become standard practice for those providing mental health services. Many of these remarkable taped interviews done by Rogers over the years have been donated to the American Academy of Psychotherapists' tape library. These invaluable teaching tools are available to therapists all over the world.

Rogers is the undisputed creator of the "non-directive" or "client-centered" approach to psychotherapy. His decades-long study of how care is provided to clients resulted in the creation of several totally new mental health therapy techniques. Looking at the classic, highly directive Freudian model of therapy, Rogers noted in *On Becoming a Person,* "Unless I had a need to demonstrate my own cleverness and learning, I would do better to rely upon the client for the direction of movement." Rogers's message to the client was also far removed from what Freud had communicated. Paraphrased, Freud's message to his patients was: I will discover the unknown flaw, developed in your earliest childhood because of psychosexual conflicts. I will root it out of your ego, superego and/or id and thus I will make you better. Conversely, Carl Rogers told clients: "I can't solve any of your problems for you, but I can help you to solve your own problems, and doing that will make you better."

Rogers was also an active participant in the development of the intensive form of group therapy sometimes referred to as the "encounter group." He is one of the first mental health professionals to conduct research regarding the effectiveness of various forms of counseling. A shy man who often refused television interviews, Rogers appeared on film interviewing clients. In 1962 he, Gestalt therapist Fritz Perls, and rational-emotive therapist Albert Ellis all were filmed during separate therapy sessions with the same client for what became known as "The Gloria Film Series." In the 1970 Academy Award-winning film "Journey Into Self," Rogers also appeared leading an encounter group.

Additionally, Rogers was instrumental in changing who provided therapy to the mentally ill. What had once been the exclusive domain of psychiatrists and psychoanalysts expanded to include all of the counseling disciplines—even educators and the clergy. His work with schools and other social support systems that provided services to children at risk affected many of the helping professions. An educator himself, Rogers never lost interest in the field of education. From his early years, during which he counseled abused and neglected children, until his death Rogers developed innovative ideas for administering mental health treatment to youth.

The unbelievable abundance of written (and published) work created by Carl Rogers from his youth to old age resoundingly shows both his amazing physical stamina and his strong work ethic. From his early college years in the early 1920s until his death in 1987, Rogers, besides maintaining a flourishing practice and lecturing all over the country, published sixteen books and more than two hundred articles. His writings embraced nearly every possible aspect of his work and his life—from therapy to scientific research, education to social issues, personal reminiscences to philosophy. The variety of publications for which he wrote speaks to the wide audience Rogers reached. He wrote articles for magazines as divergent as *The Family* and *Camping Magazine* to the *Journal of Consulting Psychology*. Several of his books have sold more than one million copies, and there are more than 60 foreign-language translations of his works.

As one of the foremost figures in the field of humanistic psychology as propounded by Alfred Adler, Abraham Maslow, and Karen Horney, Rogers expanded many of their theories to embrace an even larger audience—the world. With his unshakable belief in the inherent goodness of people, he was convinced that proper communication could potentially stop even war. Carl Rogers acted on behalf of

PRINCIPAL PUBLICATIONS

- *The Clinical Treatment of the Problem Child.* Boston: Houghton Mifflin, 1939.

- *Counseling and Psychotherapy: Newer Concepts in Practice.* Boston: Houghton Mifflin, 1942

- *Counseling with Returned Servicemen.* New York: McGraw-Hill, 1946.

- *Client-Centered Therapy: Its Current Practice, Implications, and Theory.* Boston: Houghton Mifflin, 1951.

- *Psychotherapy and Personality Change.* Chicago: University of Chicago Press, 1954.

- *On Becoming a Person.* Boston: Houghton Mifflin, 1961.

- *A Therapist's View of Personal Goals.* Wallingford, PA: Pendle Hill, 1965.

- *The Therapeutic Relationship and Its Impact.* Madison, WI: University of Wisconsin Press, 1967.

- *Person to Person: The Problem of Being Human, A New Trend in Psychology.* Lafayette, CA: Real People Press, 1967.

- *Freedom to Learn: A View of What Education Might Become.* Columbus, OH: Macmillan, 1969.

- *Freedom to Learn: Studies of the Person.* Columbus, OH: Charles E. Merrill, 1969.

- *Carl Rogers on Encounter Groups.* New York: Harper and Row, 1970.

- *Becoming Partners: Marriage and Its Alternatives.* New York: Delacorte Press, 1972.

- *Carl Rogers on Personal Power.* New York: Dell Publishing, 1977.

- *A Way of Being.* New York: Houghton Mifflin, 1980.

- *Freedom to Learn for the Eighties.* New York: Prentice Hall, 1983.

his beliefs. In the last decade of his life, he traveled to Belfast in Northern Ireland to reconcile Protestants and Catholics, and to South Africa to facilitate communication between black and white inhabitants of that country. Back home in the United States, Rogers tried to improve the dialogue between health care providers and consumers. At 85 years of age, Rogers made his last trip, to Russia. A modest man, Rogers was amazed to see how many Russians knew of his work and had read his writings.

BIOGRAPHY

Family and early years

The family into which Carl Rogers was born, according to Rogers' own description, could have posed for Grant Woods' "American Gothic," the somber portrait of two Puritanical-looking members of a nineteenth-century American Midwest farm family. But beyond his family's Bible-reading and work ethic, there seems to have been very little that was unique about the middle-class, middle-American beginnings of Carl Ransom Rogers. Oak Park, Illinois, also the birthplace of Ernest Hemingway, was a quiet suburb of Chicago when Carl Rogers was born on January 8, 1902. He was the fourth child of prosperous middle-class parents, preceded by two older brothers, Lester and Ross, and a sister, Margaret. His mother, Julia (Cushing) Rogers was descended from New England ancestors that had arrived in America on the Mayflower. She was a housewife, a highly pious Christian, and a strict disciplinarian who brought up her children to be both hard-working and God-fearing. Rogers' father, Walter Alexander Rogers, was equally devout, and a respected Chicago civil engineer. In 1901, the year before Carl was born, Walter Rogers and an associate began their own construction company that quickly met with success, assuring the family's prosperity. There would be two more children born into the Rogers family after Carl: Walter Jr. and John.

Howard Kirschenbaum, one of Rogers's several biographers, describes him as "a rather sickly child—slight, shy, prone to tears, often the target of jokes and teasing by his older brothers." In his childhood, he was extremely close to his mother. He was a precocious child, considered gifted, but also sensitive and prone to daydreams. Before he was four years old, Carl had already been taught to read by his mother and older siblings, and was already reading books, especially the Bible stories his mother encouraged him to read before he went to kindergarten. Rogers was able to skip the first grade completely. Throughout his childhood, Carl Rogers was what we would term a "loner," with no close friends. This appears to be more a factor of family expectations than any isolative

tendencies in Carl. As a means of teaching their children, Walter and Julia Rogers gave each child a province of responsibility from which they could earn money but for which they were expected to be accountable. Carl was in charge of the hens. He fed them, kept the henhouse clean, collected the eggs, and even kept records and made out bills. In return for his efforts, he could sell eggs to both his mother and the neighbors and keep the profits. Helen Elliot, his future wife, who first met him in grade school, remembered him as reluctantly heading for home after school to sell eggs while the other children played.

When Carl Rogers was 12, his father, who was comfortable financially and looking for new challenges, decided to fulfill a life-long dream and become a farmer. He bought 300 acres in Glen Ellyn, a rural community about 30 miles west of Chicago. When Carl Rogers speaks of growing up on a farm, in some ways it is a slight misnomer. The residence Walter Rogers built for his family at Glen Ellyn was an estate, complete with eight bedrooms, five baths, and a clay tennis court. Yet despite the elegance of their home, the Rogers children were still expected to do the majority of the farm chores and both attend and do well in school. Rogers spent his teenage years working on that farm, developing the work ethic, independence, and self-discipline that would characterize the rest of his life. His Bible-reading mother was a strict disciplinarian who Rogers's older brother once described as "a person you didn't tell things to." Rogers early years have frequently been described as solitary but character-building. The majority of his younger years were spent in the company of his brothers. (Margaret, being several years older, is described as having felt more maternal than sisterly toward Carl.) Rogers's own description of himself as a teenager, as presented in his 1980 book, *A Way of Being,* speaks volumes: "My fantasies during that period were definitely bizarre, and probably would be classified as schizoid by a diagnostician, but fortunately I never came in contact with a psychologist."

Education and marriage

"I have come to love my books a great deal," Rogers wrote in his diary during the summer of 1919, the year he graduated from high school. He had received a 50-dollar graduation gift from his parents, and with that money Rogers bought a set of chess pieces, some toilet articles, and 22 books. That same summer, as he prepared to enter the University of Wisconsin in the fall, he also wrote: "I have had lots of time to think this summer and I feel that I have come much closer to God, tho(sic) there are thousands of things that still perplex and baffle me." That autumn Rogers followed a family tradition and began attending the University of Wisconsin, initially majoring in agriculture. This was consistent with what he had written in that same diary a few days earlier: "I fully intend to be a farmer." Away from home for the first time in his life and clearly undecided as to his life work, Rogers managed to sustain good marks, but grew less sure about an agrarian future. Increasingly, he became involved in the Young Men's Christian Association (YMCA) and other religious activities, encouraging young people to preach the gospel all over the world. From his diary entries, Rogers burned with an evangelical fervor during that time, but he could not quite bring himself to decide to become a minister.

At the University of Wisconsin, Rogers re-established a connection from his earliest years: Helen Elliot was also attending school there. He had not seen her since the Rogers family had moved to Glen Ellyn, and now he found that she had grown into a young woman who was "tall, graceful and very attractive." A few tentative dates soon blossomed into a relationship, though Helen continued to date others as well. Due to Helen's interest in art, she left the university to attend the Chicago Academy of Fine Arts after her sophomore year, but the bond between them continued as they corresponded and saw each other as often as possible. Helen influenced Carl to take his first tentative steps away from his family's fundamentalist religious views. He learned to dance and play cards; he joined a fraternity and attended college parties—all activities frowned upon by his parents. There seems to be a difference between Carl and his siblings in the ways they viewed their parents. Carl believed that his mother "became more fundamentalist" as she grew older, while his brothers and sisters felt that after her initial disapproval of Carl's first two years in college, their mother eventually accepted the changes.

In 1921 an event occurred that was destined to change Carl Rogers's life. Rogers was selected as one of 10 youth delegates to represent the United States at the World Student Christian Federation (WSCF) conference to be held in Beijing, China. Typical of Rogers's then-inability to see himself in a positive light, for several years he believed that he was chosen only because his parents were financially comfortable enough to pay for his trip. Christian leaders involved in his selection later denied this, however, saying Rogers' intelligence, commitment, and enthusiasm were the deciding factors. In February of 1922, he and the others embarked on an experience that would

prove to be remarkably alien and broadening for a boy raised on a farm in the Midwest. He had proposed marriage to Helen before he left, but she asked him to wait. Some accounts state that Rogers's family strongly disapproved of Helen, but it is unclear if this was truly the case. They seemed more disapproving of Carl's indecision regarding his own life than of his love for Helen. Yet it is possible that they did object to the relationship. In *A Way of Being,* Rogers observed,

> I think the attitude toward persons outside our large family can be summed up schematically in this way: Other persons behave in dubious ways which we do not approve of in our family. Many of them play cards, go to movies, smoke, dance, drink, and engage in other activities, some unmentionable. So the best thing to do is to be tolerant of them, since they may not know better, but to keep away from any close communication with them.

Though the Beijing conference lasted for only a week, the WSCF voyage would also take Rogers and the others to Japan, Korea, and the Philippines, and it would keep them in Asia for over six months—from February into August. Rogers would remain nominally a Christian, but he viewed his experience in the East as a conversion of sorts because it opened up for him philosophies to which he had never been exposed. This trip to Asia also made Rogers aware of two other things that would stay in his mind and become part of him: seeing first-hand the suffering of poor and exploited people, and the similarity of all of nature. He would note that silk "lost considerable of its luster" after seeing the child labor that produced it, and the observations of nature he made while climbing Mount Fuji are quite impressive. These lessons would become part of both his psychological theories and his life's work. In Rogers's words, "I consider this a time when I achieved my psychological independence. In major ways I for the first time emancipated myself from the religious thinking of my parents, and realized that I could not go along with them." In fact, Rogers's relationship with his family would never be the same after he returned from Asia. In 1922 he also showed the beginnings of an ability that would lead him to become a prolific writer. Later that year, Rogers wrote about his Asian experience in an article entitled "An Experiment in Christian Internationalism" published in *The Intercollegian,* a magazine sponsored by the YMCA. This article would be his first successful attempt at writing for publication, but it would hardly be his last.

Though it was during this trip that Rogers first began to doubt the religious interpretations inculcated into him by his mother and others (for example, he began to question whether Jesus Christ truly was a deity or only a remarkable man, a question that horrified his parents), he still returned to the University of Wisconsin determined to become a minister. That August, after returning from China, Rogers also took a correspondence course in psychology. For the first time, he read psychologist William James' work, but he found it quite boring. Of his first psychology course, Rogers would later remember only having a long-distance argument with his professor as to whether dogs were capable of reason. Rogers states, "I was quite able to prove to my own satisfaction that my dog Shep was definitely able to solve difficult problems by reasoning." Rogers' education at the University of Wisconsin continued for his junior and senior years, and he then applied to the Union Theological Seminary in New York City, noted for its progressive and tolerant religious teachings. He was accepted there, and in 1924, following graduation, he and Helen Elliot surprised nearly everyone by marrying on August 28. Helen had chosen to give up her ambitions of becoming a commercial artist. Their honeymoon consisted of packing up everything they owned and moving to "the smallest flat" in New York City.

In the summer of 1924, part of Carl's study for the ministry included a brief stint as a pastor in a church in East Dorset, Vermont, an experience both Carl and Helen enjoyed. He noted "I found it absolutely impossible to make my sermons longer than twenty minutes, a fact that disturbed me but for which my congregation was doubtless thankful. . .". In East Dorset, Rogers also began to focus upon the multiple social problems that he observed even in a small Vermont village. He described alcoholics and psychotic people who lived there. (East Dorset also happens to have been the hometown of Bill Wilson, the founder of Alcoholics Anonymous.) For Rogers, this exposure led him to an increasing interest in psychology, and the beginnings of the process that would eventually move him across the street to Columbia University. Consistent with its reputation as an open-minded school of religion, Union Seminary in 1926 offered a student-run course entitled "Why Am I Entering the Ministry?" Rogers immediately signed up for it. "Why Am I Entering the Ministry?" proved an excellent means of winnowing the theological school's student body. As Rogers states, the majority of the attendees "thought their way right out of religious work." During those stressful years of decisions and new responsibilities, Rogers first suffered from what would become a lifelong problem: a peptic ulcer, a medical condition he shared with several other Rogers family members and which Carl suspected was caused by repressing their anger. On March 17,

1926, Carl and Helen's first child David was born. Before the year was over, Rogers had indeed crossed the street to Columbia.

Rogers, thanks to his parents' teachings, had always been enterprising. While in college after the China trip, he had run a small but lucrative importing business, sending for items from the East and selling them in the United States. While at Union Theological Seminary, he had held down a part-time job in Christian youth counseling. But now, at Columbia and the father of a baby son, an income once again became necessary. It is interesting to note that even during those busy years of working on the M.A. he received in 1928, and the Ph.D. in psychotherapy he attained in 1931, Rogers still managed to support his family. In 1928 Rogers accepted a position in clinic work at the Rochester Child Study Center under the auspices of the Rochester Society for the Prevention of Cruelty to Children. He, Helen, and baby David moved to Rochester that summer, and in the autumn their second child, Natalie, was born. Rogers would continue to work as a clinician, and eventually as the director, of both the Rochester society and its clinic. During those years, Rogers became increasingly aware of other psychotherapeutic techniques and theories then in wide usage. The work of Otto Rank, who believed that people were inevitably caught in a battle between their "will to health" and "will to illness," would greatly influence Rogers. Rank's belief that therapy was designed to aid people in accepting themselves and liberating their "will to health" seems to echo what Rogers came to believe. Yet Rogers, ever the maverick, stated on many later occasions, "I never had a mentor. I think that, to an unusual degree, my work was born out of direct experience."

Rogers also continued to write during those years. He even managed to write and publish an article entitled "Intelligence as a Factor in Camping Activities" in conjunction with C.W. Carson for *Camping Magazine* in 1930. Always prolific, Rogers continued to produce an eclectic series of articles for various journals and publications throughout the thirties. Many of these involved his ideas about clinical case work with children and psychotherapy. *The Clinical Management of the Problem Child,* a 1939 book that received little attention from the world at large or the world of psychology, was Rogers's first effort at developing his ideas into a book. It contained the seeds of many of the innovative theories that Rogers would later introduce to the world of psychology. Beginning in 1938, and culminating in 1939, Rogers became embroiled in his first professional battle. The Rochester Clinic was reorganizing, and it was suggested that it should be headed by a psychiatrist, rather than a psychologist such as Rogers. The emerging conflict eventually was decided in Rogers's favor, with his appointment as the director of the program. This incident verified his self-assessment of being "capable of dogged determination in getting work done or in winning a fight."

Teaching years

Rogers was 38 years old when he was offered a full professorship at Ohio State University in 1940. In the years prior to his university appointment, Rogers had quietly felt increasingly frustrated with and opposed to the authoritarian notions that were being proposed by Sigmund Freud and his followers. The people the Freudians called "patients" were more and more seen as "clients" by Rogers—individuals who indeed had psychological problems, but were not "sick" in the classic sense. In 1942 Rogers published a book that had a major impact on the psychotherapeutic world, *Counseling and Psychotherapy: Newer Concepts in Practice.* This work contained the first-ever references to people as clients rather than as patients. Both during and after World War II, Rogers was also actively involved in the United Service Organization (USO), helping returning veterans to cope with the psychological trauma that they had experienced. As always, Rogers put the knowledge he had acquired in working with these returning veterans into a book he wrote in 1946, *Counseling with Returned Servicemen.* In 1944, he was elected president of the American Association for Applied Psychology, an organization he had helped to found.

Rogers remained at Ohio State University until 1945, when the University of Chicago offered him joint positions teaching and setting up a center for counseling located at the university. At Chicago, Rogers conducted much of the research for which he became world-famous. This work arose from a decade-long campaign by Rogers for to explore the efficacy of and find ways to improve the various forms of mental health treatment. Prior to Rogers' time, the psychoanalytic interview, then the most common form of treatment of mental disorders, was considered sacrosanct. Psychoanalysts simply did not provide what they considered "privileged" information, and there was no measure of how effective their treatment had been except for their own version of how therapy had gone. Rogers became the counseling center's first executive secretary and managed to obtain grant funding for the research he had so strongly advocated for nearly a decade.

That same year, Rogers's newfound credibility with psychologists was enhanced when he was elected president of the more venerable American Psychological Association. Oddly enough, Rogers himself did very little of the actual research for which he has become known. He certainly was responsible for obtaining the necessary funds and for encouraging his students, providing ideas and publishing the first scientific studies of psychotherapy. But for the most part, his graduate students did the actual research. Rogers was far less interested in personal recognition, however, than in getting the job done. He often perceived himself as a facilitator of others, and in this endeavor he was highly successful. He continued working at the University of Chicago throughout the 40s and into the early 50s. During these years, as his fame grew, hordes of students from all over the world jammed his classrooms to attend his lectures. It was said that as soon as one lecture-hall was filled to overflowing, the university would provide a larger one. But soon that hall, too, would be too small and another, even larger one would be needed. He was given the least popular times to teach, such as early Saturday mornings, but still the classes were full and spilling over into the corridors.

While teaching at the University of Chicago in 1951, Rogers wrote what would become his best-known works: *Client-Centered Therapy: Its Current Practice, Implications and Theory.* In this book, Rogers for the first time spelled out his evolving personality theory.

> With all his ambivalences, the client wants to grow, wants to mature, wants to face his problems and work them through. Accept and clarify his initial expressions of feeling, and a fuller, deeper expression of feelings will follow. Accept and clarify these, and insight will follow. Accept and clarify these insights, and the client will begin to take positive actions in his life and develop self-acceptance, self-understanding, and the ability to deal with his own problems.

Rogers called his theory his "hypothesis." That hypothesis, put in its simplest terms, states that all human beings intrinsically have the power to guide their lives into modes that provide them with personal satisfaction and social usefulness. In Rogers' version of psychotherapy, people are freed to search for their own singular type of internal insight, common sense, and self-confidence.

His alma mater, Columbia University, honored Rogers with the Nicholas Murray Butler Silver Medal in 1955, and this prize was followed the next year by a special contribution award from the American Psychological Association honoring his research into psychotherapy. In 1957, 55-year-old Rogers was invited by his other alma mater, the University of Wisconsin, to return and teach there. He eagerly accepted the offer, but it was a decision he would soon regret. Returning to the school where his education had begun 37 years earlier, Rogers was totally unprepared for the discord he met there. In his words, he was beginning to wonder

> What is a university, at this stage of my career, offering me? I realized that in my research it offered no particular help; in anything educational, I was forced to fit my beliefs into a totally alien mold; in stimulation, there was little from my colleagues because we were so far apart in thinking and in goals.

In 1963, disillusioned with what we commonly call higher learning—dissatisfied with faculty diagnostic, therapeutic, and educational policies, Rogers resigned from the University of Wisconsin. It appears that Rogers maintained his disaffection with the university educational process. Although he continued to give visiting lectures and received honors from many colleges, Rogers never again was affiliated with any one school of higher learning.

Perhaps a disagreement between Rogers and the head of the psychology department at Stanford University, as described by Rogers's good friend Hobart "Red" Thomas, best clarifies part of the problem Carl Rogers had with academia. "I don't give a good god damn what the diagnosis is," Rogers is quoted as snapping in response to some statement about diagnosis made by the Stanford psychologist. "If we devote a fraction of the time we spend in diagnostic conferences to being with that person, you wouldn't need the diagnosis." Most accounts, however, describe Rogers as a man who did not argue with people. "Red" Thomas said of him: "He didn't get into arguments. He would state his position very clearly, and would listen to your position. 'Can we learn from each other?' was his basic stance." But little did Rogers know when he left Wisconsin that he was headed for much more work and fame. He was elected a fellow at the Center for Advanced Study in the Behavioral Sciences in 1962, and did work with the Western Behavioral Sciences Institute in La Jolla, California, a group that studied ways to improve human relations.

Later years

Throughout his 60s and 70s, Rogers remained remarkably healthy and mentally alert. His problems with the University of Wisconsin and others in academia apparently did not adversely affect the esteem in which he was held. He received honorary doctorates from several universities on both sides of the Atlantic, and the American Humanist Association selected Rogers "Humanist of the Year" in 1964. In 1968, the 66-year-old Rogers and some of his colleagues left the Western Behavioral Sciences Institute and founded the Center for Studies of the Person. Despite the tremendous exposure to people the world over that Rogers had enjoyed for decades, he remained basically a rather shy man. His 1970 book, *On Encounter Groups,* was judged by its publisher Harper and Row to have mass-marketing appeal. The book company wanted to set up a television interview for him, but Rogers adamantly refused. "But one show would lead to another!" an incredulous publishing executive argued. "That's what I'm afraid of," Rogers is said to have replied. He lived in California, continuing to see clients in his flourishing practice and conduct scientific studies at La Jolla. Rogers remained a frequent lecturer and prolific writer. During the last two decades of his life, between 1964 and 1987, Rogers wrote and published over 120 articles, including many that were published posthumously. In addition, Carl Rogers completed his last two books, *A Way of Being* and *Freedom to Learn for the Eighties,* in the last decade of his life.

"I am not growing old, I am old and growing" was Rogers's statement in "Growing Old—or Older and Growing," published in the *Journal of Humanistic Psychology* in the autumn of 1980, six years before his death. The last years of Rogers's life were, in many ways, the most remarkable. Consistent with his long-held belief that most human problems stem from poor communication, Rogers expanded his scope to aid the world rather than individual psyches. There is no doubt that the precarious situation in which the planet and its billions of people found themselves in the early eighties had been weighing on Rogers's mind. In the autumn of 1982, he had written a piece for the *Journal of Humanistic Psychology* entitled, "A Psychologist Looks at Nuclear War: Its Threat, Its Possible Prevention." He would soon, in keeping with the principles he had embraced all of his life, be "putting his money where his mouth was" and trying to facilitate healthy communication between the various factions in the world.

"I'm Carl Rogers. How will we use our time together?" was a typical lead-in Rogers used when conducting groups. This opening statement encouraged people to be accountable for their own knowledge, and for their part in the group process. When Rogers spoke of power, he'd explain, "I'm not interested in power over anyone. What I want is influence, to influence you to become the best you can possibly be." These are the tenets that Rogers, the master of the encounter group, brought to conflicts all over the world. During the last decade of his life, Rogers, now in his eighties, managed to visit Belgium, China, Italy,

Hungary, Mexico, Germany, Russia, Sweden, Finland, Japan, Austria, Venezuela, England, Kenya, Zimbabwe, Brazil, and South Africa. In every country that he visited, Rogers met with professionals and offered them the principles he'd spent a lifetime developing. In Latin America, Northern Ireland, South Africa, and eventually the Soviet Union, he attempted to facilitate dialogue that truly would make war-torn people "the best they could possibly be."

In Belfast, Northern Ireland, at the height of the troubles, he managed to get Protestant and Catholic leaders to meet and to have active communication for a period of several days. Over that time, the two dissenting sides came, as "Red" Thomas said, "to see each other as people." Rogers, with his usual penchant for electronic gadgets, videotaped these meetings. Sadly, both the Protestants and the Catholics attending these meetings did not want this video shown out of fear that their constituents would feel betrayed. In South Africa, Rogers met a black man named Cecil Bobibe. Bobibe today is the dean of students at a South African college and utilizes Rogerian concepts in his counseling practice. When asked what it was that Rogers brought to South Africa that so influenced him, Bobibe stated, "It (Rogers's theory) gives one faith in who we are, and shows one how to find the essential humanity in the other, whoever they might be." Rogers's last trip was to Russia in 1986, where he is still revered for his ability to facilitate conflict resolution. Carl Rogers died of a heart attack in San Diego, California, on February 4, 1987. He was quoted as saying that his last few years were the best times of his life.

THEORIES

Carl Rogers and humanist psychology

Explanation Carl Rogers was not the sole creator of what Maslow called "the third force," humanist psychology. Freud's psychoanalytic theories were considered one force, and behavioral theories pioneered by Ivan Pavlov and B.F. Skinner were a second force. Abraham Maslow, Karen Horney, and Rogers expressed an optimism regarding the human state that neither Freud nor Skinner found to be possible—humanistic psychology, or the "third force." Freud observed that "our mind is no peacefully self-contained unity." Rather he compared the mind to "a mob, eager for enjoyment and destruction . . . to be held down forcibly by a prudent superior class." Rogers, however, believed it had taken him years to undo both his early religious upbringing and Freudian

training in psychology classes at Columbia, both of which had presented human beings as being inherently evil. Rogers's own observations had shown him that people are decent; they care about the society they live in; they are capable of positive accomplishments; and they deserve to be trusted.

Early in his career, Rogers also discovered that he did not subscribe to other commonly held beliefs promulgated by Freud and his disciples; namely, that early experiences and relationships set in place fixed and inevitable mental processes leading to neurosis. Instead, Rogers seemed much more at home with the philosophy of the humanists who believed that people were capable of changing. As in all of his later work, Rogers developed the seeds of these humanistic notions from the experiences he derived in his work with abused and neglected children at the Institute for Child Guidance in the Rochester, New York area in the early days of his career. Working with these children helped Rogers see the tremendous impact of both the biology he would later write about and the negative experience of childhood on which Freud based his theories. Yet in the majority of cases, Rogers found in these young lives the hopeful, humanistic philosophy that would be his mantra for the next six decades.

Changing the labels of therapy

Rogers was one of the earliest adherents of what has been called "interactional psychology"; as a result, much of the philosophy ascribed to him less abstract, simpler, and more practical than the complex theories proposed by many of his peers. Interactional psychologists believe that a healthy psyche is the result of appropriate and beneficial communication between people. Rogers continually described how such interactions should be carried out if therapists are to help people. He also explained how psychology measures helping people, and perhaps most importantly, he re-evaluated what the goals of such therapy should be. Rogers redefined everything: the description of the person seeking help, who could provide that help, what help was actually provided, and how such help was given.

Rogers did more than change terminology when he changed what patients were called. Rogers's "patients" became "clients"—persons who were in need of assistance in reaching their innate potential. This change in perception would have far-reaching implications, and it would make Rogers the father of client-centered psychotherapy. This practice of referring to clients would spread across the world, forever altering the way the psychology profession perceives people seeking help. This model would also, in keeping with Rogers's core beliefs, improve the self-esteem of the clients whom psychologists and psychiatrists saw in therapy. It would reinforce a belief Rogers shared with his colleagues Karen Horney, Abraham Maslow, and others: that there is an ever-present capacity within each of us that instinctively seeks mental health, stability, and beyond that, the fulfillment of our potential.

Rogers's use of the reflection technique in his therapy sessions has been one of the most-parodied facets of Rogerian therapy. Rogers believed that "reflection of feelings" was one of two necessary methods used toward accomplishing what Rogers calls release, the freeing of the client from the pent-up feelings. This reflection, together with simple acceptance had to be manifested in order for the client to feel free to open up and experience catharsis—the expression of feelings previously not expressed (or sometimes not even consciously felt). Both of these techniques are designed to provide the client with assurance that the therapist is attentively involved in the psychotherapy session and is accepting of what is being expressed by the client. A classic example of simple acceptance would be the therapist's response of "Yes, I see. . . ." Reflection of feelings as Rogers practiced it was more complicated, however. The ability to listen completely and totally is demonstrated to the client by the therapist mirroring back, and restating, the emotions behind what the client says.

Example   Rogers provides the example of reflection in this interaction with one of his students who is getting failing grades. The supposed purpose of the session for this student is to make Rogers take responsibility for the student's decision to tell his parents.

Student: "Oh, I don't know if they're going to sort of condemn me . . . in the past they've said, 'It's your fault. You don't have enough will power'. . ."

Rogers: "You feel that they will be unsympathetic and condemn you for your failures."

Student: "Well my—I'm pretty sure my father will . . . He hasn't been—he doesn't experience these things; he just doesn't know what it's like . . ."

Rogers: "You feel that he could never understand you?"

The session goes on to eventually bring forth the real problem—the student's animosity toward his father and feeling of shame that this man is his father.

Because of his focus upon interaction, many of Rogers's tenets regarding therapy bring the contact between client and therapist under a microscope with a far sharper and more distinct lens. Though libertarian in his approach, refusing to be handcuffed by any pre-set protocols developed by Freud or anyone else, Rogers still actively set standards for psychotherapy. For Rogers, a pioneer in developing a complete and cogent school of psychological theory, the rationale behind the method of treatment used always remained less important than the personal qualities that the therapist possessed and brought to each counseling session. Far more than other humanists, Rogers insisted on taking a long and hard look at the attitude that the therapist brings to the psychotherapeutic session and how this affects the person being treated.

Over the years, Rogers began to experience and discover certain requirements for success in treating people. Much of what he learned and taught to others resulted from his innovative use of technology. Rogers began tape-recording therapeutic interviews with clients in 1942, long before this became a standard practice for psychotherapists. Based on what he learned from this experience, Rogers was one of the first to elaborate certain capabilities a therapist must possess in order to help clients attain their treatment goals. Rogers was also among the first to make these theoretical requirements a part of what he called "his hypothesis" of mental health care.

Rogers believed any therapist must possess four qualities, which he describes as being "necessary and sufficient":

- Congruence, or genuineness and sincerity. The quality of congruence is quite similar to one of Rogers's criteria for being "a fully functioning person," which will be discussed in more depth under Rogers's self-actualizing tendency theory. In his or her dealings with the client, the congruent therapist must present himself or herself honestly at all costs. He or she does not have to be perfect, but the therapist should never give the client the impression that they are false or "game-playing," defensive, or all-knowing.

- Empathy, the ability to feel accurately what it is that the client is expressing. Saying "I know how you feel" when the therapist actually has no idea how the person is feeling is not considered helpful by Rogers.

- Belief that the therapist also learns from the client. The therapist should be able to quietly listen, without interrupting, and be able to provide an exchange of ideas and feelings with the client.

- Unconditional positive regard, a genuine liking and acceptance of the clients as they are. It is not necessary for the therapist to agree with everything the person says or does, but he or she must be able to accept the client totally, without any reservations.

Example   Everyone, at one time or another, has tried to express to someone else how they feel when some terrible tragedy has visited them. If, for example, the person lost their spouse in the World Trade Center on September 11, 2001, and the listener responds, "Yeah, I know just how you feel . . . a distant relative that I hardly knew died two years ago in Europe and I was really sad," probably neither sincerity nor empathy is present.

Rogers's theories not only redefined who received therapy and the requirements for the provision of psychotherapy, but they also revolutionized who could provide such counseling. Prior to Rogers, mental health services were almost exclusively delivered by psychiatrists or analysts trained in psychology. Rogers's criteria for psychotherapists, however, make no mention of medical degrees or the need to have personally experienced psychoanalysis. Rogers actively encouraged the involvement of others in the provision of counseling services. For the first time, this inclusion brought social workers, teachers, clergy, and other people into the counseling area of mental health care. These innovative ideas paled in comparison, however, to the other changes in treatment that were developed by Rogers.

Initially, Rogers called the type of psychotherapy that he provided "non-directive." He perceived the therapist as accompanying the client on their journey but not leading the way. Rogers eventually changed this description to "client-centered" psychotherapy. Rogers believed that this title accurately indicated what was and was not provided by him during therapy. Rogers called his therapy "supportive rather than reconstructive." Sessions would address the client's agenda, not that of the therapist. Rogerian therapy would eventually undergo one more name change, coming less from Rogers than from others. It would become known as "people-centered," due to its increasingly wide application in so many other aspects of the real world beyond psychology—in marriage and parental counseling, child guidance, education, and even leadership seminars.

From the start of his career, Rogers developed methods to test the effectiveness of his therapy; he would continue that effort throughout life. More than any of his peers, Rogers always tried to define what

he and his client were trying to accomplish in psychotherapy. From his vast experience, he succeeded in outlining what the process of Rogerian psychotherapy should look like. These were the measures of success, the necessary and inevitable series of events that effective client-centered psychotherapy always followed.

Rogers's "people-centered" psychotherapeutic process includes all of the following steps:

- The person manifests a willingness to seek help. (Whether the person is able to identify this willingness or not, they show it by making an appointment with the psychotherapist for therapy.)
- The therapist outlines the scope of the assistance that will be provided to the client. It is made clear that the therapist does not have the answers to the client's problems, but assures the person that they have the capability, with the therapist's assistance, of finding their own answers to their problems.
- A warm, comforting, and safe environment is provided through the therapist's attitude. This encourages the client to freely assert both their feelings and insights about their problems.
- Negative feelings are identified for the client with the help of the therapist and are given free rein.
- When the negativity has been completely expressed, the therapist elicits the positive responses from the client that Rogers's experience had taught him would then be present.
- Both the negative and the ensuing positive feelings are recognized and accepted by the therapist.
- These six steps ultimately lead the client to insight into their problems. This insight is accompanied by new acceptance of self and self-understanding. New possibilities of action to solve the problem are brought forth.
- Positive actions to solve the problems and a decreased reliance on the help of the therapist occur.

Main points
- Rogers's hopeful, humanistic approach towards treating the mentally ill was born in the most unlikely of places—in his early experience working with abused and neglected children in upstate New York.
- Though Rogers was not the sole originator of the humanistic school of psychology, he added many important innovations to it; for example, that persons seeking help were "clients" rather than sick people, or "patients."

- Rogers was among the first to actually tape record therapeutic interviews for teaching purposes and to define what it was that he, as a psychotherapist, was trying to accomplish during psychotherapeutic sessions.
- Rogers developed eight criteria, or steps, listed above, for successful psychotherapy.
- Rogers believed that theory mattered less than did technique and the qualities the therapist brought to the psychotherapeutic interview. He believed that there were four qualities necessary in order for someone to successfully perform psychotherapy: congruence, or sincerity; empathy; the ability to listen and learn from the client; and a genuine liking and acceptance of the client.

Example Rogers himself provided the best metaphor for the type of therapy he spent his life practicing. He said it was similar to teaching a child to ride a bicycle. Though the teacher may initially hold onto the bicycle to steady it, eventually, in order to actually teach the child to ride, the teacher must let go of the bicycle and let the child try to ride independently. The child may take spills, yet eventually he or she will learn to ride the bicycle unassisted.

Rogers' core of personality

Explanation: The actualizing tendency For Rogers, plants and human beings gravitated toward survival in similar ways. Rogers, who in his youth had observed the plants and animals on his father's farm, had overheard the experts his father had consulted regarding breeding, learned the proper feed and environmental conditions, and observed the phenomenon of an urge for survival over and over again. In fact, in his early writings he cited mushrooms and seaweed as good examples of life struggling to live under adverse circumstances. But then Rogers began to think beyond why living organisms attempt to obtain the necessities of life, such as oxygen to breathe, water, and food. He pondered why intangibles such as safety, love, and autonomy are also valued and sought by not only human beings, but by other species as well. What Rogers came to conclude was that all living things were endowed with a genetic ability, what he terms "the core tendency" or the "actualizing tendency." This tendency not only gifted all species with a life force that made them instinctively seek to survive, but it also spurred them to go beyond survival to make the best of whatever circumstances in which they found themselves.

Rogers took this biological theory even further. He came to believe that his actualizing tendency applied not only to individual species of life but to entire ecosystems. More intricate, diverse living things, he believed, had an increased capability at survival solely because of their diversity. For example, if one species within an ecosystem such as a large forest ceased to exist, Rogers reasoned that there are most likely other species present in the forest that will take over the necessary functions to help the woodland survive. This ecological variety provided the forest with the flexibility that makes it more apt to be successful in surviving. His rural younger years had made these observations not terribly surprising and probably not much different from the observations of Darwin and others. Then Rogers took his actualizing tendency to a far different area. He ascribed this same core tendency to human personality development.

In addition to aiding survival, this actualizing tendency provides living things with a built-in capacity, developed during evolution, to know which things are good for them and which are not. The five senses are one example. Most people will not eat moldy, odoriferous food because of its offensive appearance and smell, thus saving themselves from food poisoning. Conversely, many people are tempted by the sight of a crisp apple, fresh from the tree, and most will savor the apple as they eat it. Clearly not all cases of food poisoning would be fatal and not all apples will be nutritious, but still people tend to make these choices. Observation of this behavior convinced Rogers that animals, and even babies, left to their own devices, will instinctively choose food that is right for them and necessary for their development. In other words, living beings desire and enjoy the taste of those things that they need in order to live. Rogers called such discretion "organismic valuing," and he extended the notion far beyond food choices.

Main points

- Living things have within them an innate capacity for both survival and even to go beyond survival to make the best of their lives.
- This capacity is determined by genetic factors rather than by the society in which they live.
- All living beings, animal and human, seek abstract good things such as safety, affection, and autonomy.
- Diverse living things have a greater capability of survival because they have more varied capacities to carry out functions necessary both to survival and improving life.
- Species instinctively want and enjoy the things that are necessary for their survival and growth.

- These observations of the basic needs for survival and comfort have implications far beyond the biological world. The same principles apply to the psyche.

Examples   The tree growing out of the side of a cliff or the violets growing through the crack in a sidewalk mentioned earlier are examples of life's inborn capacity and instinctual need for survival.

Wolves traveling in packs provide themselves with a necessary means of survival: strength in numbers. But the wolf pack also furnishes each creature in the group with a social milieu and relationships that are satisfying and believed to be necessary for wolves. Elephants in the wild have a similar need for, and live according to, a social structure.

The Irish potato famine is a good example of non-diversity making survival less sure. Because only one crop, potatoes, was planted in the Ireland of the 1840s, a disease specific to the potato plants obliterated entire potato fields, eventually starving those who were dependent on the potato fields for their survival.

Expansion of the actualizing tendency to human personality

The more complex the living being, the more complicated are its desires for the abstract things that are coonsidered to be good. This complexity provides human beings with an additional form of this actualizing tendency: the ability to improve, to make themselves into better people. Rogers calls this process of becoming the best we can be "self-actualization."

This core tendency for self-actualization consists of three separate areas:

- The self: A person's sense of who he or she is. The self comes into being early in life, as the person becomes aware of himself or herself as a separate entity and becomes able to describe oneself as "I" or "me." This self includes the person's personal perception of things, but it is a subjective perception rather than an objective one.

- Positive regard: Love, acceptance, and approval. Rogers perceives this need for positive regard as one universally shared by all of humankind. Though it is a requirement that is important throughout life, Rogers believes that it is most essential during infancy.

- Positive self-regard: Self-esteem, or approval and acceptance emanating from within the person that becomes a part of the person's concept of themselves.

Unlike the actualizing tendency common to all life forms, Rogers believes self-actualization is not genetically predetermined. Instead, it results from parental and societal influences on the individual, and it can be altered by family, friends, and the larger society. This self-actualization is the basis of personality development in Rogers's theory, and he manages to keep it quite simple: his personality theory recognizes only two divisions—those people whose self-actualizing capacity is active and fully functioning, and those in whom it not. In its most positive sense, self-actualization is why individuals attempt to make scientific discoveries, explore outer space, or attempt other creative endeavors. In many ways, Rogers seems more interested in describing what mental health is and how it is manifested than in looking at pathology. For Rogers, a person whose self-actualization tendency is fully functioning is a mentally healthy person, what he would call a "fully functioning person."

Rogers set up criteria that fully functioning persons would demonstrate. They are as follows:

- They would be open to the normal experience of life.

- They would be able to experience both pleasant and painful feelings that are appropriate reactions to the life situations they find themselves involved in.

- They would not use unsuitable or ineffective defense mechanisms.

- They would live existentially, that is, in the day or moment. (This does not imply that past experience is not used, only that the person uses their experience and lives in the present.)

- They would not respond with rigidity to situations. Similar to the forest described earlier, they would instead be spontaneous and able to adapt to change.

- They would possess positive self-regard, or self-esteem.

- They would have what Rogers would call "organismic trusting," that is, the ability to accept information, including experience and intuition, and trust that such information is right. Rogers values experience and intuition as being the most important. In Rogers's belief, if it feels right to the individual, it probably is right for that individual.

- They would operate with "experiential freedom": the ability to choose the most appropriate choice, based upon their experience.

- They would possess creativity, possessing a capacity for both thinking innovative and effectual thoughts and using these thoughts to produce innovative and effectual creations.

The fully functioning person probably represents a minority of the world's population, but Rogers truly believed that all people had within them the capacity for reaching this state of being. These fully functioning persons would be ones whose actualizing tendency and self-actualization would never have been thwarted by the world around them. They would have received positive regard from both parents and society as a whole, and therefore they would have developed positive self-regard. This ideal set of circumstances would lead them to what Rogers calls the "real self," the person who has achieved being both completely themselves and mentally healthy.

Main points   In human beings, the actualizing tendency has another component: self-actualization. Self-actualization has three parts: The self (the ability to recognize oneself as an individual entity, similar to Freud's ego); the need for positive regard (the need, common to all humans, for acceptance, love, and approval); and the need for positive self-regard (the individual's internal acceptance and approval of self, leading to a positive self-concept, or self-esteem). Unlike the actualizing tendency, which is genetic, self-actualization is driven by the society in which one lives.

Rogers's personality development describes only persons for whom the self-actualizing tendency is operative and those for whom it is not. Persons with an actively functioning self-actualizing tendency are described by Rogers as fully functioning persons. Among the characteristics fully functioning persons share are openness, an ability to live in the moment, a capacity to trust both intuition and experience, freedom to make choices, and the competence to be creative. Becoming the "real self," a fully functioning person faithful to their own ideals and aspirations, is the true goal of Rogers's psychotherapy.

Examples   The classic example of "the self" being subjective and dictated by the society one lives in is the young girl who has been told continually by an abusive parent that she is not pretty or that she is stupid. No matter how physically attractive she might be, or how high her IQ actually is, she will most likely continue to perceive herself as both ugly and stupid.

The need for positive regard was probably best described by a study done by researcher Rene Spitz decades ago in a South American orphanage. Some of the babies at the orphanage were not touched, held, or cuddled as babies would normally be. Eventually the babies from whom affection was withheld were noted to be failing. They died at a higher rate than infants that were given normal warmth and affection, indicating that the need for love is indeed both a psychological and physiological need.

The need for positive self-regard is basically the need to like and accept oneself. Many self-help groups address this need. One example is Al Anon, the worldwide support group for the loved ones of alcoholics and substance abusers. Al Anon literature contains 17 separate readings devoted to the subject of self-esteem.

When self-actualization isn't functioning

Explanation   Though self-actualization should be based on the inborn abilities a person possesses, it is actually very much affected by upbringing and society. Therefore, the innate potential a person has may not always be manifested if forces outside of the person harm or attempt to destroy him or her. Rogers considers one of the most important negative forces to be conditional positive regard, or withholding of love, acceptance, and approval to the child by parents unless the child complies with the parents' expectations or wishes.

Society, too, plays its role in thwarting a person's self-actualization. All of the external forces a person meets in life—family members, teachers, clergy, political leaders, even the media—send the message that the person's needs will be met only if they conform to society's expectations. In theory, how closely we conform to these expectations will determine whether or not we get the rewards society has to offer. This message, Rogers states, provides all of us with "conditions of worth."

When conditional positive regard and conditions of worth provide the framework for a person's personality development, these factors, viewed as negatives by Rogers, will eventually be internalized, leading to what he calls "conditional positive self regard," or self-esteem based solely on meeting other people's expectations. The individual will become reprogrammed to fashion themselves into an entity that is pleasing to parents and society at large, but not to themselves. Organismic valuing and experiential freedom, the basic building blocks of decision-making that lead to good mental health, will be abandoned.

Conditional positive self regard leads to the development of an "ideal self," Rogers believes. In his lexicon, "ideal" does not mean something positive, but rather a self that sets itself standards that are impossible to meet. This ideal self is an internally imposed goal that is always unattainable, and the notion leads to what Rogers calls "incongruity," and what the mental health movement prior to Rogers had called neurosis. If the real self could be described as what a person truly is, the ideal self could be characterized as what everyone else, and ultimately the person themselves, thinks they should be. The greater the difference between the real self and the ideal self, the greater the amount of mental distress that is present.

Rogers calls life events that clearly present the incongruity between the real self and the ideal self "threatening situations." If people find themselves in a situation where they are expected to be competent and calm, such as giving a speech, and instead they feel terrified, they will experience anxiety. The feeling of anxiety is a physiological response to mental discomfort, a signal that the person should physically escape from the uncomfortable predicament and run away as fast as possible. Quite often, however, people still have to do things that make them feel uncomfortable. Therefore, they develop psychological escape mechanisms that are referred to in psychology as defenses. If the person cannot run away in the physical sense, then they instead run away within their psyche.

Rogers believed that all defense mechanisms are completely based on perception, or how the person views an anxiety-producing situation. He recognizes only two defense mechanisms: denial and perceptual distortion. Rogers's denial is quite similar to Freudian denial. Rogerian denial gives the individual the capacity to completely obliterate (or deny) the existence of an unpleasant, stressful fact. Rogers's denial also includes Freudian repression, or refusal to allow the anxiety-producing thought to come into the consciousness. Perceptual distortion occurs when an individual acknowledges an anxiety-producing reality, but then (unrealistically) re-interprets it to diminish its capacity for causing stress.

According to Rogers, all human beings use defense mechanisms to some degree. The more defense mechanisms that a person employs, the less the real self is operational within the person. This leads to an even wider differentiation between the ideal self and the real self. This in turn results in an increase in incongruence, or neurosis. Rogers sees psychosis as merely an extension of this theory. When the person's defense mechanisms become completely overwhelmed, all sense of self—both real and idealized—becomes severely damaged; the psychotic person loses the ability to distinguish between the self and others.

Rogers set up similar criteria to describe the maladjusted person:

- The person lives defensively and would not be open to experiencing either pleasant and painful feelings.
- The person's life goals are based on a plan developed by someone else, perhaps the person's parents or society.
- The person does not utilize either organismic trusting or intuition.
- The person feels that they were not free to make choices and feels manipulated by others.
- The person would be unimaginative and conform to commonly held conceptions, whether these were right or wrong.

Main points

Self-actualization does not develop as it is naturally intended when forces outside of the person interfere with it. Rogers believed that if parents offered their child love, acceptance, and approval only if he or she met the parents' expectations, in his words, "conditional positive regard," that child would encounter significant road-blocks in reaching self-actualization. What Rogers called "conditions of worth," or demands put onto the person by society at large, require that the person conform to the expectations of family members, teachers, clergy, and the media, in order to receive positive things as rewards. People programmed by conditional positive regard and conditions of worth will eventually internalize these conditions for acceptance, creating conditional positive self-regard, or self-esteem entirely based upon living up to others' views of what they should be. This situation eliminates organismic valuing and experiential freedom from the decision-making process, alienating the person from their true self and from good mental health.

Conditional positive self-regard aids in the development of an ideal self, one that imposes impossible, unattainable demands upon the person. These demands, and the distance between this ideal self (what the person is conditioned to think they should be) and the real self (what the person really is) produce what Rogers calls incongruity, or neurosis. The size of the gap between the real self and the ideal self, indicates the degree of incongruity or neurosis that is present. Those events that make evident the incongruity between the real self and the ideal self are called by Rogers "threatening situations," which lead to anxiety. Anxiety produces a physiological response that calls for the person to run away from the threatening situation.

When a person cannot in reality run away from a threatening situation, they run away within their mind by using defense mechanisms.

For Rogers, there are only two defense mechanisms: denial and perceptual distortion. These defenses are based entirely upon the person's perception. Rogers's version of denial is similar to Freud's, but it also includes repression. Perceptual distortion is the re-interpretation of reality to make it less stressful. The use of defense mechanisms to some degree is a universal thing. The use of defense mechanisms makes the real self less functional, increasing the gap between real self and the ideal self. The greater this gap, the more what Rogers calls incongruence, or neurosis, that is present. For Rogers, psychosis is only an expansion of this theory, occurring when the person's defense mechanisms are completely breached and there is a shattering of both real and ideal self.

Examples Conditional positive regard is exemplified by the parents that show affection only when the child has done something that they perceive as being "good," such as washing their hands and face, and keeping their clothing immaculate while out playing. The child that comes in from playing covered with mud is then shouted at by the parents and treated in a rejecting manner.

Probably the most classic and mundane example of a condition of worth is the statement, "If you don't eat all your meat and vegetables, you cannot have dessert."

An overachiever who is never satisfied with his or her accomplishments is a person who has developed conditional positive self regard. This person's ideal self is so perfect that it is unattainable. Yet another example of a person with an ideal self is someone who wants her family to look perfect to the outside world no matter how upset and unhappy the family might actually be.

Gloria Swanson's character Norma Desmond, in the classic movie "Sunset Boulevard," exhibits several of Rogers's characteristics of a person living with an ideal self rather than a real self. Norma, a former great and beautiful movie actress, has grown old and is no longer attractive. Her ideal self is still young, beautiful, and successful in films. When reality makes her look at the actual substance of her situation, she uses denial (she is still beautiful and desirable) and perceptual distortion (everyone is jealous of her) to avoid reality. Norma Desmond eventually goes beyond incongruence, or neurosis, into psychosis.

HISTORICAL CONTEXT

When he wrote his landmark book, *Medical Inquiries and Observations upon the Diseases of the Mind,* in 1812, Philadelphia physician Benjamin Rush could not have known that he would one day become known as "the father of American psychiatry." Rush, a pious and charitable Pennsylvania physician, had advocated for some time for better treatment of the mentally ill. When he wrote his book, he was 67 years of age, and he had lived through enough adventure to fill several lifetimes. An early fighter against slavery, a patriot in the Revolutionary War, and a signer of the Declaration of Independence, Rush's battle to defeat the great yellow fever epidemic of 1793 in the United States' then-capitol, Philadelphia, probably earned him more fame and controversy in his lifetime than the book he wrote just one year before he died.

In fact, much of the controversy surrounding Benjamin Rush had nothing to do with psychiatry. He was a strong believer in the popular remedy of "bleeding" people, regardless of their diagnosis; many of his colleagues in Philadelphia, however, disagreed with his use of bleeding as a treatment for yellow fever. It is unknown if his blood-letting of mentally ill persons caused any debate. Certainly his observations regarding "Diseases of the Mind" evoked little stir. Yet Rush's book brought new thinking to an America that was considered a primitive, uncivilized backwater. Rush's observations closely mirrored those of fellow physicians Phillipe Pinel in France and Quaker William Tuke in England, who both advocated enlightened and more humane treatment for the mentally ill. Unfortunately Rush's book was flawed in two ways. It leaned heavily on astrology, a belief common in his time. But more important, it also subscribed to one of the two false theories about the cause of mental illness then in vogue: that mental illness, or "madness" as it was then called, was the result of a problem with the arteries supplying the brain with blood, causing inflammation. (The other then-popular theory was that sin caused mental illness; Rush apparently did not subscribe to this notion.) Besides his book, Rush also influenced American mental health through his invention of "the tranquilizer," a restraint that eerily resembles the electric chair. It was not as cruel as it looks, from all reports, and it was designed to decrease blood circulation to the brain.

In 1827, Thomas Upham published what is considered the first textbook of psychology: *Elements of Intellectual Philosophy*. Like Benjamin Rush's observations, Upham's book would do little to improve the quality of life for people suffering from psychiatric problems. But 30 years after Rush's death, a woman named Dorothea Dix would have appreciably more impact upon psychiatric treatment. A Massachusetts school mistress, Dix would shame Commonwealth politicians and sheriffs when she convincingly argued that the people with psychiatric illnesses in Massachusetts jails, contrary to what was then widely believed, really did feel the cold when they were shackled naked to beds in unheated cells in the dead of winter.

> I proceed, gentlemen, briefly to call your attention to the present state of Insane Persons confined within this Commonwealth, in cages, closets, stalls, pens! Chained, naked, beaten with rods, and lashed into obedience!

Dix's 1843 "Memorial to the Massachusetts Legislature" would eventually raise millions of dollars and create 32 mental hospitals in 20 states across the United States and in two Canadian provinces. Dix's castle-like stone hospitals, turreted and sitting atop hills away from the rest of the populace of cities and towns, at least provided kinder and better care for the mentally ill. They also came to be landmarks across the country. At first the medical profession had little to do with these "asylums," but gradually psychiatric care came to be seen as a specialty of medicine, and physician-superintendents became the norm. In 1844, the Association of Medical Superintendents of American Institutions for the Insane came into being.

For most Americans, psychiatric illness continued to be something both mysterious and frightening. These physicians that locked up the mentally ill in fortress-like hospitals as far removed as possible from the community did little to educate the public concerning the nature of mental illness. That lack of public education was primarily the result of a lack of knowledge. Neither Benjamin Rush, Thomas Upham, the hospital superintendents, nor Dorothea Dix really understood the causes or the effects or the treatment of emotional problems. Even as late as the Civil War, some doctors still subscribed to Rush's circulation-to-the-brain theory, while others adamantly believed mental illness was a result of wrongdoing. Harvard professor William James became America's first modern psychologist in 1890 when he wrote and published *Principles of Psychology*. The American Psychological Association came into being in 1892. In the same years, American psychologist E. L. Thorndike's studies of laboratory animals produced some of the earliest information on conditioned responses, work that Thorndike hoped to apply to education. But, echoing Dix decades earlier, it would

take another layperson to give the public the first shreds of useful information regarding mental illness.

Clifford Beers was an articulate and intelligent Yale graduate who suffered from bipolar disorder, then called manic-depressive illness. Shortly after his graduation from college in the early 1900s, he suffered a mental collapse that resulted in his being hospitalized in several of what were then called "mental asylums." Though much of the neglect and mistreatment of patients common in Dix's time had been eliminated, Beers soon discovered that confining patients in straitjackets and choking them into unconsciousness were still very much a part of mental health care in American psychiatric hospitals. Beer's mistreatment and his recovery in spite of it became the basis of his 1908 bestseller, *A Mind that Found Itself.* Two of Beers' staunchest and most influential admirers turned out to be James and famed psychiatrist Adolph Meyer. Meyer coined a new name for what was then commonly called "madness"—"mental hygiene." That same year, the Society for Mental Hygiene was founded, soon followed by a National Committee for Mental Hygiene, an organization that became international in 1919.

German education, especially regarding the study of the new-found science of psychology, was considered the best in the world at the beginning of the twentieth century. It was quite common for American students interested in the study of the mind to attend school in Europe, preferably in Germany. Wilhelm Wundt had established the first psychology laboratory at Leipzig, Germany in 1879, and American psychologist G. Stanley Hall was impressed enough with the German model to establish the first American psychology laboratory at Johns Hopkins Hospital in Maryland the next year. Hall moved on to Clark University in Worcester, Massachusetts, where he incorporated the German concept of graduate education. Hall's interest in psychology led to his inviting Sigmund Freud and Carl Jung to lecture at Clark in 1909, Freud's only trip to the United States, and one that deeply influenced American psychological thought. The first psychological studies of learning, with rats negotiating mazes, occurred at Clark University under Hall's auspices, and he was an early pioneer in the field of psychological studies regarding children.

For the majority of mentally ill Americans in the early twentieth century, however, neither psychiatry nor psychology significantly improved their treatment. In fact, both areas of learning remained the exclusive domain of intellectuals that shared their findings only among themselves. Furthermore, most practitioners of the newly discovered science of psychology discriminated against women. Three American women psychologists faced overwhelming sexual discrimination in the early years of the twentieth century, yet Mary Whiton Calkins, Christine Ladd-Franklin, and Margaret Washburn all managed to make major research contributions in their field. Calkins was banned from graduation from Harvard University, even though she had taken classes there, had passed all her courses, and was considered one of the university's most brilliant students. Both Ladd-Franklin and Washburn also were victimized by discriminatory practices several times during their careers. Yet, with incredible effort, these three women still managed to leave a lasting impression on American psychology. Calkins developed a memory procedure that is still used today, and she was the first woman president of the American Psychological Association. Ladd-Franklin was responsible for an evolutionary theory regarding color vision, and Washburn did impressive work in the field of comparative psychology.

Gender bias ran rampant within both psychiatry and psychology. American psychologist E.B. Titchener, who was educated in Germany, returned to his native country to write a 1909 book called *Titchener's Textbook of Psychology* and initiated the psychological approach known as structuralism. To pursue his passion for psychological research, he led a group of male-only researchers that called themselves "experimentalists." Both Columbia University and the University of Chicago, schools that would later employ Rogers, became quite active in the development of psychology in the United States, but neither school did much to encourage women's participation, educate the public regarding mental illness, or actually help troubled people. An example of one of the very few understandable public statements regarding psychological theory was made by James Angell, one of the first presidents of the American Psychological Association. Two schools of psychology had developed within American universities: the previously mentioned structuralism and another called functionalism. Angell explained the difference between the two schools of thought this way: "Structuralists ask, 'What is consciousness?' while functionalists ask, 'What is consciousness for?'" Few of his contemporaries made things as simple.

Despite its researchers' lack of communication with most of the American public, psychology became an important component of higher education. Mental testing for educational purposes was among the earliest psychological testing to have been developed and employed in the United States, but unfortu-

nately it quickly proved to be flawed. Henry Goddard (the originator of the term "moron") brought European intelligence testing to America. Alfred Binet's methodology had originally been developed to identify academically weaker students so that special programs could be developed to help them learn. Unfortunately, these early Binet tests were perverted and used to discriminate against certain Southern and Eastern European immigrants who came to America during the early years of the twentieth century. Eventually, this mode of testing developed into a more useful form, the Stanford-Binet IQ test, which is still used today. But in spite of these small steps forward, neither psychology nor psychiatry in the early twentieth century seemed capable of developing or carrying out concepts that would improve life for people with mental illness. Psychology had an image of rats in mazes or of flawed tests that proved skewed racial theories rather than a field that could help human beings. It would take Carl Rogers and others like him to put a more human face on the field of psychology.

CRITICAL RESPONSE

Disfavor among academics and parts of society

The contrast between Rogers's strong positive impact on clinical psychology in the real world and the lack of regard he enjoys among psychology professors in academia is impressive. Biographers Howard Kirschenbaum and Valerie Henderson note in their 1989 book, *The Carl Rogers Reader,* that

> Rogers spent his whole life not only asserting the importance of the democratic and libertarian ideal in all human relationships, but seeking ways to accomplish that ideal. He innovated, he described, he modeled, he even proselytized. For that he won hundreds of thousands of appreciative students whose work touches millions of lives each year. . . . he also won thousands of influential critics who have prevented Carl Rogers and the people-centered approach from becoming the mainstay of professional training in the academic institutions of the United States.

Yet, as noted previously, a 1982 study conducted by the American Psychology Association that polled practicing psychologists and psychotherapists ranked Rogers first in a rating of "The Ten Most Influential Psychotherapists."

Kirschenbaum and Henderson go on to state that "not all professionals have been pleased with Rogers's influence. Many find his theory and methods oversimplified. Others argue that trusting the individual's resources for self-help will not work and might even do harm." Psychologist and college professor C. George Boeree investigates this criticism in more detail. He refers to Rogers's "organismic trusting" as "a major sticking point" in Rogers's theories—not only for academics but also for those lay persons with a fundamentalist ethos. If the definition of organismic trusting is, as Rogers would say, having faith in ourselves that if we do what feels naturally right it will prove to be the right thing to do, it becomes clear that this could indeed become a slippery slope. To paraphrase Dr. Boeree, this could mean that if you are a sadist, you should hurt other people; masochists should hurt themselves; if you like drugs or alcohol, go for it; and if you're feeling depressed, kill yourself. This "If it feels good, do it!" attitude, often expressed by young adults but criticized by society at large during the 60s and 70s, has frequently been blamed on Rogers. Dr. Boeree further reflects, however, that organismic trusting would of necessity be in keeping with knowledge of the real self; consequently, by Rogers's definition, the real self would most likely not be compatible with sadism, masochism, substance abuse, or severe depression.

Rogerian therapy also often faced ridicule based upon its use of reflection of feelings. Rogers always said that the ability of the therapist was the most important facet of any Rogerian psychotherapy; still, there were those who believed that they were following Rogers's tenets but actually were not. Two common anecdotes prevalent among the psychological community in the 1950s, as reported by Howard Kirschenbaum in his earlier (1979) book *On Becoming Carl Rogers,* illustrate the common perception and criticism:

> I once went to a Rogerian counselor. I started talking about my problems and all he did was repeat back, word for word, everything I said. I couldn't figure out who was the crazy one, him or me. I said, I know that. That's what I just told you. So he said, You know that. That's what you just told me. After a while, I started getting really angry. So then he tells me I'm getting angry.

The following anecdote is both frightening, darkly humorous, and totally untrue. However, this mocking spoof of Rogers's type of therapy was a particular favorite of his critics during those years. It describes a fictional client's interaction with Carl Rogers during an appointment with Dr. Rogers in his office, on the 34th floor.

Client: "Dr. Rogers, I've been feeling awfully depressed lately."

Rogers: "Oh, you've been feeling very depressed lately?"

Client: "Yes, I've even seriously been considering suicide."

Rogers: "You feel you might like to kill yourself."

Client: "Yes, in fact I'm going to walk over to the window here."

Rogers: "Uhumm, you're walking over to the window there."

Client: "Yes, I'm opening the window, Dr. Rogers."

Rogers: "I see. You're opening the window."

Client: "I'm about to jump."

Rogers: "Uhumm. You're about to jump."

Client: "Here I goooooo. . . . ." (the client jumps).

Rogers: "There you go."

A loud crash is heard below. Dr. Rogers walks over to the office window, looks down, and says, "Splat!"

But perhaps the bias against Rogers's tenets arises not just from the prejudice of intellectuals or society's fear of pleasure-seeking and self-indulgence, but rather from Western culture's love affair with technology. Kirschenbaum and Henderson further observe in *The Carl Rogers Reader,* that "Rogers's message points us in a different direction (from technology). . . .what really matters is trust in ourselves and others, in communication, in how we handle our feelings and conflicts, in how we find meaning in our lives." They note that it is not only the professors in universities who have resisted Rogers's body of work. Ironically, it seems that the man who was such an innovator in the use of the twentieth century's gadgets—tape recordings, films and other media—is also the victim of society's fascination with this same technology. As a humanist, Rogers's belief in good communication and understanding between people is, in the end, more difficult and takes longer than technology's quick fixes. Rogers leads people away from computer programs, pills that provide chemical solutions to behavioral problems, and all the other proposed technocratic solutions to humanity's woes.

Rogers's common ground with other humanist psychologists

Humanistic philosophy of mental health treatment can be defined in many different ways. Most experts generally agree, however, that it includes three commonly held tenets: the importance of the person's perception of reality; the importance of helping people to understand both the significance and the definition of good mental health; and the need to encourage humanness and the ability to choose. Based on those criteria, it is clear that Rogers qualifies as a humanist. But going beyond the label, if often appears that the differences between Rogers and other humanist psychologists are more a matter of terminology than actual philosophical differences. Whether referred to as the actualization tendency by Rogers, self-realization by German-American psychoanalyst Karen Horney, or self-actualization by Abraham Maslow, the notion that human beings possess both an inborn desire for mental health and the capacity to realize that health is the common thread among the humanists.

Rogers' "conditional positive self regard," or the development of a person's self-esteem that is based on complying with the requirements of others, is remarkably similar to the theory propounded by Karen Horney. As did Horney, Rogers believes that this society-induced betrayal of the self is one of the building-blocks for the development of neurosis, or what Rogers called incongruence. The conditional regard of parents as described by Rogers is quite similar to the basic evil as described by Horney: parental indifference unless the child complies with their wishes. Maslow's "hierarchy of needs," progressing from basic physiological requirements such as hunger, thirst, and sex to self-actualization is very similar to Rogers' transition from the "actualizing tendency" to the "fully functioning person."

It is worth noting, however, that Rogers, humanist though he was, did not actually describe human beings as being basically good. In his 1977 book *A Way of Being,* Rogers explained his theory, as he so often did, in terms of a remembered perception from his teenage farming years. He talks about the family's winter storage of potatoes in a bin in the cellar, a few feet from a window. As spring approached and the light and temperature increased, these potatoes would put forth white, spindly shoots reaching toward that window. These sprouts would be totally different from the healthy green growth that a potato would put forth when planted in the rich soil outdoors. These unhealthy buds, reaching toward the light, though they would not be destined to flourish, would also not give up. Rogers noted that these potato sprouts made him think of

> clients whose lives had been terribly warped . . . men and women on back wards of state hospitals. So unfavorable have been the conditions in which these people have developed that their lives often seem abnormal, twisted, scarcely human. Yet the directional tendency in them (the wish to be mentally healthy) is to be trusted.

Yet Rogers surely did share with other humanists their disagreement with Freud's conception of the inherent malevolence of the human race. He addressed this contention, specific to the Freudian beliefs of famed psychiatrist Karl Menninger, in Rogers's article, "A Note on the Nature of Man," published in the *Journal of Counseling Psychology* in 1957. Menninger had reportedly told Rogers that he viewed man as being "innately destructive," a premise that made Rogers "shake his head in wonderment." In the article, Rogers looked to the animal world for comparison regarding inborn characteristics, believing that most people have fewer preconceived prejudices there. He described the lion, often perceived by people as being a "ravening beast," as in reality a well-adjusted creature. He noted that in their natural habitat lions kill only for food, are never gluttonous, and do not become obese. Furthermore, most lions develop into mature, independent, and self-responsible creatures that care for their young and understand about working cooperatively to survive. Similarly, Rogers stated that the human beings he had counseled had taught him that

> to discover that an individual is truly and deeply a unique member of the human species is not a discovery to excite horror. Rather I am inclined to believe that fully to be a human being is . . . [to be] one of the most widely sensitive, responsive, creative and adaptive creatures on this planet.

Relationship to Gestalt therapy

Freud and his disciples tend to look at their patients from the outside inward, trying to understand their patients' distorted view of reality. Conversely, Gestalt therapists do their best to go inside their patients and look outward, viewing the world from the person's internal vision of things. Early in the twentieth century, prior to World War I, German psychologists Max Wertheimer, Wolfgang Kohler, and Kurt Koffka began to perform experiments on monkeys and other animals and apply the results to human beings. In one experiment, researchers placed a banana (the reward) in an unreachable but visible place outside of the laboratory monkey's cage. If the monkey was given a sufficient number of sticks, Gestalt researchers learned that the creature would figure out how to assemble the sticks in order to successfully get hold of the banana. This outcome made Gestalt therapists believe that human beings, too, were innately capable of reasoning their way toward goals or solving problems. This belief is quite similar to Rogers's self-actualizing tendency.

Debates with behaviorist B.F. Skinner

In the late nineteenth century, American psychologist E.L. Thorndike began laboratory work that produced some of the earliest information on conditioned responses. Thorndike's interest was primarily in regard to education. In the early twentieth century in Czarist Russia, a psychologist named Ivan Petrovich Pavlov was also conducting animal research that showed the ability to produce emotional states by repeated conditioning. Thorndike and Pavlov's research was the beginning of behaviorist psychology, but most Western psychologists initially were unaware of Pavlov's contributions, as his work was not translated in the West until 1920. This research led to B.F. Skinner's efforts in the 1930s. The basic premise behind Skinner's research was that the more a certain behavioral response was rewarded, or "reinforced," the more that response was likely to happen again. This principle, called "operant conditioning" by Skinner, became the most common and popular version of behavioral psychology.

Skinner would take this notion even further, into political and social spheres, in his novel, *Walden Two.* This book proposed a utopian society that would be populated by ideal people who would be created as a result of operant conditioning. These Walden Two inhabitants would be mentally healthy, productive, and happy, and thus they would no longer need such abstract concepts as democracy or capitalism because there would be no class struggles.

Rogers took issue with much of behaviorist theory. As early as 1946, he had noted that, although behavior could be determined by the external influences to which an organism is exposed, "it also may be determined by the creative and integrative insight of the organism itself." In 1956, Rogers and Skinner met for the first time to debate their differences at the American Psychological Association's annual convention. Two more debates took place in the early 1960s.

From most reports, there was no winner in any of the three debates. Both Rogers and Skinner were remarkably articulate and informed presenters of their positions. In nearly all of these discussions, Rogers brought up *Walden Two,* and at one point noted that he saw little difference between that book and George Orwell's science-fiction classic *1984,* wherein all people are conditioned by punishment to be the same and to obey a dictator known as "Big Brother." Though they met for only those three debates, the dispute between Rogerian libertarianism and behavioral conditioning has continued. Rogers' position is probably best expressed in a statement he wrote in 1947:

> Significant problems of social philosophy are also involved in these diverging attitudes regarding therapy. If objective study supports the conclusion

that dependence, guidance and expert direction of the client's therapy and life are necessary . . . then a social philosophy of expert control is clearly implied. If further research indicates that the client has at least the latent ability to understand and guide himself, then a psychological basis for democracy would have been demonstrated.

THEORIES IN ACTION

For over 50 years, Rogers's work has continued to exert an major impact upon all aspects of psychology, and that impact has even spread far beyond the borders of what most people would term mental health. In nearly aspect of life in the twenty-first century, his legacy continues. His beliefs have influenced diverse groups, such as teachers, motivational speakers, and social workers. Rogers's encounter group ideas have been applied by both Rogers himself and others in efforts to bring about peace within communities and throughout the world. The multitudes of groups that try to discover each others' humanness and thus defuse ignorance and hate are the direct result of Rogers's ideas. The specific group discussions that Rogers facilitated in Northern Ireland and South Africa are examples of this, as are community groups in poor, urban areas that meet regularly with local police to discuss problems and feelings.

Research

Rogers worried from the beginning that Rogerian therapy could become dogmatic, as had other forms of psychotherapy and analysis. (The best example of this dogmatism would be Freudian theory.) Increasingly, Rogers became convinced that "psychotherapy may become a science, applied with art, rather than an art which has made some pretense of being a science." The only way that psychotherapy could be a science would be through research, developing measures of the success of psychotherapy sessions. From the beginning of his practice and writing in the 1930s, Rogers advocated for the inclusion of such study. What made the research possible was Rogers's tape-recording of his client's psychotherapeutic interviews, which he began in 1941. In the ten years that followed, Rogers would record more than 40 complete cases. By 1957, he had taped over 200.

The first phase of Rogers's research ran between 1940 and 1948. These studies were admittedly random and subjective, based on the ideas and needs of the individual researchers (usually graduate students) that worked with Rogers during those years. These investigations sought to identify what happened

FURTHER ANALYSIS:
The "Q Technique"

When Carl Rogers put together a group of graduate students and other professionals at the University of Chicago in 1940, he was beginning a study of psychotherapy that he had been advocating for over a decade. As the initial two studies unfolded, he and the other researchers became acutely aware that there was no tool in existence that measured whether clients believed that they had become better. For Rogers, this measure was by far the most important measurement of all, but no psychological test then used captured this information. William Stephenson, an English researcher then working at the University of Chicago, had developed a system of cards called "Q cards" that Rogers and his group used. Rogers calls the information on these Q cards "a population of self-referent items." They contained statements that were originally extracted from client interviews—self-descriptions gleaned from them during their psychotherapeutic interviews.

Examples of the type of statements to be found on these cards are:

- I am a submissive person.
- I'm afraid of a full-fledged disagreement with a person.
- I am a hard worker.
- I am really disturbed.
- I am likable.

Each client involved in the Phase III study would be given 100 of these Q cards and asked to sort them, usually into nine separate categories. The research subjects sorted the cards according to how similar to themselves the statements were. That is, the first stack would hold cards with descriptions that they felt were the most like themselves, the next stack a little less so, and on until by the ninth pile, the person would feel that most of the expressions on the Q cards did not actually apply to them. As only a set number of cards could be sorted into any one pack, the responses were set up to provide a bell-shaped curve which made for more manageable development of statistics. These "Q Sorts" as they were called were done several times during therapy, and in three different ways. The test that Rogers and the others developed from this method came to be called the "SIO (self, ideal, and ordinary) Q Sort" test.

The three methods of sorting the Q cards performed by the study subjects (and the controls) were:

- Categorizing the self-referent statements as to which were the most descriptive of them to those that were least like themselves. This first sort would establish a self-concept.

- Dividing the cards based upon the subject's perception of which cards described best what they would want to be like. This process would extend to a ninth stack that contained statements expressing what the person would least want to be like. This second sort would provide the person's perception of their ideal self.

- Sorting the cards based on the clients' perceptions of "ordinary people." This third sort represented the ordinary data point.

This self-test, given at key points both before, during, and after a client underwent psychotherapy for the first time produced a means of measuring whether or not a person's self-concept actually changed as a result of psychotherapy. The control subjects provided the means of assuring that changes in the people studied were not simply random phenomena, or changes that could have happened anyway, with or without therapy. The Rogers group researchers produced results that were among the most definitive and dramatic ever demonstrated. They showed through their testing methods that people involved in client-centered therapy reduced the gap between their self-concept and their idealized version of themselves. Self-concepts in particular showed drastic improvement.

---

during therapy, measured how directive or non-directive the therapist was, tried to determine how much emotional expression and insight were developed by the client, and estimated how the researchers perceived the success of the therapy. There were a total of 13 of these early studies done, and these were considered by most to be merely explorations of Rogerian psychotherapy. Elias Porter, a student from Ohio State University, conducted and published the first of these studies in 1943. Based upon Rogers' often-repeated and published statements that the process and progress of therapy was a predictable thing, these graduate student researchers attempted to confirm or invalidate his vision of what happened in psychotherapy sessions. It was considered an exploratory form of research only, and it had obvious failings. Even if insight were measured, there was no means of calculating how increased insight improved the client's life situation. Equally, no measurement in Phase I demonstrated whether non-directive therapy was any more effective than any other type.

The second phase of research looked at the efficacy of Rogerian psychotherapy by using more sophisticated, time-tested psychological evaluation. The problem with Phase II, even with the use of improved testing, was twofold: the number of clients involved in the study was small; and there were no experimental "control" subjects involved. Yet, it represented an improvement over the earlier phase of testing.

Among the psychological tests used in Phase II were:

- The Rorschach, or "inkblot" projective test, designed to reveal the subject's inner personality structure, including introversive and extroversive tendencies.

- The MMPI (Minnesota Multiphase Personality Inventory), a questionnaire designed to sort the person's response into certain diagnostic categories in order to indicate his or her tendency toward that diagnosis.

- A client self-rating of improvement scale developed by the researchers.

Ever persuasive, Rogers managed to obtain several hundreds of thousands of dollars in funding from various foundations and from the U.S. Public Health Service to carry out Phase III. Though 15 to 30 people worked on various phases of this research over the years, only 10 of them, including Rogers, remained involved from the project's earliest days until the completion of the third phase. The others were graduate students that became involved for a time and eventually moved on. As noted previously, rather than conduct the research himself, Rogers preferred to facilitate, providing funding, ideas, and simple encouragement. Most of his graduate students came from what was known as "The Rogers Group" at the University of Chicago Counseling Center.

Phase III, the final and most definitive phase of Rogers's research into the efficacy of psychotherapy, was characterized by several innovative ideas, organized as follows:

- The study was divided into two "blocks" of clients, people who had come to the counseling center for help and had agreed to be involved in several batteries of psychological tests during their treatment.

- Block I contained 25 clients who had come for therapy.

- Block II, assembled later, contained at least 25 more clients.

- The ethical problem concerning finding "controls," people not receiving therapy to measure against those receiving therapy, was resolved in two ways: volunteers not receiving therapy but taking the psychological tests used were "matched" to clients in therapy; and prospective clients were put on a waiting list for therapy, and also received the same psychological testing.

- The measurement that Rogers considered the most important—the client's self-rating of the efficacy of therapy—still needed to be developed. All previous such self-rating scales had proven inaccurate and unscientific. A British researcher, William Stephenson developed the "Q Technique" that finally solved this quandary. (See sidebar)

With the Q Technique in place, Rogers's researchers were ready. "Test Points," times that tests would be administered, were established at key times both before, during, and after therapy. The same battery of tests was administered to the control subjects on much the same schedule: before their wait began, during the clients' psychotherapy treatment, and afterward. The thoroughness of the testing and follow-up clearly demonstrate the painstaking accuracy that was involved in completing this research (as shown below). The detail involved is both impressive and shows clearly why Rogers's research was so heralded by nearly everyone in the mental health field.

Testing and other data collected during Phase III of Rogers' research included:

- A short personal history form filled out by both clients and controls prior to the beginning of treatment.

- A psychological test known as the Willoughby Emotional Maturity Test completed by two of the subject's friends or relatives, assessing the person's emotional maturity during therapy.

- Recording and transcription of all therapy sessions.

- A SIO (self, ideal, and ordinary) sorting of Q cards prior to therapy, after counseling was

CHRONOLOGY

1902: Carl Rogers is born in Oak Park, Illinois.

1914: Moves to a rural Illinois community with his family.

1921: Travels to the Far East with a religious student group.

1924: Graduates from the University of Wisconsin and marries Helen Elliot.

1926: Son David is born. Leaves seminary to attend Columbia University.

1931: Earns a PhD in psychotherapy from Columbia University.

1940: Receives a full professorship at Ohio State University.

1945: Joins faculty at the University of Chicago. Elected president of the American Psychological Association.

1964: Elected "Humanist of the Year" by the American Humanist Association.

1970: *On Encounter Groups* published. He would publish two more books before his death.

1986: Travels to Russia to facilitate conflict resolution.

1987: Dies of heart attack.

---

completed, and then again six months later. (This was in addition to Q sorts at the seventh, twentieth and, if necessary, at the fortieth counseling session.)

- The Willoughby Emotional Maturity Test to the client administered before, after, and six months after completion of therapy.

- The Thematic Apperception Test (known as the TAT), a projective psychological test similar to the Rorschach, given before, after, and six months after completion of therapy.

- The Self-Other Attitude Scale, a test that measured several social and political attitudes of the person, given on that same schedule of before, after, and six months after completion of psychotherapy sessions.

- A role-playing activity, developed to determine how the client would respond to those around him or her in certain situations.

- In order to assess the therapist's empathy, at the end of the therapy the person conducting the therapy was asked to sort the Q cards as he or she believed the client would.

- A self-rating scale for the therapist appraising their view of the relationship between therapist and client, as well as the entire therapeutic process.

- Two follow-up interviews: one between the client and therapist and one with the client and the person performing the tests to determine the client's assessment of the efficacy of the therapy.

- A follow-up questionnaire sent to clients after the termination of therapy.

This research, the culmination of years of work and the collaboration of many was, as Rogers freely admitted in his 1954 book *Psychotherapy and Personality Change,* "far from perfect." However, no one had ever before come close to actually measuring what occurred in psychotherapy. The Distinguished Scientific Contribution award given by the American Psychological Association to Rogers in 1956 cited him

> for developing an original method to objectify the description and analysis of the therapeutic process, for formulating a testable theory of psychotherapy and its effects on personality and behavior. . . . His imagination, persistence and flexible adaptation of scientific method in his attack on the formidable problems involved in the understanding and modification of the individual person has moved this area of psychological interest within the boundaries of scientific psychology.

Rogers cried when he received this honor and even years later said, "Never have I been so emotionally affected . . ."

Case studies

This description of the group process as perceived by Rogers, then 75 years of age, is taken from his 1977 book *Carl Rogers on Personal Power.* It concerns a group held during a workshop Rogers was attending. He describes two of the people in the group, and with tremendous self-honesty, explains how he feels about the interactions occurring between him and these two people. Ben is an elderly psychiatrist attending the group who seems to want Rogers to be an authority and impart wisdom about therapy. Ben also wishes to tell the group his own philosophy—that feelings create nothing but problems and he has been able to live successfully for several years holding all of his emotions in check. Rogers sees the attempt to

BIOGRAPHY:

Hazel Markus

"It struck me as an interesting possibility."

That was how, in an interview, Hazel Rose Markus described her initial decision to make social psychology her life work. It is clear Markus' work and ideas had their early development in the theories of Carl Rogers. Like Rogers, Markus began her career in the Midwest, at the University of Michigan. She had received her B.A. from California State University in San Diego, and in 1975 she earned her Ph.D. from the University of Michigan. Unlike Rogers, Helen Markus married a fellow academic; University of Michigan professor Robert Zajonc. She joined the faculty of Stanford University as a professor of psychology in 1994. Markus's career has also included a stint as a research scientist at the Institute of Social Research. Also, like Rogers, Markus has traveled worldwide in the course of her work, has written extensively, and much of her career has been spent studying the self—specifically, self-concept and self-esteem, and how these relate to a person's behavior and his or her interactions with the world.

Markus' other field of endeavor has been one that humanist (and social) psychologists such as Rogers,

Karen Horney, and Erich Fromm could surely relate to: the study of how environment and culture relate to the development of the personality. Her research has taken her to places as diverse as Japan and Jamaica. As she describes it, "Specifically, my work is concerned with how gender, ethnicity, religion, social class, cohort, or region or country of natural origin may influence thought and feeling . . . particularly self-relevant thought and feeling." A recent study by Markus addressed the differences in both functioning and self-concept between Japanese and American university students. In combination with Kitayama, Heiman, and Mullally, Markus has written several books and articles, including "A Collective Fear of the Collective: Implications for Selves and Theories for Selves," published in 1994 in the *Personality and Social Psychology Bulletin, Culture and Basic Psychological Principles,* and *Social Psychology: Handbook of Basic Principles.* Markus has also worked on research into shyness, midlife, and aging. Her most current writing, also in conjunction with S. Kitayama, is a book called *Collective Self-Schemas: The Socio-Cultural Grounding of the Personal.*

---

make him an authority by Ben as "dependency" and admits that it annoys him. Others in the group, especially the women, are angered by Ben's credo regarding feelings and attack him on this score. Rogers feels very impatient, keeps thinking that the group is moving very slowly, and they should pick up the pace.

Michelle, a pretty 30-something divorced woman, expresses both her desire for, and fear of, getting into another relationship. She spoke of going to a swimming pool with a male acquaintance and feeling panic, which caused her to just leave without any explanation. She refers to her ambivalence regarding getting into another relationship by saying, "I'm always doing this push-pull thing. It's awful. I can't bear this stress." Ben then spoke up again, stating that he had been thinking about his no-emotions stance, and realizing that perhaps he was wrong. He goes on to remember that his wife bitterly complained about his being cold and unfeeling, and he now wonders if he is not doing the same thing with this group. Rogers is skeptical of this sudden transformation in Ben. He is also feeling a

strong urge to hug Michelle. He tries to question his own reasons for this, and he considers that it is possibly a sexual attraction for her that he is feeling. He finally asks her if she would like a hug, and she replies, "I'd love it!" Rogers hugs her and she says, "Maybe I won't fly home tomorrow after all." (She apparently was having so much difficulty interacting with others that she had considered just leaving the group.)

Based upon the group interactions that Rogers experienced while attending this group, he was able to make the following conclusions about the group process:

- There is power built into a group. The group proceeds at its own pace, and it will not be manipulated or pressured to go either faster or more slowly.

- Risk-taking leads to trust between people in the group. Rogers took responsibility for honestly sharing how he felt and was accepted by the group.

- The psychiatrist Ben also took the risk of sharing, and even though the group was critical of his stance regarding feelings, they were also able to demonstrate to him that they cared.

• Michelle, too, shared her pain and confusion regarding her feelings with the group and felt accepted and cared for by the group.

• Rogers's intuitive action of hugging Michelle proved to be an example for him that his intuition was indeed trustworthy and the group's reaction could also be trusted.

• In the group, closeness was found to be safe.

• The group comes to understand that it is accountable for itself; each member is responsible for expressing themselves to make the group useful to all.

BIBLIOGRAPHY

Sources

Boeree, C. George. *Personality Theories/Carl Rogers*. 2000. http://www.ship.edu/~cgboeree/fromm.html.

Coleman, James. *Abnormal Psychology and Modern Life*. Chicago: Scott, Foresman and Co.,1956.

Goodwin, C.J. *A History of Modern Psychology*. New York: John Wiley and Sons, 1999.

Hazel Markus, Professor of Psychology. 2001. http://www.stanford.edu.

Humanistic Psychologists. *Carl Rogers: His Life and Background*. 2000. http://www.facultyweb.cortland.edu.

Kaplan, Harold I., MD, and Benjamin J. Sadock, MD. *Synopsis of Psychiatry, Behavioral Sciences and Clinical Psychiatry*. Baltimore, MD: William and Wilkins, 1991.

Kirschenbaum, Howard. *On Becoming Carl Rogers*. New York: Delacorte Press, 1979.

Kirschenbaum, Howard and Valerie Henderson. *The Carl Rogers Reader*. Houghton Mifflin, 1989.

Notes on Carl Rogers. 2002. http://www.sonoma.edu.

O'Hara, Maureen. *About Carl Rogers*. 2002. http://www.saybrook.edu.

Rogers, Carl. *Carl Rogers on Encounter Groups*. New York: Harper and Row, 1970.

Rogers, Carl. *Carl Rogers on Personal Power*. New York: Dell Publishing, 1977.

Rogers, Carl. *Client-Centered Therapy: Its Current Practice, Implications and Theory*. Boston: Houghton Mifflin, 1951.

Rogers, Carl. *Counseling and Psychotherapy: Newer Concepts in Practice*. Boston: Houghton Mifflin, 1942.

Rogers, Carl. *On Becoming a Person*. Boston: Houghton Mifflin, 1961.

Rogers, Carl. *Psychotherapy and Personality Change*. Chicago: University of Chicago Press, 1954.

Rogers, Carl. *A Way of Being*. New York: Houghton Mifflin, 1980.

Further readings

Rogers, Carl. *The Clinical Treatment of the Problem Child*. Boston: Houghton Mifflin, 1939.

Rogers, Carl. *Counseling with Returned Servicemen*. New York: McGraw-Hill, 1946.

Rogers, Carl. *A Therapist's View of Personal Goals*. Wallingford, PA: Pendle Hill, 1965.

Rogers, Carl. *The Therapeutic Relationship and its Impact*. Madison, WI: University of Wisconsin Press, 1967.

Rogers, Carl. *Person to Person: The Problem of Being Human, A New Trend in Psychology*. Lafayette, CA: Real People Press, 1967.

Rogers, Carl. *Freedom to Learn: A View of What Education Might Become*. Columbus, OH: Macmillan, 1969.

Rogers, Carl. *Freedom to Learn: Studies of the Person*. Columbus, OH: Charles E. Merrill, 1969.

Rogers, Carl. *Becoming Partners: Marriage and its Alternatives*. New York: Delacorte Press, 1972.

Rogers, Carl. *Freedom to Learn for the Eighties*. New York: Prentice Hall, 1983.

Burrhus Frederic Skinner

BRIEF OVERVIEW

Burrhus Frederic (B.F.) Skinner (1904–1990) is considered by most to be one of the pivotal psychologists of the twentieth century. Both his followers and detractors alike agree that his tireless work in behaviorism has significantly changed the landscape of psychology in general and the perception of how behavior is understood by both scientists and common people. His theories, though modified in various ways over the years, still continue to be widely applied in all walks of contemporary life.

Skinner was an American psychologist best known for the theory he developed over many years, which he called operant conditioning. Operant conditioning was a refinement of Ivan Pavlov's earlier concept of classical conditioning. Operant conditioning states that learning occurs as a result of the rewards and punishments the subject receives in response to a particular behavior. If the result of the behavior is a reward, the same behavior is likely to be repeated. If the result is a punishment, the behavior is less likely to be repeated.

Skinner had an initial interest in becoming a writer and received a bachelor's degree in English from Hamilton College in New York. After some time out of school writing newspaper articles, Skinner enrolled in the experimental psychology program at Harvard University and earned his masters and doctoral degrees in 1930 and 1931, respectively.

It was while Skinner was at Harvard that he was heavily influenced by the work of John B.

1904–1990

AMERICAN PSYCHOLOGIST, WRITER

HARVARD UNIVERSITY, Ph.D., 1931

B. F. Skinnner. *(Courtesy of the Library of Congress.)*

(1971). In *Beyond Freedom and Dignity*, Skinner advocated mass conditioning as a means of social control, which created a great stir of controversy when it was published.

Skinner is also known for his invention of "the Skinner box," which is used in behavioral training and experimentation of animals to test and record the results of operant conditioning. For years it was rumored that Skinner kept his own daughter in one of the experimental boxes for an extended period of time, but historical records show this to be false.

Although Skinner's research was predominantly conducted with laboratory rats, he believed that his results could also be extrapolated to the behavior of human beings. As a behaviorist, he viewed human behavior as largely a response to environmental stimuli.

At the time of his death in 1990 from leukemia, Skinner had become one of the most notable figures in the field of psychology. The principles of operant conditioning and reinforcement that he outlined were built upon by clinical psychologists and applied to the treatment of disorders such as phobias, panic disorders, and child conduct problems.

Watson, who is commonly referred to as the "father of behaviorism" and the one responsible for initially popularizing many behavioral principles in the culture. Stemming from this and other influences, Skinner dedicated his life's work to studying the relationship between reinforcement and observable behavior. Throughout his career, he insisted that psychology was a scientific, empirically driven discipline.

In 1936, Skinner joined the faculty of University of Minnesota and later (1945) took up a position as chairman of the psychology department at Indiana University. In 1948, however, Harvard offered him a faculty position, which he accepted, and he remained there for the rest of his life.

Skinner is perhaps best known for several of his books. The first, entitled *Walden Two* (1948), describes a utopian community where the members of the community lived by the principles of operant conditioning and reinforcement. It received great praise from those receptive to his radical ideas and harsh criticism from those opposed to the mechanistic application of his theory to life. A prolific but slow writer, Skinner penned a combined total of nearly 200 articles and books over his long and influential career. His other important works include *Behavior of Organisms* (1938), and *Beyond Freedom and Dignity*

BIOGRAPHY

The early years

B.F. Skinner was born on March 20, 1904 in Susquehanna, a small railroad town located in northeastern Pennsylvania. Skinner wrote three volumes of autobiography during his later years, and much of what we know of his earliest years comes from his own recollection.

Skinner was the older of two children and was brought up in a home with "rigid standards" enforced by his mother Grace Burrhus. Like most children in the early 20th century, Skinner and his younger brother Edward (called "Ebbie") grew up in an atmosphere where a strict code of conduct was followed. Grace clearly attempted to pass this strong social code to Skinner (called Fred), by expressing disapproval when he wavered from the expected norm. Skinner seemed to be especially receptive to praise from his parents, though it was apparently not given in great quantity. It is an interesting parallel that later his theory of operant conditioning would emphasize the crucial effect of "positive" reinforcement on behavior.

Skinner's father, William, was an only child and lived most of his life in Susquehanna. After finishing high school, William worked for a short period as a draftsman in the Erie Railroad Engineering Department. Because he showed little mechanical aptitude, he decided in 1895 to enroll in law school in New York. After passing the bar examination in 1896, he opened a law practice and was interested in making his mark amid the opportunities that were present in the ever-changing cultural landscape of the early twentieth century. He was successful as an attorney, political orator, and town booster, but was also notoriously boastful about his accomplishments to peers and underlings.

Skinner recalled his father as a gentle parent who never physically punished him, preferring verbal disappointment or good-natured ridicule as the preferred form of discipline. His father never missed an opportunity, however, to inform him of the punishments which were waiting for him if he turned out to have a criminal mind. His father once took his eldest son through the county jail to show what life would be like inside a prison.

Despite William's verbosity in the community, at home he seemed to live under the control of his wife's domineering personality. She acted in a condescending way toward her husband, and according to Skinner's account, the two were never very close emotionally.

Grace, Skinner's mother, was the oldest of four children and three years younger than her husband. She apparently was quite attractive and had a gifted singing voice, which she regularly used in her performances at the Susquehanna Hogan Opera. She attended Susquehanna High School and had ambitions to become a secretary, which she eventually realized when she was hired by the Erie Railroad in 1901. It was during this time that she met William and was impressed by his rising reputation as a lawyer and political speaker. They were married in 1902 and had a much more promising future since the economic depression and widespread labor unrest of the 1890s had abated. American women of that era were expected to sacrifice their careers when they married, and Grace was no exception. Even though she still cared a great deal about her standing in the community, her status would be associated with William's professional position.

Skinner's brother Ebbie was two and a half years younger than he and appeared to be the favored child of his parents. Ebbie was an affable child who raised pigeons and played the clarinet. Ebbie was more outgoing than Fred and seemed to have a social grace that Fred lacked. Yet Fred was apparently not jealous of his brother and even appeared to like him. As Ebbie

PRINCIPAL PUBLICATIONS

- *About Behaviorism.* 1974.
- *The Analysis of Behavior: A Program for Self-Instruction.* 1961.
- *The Behavior of Organisms: An Experimental Analysis.* 1938.
- *Beyond Freedom and Dignity.* 1971.
- *The Contingencies of Reinforcement: A Theoretical Analysis.* 1969.
- *Cumulative Record: Definitive Edition.* 1959, 1961, and 1972.
- *Enjoy Old Age: A Program of Self-Management.* 1983.
- *A Matter of Consequence.* 1983.
- *Notebooks.* 1980.
- *Particulars of My Life: Part One of an Autobiography.* 1976.
- *Recent Issues in the Analysis of Behavior.* 1989.
- *Reflections on Behaviorism and Society.* 1978.
- *Schedules of Reinforcement.* 1957.
- *Science and Human Behavior.* 1953.
- *The Shaping of a Behaviorist: Part Two of an Autobiography.* 1979.
- *Skinner for the Classroom.* 1982.
- *The Technology of Teaching.* 1968.
- *Upon Further Reflection.* 1987.
- *Verbal Behavior.* 1957.
- *Walden Two.* 1948.

grew older, he proved to be much better at sports and more socially popular than his older brother. Ebbie often would tease Fred about his literary and artistic interests. Tragically, Ebbie died when he was 16 years old due to a massive brain aneurysm. The loss of Ebbie was devastating to the Skinners, especially William, who seemed thereafter to lose a part of himself he was never quite able to recover. Perhaps

FURTHER ANALYSIS:
The operant chamber

An operant-conditioning chamber, also commonly known as a "Skinner box," is an experimental apparatus that was invented by B. F. Skinner in 1935 and was the basis of operant conditioning theory. Operant theory suggests that humans and animals "operate" on their environment and in doing so, encounter reinforcing stimuli that shape behavior. In operant conditioning, the behavior is followed by a consequence, which reinforces the behavior and makes it more likely to be repeated.

Skinner used the operant chamber to study the learning process of small animals. The chamber was a soundproof, light-resistant box or cage used in laboratories to isolate an animal for experiments in operant conditioning, and usually containing only a bar or lever to be pressed by the animal to gain a reward, such as food, or to avoid a painful stimulus, such as a shock. The chamber was large enough to easily accommodate the animal while allowing for easy viewing of the subject.

Most subjects that Skinner used in the operant chamber were smaller animals such as rats and pigeons. However, many other researchers have subsequently used the chamber with monkeys, raccoons, a variety of birds, and a host of other animals. Skinner began his research, like most at the time, using rats. But he soon found pigeons to be superior subjects because they could be conditioned more quickly using operant techniques. After this discovery, he used pigeons exclusively in his experiments.

The typical operant chamber includes a bar-press lever that is attached to a wall, adjacent to a food-cup or dish. During the exploration of the box, the subject may come across the lever and activate it, which triggers the release of a food pellet in the food cup or opens a door in the chamber that reveals food. Depending on the type of animal used, the chamber will incorporate different types of feeders and an operandum. An operandum is a device that automatically detects the occurrence of a behavioral response or action in the subject. The operandum is typically hooked up to a computer or other monitoring device to record the responses of the subject.

A modern operant chamber is more complex than those used by Skinner. Typically it would contain one or more levers that an animal can press; more than one stimulus, such as light or sound; and depending on the experiment, the chamber may include several means of reinforcing the behavior with food. The animal's interaction with the levers can be detected and recorded automatically. It is also possible to deliver other reinforcers such as water, or a form of punishment like electric shock through the floor of the chamber. With this configuration of multiple operandii and reinforcers, it is possible to investigate countless psychological phenomena.

In principle, the goal of the operant chamber is to measure an animal's ability to learn the association between the behavior (pressing a bar) and receiving a reward or reinforcer of the behavior (food). In operant terms, if the organism is learning this association, then the reinforcer (food) is likely to cause the behavior to repeat.

The use of the operant chamber was one of Skinner's most important developments and formed the basis for much of his theory of operant conditioning, which he has generalized to human behavior as well. Behavioral psychologists around the world still use variations of the operant chamber in ongoing research with subjects.

---

this was related to William's secret favoritism of his younger son over Fred. Years later, while reflecting on this tumultuous period, Frederic Skinner admitted that he was "not much moved" by his brother's death and subsequently felt guilty for his lack of emotion.

Much of Skinner's early years were spent building things. Whatever control his parents exercised, they still allowed Fred substantial freedom to explore, observe, and invent. A sampling of his inventions included musical instruments, roller-skate scooters, merry-go-rounds, model airplanes, and even a glider, which he tried to fly. As an early business venture, Skinner invented a flotation system that separated ripe elderberries from green ones so that he and a friend could sell the ripe berries door-to-door. In retrospect, these early inventions were an indication of Skinner's immense curiosity of how things worked. He would later shift this same curiosity from the mechanics and interrelationship of objects to the mechanics and reinforcement of behavior.

As part of life in a small town, Skinner attended the same school during his first 12 years of education. There were only eight students in his graduation class. His keen mind and literary interests allowed him to excel academically. One teacher in particular, named Mary Graves, would prove to be an important figure in his life. Her father was the village atheist and an amateur botanist who believed in evolution. Ironically, Graves also taught Skinner and a handful of other boys most of the Old Testament in a Presbyterian Sunday school class she lead for years. Despite her efforts, Skinner would, years later, announce to Graves that he did not believe in the existence of God.

Graves was a dedicated person with cultural interests that far exceeded those of the average person in town. She organized what was known as the "Monday Club," a literary society to which Skinner's mother belonged. Graves also introduced Skinner to a wide range of classic literature ranging from Shakespeare to Conrad's *Lord Jim*. Graves taught Skinner many subjects during his years in that schoolhouse. She taught him drawing in the lower grades, and later English, both reading and composition. Skinner attributed his interest in literature and later his choice of English as his major study in college to Graves' influence.

College

Skinner attended Hamilton College on the recommendation of a friend of the family and majored in English. He minored in Romance languages. Hamilton was proud of its reputation for public speaking, and required all of its students to be trained in oratory skills throughout their stay. Skinner reluctantly complied with the four compulsory years of public speaking. Though a good student, Skinner never felt like he fit into student life at Hamilton. He joined a fraternity without knowing what it entailed. He was admittedly not good at sports and complained that the college was "pushing him around" with unnecessary requirements, such as attending daily chapel. He observed that most students showed almost no intellectual interest in the subjects taught and by his senior year was in open revolt of the school's system.

Skinner claims that the most important thing that happened to him while at Hamilton was getting to know the Saunders family. Percy Saunders was dean of Hamilton College at the time and through a series of conversations, Skinner was chosen as a mathematics tutor for the Saunders' youngest son. The Saunders family lived in a large frame house alongside the campus, and they exposed Skinner to a world of art and culture he had previously not known. The Saunders' home was full of books, pictures, sculpture, musical instruments, and huge bouquets of peonies in season. His visits to the Saunders' home exposed him to writers, musicians, and artists. It would be commonplace during his visits to hear beautiful music playing in the background composed by Schubert or Beethoven, or to hear poetry recited. According to Skinner, "Percy and Louise Saunders made an art of living, something I had not known was possible."

Literary interests

As a child, Skinner had an inclination to become a writer. He had used an old typewriter to compose poems and stories. He even started a novel or two. In high school he worked for the local newspaper, called the *Transcript*. In the morning before school he would crib national and international news from the Binghamton, New York, papers that came in on the morning train. The summer before his senior year he attended the Middlebury School of English at Breadloaf, Vermont. He took a course with Sidney Cox, who one day invited him to have lunch with the poet Robert Frost. During lunch, Frost asked Skinner to send him some of his work, which he did—three short stories. Frost responded with encouragement to continue writing, and it was at this point that Skinner made a definite decision that he would be a writer.

Unfortunately, Skinner's decision to become a writer was not supported by his father. William, from the time his son was born, had hoped his eldest son would follow in his footsteps and join him in the practice of law. Skinner cites his birth notice as an indication of his father's long-held eagerness for his son to join his profession. It read: "The town has a new law firm: William A. Skinner & Son." Skinner's father thought that Fred should first prepare himself to earn a living as a lawyer and then try his hand at writing after he was established. But William eventually conceded and agreed to let young Skinner live at home—which at the time was in Scranton, Pennsylvania—and write for a year or two to set his career in motion. Skinner spent a great deal of time building a small study in the attic, which included bookshelves, a desk, and other furniture. Though he had comfortable surroundings in which to write, he never seemed to make time to do it. He used his time poorly, read aimlessly, built model ships, played the piano, listened to the newly invented radio, contributed to the humorous column of a local paper, but wrote almost nothing else, and even thought about seeing a psychiatrist. He later referred to this period as the "dark year."

Before the year was out, Skinner ended up taking a job with the government. The job required him to read and write abstracts for thousands of legal decisions handed down by the courts that pertained to grievances over highly publicized coal strikes in previous years. His work was compiled and used as a reference book on the subject. After finishing the book, Skinner went to New York for six months of bohemian living in Greenwich Village, then to Europe for the summer, and on to Harvard in the fall to begin the study of psychology.

During the "dark year" Skinner developed a growing curiosity about writers who embraced a behavioristic philosophy of science. Foremost among these was John B. Watson, the founder of behaviorism. Skinner probably first read about Watson in the summer of 1926, when he was 22 years old, but this exposure only whetted his appetite and did not exert profound influence on him until several years later. Perhaps it was his own depression or lack of understanding about his failure as a writer, but the science of psychology was becoming increasingly intriguing to him.

Growing interest in psychology

Human behavior had always interested Skinner, but college did little to further his interest in psychology. The only formal instruction he recalled receiving at the university "lasted 10 minutes." After college, Skinner's literary interests did more to carry him in the direction of psychology than formal studies. Yet he did owe a debt to one of his college instructors for exposing him to the material that would start him down a path he would follow the rest of his career.

A biology teacher at Hamilton called Skinner's attention to Jacques Loeb's *Physiology of the Brain* and *Comparative Psychology*, and later showed him a copy of Pavlov's *Conditioned Reflexes*. Skinner bought Pavlov's book and read it while living in Greenwich Village. Skinner also read the literary magazine called *The Dial*, which at the time was publishing articles by the philosopher Bertrand Russell. Russell's book, *Philosophy*, which Skinner read shortly thereafter, devoted a good deal of space to John B. Watson's theory of behaviorism. After reading these books, Skinner was able to begin putting pieces of his fragmented thoughts into place and envision a direction for the kind of work he believed might explain human behavior. Skinner was not interested in traditional psychological theories that were reminiscent of the Freudian emphasis on the inner self, however. He was much more captured by the outward manifestation of behavior.

At the age of 24 Skinner enrolled in the psychology department of Harvard University. Still rebellious and impatient with what he considered unintelligent ideas, Skinner found an equally caustic and hard-driving mentor. William Crozier was the chair of a new department of physiology. Crozier fervently adhered to a program of studying the behavior of "the animal as a whole" without appealing, as the psychologists did, to processes going on inside. That exactly matched Skinner's goal of relating behavior to experimental conditions. Students were encouraged to experiment. Given Skinner's enthusiasm and talent for building new equipment, he constructed various gadgets to use in his lab work with rats. After creating a dozen pieces of apparatus and stumbling onto some lucky accidents, Skinner discovered something new. He found that the rats' behavior was not just dependent on a preceding stimulus (as Watson and Pavlov insisted), but was more influenced by what happened after the rat pressed the bar. In other words, the type of reinforcement the rat received *after* the behavior was perhaps more important than the stimulus that occurred before. Skinner named this new process operant conditioning.

After completing his doctoral degree in 1931, Skinner was awarded a series of fellowships that lasted five years at Harvard. These enabled him to continue his experiments in the laboratory without the burden of teaching responsibilities.

Minnesota

In 1936, then 32 years old, Skinner married Yvonne Blue, and the couple moved to Minnesota where Skinner had his first teaching job. Busy with teaching and his new family, which in 1938 included a daughter, Julie, he did little during these years to advance the science he had started. That changed with the advent of war.

In 1944, World War II was in full swing. Airplanes and bombs were common during this time, but there were no missile guidance systems yet available. Anxious to help, Skinner sought funding for a top-secret project to train pigeons to guide bombs to their target. He knew from working with animals in the lab that pigeons could be quickly trained to perform a desired task. Working intently, he trained pigeons to repeatedly peck a point of contact inside the missile that would in effect hold the missile on its intended trajectory toward the target. The pigeons pecked reliably, even when falling rapidly and working with warlike noise all around them. But, Project Pigeon, as it was called, was eventually discontinued because a new invention, radar, proved to be far more useful. Though Skinner was disappointed at the discontinuation of his experiment, it did strengthen his determination to continue using pigeons in future experiments

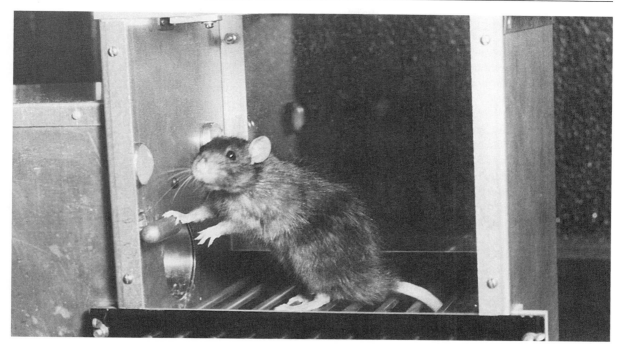

This rat has been conditioned to press a metal lever in order to receive a reward of food in this Skinner box.
(*Photo Researchers, Inc. Reproduced by permission.*)

because they responded more quickly to reinforcement than did rats. He never again worked with rats from that point forward.

The baby box

In 1944, near the end of the Second World War, Skinner and Yvonne decided to have a second child. Knowing that Yvonne found the first two years of caregiving for a child arduous, Skinner suggested they "simplify the care of the baby." This suggestion evolved into an invention that would later become known as the "baby box," or baby tender, as Skinner called it. The baby box was intended to be a superior alternative for the traditional baby crib. Skinner's baby box consisted of a thermostatically controlled enclosed crib with safety glass on the front and a stretched-canvas floor. It provided restraint and protection for the infant while also allowing great freedom of movement for the child. This baby box would be the sleeping space for their second daughter, Deborah, for the next two-and-a-half years. Skinner reported his invention and its use with his daughter in an article he submitted to *Ladies Home Journal* during that time period. As a result of this exposure, hundreds of other babies would eventually be raised in similar devices that would come to be known as Aircribs, for the increased air flow that resulted from the design.

To the end of his life, however, Skinner was plagued by rumors that he had used his second daughter as one of his experimental subjects in putting her in the baby box, causing harm that ranged from mild to severe. These rumors proved to be untrue. Skinner was in fact an affectionate father and never experimented on either of his children.

Walden Two

In the spring of 1945 at a dinner party in Minneapolis, Skinner sat next to a friend who had a son and a son-in-law in the South Pacific. They discussed difficulties facing returning soldiers as they attempted to transition back into a civilian lifestyle. This started Skinner thinking about an experimental attitude toward life that led him to write a fictional account of one. The community he envisioned would live by the principles of operant conditioning and reinforcement that he was working forging in his experiments. He called the book *Walden Two* (1948), as a loose extension of Henry David Thoreau's book about his outdoor experiences in *Walden* published much earlier. Skinner's book began simply as a description of a feasible design for community living and evolved into something that his characters seemed to dictate once he began writing.

Skinner was known as a slow writer and typically wrote longhand. In general, he would claim that it would take him about three or four hours of writing each day to produce about 100 publishable words. *Walden Two* was an entirely different experience. He wrote it on the typewriter in seven weeks. In fact, he stated afterward that writing *Walden Two* was a "venture in self-therapy." Some of it was written with great emotion. After the publication of *Walden Two*, Skinner received many letters from individuals wanting to know whether the community he described actually existed; some even wanted to join. For a period of time he seriously entertained the idea of such an experiment, but abandoned it, citing his age as the biggest hurdle to seeing such an involved experiment to completion.

Indiana

In the fall of 1945, Skinner moved from Minnesota and took the position as chairman of the Department of Psychology at Indiana University. It was an administrative position that exempted him from teaching duties but still allowed time for a number of experiments, all of which used pigeons. Although Skinner was well-connected with other faculty members at Indiana University, his wife felt isolated and unhappy. It was not uncommon for her to pass her days reading novels. When it was apparent that they would be leaving Indiana University, both of them were enthusiastic about moving back east.

Back to Harvard

While giving the William James Lectures at Harvard in 1947, Skinner was asked to become a permanent member of the department. So in 1948, Skinner and his family moved to Cambridge, where he would finish his career at prestigious Harvard University. Before agreeing to come, Skinner had negotiated with Harvard that his presence as faculty member would entail more than teaching. He was given sufficient funds to purchase and maintain a laboratory where he could conduct experiments and actively promote operant science.

In the early 1950s Dr. Harry Solomon, then chairman of the Department of Psychiatry at the Harvard Medical School, helped Skinner set up a laboratory for the study of the operant behavior of psychotics at the Metropolitan State Hospital in Waltham, Massachusetts. By this time, a number of others had extended operant principles to the management of psychotic patients in hospital wards, and there was increasing interest in its applications to personal therapy.

Teaching machines and programmed instruction

By 1953, Skinner's children were growing up; his youngest child was now in the fourth grade. Skinner attended his daughter's class one November day at the school's invitation for fathers to observe their children. He had no idea that this visitation would alter the direction of his career.

As Skinner sat at the back of this typical fourth grade math class, what he saw suddenly hit him with an unnatural force of inspiration. As he put it, "through no fault of her own the teacher was violating almost everything we knew about the learning process." In other words, Skinner's concepts of operant conditioning were being violated right before his eyes in the classroom. The students were not being reinforced positively if they came up with the correct answer. But according to operant theory, shaping a desired behavior required immediate reinforcement. The other problem he became aware of was the dilemma of the teacher to shape the mathematical behavior of 20 or 30 children simultaneously. Clearly, the teachers needed help to facilitate learning for so many students. That afternoon, Skinner constructed his first teaching machine.

Skinner's teaching machine simply presented mathematics problems in random order for students to perform, with feedback after each one. This machine did not teach new behavior; it provided practice on skills already learned. Within three years, however, Skinner developed a program of instruction where, through careful sequencing, students responded to material broken into small steps. The steps were similar to what a skilled tutor would present if working one-on-one with a student. The first responses of each sequence were prompted, but as performance improved, less help was given. By the end of the material, a student was doing work beyond what they could have accomplished at the beginning. For about the next 10 years, Skinner was caught up in the teaching-machine movement, answering every one of thousands of letters from parents, schools, and business and industry.

After securing a grant, Skinner hired James G. Holland, who with Skinner's supervision, created the book called *The Analysis of Behavior* for use in Skinner's classes at Harvard; it was designed to be used with a teaching machine. The field of education embraced this newest teaching method, but many of the materials were poorly written, and companies were reluctant to spend much money designing materials for a teaching machine that might go out of production. By around 1968 education publishers stopped printing programmed instruction for the machine. That same year Skinner published *The Technology of Teaching*, a collection of his writings on education. Some of the better programs from the

1960s are still used. With the advent of the computer and Internet, the sophisticated machine that Skinner lacked is now available. Increasingly, instructional designers are realizing that, as Skinner insisted, tutorials must do more than present blocks of content with quizzes at the end. Effective instruction requires learners to respond to what each screen of information presents and to get feedback on their performance before advancing to the next segment of instruction.

Skinner's analysis of how to design sequences of steps for teaching came to him as he was finishing a book on which he had worked, on and off, for 20 years. He eventually named the book *Verbal Behavior.* Published in 1957, it was an analysis of why people speak, write, and think the way they do. It took another 20 years before researchers used Skinner's categories and found that the different controlling variables he postulated were, indeed, independent. His work in this area has contributed significantly to establishing methods of teaching children, especially those with autism, to communicate effectively.

Later life

An interest in the implications of behavioral science for society at large turned Skinner to philosophical and moral issues. In 1969 he published *Contingencies of Reinforcement* and two years later, perhaps his most well-known book, *Beyond Freedom and Dignity,* which prompted a series of television appearances. Still, the lack of understanding and misrepresentation of his work prompted him to write another book entitled *About Behaviorism* in 1974. Toward the end of his life he was still active professionally. In addition to professional articles, he wrote three autobiographical volumes, *Particulars of My Life, The Shaping of a Behaviorist,* and *A Matter of Consequences.*

After finishing *Beyond Freedom and Dignity,* at age 67, he was especially exhausted. He had previously felt symptoms of angina and was told by his physician that he might not survive another five years if he didn't change his lifestyle. His daughters put him on a strict diet to lower his cholesterol. By the mid-1970s, although his general health remained good, he had lost much of his hearing. In addition to wearing a hearing aid, he devised an amplification system in his basement that allowed him to continue listening to music. More health concerns followed with the discovery of a cancerous lesion in his head in 1981, a fall that required two surgeries in 1987, and other difficulties. But despite these temporary setbacks, Skinner continued working.

In 1989 he was diagnosed with leukemia, which would eventually take his life. He kept as active as his increasing weakness allowed. At the American Psychological Association, 10 days before he died, he spoke before a crowded auditorium. He finished the article from which the speech was taken on August 18, 1990, the day he died.

Skinner was the uncontested champion of behavioral psychology from the 1950s to the 1980s. During this period, American psychology was shaped more by his work than by the ideas of any other psychologist. In 1958, the APA bestowed on Skinner the Distinguished Scientific Contribution Award, noting that "few American psychologists have had so profound an impact on the development of psychology and on promising younger psychologists." In 1968, Skinner received the National Medal of Science, the highest accolade bestowed by the U.S. government for contributions to science. The American Psychological Foundation presented Skinner with its Gold Medal Award, and he appeared on the cover of *Time* magazine. In 1990, Skinner was awarded the APA's Presidential Citation for Lifetime Contribution to Psychology.

THEORIES

B. F. Skinner's entire theoretical system is based on what he called operant conditioning. Operant conditioning is one of the most basic forms of learning and affects virtually all forms of human behavior. It states that learning occurs as a result of voluntary responses that are *operating* on the environment. These behavioral responses are either strengthened (more likely to recur) or weakened (less likely to recur) depending on whether the consequences of the response are favorable or unfavorable. Unlike classical conditioning, which depends on the biological responses to some stimulus such as food (Ivan Pavlov's dogs salivating at the sight of meat powder), operant conditioning applies to voluntary responses, which an organism deliberately performs in order to achieve a desired outcome.

One way to understand operant behavior is it *operates* on the environment in ways that produce consequences. If a person is playing the piano, that person is operating on the environment (the keys on the piano) in such a way as to produce music. The quality of the music and comments from listeners are the consequences that condition the person's operant performance at the piano. Well-played music elicits social approval that reinforces the skills needed for

B. F. Skinner in his later years. (Psychology Archives—The University of Akron.)

playing well. In contrast, poor playing is likely to be criticized and thus negatively reinforced.

Operant conditioning is sometimes called instrumental conditioning because it is *instrumental* in changing the environment and producing consequences. Working late at the office may be instrumental in getting a particular project finished by the deadline.

Skinner's research was concerned with describing behavior rather than explaining it. His research dealt only with observable behavior. He was also unconcerned with speculations about what might be occurring inside the organism. His program of operant conditioning included no assumptions about drives or physiological process that characterized other theories. Whatever might happen between stimulus and response was not the sort of objective data with which Skinner was concerned.

Skinner's behaviorism assumes that humans are controlled and influenced by forces in the environment and the external world, not by forces from within. He did not go as far as denying the existence of internal physiological or even mental conditions, but he did deny their usefulness for the scientific study of behavior.

It is also worth noting that Skinner did not use large numbers of subjects to make statistical comparisons between the average responses of subject groups. His method was the comprehensive investigation of a single subject.

Main points

Reinforcement

Reinforcers are the prime movers of operant conditioning. Reinforcers that follow an operant behavior increase the likelihood that a similar response will occur in the future. A reinforcer is also called a reinforcing stimulus. The speed in which a person learns an operant behavior depends on the complexity of the behavior, the person's level of skills, the reinforcer involved, and many other variables.

There are two kinds of reinforcement: positive and negative. To reinforce means to strengthen; both positive and negative reinforcement strengthen behavior. Both increase the likelihood that a subject will repeat the behavior in the future. The critical difference between the two is that positive reinforcement occurs with the addition of a reinforcing stimulus. Negative reinforcement consists of removing an aversive stimulus.

Explanation   In its simplest form, reinforcers can be thought of in terms of rewards: both a reinforcer and a reward increase the probability that a preceding response will occur again. The term "reward," however, is limited to positive support. Reinforcement, as Skinner used it, can be either positive or negative.

A positive reinforcer is a stimulus added to the environment that brings about an increase in a preceding response. For instance, if food, water, money, praise, or any number of other stimuli follow a particular response, it is very likely that this response will occur again in the future. Positive reinforcement can be given in natural or artificial ways. Unnatural praise and artificial rewards are not very effective in reinforcing behavior. Highly contrived, unnatural rewards can even decrease the frequency of an operant behavior if used in a manipulating manner. However, natural and sincere positive feedback is usually both pleasurable to receive and effective in reinforcing behavior.

In contrast, a negative reinforcer refers to an unpleasant stimulus whose removal from the environment leads to an increase in the probability that a preceding response will occur again in the future. The two main classes of behavior produced by negative reinforcement are escape and avoidance. Escape responses are those operants that allow a person to get away from aversive stimuli after the stimuli are present. Avoidance responses are those operants that allow a person to prevent the occurrence of aversive stimuli *before* the aversive stimuli appear. In other words, escape involves reacting after an aversive event is present. Avoidance involves *proacting,* or taking preventative steps before an aversive event arises. People react to getting a splinter in their finger by pulling it out; they proact by putting on gloves before handling rough wood. Escape behaviors are usually learned before avoidance behaviors.

Examples An example of positive reinforcement is a student who diligently plans and follows a disciplined schedule of study in order to get good grades. The positive reinforcer is the achievement of good grades. In other words, the good grades reinforce the disciplined study habits of the student so he or she is likely to continue the study regimen with hopes that good grades will continue.

Positive reinforcement can also come from nonsocial sources by virtue of an operant principle termed "selective perception." Selective perception describes a person's ability to pay attention to only a fraction of all the stimuli in their environment, neglecting the others. So, for instance a person is walking down a sidewalk when he notices a dollar bill lying in the curb. He sees no one around to whom it may belong and puts it in his pocket. Moments later he notices a change in his own behavior. He is no longer looking at the trees or houses, but is scanning the ground as if looking for another lucky find. The behavior of looking down was followed by the positive reinforcement of finding the money.

Negative reinforcement could be illustrated by a child who begrudgingly does his chores simply to escape the nagging of his parents. In this example, the nagging is the negative reinforcer. So, as the child performs the assigned chores, he finds it eliminates the nagging, which in turn reinforces the likelihood that he will continue doing the chores.

An example of escaping could involve a married couple who repeatedly find themselves in verbal arguments with each other. They react by trying to escape the aversive situation through marital counseling. Other couples who see their friends having marital troubles may proact by working on improving their communication and resolving differences before problems arise, thereby avoiding some arguments and possible long-term damage to their marriage.

Punishment

When an operant behavior is followed by a response that reduces the frequency of a similar response in the future, that stimulus is called punish-

PUNISHMENT	
Positive punishment	**Negative punishment**
When the subject—a person or animal—engages in a behavior and something negative is applied as a result, the behavior is less likely to be repeated.	When the subject—a person or animal—engages in a behavior and something positive is taken away, that behavior is less likely to be repeated.

(Courtesy Thomson Gale.)

ment. If a person receives a significant fine after driving through a red light, the punishment is likely to reduce the tendency to speed through red lights in the future. Both punishment and extinction reduce the frequency of behavior, but punishment usually does so more rapidly and more completely than extinction does. Punishment produces the fastest reduction of the behavior when it is strong, immediate, and not opposed by reinforcement.

There are two types of punishment: positive punishment and negative punishment, just as there are both positive and negative reinforcement. In both cases, the term "positive" refers to something that is added, whereas "negative" implies something that is removed.

Explanation The terms "positive" and "negative" indicate whether punishment occurs with the onset or termination of the stimulus that follows the operant. "Positive" indicates onset, and "negative" indicates termination. Positive punishment occurs when the onset of an aversive stimulus suppresses behavior. For instance, if you spill hot coffee on your hand while carrying a cup to a nearby table, the onset of an aversive stimulus (hot coffee) punishes the clumsy act. This is considered a positive form of punishment. Negative punishment occurs when the termination of a rewarding stimulus suppresses behavior. If a haphazard action results in your dropping and losing an important document, the loss serves as punishment for the act. Therefore the loss of a positive reinforcer is a negative punishment. It is important to distinguish between negative reinforcement and punishment. The two are not the same in operant conditioning. Punishment refers to a stimulus that *decreases* the probability that a prior behavior will occur again. This differs from negative reinforcement, which *increases* the likelihood of a recurrence in the behavior.

Punishment does not cause behavior to be unlearned or forgotten. It merely suppresses the frequency of responding. Often the effects of punishment are only temporary. When the punishment no longer occurs, the rate of responding usually increases. This phenomenon is called recovery. Recovery is fastest and most complete when the original punishment was mild or infrequent and there is reinforcement for reinstating the behavior. The milder the original punishment, the sooner a behavior is likely to recover after the end of punishment.

Positive punishment *weakens* a response or makes it less likely to recur through the application of an unpleasant stimulus. On the same track, but coming from the opposite direction, is negative punishment. This consists of removing something that is pleasant in order to weaken the response or make it less likely to be repeated.

Although Skinner recognized the role of punishment in response to behavior, he was against using it because he did not believe it had a permanent effect on altering behavior except in extreme cases. Although it may initially stop the particular behavior in question, Skinner believed that the prior response was likely to reappear over time. In addition, punishment may actually cause a resulting fear or anxiety to emerge that wasn't present before the application of the punishment.

A very effective non-punitive method of decreasing the frequency of a behavior is the use of differential reinforcement of other behavior. This means that reinforcement is provided for behaviors other than the one that is problematic, with the hope the behaviors reinforced will be repeated and the problematic behavior will decrease or cease. Differential reinforcement works best when the desired behavior is incompatible with the undesired behavior.

Examples   Positive punishment can be illustrated by thinking of a young child who disobeys a parent and receives a spanking for his response. Here the parent is *adding* an unpleasant stimulus (the spanking) with the hope that is will weaken the future response of the child and make it less likely to recur.

A good example of negative punishment is when a teenager is told she is "grounded" and will no longer be able to use the family car because of her poor grades. The negative punishment entails the removal of what is pleasant or desirable (using the car). The hope behind the use of negative punishment in this case is that removal of the privilege will make poor grades less likely to recur.

If a child is being overly aggressive with his playmates, his parent can use differential reinforcement by providing rewards or reinforcement for nonaggressive behavior such as helping, consideration, or concern for others. This not only draws the child away from aggression, but gives him a new style of interpersonal relations which make aggression much less likely to occur.

Extinction

Once an operant has been reinforced and become common, there is no guarantee that the frequency of the response will remain the same in the future. Either extinction or punishment will cause a response to become less frequent. Regardless of which one is in effect, both work in the opposite direction from reinforcement. Extinction consists of the discontinuation of reinforcement, whether positive or negative, that once maintained a given behavior. This withholding of the reinforcement will, in theory, cause the behavior to cease.

Explanation   Extinction can take place because there is no reinforcement associated with a certain behavior, or there is less reinforcement associated with that behavior because there is some superior alternative. The idea behind extinction is that without the reinforcement, either positive or negative, the behavior will cease because the reward is no longer present. The rate at which a response ceases depends on the individual's prior history of reinforcement. When extinction begins, people usually give up a pattern of behavior much faster if the behavior had been rewarded all the time (continuous reinforcement) in the past instead of rewarded only part of the time (intermittent reinforcement).

The question becomes: Once a conditioned response has been extinguished, can it return? Pavlov discovered during his experiments with dogs that the conditioned behavior that had stopped being reinforced and ceased could be engaged again with the commencement of the conditioned stimulus. This effect is known as spontaneous recovery, or the reemergence of an extinguished conditioned response after a period of rest. With each successive reduction of the behavior due to removal of the conditioned stimulus, the conditioned response can spontaneously recover more rapidly once the conditioned stimulus is reused. This concept is called saving, which implies that some of the learning is retained from previous conditioning.

Behavior modification practitioners often advocate extinction as an alternative to punishment. The danger in using extinction, however, is that it may produce frustration in the respondent and as a result, temporarily increase the behavior that is supposed to stop. The potential benefit of using extinction is that once the old behavior is not reinforced, the person looks for new behaviors to try and restore the reward. These behaviors are more likely to be in line with the desired behavior. If reinforced, these new behaviors should repeat.

Examples   Two businessmen (Tom and Joe) strike up a friendly rapport due to their frequent phone calls with each other related to business matters. One day Joe calls Tom to discuss a new product he has just received, but gets voice mail. Joe leaves a message asking for a return call. When no return call is received he makes several more calls to Tom over the course of the next few weeks. None of these are returned. Because the reinforcement of a return phone call from Tom no longer exists, Joe eventually ceases to call Tom anymore, not expecting to hear from him.

If a person's car has always started on the first try (continuous reinforcement), that person is more likely to give up and call a garage if one morning the car doesn't start. In another case, the person used to trying a dozen times or more to start the car is less likely to give up quickly on a given day when he or she is unable to start the car. This latter person has been rewarded intermittently, which makes extinction of a particular behavior more difficult.

Shaping

Shaping is a technique that is used in behaviorism to train an organism to perform a behavior that is completely new. Shaping teaches a complex behavior by rewarding or reinforcing each step of the learning process rather than the final outcome.

Explanation   Shaping works from the principle that a little can eventually go a long way. The final goal or target response is beyond the realistic reach of the organism because the behavior is not yet in their behavioral repertoire; it is completely new. The concept of shaping breaks down the learning process into smaller pieces. Skinner used incremental stages to reinforce the desired behavior. At first, actions even remotely resembling the target behavior, which he termed successive approximations, are followed by a reward. Gradually, closer and closer approximations of the final target behavior are required before the reward is given. Shaping, then, helps the organism acquire or construct new and more complex forms of behavior from simpler behavior. By the time shaping is complete, the reinforcement need only be given at the completion of the desired behavior in order for the behavior to recur.

Examples   Textbooks for students are often written using the concept of shaping. Typically, information is presented so that new material builds on previously learned concepts or skills. If this were not the progression, most students would become confused and perhaps abandon the attempt to learn the concepts under study.

Teachers are continually in the position to shape the behavior of their students. An art student begins a series of drawings while the teacher assesses the various skills of the student. The teacher gives positive feedback for the areas in which the student performs well and looks for ways to reinforce small steps (successive approximations) toward the desired outcome. During the shaping process, praise (reinforcer) is given for the skills the student can do at present. The teacher may compliment the student on his shading techniques and at the same time suggest he try to expand his shading to another portion of the drawing to perhaps work on perspective. This allows the shaping to occur in increments while being positively reinforced through the learning process.

Chaining

Chaining refers to a type of conditioning that is similar to shaping but requires a more complex sequence of behaviors. This process is referred to as chaining because each response is like a link in the chain. The reward is presented after the entire sequence of behaviors is completed, thus reinforcing the sequence and not the individual behavior.

Explanation   Chains can be trained in the forward direction, that is, by practicing the first response in the chain and then adding successively the next elements. It can also be learned backwards, beginning with the last element and working toward the front. Sometimes the entire chain is learned simultaneously. Training that starts at either end tends to place a greater emphasis on the skills or knowledge that lies at those places for the overall mastery of the chain. Training that attempts to learn the entire chain simultaneously leads to more total errors but affords more practice on all links of the chain.

Examples   Backward chaining is often used with pilot trainees when using a flight simulator. They practice landings first, followed by landing approaches and then other flight specific behaviors such as mid-air maneuvers. The purpose of the backward chaining is that landings are the most difficult behavior to master in the chain and by starting there, this behavior receives the most practice as the behavioral links are put in place. Forward chaining might be used by physical therapists to teach disabled individuals to transfer themselves from a wheelchair to another chair or bed.

A forward chain is often preferable when the skills learned in the first link are needed to build successively from that point.

Discrimination and generalization

People and animals learn to pay attention to cues in the environment that reliably signal certain consequences for their actions. Learning to distinguish one stimulus from another is called stimulus-control training. For instance, it doesn't take a child very long to distinguish that a red light at an intersection means stop and a green light means go. In stimulus-control training, a behavior is reinforced in the presence of a specific stimulus but not in its absence.

Stimulus generalization happens when an organism learns a response to one stimulus and applies it to another similar stimulus. Even though the stimuli may be different, the familiarity that accompanies the initial learning can be applied to other stimuli as well.

Explanation   A discriminative stimulus signals the likelihood that reinforcement will follow a particular response. Some discriminations are relatively easy, while others extremely complex. For instance, it is easy to distinguish between the facial features of two people who resemble one another in appearance if the observer looks carefully. It is far more difficult, however, for that same observer to discriminate when a facial expression is communicating friendliness versus love. Certain cues must be present or absent for the observer to draw a convincing conclusion. Perception plays a large part in a person's ability to discriminate one stimulus from another. The ability to effectively discriminate plays a considerable role in human behavior.

Stimulus generalization enables organisms to take previous learning and apply it to new, but similar, situations. The ability to utilize previous learning keeps the organism from having to start over in the learning process. Generalizations can be less effective when the stimulus has an element of newness unassociated with the familiarity. For example, when a person learns to drive a car, this training can be generalized to driving most other cars. If the initial training was on an automatic transmission, though, and now the driver must drive a manual transmission, generalization of the prior skills is limited. The respondent must then use stimulus discrimination to distinguish between the familiar and the new information, and make the appropriate adjustments to generalize the new learning.

Examples   Children, for example, may learn that when their father whistles, he is in a good mood and therefore he is more likely to respond favorably if asked for

money or permission to do something fun with friends. The children learn to discriminate the good mood from the bad mood by the presence of the cue (whistling). Over time the children learn to make requests only in the presence of the signal for a good mood.

If a person has learned that being polite produces the reinforcement of granting them what they want in certain situations, that person is likely to generalize that response to other situations.

Reinforcement schedules

In his early research, Skinner discovered that reinforcement need not be given for each response, but instead could be given after some number of responses according to various schedules of reinforcement. A schedule of reinforcement refers to the specific relationship between the number, timing, or frequency of responding; and the delivery of the reward. In other words, once a behavior has been shaped, it can be maintained by various patterns of reinforcement. Depending on the particular schedule, the reward may follow the response immediately or have varying degrees of delay.

Schedules are among the most powerful determinants of behavior. All reinforcers and punishers are embedded in one schedule or another and each schedule has its own characteristic effects on behavior.

Reinforcement can be given for each occurrence of the response or only for some of the responses. The two broad categories of schedules are continuous and partial (also called intermittent) reinforcements. With continuous reinforcement, each response of a particular type is reinforced. In a partial reinforcement schedule, only a portion of the responses are reinforced.

Explanation   When attempting to instill a particular behavior, a continuous schedule of reward generally produces more rapid conditioning or a higher level of responding than a partial-reinforcement schedule. Though a continuous schedule may condition more rapidly, partial schedules are often more powerful in sustaining the behavior, depending on the interval of reward. Extinction does tend to occur more quickly if a behavior that has received continuous reinforcement is no longer reinforced.

There are again two broad types of partial-reinforcement schedules: interval schedules, which are based on the passage of time; and ratio schedules, which are based on the number of responses. On an interval schedule, the first response made after an interval of time has passed is reinforced. Responses made before that interval of time are not reinforced. There are two types of interval schedules: fixed and variable. In a ratio schedule, time is not a factor. Instead, reinforcement is given only after a certain number of responses. Ratio schedules also have two types: fixed and variable.

Examples A fixed-interval schedule applies the reinforcer *after* a specific amount of time. An example might be an employee who gets a raise once at the end of each year but no increase in pay during the course of the year. The reinforcer (increase in pay) comes only at a predetermined time regardless of the employee's work performance during the year. Fixed-intervals have built-in problems that manifest in certain situations. Using the example of the employee's end-of-the-year raise, the employee, because he knows when the reinforcement is to come, may tend to lower his performance immediately after the reinforcement and tend to increase performance right before the reinforcement period. In this case, he might improve his performance near the end of the year to "look good" when it comes time for the review that determines the amount of pay raise.

Reinforcement is also controlled mainly by the passage of time in a variable-interval schedule. In contrast to the fixed-interval, in which the person knows the time the reinforcement will be given, the person does not know when the reinforcement will appear in a variable-interval schedule. An example of this schedule might be the supervisor who checks an employee's work at irregular intervals. Because the employees never know when such checks will occur, they must perform in a consistent manner in order to obtain positive outcomes, such as praise; or avoid negative ones, such as criticism or loss of their job. The advantage of variable-interval schedules is that it often eliminates the inconsistencies of performance associated with the fixed interval. Because of this, variable schedules are usually considered more powerful and result in more consistent behaviors than fixed intervals schedules.

Another modern example of variable-interval scheduling is the use of random drug testing. Athletes are routinely tested as well as people whose impaired performance could endanger the lives of others, such as airline pilots, security personnel, and healthcare workers. Because the participants cannot predict the day when the next test will be given, these individuals are more likely to refrain from using drugs.

Reinforcement is determined in a very different manner on a fixed-ratio schedule. Here, reinforcement occurs only after a fixed number of responses. For example, some individuals are paid on the basis of how many pieces of goods they produce. A factory worker who drills a series of holes for a particular product is paid a certain price for every product they complete. Or consider the person who collects recyclable aluminum cans or scrap metal and is paid based upon the number of pounds they turn in. Generally, a fixed-ratio schedule yields a high rate of response, though there is a tendency for brief pauses immediately after reinforcement. In the examples above, the reinforcement would be the fixed amount of pay obtained in good produced.

On a variable-ratio schedule, reinforcement occurs after completion of a variable number of responses. Since the person using a variable-ratio schedule cannot predict how many responses are required before reinforcement will occur, they usually respond at high and steady rates. Perhaps one of the best examples of the variable-ratio schedule is found in casinos across the country. The person who repeatedly plays the slot machine knows at some point the machine will have a payoff, but they are not sure when it will occur. The anticipation that it could happen on the next pull compels many to keep playing beyond the point of good reason.

Variable-ratio schedules also result in behaviors that are highly resistant to extinction. This means that even in the absence of reinforcement, the behavior might persist. In fact, resistance to extinction is much higher after exposure to a variable-ratio schedule than to a continuous-reinforcement schedule. This would help explain why gambling can be so addictive for certain individuals.

HISTORICAL CONTEXT

Skinner's theory of operant conditioning did not spring from his mind alone. Several theorists were profoundly influential in laying a foundation for the work Skinner was to build on.

All behavioral theories owe some debt of gratitude to Ivan Pavlov for developing the principles of classical conditioning. Pavlov, who won the Nobel Prize in 1904 for his work on digestion, was best known for his experiments on basic learning processes. While studying the secretion of stomach acids and salivation in dogs in response to eating various amounts of food, he discovered that even the mere sight of a person who normally fed the dogs could elicit an anticipation of food by the canines. In other words, the dogs were not only responding to the biological need to eat but also demonstrated that there was learning going on in the process of feeding. A neutral stimulus such as the experimenter's footsteps, when paired with food, could bring about a similar response as the food alone. This type of learning Pavlov called classical conditioning.

The basic process of classical conditioning can be described in several steps. It first needs the presence of a neutral stimulus that does not elicit specific response in the participant prior to the experiment. In Pavlov's classic experiment, the neutral stimulus was the sound of a bell. Ringing the bell prior to the experiment did not elicit salivation in a dog. The second component is the unconditioned stimulus, which in this experiment was meat. At the mere sight of meat the dog would salivate. It is called the unconditioned stimulus because the dog salivates instinctively and needs no training for this response. Hence, the dog's response is an unconditioned response. During the conditioning process, the bell is routinely rung just before the presentation of the meat. Over time, the ringing of the bell alone will bring about salivation. Conditioning is complete when the previously neutral stimulus of the bell (now the conditioned response) is now able to elicit salivation (conditioned stimulus).

Although the initial conditioning experiments performed by Pavlov and others were conducted on animals, classical conditioning principles were soon being used in various ways to explain everyday human behavior. Pavlov's conditioning techniques provided psychology with behavioral ways in which complex behavior could be better understood and built upon by other theorists.

At approximately the same period of time that Pavlov was experimenting with animals and developing his classical conditioning theory, a man by the name of Edward Thorndike was conducting ground-breaking experiments of his own. Thorndike is one of the most influential theorists of the early twentieth century and considered a very important researcher in the development of animal theory. Thorndike believed that psychology must study behavior, not mental elements or conscious experiences, and thus he reinforced the trend toward greater objectivity within the emerging field of psychology.

One of Thorndike's major contributions to the study of psychology was his work with animals. Through long, extensive research with these animals, he constructed devices called "puzzle boxes." These were essentially wooden crates that required the manipulation of various combinations of latches, levers, strings to open. A cat would be put in one of these puzzle boxes and would eventually manage to escape from it by trial and error. On a successive attempt, the amount of time it took the cat to escape decreased. Thorndike compared the results of several

cats and found a similar pattern. If he rewarded the behavior of the cat, the behavior was repeated, if he did not, it would cease. He surmised that certain stimuli and responses become connected or dissociated from each other in the process of learning. This learning principle he termed the law of effect.

This evaluation led Thorndike to conclude that animals learn by trial and error, or reward and punishment. Thorndike used the cat's behavior in a puzzle box to generalize what happens when all beings learn anything. All learning involves the formation of connections, and connections were strengthened according to the law of effect. Intelligence is the ability to form connections, and humans are the most evolved animal because they form more connections then any other being. He continued his study with learning by writing his famous book called *Animal Intelligence*. In this he argued that we study animal behavior, not animal consciousness, for the ultimate purpose of controlling behavior.

A subtle but important distinction should be made between trial and error learning (instrumental learning) and classical conditioning. In classical conditioning, a neutral stimulus becomes associated with part of a reflex, which is either the unconditioned stimulus or the unconditioned response. In trial and error learning, no reflex is involved. A reinforcing or punishing event, which is also a type of stimulus, alters the strength of the association between a neutral stimulus and the arbitrary response.

Thorndike's early research served as the foundation for Skinner's work that was beginning in the latter years of Thorndike's career. Whereas Thorndike's goal was to get his cats to learn to obtain food by leaving the box, animals in Skinner's box learned to obtain food by operating on their environment within the box. Skinner became interested in specifying how behavior varied as a result of alterations in the environment.

One of the biggest influences on Skinner's ideas came from the work of John B. Watson, often referred to as the "father of behaviorism." Watson carried the torch of the behaviorist position, claiming that human behavior could be explained entirely in terms of reflexes, stimulus-response associations, and the effects of reinforcers. His 1914 book entitled *Behavior: An Introduction to Comparative Psychology* became the official statement of his theory and was widely read at the time.

Watson's lab work with rats enabled him to discover that he could train rats to open a puzzle box like Thorndike's for a small food reward. He also studied maze learning but simplified the task dramatically. One type of maze he used was a long straight alley with food at the end. Watson found that once the animal was well trained at running this maze, it did so almost automatically. Once started by the stimulus of the maze, its behavior becomes a series of associations between movements rather than stimuli in the outside world. The development of other well-controlled behavioral techniques by Watson also allowed him to explore animal sensory abilities.

Watson's theoretical position was even more extreme than Thorndike's. He would have no place for intellectual concepts like pleasure or distress in his explanations of behavior. He essentially rejected the law of effect proposed by Thorndike, denying that pleasure or discomfort caused stimulus-response associations to be learned. For Watson, all that was important was the frequency of occurrence of stimulus-response pairings. Reinforcers might cause some responses to occur more often in the presence of particular stimuli, but they did not act directly to cause their learning.

After Watson published his second book *Psychology from the Standpoint of a Behaviorist* in 1919, he became the founder of the American school of behaviorism. In this book he addressed a number of practical human problems such as education, the development of emotional reaction, and the effects of factors such as alcohol or drugs on human performance. Watson believed that mental illness was the result of "habit distortion," which might be caused by fortuitous learning of inappropriate associations. These associations then go on to influence a person's behavior so that it became ever more abnormal.

Watson became a very controversial figure in psychology for several reasons. He was credited with wedding behavioral techniques with celebrity endorsements of products and services to manipulate motives and emotions. Now a widely used strategy for marketing and advertising, during the 1920s, it was not well received by many people. In a larger sense, Watson was a pivotal figure in shaping public perception away from the dominant view of psychoanalysis and the internal processes of behavior. His call was for a society based on scientifically shaped and controlled behavior. His ideas offered hope to those disenchanted with old ideas.

Skinner probably first read some of Watson's work in the summer of 1926, when he was 22 years old, but it wasn't until the spring of 1928 that Skinner took the writings of Watson more seriously. Years later, when Skinner had established himself as an independent thinker and writer on radical behaviorism, he said that Watson had brought the "promise of

a behavioral science," but this was not the same thing as delivering the science itself. But Skinner agreed with Watson in that he denied that behavior is determined by processes with the physiology of the organism.

By the 1920s, the field of psychology had already captured the public's attention. Given Watson's charisma, personal charm, persuasiveness, and message of hope, Americans were enthralled by what one writer called an "outbreak" of psychology. Much of the public was convinced that psychology provided a path to health, happiness, and prosperity. Psychological advice columns sprouted up in the pages of the daily newspapers. Watson's behaviorism was the first stage in the evolution of the behavioral school of thought. The second stage, sometimes referred to as neobehaviorism, can be dated from about 1930 to about 1960 and includes the work of Edward Tolman, Clark Hull, and B. F. Skinner.

Edward Tolman was one of the early converts to behaviorism and like Watson, rejected the notion of introspection and inner processes for determining behavior. He was firmly committed to working only with those behaviors that were objective and accessible to observation. Tolman is recognized as a forerunner of contemporary cognitive psychology, and his work had a great impact, especially his research on problems of learning. Some of his core principles were later used by Skinner and other behaviorists.

Clark Hull and his followers dominated American psychology from the 1940s until the 1960s. Hull had a proficient command of mathematics and formal logic and applied this knowledge to psychological theory in a way that no one had before. Hull's form of behaviorism was more sophisticated and complex than Watson's. Hull described his behaviorism and his image of human nature in mechanistic terms and regarded human behavior as automatic. He thought behaviorists should regard their subjects as machines and believed the machines would one day replicate many human cognitive functions. As might be guessed, Hull drew much criticism for his hard-line approach to the mechanism of human processes, but his influence on psychology at the time was substantial.

Beginning in the 1950s, Skinner became the major figure in American behavioral psychology. He attracted a large, loyal, and enthusiastic group of followers. His influence extended far beyond the professional community of psychologists at work in laboratories. His popularity was largely as a result of the advent of television in the early 1950s. His two most widely read books, *Walden Two* and *Beyond Freedom and Dignity*, thrust him into popular culture.

It was the modern medium of television, however, that made him a household name. He would regularly appear on television talk shows to advance his views on operant conditioning and how it applied to everyday life. In a short period of time, he became a celebrity and arguably the best-known psychologist of that era.

Skinner's system of psychology reflects his early life experiences. According to his view, life is a product of past reinforcements. He claimed that his life was just as predetermined and orderly as his system dictated all human lives should be. He believed his experiences could be traced solely and directly to stimuli in his environment. Having been raised by a mother who was rigid in her discipline and by a father who tended toward being verbally critical of Skinner, praise was not common in his home life. Perhaps there is a correlation in his theory with his most important concept of reinforcement. Operant conditioning states that for a behavior to be repeated, it must be positively reinforced. The centrality of that theme in his theory has been mentioned by some scholars as a response to his own desire for more praise and encouragement from his parents.

In 1938 Skinner published what was arguably the most influential work on animal behavior of the century, entitled *The Behavior of Organisms*. Skinner resurrected the law of effect in more starkly behavioral terms and provided a technology that allowed sequences of behavior produced over a long time to be studied objectively. His invention of the Skinner box was a great improvement on the individual learning trials of both Watson and Thorndike. Skinner's theory would eventually become known as operant conditioning and would become one of the most enduring theories of the twentieth century.

CRITICAL RESPONSE

Skinner has aroused more than his share of controversy. Those who are familiar with Skinner's ideas tend to have a strong positive or negative reaction depending upon their own presuppositions about human nature. The most common critical responses follow.

Free will and personal responsibility

Skinner's operant conditioning opposes the concepts of free choice and personal responsibility. He maintained that it is the environment that determines what a person was, is, and will be in the future.

He accounts for genetic inheritance by referring to the environments that existed during evolutionary history. In short, he claims that environmental factors determine behavior in a way that free will and individual choice play no causal role.

According to Skinner, each person is unique, but not because of choices the individual makes. Rather, personality arises from genetic makeup and the different experiences each person is exposed to during their lives. In addition, individuals remain under the influence of their environment throughout the lifespan, regardless of the degree of learning that has preceded.

There is agreement among many of Skinner's critics that environmental factors are important. The extreme position that Skinner takes (that environment alone shapes behavior) causes much controversy. His view of environmental reinforcement as the basis of behavior violates what most people believe regarding the presupposition of "freedom of choice" and personal accountability for one's actions. Though many critics would agree that the environment is a shaping entity for some human behavior, only a minority are willing to agree that the totality of human behavior can be explained in operant terms.

A question naturally arises in regard to control: If humans are controlled by their environments and have no free choice, how must people go about the process of "deciding" to follow the principles of operant conditioning? It appears a contradiction on the one hand to say we have no free-will choice, and on the other hand to imply that choices must be made to reinforce certain behaviors.

Generalizing findings to human behavior

Skinner conducted nearly all of his experiments with laboratory animals, most of which were rats and pigeons. Although there have been a number of successful applications of Skinner's concepts with humans, criticism has been leveled over how much of the results of Skinner's experiments can actually be generalized to human beings. The criticism basically states that humans are far more complex and advanced than the animals used in the operant experiments, so how can Skinner so confidently generalize the outcomes to humans? In using animals as substitutes for humans in the exploration of human behavior, Skinner was making the huge assumption that general laws relating to the behavior of animals can be applied to describe the complex relations in the human world.

Could it be possible, critics add, that even though the behavior of both rats and humans tends to increase in frequency when certain consequences occur, that humans still have higher and perhaps different cognitive processes? Perhaps humans can assess what is going on by using rational thought processes and then decide which behavior they will do to be reinforced. In contrast, rats may process the information more mechanically, with no conscious or rational self-determination. The final answer to these questions is not yet available. Those psychologists who hold this view believe more experiments with human participants must be done to prove the validity of this theory.

Operant conditioning is overly simplistic

Skinner's concepts of operant conditioning have often been interpreted as being simplistic because he either ignores or negates the richness of life. The assumption is often made that Skinner doesn't deal with human emotions and thoughts and has virtually nothing to say about the complex behaviors of life that are displayed in creative activities. In general, Skinner seems to ignore the realm deemed "creative," which includes the imagination, because it is not easily open to direct observation and presents difficulties on the experimental level. Skinner saw the creation of a poem, for instance, as being analogous to having a baby or to the process of laying an egg by a hen. He believed that there is no creative act that is autonomous. The person who writes the poem has a particular background and is living under certain conditions that reinforce one's view of the world. Therefore the creation of the poem is merely a function of how the environment has treated that person, as opposed to some uncaused event that sprung from nowhere. The criticisms of Skinner on this point have more to do with his mechanistic view of human nature than the resulting conclusions about creativity. It follows logically that if a human being is nothing more than a machine of sorts, then there is no need for an inner life of which imagination and creativity are parts. These aspects of life bring a multi-dimensional enjoyment of life that many people cannot reconcile with operant-conditioning principles.

Development of human language

Although Skinner's ideas on operant conditioning are able to explain phobias and neurosis, a number of critics find the applicability to the more complex human behaviors of language and memory sadly lacking. The argument centers around the idea that some portion of language acquisition in young children must be inherited. Infants do not learn language on a word-by-word basis. Instead they learn grammatical rules necessary to produce sentences over time.

Skinner's inability to explain the language phenomenon in a satisfactory way has caused a number of critics to dismiss the theory altogether. While observable objective stimuli for verbal responses are more clear-cut, private stimuli or concepts such as "I'm hungry" are harder to explain. According to Skinner, the acquisition of verbal responses for private stimuli can be explained in four ways. First, he claims that private stimuli and the community do not need a connection. As long as there are some sorts of public stimuli that can be associated with the private stimuli, a child can learn. Also, the public can deduce the private stimuli through nonverbal signs, such as groaning and facial expressions. The critics claim that these nonverbal signs associated with public and private events can often be misinterpreted. His third theory states that certain public and private stimuli are identical; therefore there is no need for interpretation. Finally, he says that private stimuli can be generalized to public stimuli with coinciding characteristics. Although Skinner attempted to respond to ongoing criticism of these claims during his lifetime, his arguments were considered by many to be weak and relatively unproven.

Misuse of reinforcement

A number of criticisms have arisen relating to operant conditioning and the use or misuse of reinforcement. One objection states that the use of reinforcement, as outlined by Skinner's theory, is manipulative. Granting and withholding reward is a form of control. The concept of control is central to Skinner's thinking, however, and appears repeatedly in his writing. When he uses the term, he claims that individuals are controlled by environmental forces, which include the actions and behaviors each person displays to others. He would simply say that these forms of control are necessary ways of interaction or operating in the world. For a culture of freedom-loving, self-directed people, however, the concept of being controlled by forces beyond voluntary choice is not popular.

Another criticism of reinforcement argues that certain behaviors should be performed by individuals in society regardless of the rewards or reinforcements that are associated. Appropriate behavior, such as responsible parenting, civil duties, altruistic help, and many others, should be expected as the norm for community behavior and not depend on bribery or the enticement of a reward. Skinner would respond by saying that reinforcements or rewards are always being used in daily living, whether individuals are consciously aware of them or not. Even if explicit rewards are not given, internal reinforcement may be present. Self-praise, or feelings of self-esteem from doing well at a chosen task, could provide a form of reinforcement.

A third objection is that reinforcement undermines intrinsic motivation, or an internally motivated desire to perform a given behavior for its own sake. With intrinsic motivation, the incentive to perform comes from the activity itself. In extrinsic motivation, the drive to perform stems from the rewards attached to the task. In recent years, more researchers have questioned the validity of rewards as a counterproductive means toward fostering intrinsic motivation, especially in children.

Finally, some critics challenge the effectiveness of reinforcement, saying that reinforcement often produces short-term changes, which disappear when the reinforcement ceases or becomes infrequent. True learning, according to many learning specialists, is supposed to produce relatively permanent changes in behavior.

Antitheoretical contradiction

Skinner made confident assertions about economic, social, political, and religious issues that derived from his system. In 1986, he wrote an article with the all-embracing title "What is Wrong with Life in the Western World?" He stated that "human behavior in the West has grown weak, but it can be strengthened through the application of principles derived from an experimental analysis of behavior." This willingness to draw conclusions from the data, particularly as it pertained to solutions to complex human problems, is inconsistent with Skinner's antitheoretical stance. In other words, Skinner went beyond the central premise of his theory, which was that only observable behavior was important, and presented a theoretical blueprint for the redesign of society.

Although Skinner suggests that his behavioral principles can be applied at the societal level, he appears to sidestep the issue of who will put these principles into effect. Who will exert the power to set up certain reinforcement contingencies, and who will decide which behaviors are to be reinforced? He has addressed some of these issues, but more in a philosophical manner and not in practical or concrete terms.

Limitations of applications

Despite the fact that Skinner's principles have been used quite effectively in various settings, including therapeutic, educational, and business, there are still shortcomings even in environments that are carefully controlled. Behavioral management has not always been as effective as some claim. When neurotic behaviors improve but not to the extent that the person can function normally, or when a child learns more using behavioral principles but still cannot master certain concepts, is it the individual's limitations that are at fault or simply the realization that all behavior

is not subject to control through reinforcement? Skinner would say that all behavior can be shaped given the appropriate reinforcements, but this is seriously questioned in real-life situations when some variables seem outside the realm of what can be controlled.

Punishment

Skinner's position on punishment is another point that has been commonly criticized. He has asserted that punishment has detrimental effects and that it does not permanently eliminate unwanted behaviors. Although these views might be interpreted as being sensitive to the organism's aversion to harsh treatment, the conclusions are questionable from a scientific perspective. Studies have shown that under certain conditions, punishment does seem to be effective in controlling behavior and does not seem to have long-lasting negative effects. Punishments sometime curtail undesirable behaviors so that alternative, desirable behaviors can be shaped with positive reinforcers. Of course, unless the alternatives are available, applying punishment is not likely to produce the desired outcomes. The point here is not that punishment is more desirable than positive reinforcement as a general technique of control, but rather that Skinner perhaps has neglected to give punishment a viable place in shaping behavior.

Instinctual vs. learned behavior

Skinner's view was that all behavior was learned through the process of reinforcement, whether it was positive or negative. Yet, research completed by Keller and Marian Breland in the early 1960s found that pigs, chickens, hamsters, porpoises, whales, cows, and other animals all demonstrated a tendency toward "instinctive drift." This means that animals tended to substitute instinctive behaviors for behaviors that had been reinforced, even when instinctive behaviors interfered with obtaining food. The animals were quickly conditioned to perform a number of tasks followed by unwanted behaviors. The conclusion is that the animals were reverting to innate behaviors that took precedence over the learned behaviors, even though this delayed receiving food, which supposedly was reinforcing the conditioned behavior. Clearly, in these cases, reinforcement was not as powerful an incentive for the animals as Skinner claimed.

Limitations of behavioral therapy

Behavioral therapy is a natural extension and application of many of Skinner's views focusing on observable behavior. The first criticism pertains to the lack of attention that behavior therapy gives to emotion. Behavioral practitioners hold that empirical evidence has not shown that feelings must be changed first in order to achieve measurable progress. In general, behavioral practitioners do not encourage their clients to experience their emotion, although some will work with aspects of emotion. Critics argue that emotions play a significant part in behavioral responses and should not be ignored. The strict emphasis on overt behavior to the exclusion of an inner life was a core concept that Skinner held throughout his career.

So hence, if there is not an inner life or at least one worth attending to, then it would follow that insight into one's motives or origins of behavioral responses would be of little value. This criticism states that behavior therapy ignores the importance of self or self-consciousness to the exclusion of overt behavioral responses. Skinner rejected the idea that such internal agents such as an ego or self allow us to make independent and free choices or derive any true benefit for examination of internal processes. This viewpoint, however, does not adequately take into account the reflective nature and imagination of the individual. A person cannot, as critics suggest, simply turn off his or her ability to reflect on past events or what propels them toward or causes them to back away from various choices.

Another criticism of behavior therapy is that it treats symptoms rather than causes. The psychoanalytic assumption is that early life events are the source of present difficulties. Behavior therapists may acknowledge the existence of past life events but do not place particular importance to those events in the maintenance of current problems. Instead, the behavioral practitioner emphasizes changing environmental circumstances and how those environmental forces reinforce particular behaviors. Critics respond with the argument that it is natural for humans to conceptualize a cause and effect relationship in behavior. This is an example of sequential learning and is used in many ways to describe the process of progress.

A final therapeutic criticism of behavior therapy involves the use of control and manipulation by the therapist toward the client. The therapist assumes a position of power with the client where he or she, through the process of reinforcement, can potentially manipulate the client's behavior responses. This criticism is largely a misunderstanding of contemporary behavior therapy. If applied in a strictly Skinnerian model, the potential for manipulation would be greater. However, all therapeutic approaches give some degree of control to the therapist, who hopes to facilitate change in the person seeking help. Most modern behavior therapists are not attempting to control their clients or manipulate them. In fact, many use techniques aimed at increased self-direction and self-control.

Ambiguity about human aspects of his theory

Skinner admits that the science of human behavior is not complete and needs further development. He also admits that rats and pigeons are not perfect models of humans. It would seem then that what is needed are some psychological principles that help bridge the gap from animal data to human functioning. Skinner believed, though, that the foundation of a science of human behavior has been set forth in his theories that deal adequately with human behavior.

THEORIES IN ACTION

Operant conditioning has become a very influential area of psychology, because it has successfully provided practical solutions to many problems in human behavior. Operant principles discovered in the laboratory are now being employed in a vast number of areas that include healthcare, education, mental health, prisons, and animal training, among many others.

Research

Applied behavior analysis Skinner was primarily concerned with understanding behavior and the process of learning. Although his experiments were largely with animals, he did generalize his findings to humans. Contrary to some criticisms of Skinner's deterministic principles, he did acknowledge that people could determine the causes of most behavior by identifying environmental conditions that support the behavior and then manipulate these conditions to influence the behavior in desired directions. Skinner's views led to a distinct branch of psychology called applied behavior analysis. Research in this area is directed primarily toward solving problems of everyday life.

Applied behavior analysis is a research method that uses a four-step process:

- define
- observe
- intervene
- test

Since operant conditioning is focused on observable behavioral outcomes, the first step is to define the target behaviors that need to be changed. Doing so allows researchers to develop procedures to then observe how often the behaviors occur under existing conditions. Once a stable measure of behaviors is maintained, researchers intervene to change the target behavior in the desired direction. For example, they may begin to reward behaviors they wish to increase, or withhold rewards following inappropriate behaviors they wish to decrease. Finally, they test the impact of the intervention by continuing to observe and record the target behavior during the intervention and beyond. Testing allows researchers to see the evidence of the intervention over time.

Computer assisted technology   Operant conditioning has also been applied to the field of education. One of the most impressive operant-based techniques involves the use of computers in the classroom. This is often referred to as computer-assisted instruction, or CAI. In CAI, students interact with sophisticated computer programs that provide immediate reinforcement of correct responses. With certain restrictions, these programs are paced according to each student's progress. CAI has been enhanced to now include lecture-based distance learning through the Internet, so that simultaneous learning can occur in virtually any geographic location through high-speed communication technology.

Biofeedback   Another area where operant conditioning is being studied and applied is in the realm of biofeedback. This is a technique that enables people to monitor and alter bodily responses such as skin temperature, muscle tension, blood pressure, and electrical activity of the brain. For example, a rise in blood pressure or muscle tension is indicated by a signal such as a loud tone, which acts as the feedback stimulus. As one lowers the blood pressure or relieves the muscle tension, the tone becomes softer. Reinforcement can play several roles, from reward to incentive. In biofeedback, the information given by the changing tones helps the subject know how much the behavior has changed.

Biofeedback research has influenced basic and theoretical ideas about learning. Responses of the autonomic nervous system were once thought to be outside the realm of operant conditioning. Research has demonstrated, though, that instrumental training of autonomic responses is possible with this technique.

Behavior modification   The most frequently cited examples of reinforcement can be found in the field of behavior modification. Behavior modification, also

known as behavior mod, seeks to apply the principles of operant learning to changing behaviors in a variety of settings.

An application of behavior modification through secondary reinforcement has been used in institutions across the country and is known as a token economy. For example, the staff of a psychiatric hospital is faced with the problem of motivating residents to perform a number of daily living behaviors: dressing and basic grooming, among other simple tasks. The patients are given tokens for each desired behavior or set of behaviors that they complete. The tokens have no inherent worth but can be exchanged for candy, movie tickets, outdoor activities, or other privileges. In this way, the tokens are secondary reinforcers of the behavior. The token economy is one of the few behavior modification techniques that work well with large numbers of subjects at one time. It is based on the concept of positive reinforcement.

Another prevalent use of behavior modification is applied in the school system. Teachers frequently structure reward-giving situations to help them accomplish their learning objectives for students. When teachers want to shape a behavior with a low response rate and make it a high response rate, they often employ behavior modification techniques by associating the two. For instance, a teacher might observe a child for some time to determine which behaviors occur at a high frequency and which occur at a low frequency. If the child has a high frequency with art but a low frequency with math, the teacher will make art contingent upon completing the work dealing with math.

Learned helplessness   Research on learned helplessness seems to suggest that its onset stems partly from one's perception of control. When people believe they have no control over their environment, they stop trying to improve their situation. For example, children growing up in urban slums may perceive that they have little control over their environment and even less hope of escaping it. As a result, they may simply resign themselves to a lifetime of exclusion and hopelessness. Operant principles of reinforcement would especially apply with individuals dealing with learned helplessness. Studies have shown that some behavior is influenced not only by the level of rewards a person receives but by the person's evaluation of those rewards. For a reward to be effective, it must match the perceptions of the individual and shape the behavior in a positive manner. For instance, if a teen has learned helplessness about his ability to develop a marketable skill to get a job, the reinforcement cannot be indiscriminate. It must specifically address the need for competence in a potential area of strength, in order to effectively reshape the learned helplessness.

Case studies

A study that illustrates applied behavior analysis involved the task of trying to reduce the amount of graffiti on the walls of three public restrooms on a particular university campus. The increase of graffiti had caused the school to repaint these rooms repeatedly. The researchers began by objectively defining what constituted graffiti and what did not. Then they made daily counts of the graffiti to determine the number of occurrences. The researchers then introduced an intervention they felt might help reduce the amount of graffiti. The intervention consisted of a sign taped to the bathroom wall that read: "A local licensed doctor has agree to donate a set amount of money to the local chapter of the United Way for each day this wall remains free of any writing, drawings, or other markings. Your assistance is greatly appreciated in helping to support your United Way." The intervention was successful and kept the walls free of graffiti for the next three months.

Teaching machine   In one significant way, Skinner was well ahead of his time in the development of his teaching machine. It began as a simple observation while attending his daughter's math class. He noticed that the teacher was not reinforcing the answers students provided partly because she was unaware of the importance of such behavior and partly because she could not adequately reinforce so many students' responses simultaneously. This gave him an idea, an invention Skinner was to call the teaching machine.

Skinner's teaching machine presented problems in random order for students, with feedback (reinforcement) after each one. While it did not attempt to teach new behavior (and thus replace the human instructor), it was seen as an excellent tool for reviewing previous material and building on previously learned concepts. Within three years of his initial idea Skinner had developed a complete program of instruction. For the next 10 years, Skinner was very involved with his work on the teaching machine, attempting to perfect it. Unfortunately, the technology he longed for to make his teaching machine didn't arrive until the latter years of his life. The advent of the personal computer would eventually allow many of Skinner's ideas regarding learning to be applied in the way he envisioned them.

Behavior modification   The techniques of operant conditioning were primarily used on animals in the early experiments. In 1953, though, Skinner and a colleague began experimenting with some of the principles of operant conditioning, now called behavior modification, at the Metropolitan State Hospital in Waltham, Massachusetts. The purpose of the studies was to determine how applicable operant conditioning techniques were in the experimental analysis of psychotic patients. Fifteen male patients were conditioned to pull levers for candy and cigarettes. Skinner and his colleague were able to demonstrate highly stable individual differences in overall rate of lever-pulling per hour in the subjects. For the first time, medically useful and objective measures of the psychoses were available.

The most intriguing aspects of the studies suggested that psychotic behavior is controlled by reinforcing properties within the immediate environment. From this basic premise came a whole new understanding of the origin of deviant behavior. Previously, the dominant view of deviance was understood in dynamic terms as an internal state of mental illness. The behavior modification study suggested a learning model that involved symptoms that might have been learned at some point in the person's past through accidental reinforcement.

Dolphin-human therapy   Dolphin-human therapy was created and developed by David Nathanson, Ph.D., a psychologist with almost 30 years experience working with disabled children. This therapy was developed with a series of carefully controlled language experiments using dolphins as teachers for children with Down syndrome. The key to learning for all people, but especially for the mentally retarded, is to increase sensory attention—i.e., sight, sound, touch, taste, smell—so that increased learning will occur. Most mentally handicapped children have difficulty paying attention to a stimulus, and as a result, learning is impaired. The theory and research behind dolphin-assisted therapy is that children or adults will increase attention as a result of a desire to interact with dolphins. By interacting with the dolphins and using a behavior modification procedure that rewards the child for correct cognitive, physical, or affective responses, the therapy incrementally teaches children skills they may not be able to learn in more conventional ways.

Organizational behavior management   Behavior modification has also been used successfully in organizations to help facilitate greater efficiency. One study sought to use behavior modification techniques with an existing hotel-cleaning staff, to determine how to improve and maintain a standard of cleanliness with

CHRONOLOGY

1904: B.F. Skinner born March 20.

1930: Initiates research in reflexes.

1936: Marries Yvonne Blue.

1938: *The Behavior of Organisms* is published.

1942: Awarded the Warren Medal by the Society of Experimental Psychologists.

1945: Takes over the Psychology Department at the University of Indiana, where he developed the Teaching Machine and Aircrib.

1948: *Walden Two* is published.

1956: Fixed interval schedule of reinforcement described.

1966: Introduces the concept of critical period in reinforcing an event.

1968: Identifies the critical characteristics of programmed instruction.

1971: Publishes *Beyond Freedom and Dignity*.

1972: Receives the Humanist of the Year Award by the American Humanist Association.

1983: Publishes *Enjoying Old Age*.

1990: Dies on August 18.

---

minimum turnover and cost. The study was initiated because of the very high turnover rate of cleaning staff and the substandard work carried out. To further exacerbate management's situation, the hiring, training, outfitting, and maintenance of a housekeeping staff is one of the largest budget line items for most hotel/motel operations. During the assessment it was discovered that a standard of cleanliness had not been established, feedback to the cleaning staff was essentially nonexistent, and aversive managerial practices were common, leading to low morale. The applications of behavior modification began by establishing clear standards that could be objectively measured regarding cleanliness. Management then chose to positively reinforce the role of the cleaning staff by rewarding their performance with merit-pay increases when they adhered to the cleanliness standards set forth. Regular feedback was given to staff to keep

them informed of training and expectations. The program was successful in improving worker morale, raising the level of cleanliness, and saving a substantial amount of money in the long term.

Relevance to modern readers

Skinner's work is considered by some to be the most important contribution to date on learning and the process of behavioral change. Though his work was largely with animals, his concepts have been among the most researched of all the psychological theories. Because the emphasis is on observable behavior, new studies are continually being devised that build from the concepts established by Skinner, expanding upon and adapting the original principles to various types of human behavior. In fact, operant-conditioning principles are apparent in virtually every sphere of modern life. Most noticeable are variations of behavior modification. The modern reader may not immediately recognize the relationship between operant principles and everyday behavior, but once these patterns are identified, it is hard to underestimate the influence of Skinner's ideas on contemporary life. Following are some of the most obvious realms where operant conditioning techniques are at work.

Behavioral shaping   Behavioral shaping is commonly used to change a behavior in response to rewards known as positive reinforcements. This technique is often used by parents in their attempt to modify their child's behavior. For instance, if a child is learning a new skill, such as riding a bicycle, the parent can reinforce the progress incrementally through praise and supportive encouragement until the skill is mastered. Behavioral shaping can also employ negative reinforcement. For instance, the child who disobeys his or her parent may receive a "time-out." The mandatory time spent away from the child's preferred activity is a negative reinforcement. In other words, to avoid this consequence again, the child needs to change his or her behavior so that it complies with the parent's wishes. Both positive and negative reinforcements can be used effectively to shape behavior in children, teens, and even adults. One example of how this technique is commonly used with adults is weight loss. Positive reinforcements or rewards play a significant role in one's ability to continue the disciplined task of losing weight. One example of behavior modification at work would be the following: each time a person abstains from eating out at lunch hour, they deposit the amount of money they would have spent into a "rewards jar." The money that accumulates will be used for a non-food reward

FURTHER ANALYSIS:
The baby box: Myth and reality

B. F. Skinner, the dominant behavioral psychologist of the 20th century, contributed many insights into the understanding of animal and human behavior during his career. But one "experiment" attributed to him is among the most controversial of all his work. It involved his second daughter Deborah whom he was accused of using for one of his psychological experiments. Throughout Skinner's life, he was routinely charged with accusations regarding this incident and made many attempts to set the record straight. Here's the real story.

Skinner began his career in the 1930s and is best known for the operant chamber, more commonly referred to as the "Skinner box." It was a small laboratory apparatus used to conduct and record the results of operant-conditioning experiments with animals. These experiments typically required an animal to manipulate an object such as a lever in order to obtain a reward.

When Skinner's second daughter, Deborah, was born in 1944, Skinner (who then lived in Minnesota) constructed an alternative type of crib for her that was something like a large version of a hospital incubator. It was a tall box with a door at its base and a glass window in front. This "baby tender," as Skinner called it, provided Deborah with a place to sleep and remain comfortably warm throughout the severe Minnesota winters without having to be wrapped in numerous layers of clothing and blankets. Deborah slept in her novel crib until she was two and a half years old, and by all accounts grew up a happy, healthy, thriving child.

Skinner invented the baby tender not as a lab experiment but as a labor-saving device. Because it was equipped with filtered and humidified air it allowed Deborah to have less risk of airborne infection. The sound-proof walls provided for sounder sleep and the warm air that continually circulated through the crib allowed the child to wear only a diaper to bed. There was also a shade that could be drawn to keep the light out of the crib while the baby was sleeping.

Skinner claimed that his invention was used in the same way that a traditional crib would be used.

Deborah was taken out of the crib for short periods throughout the day so that she could eat and interact with her older sister, Julie, and her parents. Friends and neighbor children who visited the house could view the young child in her enclosed crib while keeping her in a germ-free environment.

The trouble began in October 1945, when Skinner submitted an article on the baby tender to the popular magazine *Ladies Home Journal*. The article featured a picture of Deborah in a portable (and therefore smaller) version of the box, her hands pressed against the glass and the headline read: "Baby in a Box." People who didn't read the article carefully, or who merely glanced at the picture or heard about the article from someone else, tended to confuse the baby tender with a Skinner box, even though the article clearly explained that the baby tender was something quite different.

Nonetheless, many people jumped to the conclusion that Skinner was raising his daughter in a cramped box equipped with bells and food trays. It was viewed by many as just another of Skinner's psychological experiments measuring the reinforcement of reward and punishment. Outraged readers of the magazine wrote letters protesting such behavior and started a landslide of rumor that Skinner was never quite able to put to rest during his lifetime.

Over the years, the details about Skinner's baby tender, which was unsuccessfully marketed under the name "Aircrib," faded somewhat. But by the mid-1960s, about the time Deborah turned 21, the rumor emerged again this time saying that Deborah had become psychotic and was suing her father. Some reports stated that she had committed suicide.

The truth of this story is that Deborah Skinner (now Deborah Skinner Buzan) grew up having a very normal life and remained close to her father while he was alive. She has been living and working in London as an artist since the mid-1970s. She is not psychologically scarred as a result of her use of the baby tender. She claims that most of the criticisms of the box are by people who do not understand what it was.

when they reach their target weight. Thus, each deposit of money is a positive reinforcer for continuing the behavior.

Systematic desensitization Operant-conditioning techniques are also at work in helping those with significant fears and anxiety learn to live more effectively. A process called systematic desensitization is used to overcome the fear or anxiety associated with a particular stimulus. The premise behind systematic desensitization is that if a fear is learned or conditioned, it can then be unlearned by the process of extinction or by not reinforcing the behavior. The person undergoing this treatment is asked to either imagine the anxiety-producing situation or confront the real-life situation incrementally, while positive reinforcement is provided to help establish the perception of control over the stimulus. Occasionally, relaxation training accompanies the use of systematic desensitization whenever the anxiety-producing stimuli are present. It helps to increase the likelihood of a relaxed response to the feared stimulus. This behavior-modification treatment has been very successful at extinguishing the stimulus that triggers the fear or anxiety.

Other applications Behavior modification techniques are also being used to help people with a wide variety of everyday behavior problems, including those with addictive behaviors, aggression, attention deficit disorder, teen delinquency, and learning disabilities, among others. These methods have been used successfully in schools systems, prisons, mental health institutions, the workplace, and many other environments. Behavior modification has become so popular because it has been shown to be extremely effective in various situations and it empowers the individual using the techniques to change unwanted behavior. Though Skinner would attribute behavior change to environmental reinforcements in one's life to which a person has only limited control, modern adaptations of behavior modification instill the perception of control in the person attempting to make the behavioral change.

BIBLIOGRAPHY

Sources

Baldwin, John D., and Baldwin, Janice I. *Behavior Principles In Everyday Life.* Englewood Cliffs, N.J.: Prentice Hall, 1986.

Bjork, Daniel. *B. F. Skinner: A Life.* New York: Basic Books, 1993.

Carpenter, Finley. *The Skinner Primer.* New York: The Free Press, 1974.

Evans, Richard. *B. F. Skinner: The Man and His Ideas.* New York: E. P. Dutton and Co., 1968.

Epstein, Robert, ed. *Skinner for the Classroom: Selected Papers.* Champaign, IL: Research Press, 1982.

Geiser, Robert L. *Behavior Modification and the Managed Society.* Boston: Beacon Press, 1976.

Green, Christopher. *Classics in the History of Psychology: The Misbehavior of Organisms.* University of Toronto. http://psychclassics.yorku.ca/Breland/misbehavior.htm.

Nye, Robert D. *Three Views of Man.* Monterey, CA: Brooks/ Cole Publishing Company, 1975.

Nye, Robert D. *What is B. F. Skinner Really Saying?* Englewood Cliff, N.J.: Prentice Hall, Inc. 1979.

Radford University. *What is wrong with Daily Life in the Western World.* http://www.radford.edu/~jmontuor/Skinner_Article.htm.

Sagal, Paul T. *Skinner's Philosophy.* University Press of America, Inc., 1981.

Schultz, Duane P., and Sydney Ellen Schultz. *A History of Modern Psychology.* Belmont, CA: Wadsworth, 2004.

Skinner, B. F. *About Behaviorism.* New York: Alfred A. Knopf, 1974.

Skinner B. F. *A Matter of Consequences.* New York: Alfred A. Knopf, 1983.

Skinner, B. F. *Particulars of My Life.* New York: Alfred A. Knopf, 1976.

Skinner, B. F. *Reflections on Behaviorism and Society.* Englewood Cliffs: Prentice Hall, Inc., 1978.

Skinner B. F. *The Shaping of a Behaviorist.* New York: Alfred A. Knopf, 1979.

Slater, Lauren. *Opening Skinner's Box.* New York: W. W. Norton and Company, 2004.

Further readings

Bjork, Daniel. *B. F. Skinner: A Life.* New York: Basic Books, 1993.

Carpenter, Finley. *The Skinner Primer.* New York: The Free Press, 1974.

Epstein, Robert, ed. *Skinner for the Classroom: Selected Papers.* Champaign, IL: Research Press, 1982.

Sagal, Paul T. *Skinner's Philosophy.* University Press of America, Inc., 1981.

Skinner, B. F. *About Behaviorism.* New York: Alfred A. Knopf, 1974.

Skinner B. F. *A Matter of Consequences.* New York: Alfred A. Knopf, 1983.

Skinner, B. F. *Particulars of My Life.* New York: Alfred A. Knopf, 1976.

Skinner, B. F. *Reflections on Behaviorism and Society.* Englewood Cliffs: Prentice Hall, Inc., 1978.

Skinner B. F. *The Shaping of a Behaviorist.* New York: Alfred A. Knopf, 1979.

Max Wertheimer

1880–1943

GERMAN-AMERICAN PROFESSOR, LECTURER

UNIVERSITY OF PRAGUE, PHILOSOPHY, 1902; UNIVERSITY OF WÜRZBURG, PhD IN PHILOSOPHY, 1904

BRIEF OVERVIEW

Science is rooted in the will to truth. With the will to truth it stands or falls. Lower the standard even slightly and science becomes diseased to the core. Not only science, but also man. The will to truth, pure and unadulterated, is among the essential conditions of his existence; if the standard is compromised, he easily becomes a tragic caricature of himself.

—Max Wertheimer, "On Truth," published in *Social Research* in 1934.

For Max Wertheimer and the Gestalt therapy for which he became best known, truth began with a train trip and a simple child's toy. When 30-year-old Wertheimer left Vienna, Austria for a vacation in Germany's Rhineland in 1910, he had no idea that his holiday would never come to be. Equally he had no idea that his idle thoughts on that train trip would lead to a discovery that would irrevocably alter not only his own life, but produce profound changes in psychology-related disciplines all over the world. Gestalt, the notion that the whole is not only greater than its components, but also different from those components; was little more than a lone, obscure, and struggling concept that summer day in 1910 as Wertheimer rode the train.

On that day, psychology was little more than a fledgling discipline, still widely considered a sideline for philosophers. "Gestalt" was the name Christian von Ehrenfels, one of Max Wertheimer's teachers, had coined to describe the philosophical concept nearly

Max Wertheimer. (Corbis Corporation. Reproduced by permission.)

25 years earlier. Yet so impressive was Wertheimer's work on the subject that he would become to be known as the father of the movement. Much of Wertheimer's research and unique experiments were merely the initial battles in a rebellion against a notion prevailing in European psychology at the time: the "Elementalism or Structuralism" of famed German psychologist Wilhelm Wundt. But Max Wertheimer's version of Gestalt psychology would do far more than negate previous psychological assumptions. It would profoundly change the way educators, psychiatrists, psychologists, rehabilitation specialists—anyone involved in the helping professions—look at their clients and their work.

Wertheimer's train trip exposed him to a phenomenon that would ignite his imagination. As he rode from Vienna to Frankfurt, he became aware of two separate and alternating light patterns from the train's window. As he watched, Wertheimer discovered that if the spacing, on-time, and off-time were just right for these lights, his mind would perceive the dual lights as one single flashing light moving back and forth. Reaching Frankfurt, Wertheimer disembarked from the train and put an end to his vacation plans. He proceeded to a store and bought a toy stroboscope, then a popular child's toy, and checked himself into a hotel room.

There he repeated his visual perception experiment over and over to test the validity of what he had seen on the train. Stroboscopes, the precursors of motion pictures, were a revolving disk that can be synchronized with movement to make an object appear either to be standing still or moving slowly forward or backward. This simple experiment, not even terribly original in its nature, would lead Wertheimer to an original name for what he had just observed—the phi phenomenon. His observations, though, would go far beyond what researchers and thinkers before him had seen or realized. From the phi phenomenon Wertheimer would go on to rethink and revolutionize psychology's notions about how human beings see and experience things. It would also make him one of the many people responsible for the creation of early cartoons and motion pictures.

It was in those early years in Frankfurt that Wertheimer also found two soul mates. His two research partners at the University of Frankfurt, Wolfgang Köhler and Kurt Koffka, would become his lifelong colleagues in both their testing and formation of the Gestalt theories. They would revolutionize the psychological world with their new way of looking at things. Though Wertheimer believed in Gestalt psychology as avidly as any of his disciples, he appears to have acted more in the role of a facilitator than preacher. He never published a definitive summation of the Gestalt psychology he made famous. Though he was a man given to passionate beliefs, neither did he engage in the tiresome dialogues about the efficacy of his hypotheses that seemed to have plagued so many of his contemporaries. He wrote far less prolifically and therefore was far less known than many other mental health figures of his time, notably Carl Jung, Sigmund Freud, or Carl Rogers. Yet his impact upon psychology is undeniable.

Wertheimer was rather like a shooting star that streaked across the study of the mind, shooting off sparks of brilliant insights and then moving on, leaving others to fill in the more mundane facts and procedures deduced from his insights. As his friend Edwin B. Newman noted in his 1944 *American Journal of Psychology* article, "Max Wertheimer: 1880–1943," "He tended to be impatient with experimental plans that called for meticulous care in their details. The neatest of plans was invariably upset and rearranged after he had finished with them. It was not easy to work under Wertheimer just because of this restlessness."

In addition, the early papers that he did manage to publish, many written during the years that Germany was a combatant nation in World War I, did not receive worldwide recognition until well after the war, in the early 1920s. Yet quietly and with humility, Max Wertheimer influenced his colleagues and countless students. It would be those students who would carry on the research and develop the principles that would become an accepted worldwide school of psychological thought. But both Wolfgang Köhler and Kurt Koffka, who provided so much of the structure for Gestalt psychology, would always acknowledge that it was Wertheimer who originally saw the flaws in the then-current psychological ideas and recognized the significance of what he had observed for a brief time on a train. Koffka referred to Wertheimer as "the first founder" (of Gestalt theory).

As had happened to so many other German Jewish intellectuals, Hitler and the Nazis would force Wertheimer out of Germany and across the Atlantic Ocean to the United States. Initially the language and cultural barriers he experienced would mask a brilliant mind. But like many of the other intelligentsia, Wertheimer would find a second home in the New School of Social Research initiated in New York City in the 1930s. A well-rounded individual who deeply cared about the social issues of his time, Wertheimer became an intellectual giant operating at the new school.

He would go on to write and lecture on an eclectic array of psychological and philosophical subjects ranging from ethics and morality to the meaning of freedom. In all of his philosophical discourses, he would demonstrate how Gestalt principles applied to even these ethereal philosophical concepts. Many observers have described Wertheimer's Gestalt psychology as applicable only to how we perceive things. For Wertheimer, howver, perception was only one side of the equation. Thinking and problem-solving were the other aspects of that equation, something Wertheimer would demonstrate again and again. He would show it in his much-publicized conversations with Albert Einstein on the development of the theory of relativity, which became part of his last work, published posthumously as *Productive Thinking*.

BIOGRAPHY

The early years

Prague, the capitol of the Czech province of Bohemia, had been a German city for 14 years when Max Wertheimer was born there on April 15, 1880. Bohemia had alternated between German and Austrian rule over most of the century, and in 1866, Prussian troops had besieged Prague and won the

PRINCIPAL PUBLICATIONS

- "Experimentelle Untersuchungen zur Tatbestand-diagnostik." *Archiv für die gesamte Psychologie* 6 (1905): 59–131.

- "Musik der Wedda." *Sammelbãnde der internationalen Musikgesellschaft* 11 (1910): 300–09.

- "Experimentelle Studien über das Sehen von Bewegung." *Zeitschrift für Psychologie* 61 (1912): 161–265.

- "Über das denken der Naturvölker. I. Zahlen und Gebilde." *Zeitschrift für Psychologie* 60 (1912): 321–28.

- "Untersuchungen zur Lehre von der Gestalt. 1. Prinzipielle Bermerkungen" (A Source Book of Gestalt Psychology). *Psychologische Forschung* 1 (1922): 47–58.

- "Untersuchungen zur Lehre von der Gestalt." 2. *Psychologische Forschung* 4 (1923): 301–50.

- "Gestaltpsychologische Forschung." *Einführung in die neuere Psychologie.* Osterwieck am Harz, 1928.

- "Zu dem Problem der Unterscheidung von Einzelinhalt und Teil." *Zeitschrift für Psychologie* 129 (1933): 353–57.

- "On Truth." *Social Research* 1 (1934): 135–46.

- "Gestalt Function in Visual Motor Patterns in Organic Disease of the Brain." *Archives of Neurology and Psychiatry* 33 (1935): 328–29.

- "Some Problems in the Theory of Ethics." *Social Research* 2 (1935): 353–67.

- "Freedom: Its Meaning." *A Story of Three Days,* edited by R. N. Ashen. New York: Harcourt, Brace, 1940.

- "Gestalt Theory." *Social Research* 11 (1944): 78–99.

- *Productive Thinking.* New York: Harper, 1945.

battle that would end what was then called "The Seven Weeks War." That defeat had left Bohemia completely under Germany's control. Very little has been written of Wertheimer's early years. It is known that his father was a schoolmaster who had charge of a commercial high school in Prague, and that both of his parents wanted him to be a musician. He attended a local gymnasium, a school that prepared students for the university, and in 1898, at the age of 18, he began his studies at the University of Prague. For two and a half years, Wertheimer studied law there, but then came to realize that a legal career was not for him. In those first two years at the university, he had already shown an interest in philosophy, attending several lectures on the subject. In the spring of 1901, the 20-year-old Wertheimer made the study of philosophy his major.

Though the University of Prague did not have its own psychological laboratory, it certainly did boast some of the luminaries of European psychology and philosophy as members of its teaching staff. During his time at Prague University, Wertheimer listened to the lectures of Christian von Ehrenfels and Ewald Hering, two of the foremost names in psychology and philosophy of that era. Prophetically, von Ehrenfels's primary intellectual pursuit concerned what he called *Gestaltqualidt,* or "form quality," the forerunner of Wertheimer's later credo, Gestalt psychology. Wertheimer became acquainted with the field of experimental visual psychology through hours spent in the Physiology Institute, working in Ewald Hering's visual laboratory on the study of color perception. In 1902, Wertheimer completed his studies at Prague University and moved on to the University of Berlin. Here psychology was a well-established field, and Carl Stumpf, a good friend of American psychologist William James, was his teacher. But Stumpf apparently was much involved at the time in his study of the psychology of music. Stumpf's assistant Friedrich Schumann, though well-known for his collaboration with G. E. Muller in the invention of the Memory Drum, was a teacher who failed to provide the intellectual stimulus Wertheimer sought. From his own accounts, Wertheimer spent his first semester in Berlin studying volume after volume of the still-growing German psychological textbook *Zeitschrift für Psychologie.*

Wertheimer moved on to the University of Würzburg in 1903. Once again at Würzburg, he was fortunate to have as teachers Karl Marbe, well-known in his time for his work on imageless thought and industrial psychology; and Oswald Kulpe, considered the father of the modern study of thought processes. In an era when philosophy and psychology were considered to be closely interrelated, Wertheimer was awarded his doctorate in philosophy *summa cum laude* from Würzburg in 1904. His doctoral dissertation was

on an old interest, the law. He discussed the use of word association techniques in determining the guilt or innocence of defendants in criminal cases. But even then, his interests were not only psychology and philosophy. Wertheimer had an equally sustained interest in both mathematics and languages. Interestingly, though he chose not to follow his parents' wishes and become a musician, he maintained an avid love for music as well. It was a pursuit that would stay with him for the rest of his life.

The period between 1904, when Wertheimer received his Ph.D; and 1910, when he took his memorable train ride, appear to have been years of restlessness. In an article written for the magazine *Social Research* by Wertheimer's good friend Horace Kallen in 1948, he described those years as "a period of wandering from place to place and task to task." Parts of the first two years were spent in both Prague and Vienna, and some of that time apparently was spent working in psychiatric hospitals. But there is no record of the actual projects he was involved in during this time. It is known that in 1906 he (uncharacteristically) became involved in a dispute with Carl Jung over Jung's word association technique. Though he had decided not to become an attorney, Wertheimer apparently continued to embrace a fascination with law. Many of his earlier papers, written with a young lawyer identified only as "M. Klein," concern the mental processes of court testimony. Klein and Wertheimer attempted to use the Jungian free association idea as a means of distinguishing the truthfulness of testimony. These papers seem far removed from the Max Wertheimer of Gestalt theory. As Edwin Newman notes in "Max Wertheimer—1880–1943" in the July 1944 *American Journal of Psychology*, "Only one thing in it (one of these papers) foreshadows his later interests: That is the emphasis on the problem of truth, a problem which becomes even more acute in the realm of logic and reasoning."

Wertheimer shortly moved on again to Berlin, where he was reintroduced to an earlier love, music. In Berlin, he quickly formed a close and abiding friendship with Erich von Hornbostel, an Austrian music scholar who had been Carl Stumpf's assistant at the Berlin Psychological Institute. During the time he spent there, Wertheimer worked with both Stumpf and von Hornbostel at the Phonogramm Archives, a Berlin institute for the study of music and culture. The Phonogramm Archives was among the first places to record various ethnic music (including that year, Siamese opera) with the American Thomas Edison's new phonograph recording equipment. Like many of the other friendships in Wertheimer's life, his alliance

BIOGRAPHY:
Kurt Koffka

Kurt Koffka (1886–1941) was born into a comfortable, upper-class family in Berlin on March 18, 1886. His father, an attorney, had served as a royal legal councilor. Koffka had governesses as a child, one of whom was English-speaking. He attended the University of Berlin and used the English he had learned as a child when in 1904 he took a year to study at the University of Edinburgh. Like Max Wertheimer before him, he changed his major from philosophy to psychology when he returned to Germany in 1905. Koffka's earliest published work studied color blindness, a subject he knew something about due to his own color blindness. In 1909, Koffka served as assistant to two of Germany's luminaries in psychology: Karl Marbe and Oswald Kulpe. That same year he married Mira Klein, whom he had gotten to know when she served as a subject for experiments related to his doctoral dissertation.

The next year, 1910, newlywed Koffka moved to Frankfurt and found employment as an assistant to Friedrich Schumann at the Psychological Institute there. That move proved to be the most fateful of his career. Max Wertheimer had unexpectedly shown up there earlier that year, and Koffka soon became one of the subjects for Wertheimer's experiments in apparent motion. By the time the study was finished, Koffka, too, had become a believer. He moved on to the University of Giessen in 1911, but he continued to

spread the Gestalt ideas throughout Germany. With Wertheimer and Wolfgang Köhler, he founded the first psychological journal completely devoted to Gestalt psychology, *Psychologische Forschung*. He remained at the University of Giessen with intermittent trips to the United States for the next 16 years. His book on child psychology, *Growth of the Mind,* was written during the Giessen years. As noted earlier, Koffka had a special interest in education, and was a strong opponent of rote learning. In 1922 he wrote an article for *Psychological Bulletin*, which first introduced Gestalt theory to the United States. He left

Kurt Koffka. (Archives of the History of American Psychology. Reproduced by permission.)

Germany in 1927, far ahead of the exodus created by Adolph Hitler and the Nazis, and moved to the United States. He became a professor at Smith College that same year and continued there until his death, involved in research on color vision in relation to the organization of perception. Koffka did not survive his old mentor Wertheimer. He died in 1941, at the age of 55.

and collaboration with von Hornbostel would continue even after both men came to the United States.

The train trip that led to Gestalt psychology

In 1910, Wertheimer was once more back in Vienna, when he boarded a westbound train for the Rhineland and a vacation. As the train chugged along through the night that he became aware of a strange illusion. Two separate lights were visible from his train window. But because the on-times and off-times for these lights were synchronized in a certain manner, Wertheimer found that his mind would not distinguish them as being two lights, but rather one light in motion, rather like changing neon lights or rotating lights on a Christmas tree. It was Wertheimer's nature to immediately become enthusiastic about some phenomenon

that his curious mind encountered, and this observed light pattern was no exception. At the next train stop, which happened to be the city of Frankfurt, Wertheimer left the train and his vacation plans behind.

Wertheimer first found a hotel, paid for a room, and deposited his suitcases there. Then he went shopping. What he purchased was a toy stroboscope, a child's drum-shaped toy that spun. The stroboscope had regularly spaced slots and pictures inside for viewing, similar in manner to a very simple movie machine. He spent several days in that Frankfurt hotel room, repeating over and over again his experiment in perception based upon his experience on the train. Then he was ready to act. His former teacher in Berlin, Friedrich Schumann, was now a professor at Frankfurt's Psychological Institute. Wertheimer brought his novel idea to Schumann, who was immediately supportive of the research. In place of the child's stroboscope, Wertheimer was now offered the use of the university's tachistoscope, a psychology lab device that provides a visual stimulus. This stimulus could be adjusted to afford brief interval exposures through the use of a gravity-operated shutter. But far more importantly, Wertheimer was offered the help of Schumann's 25-year-old assistant, Wolfgang Köhler. Within a short time, Kurt Koffka, then 26, joined the research group. Both Köhler and Koffka had earned their PhDs at the University of Berlin, under the tutelage of Friedrich Schumann.

Before their fateful meeting with Wertheimer, both Köhler and Koffka had already been involved in other psychological research. Köhler's work had been related to hearing, and Koffka had studied imagery (in particular, color perception) and thought. As is the accepted procedure, neither of Wertheimer's subjects was told anything about the research in which they were involved. But in 1911, when Wertheimer's study was completed, he met with both young men to discuss the study that had just been completed. It was during this conversation that the first two disciples of Gestalt therapy were made. What Wertheimer told them convinced both young men sufficiently that they would spend the rest of their lives researching, modifying, and explaining Wertheimer's Gestalt ideas.

The World War I years and his early teaching

In 1912, Max Wertheimer published his groundbreaking paper, "Experimental Studies of the Perception of Movement." He stayed on at the emerging University of Frankfurt, the place he had come to so impulsively from a trip on a train. His stay in Frankfurt was the result of Schumann and the faculty there inviting Wertheimer to remain as a *Privadozent* (called PD for short). A *Privadozent* is a unique position in the university system of Europe and most common specifically in German academic life. Begun in Prussia in the early 1800s, it is a title bestowed on a scholar who has earned a PhD, written a second thesis, and lectured on the scholar's area of expertise at the university for which he is a candidate. Following the lecture, the faculty then votes whether they wish the person to remain at the school as a PD.

If voted in, the new PD is both permitted, and expected, to teach at the university. A PD gives lectures and advises PhD candidates on their theses. It is a typical way for an aspiring professor to begin his or her career. The down side of such a position in Wertheimer's time—what Simmel called "the purgatory of *Privadozent*-ship"—was that PDs received

no salary and had no formal position or status. Wertheimer did receive lecture fees or payment for classes taught, but that was all. PDs are less common in Europe today, and especially since university reform in Germany in 1968. For those that remain, there has been massive improvement in working conditions over the years since Wertheimer served in this position. Currently it is most common for PDs to receive a modest stipend.

The assassination of Austrian Archduke Franz Ferdinand in 1914 by a Serbian revolutionary plunged Europe into the "war to end all wars," World War I. For the first two years of the war, Max Wertheimer remained in Frankfurt. But in 1916 his old friend Erich von Hornbostel invited him to come to Berlin. He was placed on leave from his Frankfurt *Privadozent* position and collaborated with von Hornbostel on war-related research. Much of this work had to do with the development of listening devices to be used in locating enemy sounds both on land, sea, and air. Some of their work, apparently related to early studies of sonar, was conducted aboard submarines, and other portions involved being stationed at harbor defense installations. The war ended in 1918, but Wertheimer and von Hornbostel's work did not become published until 1920, when a paper describing their findings during the war was presented to the Prussian Academy of Sciences. During this same period of time, Wertheimer was elected a *Privadozent* at the University of Berlin.

Career and marriage in Germany

However, this time Wertheimer's career as a PD was a short one. He was made "Professor Extraordinarius" at the University of Berlin in 1922. This assurance of having an income solved one problem for Wertheimer: It finally made it financially feasible for him to marry. In 1923 he married Anna Caro, one of his Berlin University students with whom he had fallen in love. Wertheimer was then 43 years of age, considerably older than his wife. The Wertheimers remained in Berlin for the next seven years, and it was during those years that their four children were born. Two sons, Rudolph and Valentin, were born in 1924 and 1925, soon followed in 1927 by another son, Michael. Their daughter, Lise, came into the world the next year, in 1928.

Wertheimer became an immensely popular teacher at the University of Berlin. One of the characteristic components of all his classes was himself at the piano, playing music and querying his students as to what philosopher or even cartoon character he was musically portraying. It was also during these years in

Berlin that Wertheimer made the acquaintance of a man who would remain his friend for the rest of his life, physicist Albert Einstein. It appeared that Wertheimer had found his academic niche in Berlin. But events would soon change all of that. In 1929, he accepted the position of professor where his career could be said to have begun, the University of Frankfurt.

In some ways, it seems odd that Wertheimer accepted a teaching position back at the University of Frankfurt. The head of the Psychological Institute there, his old teacher Friedrich Schumann, and Wertheimer had by then developed a rift that was destined to deepen. Schumann apparently was less than pleased by, and disagreed with, the growth of Gestalt psychology. When Schumann assigned one of his students named Fuchs to assist him in research on the phenomenon of transparency, Fuchs told him that it could only be understood by using Wertheimer's Gestalt principles. Schumann immediately showed great antipathy towards Fuchs's ideas simply because they embraced Gestalt theory. The animosity between Schumann and Wertheimer only deepened when Schumann refused to allow Fuchs to publish his work on the project. By 1933, however, the disagreement between the two academics had become a moot point with the coming to power of Adolph Hitler and his National Socialist (Nazi) party.

Emigrating and adjusting to America

Wertheimer seems to have understood from the beginning that Germany would no longer be a safe place for intellectuals—let alone Jewish intellectuals—after Hitler and the Nazis took charge of the German government. In 1933, the same year that Adolph Hitler was elected chancellor, Wertheimer, his wife, Anna, and their four children traveled from Germany to his native Czechoslovakia, an independent country since the end of World War I. It was part of a prearranged plan. Their next journey would take them across the Atlantic to the United States. The Wertheimers settled in New York, and the next year Max accepted a previously made invitation offered while he was still in Germany: to join the "University in Exile."

The notion of an entire European-style university functioning in New York as part of the New School for Social Research had been the idea and dream of several German refugees from Nazism. The New School itself was an innovative place that had been developed in 1918, long before Hitler and the Nazis had become an issue. But the New School's "University in Exile" came into being in 1933 through

the efforts (and donations) of several American and European philanthropists determined to find a safe place for some of the brightest minds in Europe, many of whom were German Jews, now at risk for their lives. Initially only two from each of several different disciplines were invited to teach there. Wertheimer was one of the two psychologists invited to put together a masters degree and doctoral program in psychology for the new university. Later the school would enlarge its teaching roster to include a greater diversity of nationalities and thinking.

At the outset of the 10 years Wertheimer would spend at the University in Exile, he was very much hindered by the strangeness of everything American and the New School. He learned English as thousands of other immigrants before him had done—through exposure to it. It is said that despite his brilliance in so many areas, he never did get English exactly right. Yet Wertheimer quickly developed a love for America, his new home. Always a man of many interests, he became passionately interested in American politics. He made many new friends as well as maintaining several of the friendships that had begun in Germany. This was possible because so many of his former colleagues were now also his fellow refugees. His old friend from pre-World War I days, Erich von Hornbostel, was one of these. Von Hornbostel had also come to the University in Exile in 1933 as a musicologist. Nominally a Christian, von Hornbostel's "sin," making emigration the only safe course, had been that his mother was Jewish. Sadly, von Hornbostel only spent two years in America before he died.

One of the immediate differences Wertheimer and the other refugee academics encountered at the New School was the transition of psychological and philosophical studies from the humanities to the realm of social science. This particular change seems to have been one to which Wertheimer easily adapted. He increasingly studied, taught, and wrote about how Gestalt theory applied to other social issues. His eloquent essays about ethics and the meaning of freedom are evidence of this shift. It is said that Wertheimer continued to do small psychological experiments informally, but he published none of this work.

The American students Wertheimer eventually taught were also mostly of a far different category than those that he had taught in Germany. They were most often practicing psychologists who were furthering their education or just interested in hearing Wertheimer's lectures because of his fame as the founder of Gestalt psychology. In the same way that Wertheimer had won over his students in Germany, he soon began to make his classes at the University in Exile among the most popular classes held there. The golden age of psychology had passed back in Germany thanks to the Nazis, but Wertheimer's impact remained. Despite Nazi efforts to write him out of psychology literature in Europe, his influence was still strongly felt among students on both sides of the Atlantic. Friends have said that Wertheimer never was very concerned with dignity and pomp. He was simply a natural-born teacher who always seemed to be more excited about learning than most of his students.

Some have suggested that the 53-year-old Wertheimer had become weary by the time he reached the United States. His friend Horace Kallen describes him as "frequently exhausted." However, his child-like spirit was still capable of giving him the enthusiasm for which he was famous. Another friend, Edwin B. Newman, states that "the dreariest experiment would become cosmic in its scope as he would brush aside details and keep pushing you on, insisting that you get to the heart of the matter." Wertheimer made research studies into games, debates into a test of his students' resourcefulness. One of his students, quoted by Horace Kallen in *Social Research*, described him thus:

> The impact of his personality was so strong that the whole atmosphere seemed to change. . . . Most of us experienced a refreshing and stimulating adventure in which Wertheimer himself took an active part. Shouting and gesticulating, walking between the benches, he was indifferent to all demands of dignity; his carefree and completely natural manner made us forget his age and his fame. His words had the power to bring to life even figures and geometrical drawings.

Another of his students noted that Wertheimer was "an extremist . . . either passionately for or passionately against (whatever issue he became interested in)."

During his 10 years at the New School, Wertheimer functioned as both professor of psychology and philosopher. He led a joint seminar on social sciences each week as well as being involved in what was called a "General Seminar." This group met and discussed problems in all the areas covered by the University in Exile, and attempted to find Gestalt theory solutions to these difficulties. When Japan bombed Pearl Harbor on December 7, 1941, and the United States declared war on the Axis powers, 61-year-old Wertheimer immediately contacted the War Department and volunteered his services. It is said that he and his students at the University in Exile did psychological research for the armed forces during the early part of World War II, but the exact nature of that work is unknown.

Max Wertheimer and Albert Einstein

Another of the brilliant minds that Wertheimer remained in contact with in the United States was physicist Albert Einstein. Arthur I. Miller states in *Albert Einstein and Max Wertheimer: A Gestalt Genesis of Special Relativity Theory, History of Science* that Einstein, throughout his life, stayed in contact with many of the intellectual luminaries of his time. There are archival records of his correspondence with Sigmund Freud. Contained in these letters is the disagreement he expressed to Freud as to whether psychoanalysis was truly science. Einstein's relationship with Wertheimer was different. They first met in Berlin in 1916, and liked each other immediately. They shared similar interests, including physics and a passion for sailing.

Their proximity after coming to the United States—Einstein was at Princeton University and Wertheimer at the University in New York—made it feasible for the two men to continue their friendship. Much of Wertheimer's work was based on Einstein's forte, physics. Wertheimer would later try to reconstruct the conversations he had had with Einstein over 20 years earlier in Berlin. These discussions on how the mind must abandon old, unproductive ways of looking at things and develop new ways in order to make discoveries would become part of Wertheimer's book *Productive Thinking*. He showed how Gestalt ideas applied to Einstein's vision that produced the theory of relativity.

The last years

Over the years, Wertheimer had in many ways acted like a butterfly, flitting from project to project, leaving little that was tangible. He had never written a cogent, complete statement on Gestalt theory, nor shown any interest in doing so. Yet all of his work had consistently remained within the parameters of the Gestalt theory that he had published in 1912. He had published as many articles on ethics, music, and other non-psychological subjects as he had on Gestalt psychology over the years since. With typical abandon regarding the details, much of his work on mental illness and brain damage had been published under others' names either because they had helped with the research or because the data had been transcribed by others since Wertheimer did not take the time to write it down. Prime examples of this are "A Gestalt Theory of Paranoia," "A Case of Mania with its Social Implications," and "Some Aspects of the Schizophrenic Formal Disturbance of Thought," all of which have listed as their author Erwin Levy. In fact Wertheimer wrote all three of these articles, if not completely, then for the most part.

Wertheimer also contributed lectures such as "Understanding Psychotic's Speech" that were later published by A.S. Luchins, one of his biographers; and *Max Wertheimer's Research on Aphasia and Brain Disorders: A Brief Account*, published posthumously by his son Michael, also a psychologist, and Viktor Sarris. There remained, however, one more important contribution that Wertheimer wished to make to the province of psychology. During the same period of time that he was assisting the War Department, in 1942, he also began working on the only book he ever published, *Productive Thinking*. *Productive Thinking* was initially envisioned as the first in a series of three books explaining how Gestalt psychology helped people come up with innovative solutions to old problems.

Horace Kallen describes Wertheimer as "sweating and suffering" over this book. He was a perfectionist, and always felt that language was an imperfect "vehicle" in which to express the truth. However for the most part, the man that hated details managed to put the relevant ones into this work. Sadly, he did not live to create the two books that he had hoped would follow. He had barely completed *Productive Thinking* when he suffered a heart attack. Wertheimer never saw his book in print. He died at his home in New Rochelle, New York, on Columbus Day, October 12, 1943. As R. I. Watson noted in *The Great Psychologists*, "His spontaneity and brilliance made for his productive contributions to psychology. Paradoxically, he was compulsively careful about gathering and analyzing data. Only when the data was crystal clear and unequivocal would he publish his results." This compulsiveness made his co-workers and the students who actually heard him lecture the only people who were fortunate enough to truly appreciate the brilliance of his mind.

THEORIES

Wilhelm Wundt's theory of structuralism
Explanation   It is difficult to discuss Wertheimer's research and theories without explaining what he and other psychologists of his time were trying to disprove. Wilhelm Wundt was the first person that history records as having been called a psychologist. Born in 1832, psychology prior to his time was considered one small division of the larger and more illustrious field of philosophy. Wundt, a trained medical doctor, was well aware that he was creating a new field—the science of psychology—when he wrote the first edition of his *Principles of Physiological Psychology* in 1874. In its preface he notes that the book was written to "mark out a new domain of science." It was his strong belief that since psychology was science, there was no room within it for metaphysical hypothesis. Though he believed that there were indeed psychic processes that went on within the mind, he was equally convinced that the physiologic (brain) processes were separate, parallel activities. At the University of Leipzig where he taught, Wundt established the first psychological laboratory in 1875. (It is worth noting that 1879 is usually cited as the year that Wundt began his laboratory. However, that is actually the year the University of Leipzig formally acknowledged his psychological lab. It had then been in operation for four years. It is also worth noting that American psychologist William James had also equipped a small laboratory in that same year, 1875.)

Wundt perceived philosophy as being part of psychology, a view that was the total reverse of what most academics of his time believed. In 1881, a year after Wertheimer was born, Wundt began publishing *Philosophische Studien (Philosophical Studies)*, a journal devoted to the reporting of the psychological research being conducted at his new laboratory. This new lab and Wundt's approach brought students to Leipzig from all over Europe and even North America and extended his ideas all the way to the same locations. He adamantly denied that psychology should be involved in anything other than physiological and psychological research. Students who deviated from that belief, according to R. I. Watson in *The Great Psychologists*, were viewed by Wundt as if "this were desertion in the face of the enemy." Wundt's "school" of psychology was profoundly physical (often called "structural" or "elemental"). Painstaking research was carried on, examining feeling through measuring pulse, breathing, and muscular strength. But if Wundt studied the minutest details of sensation, perception, reaction, attention, and feeling; he equally ignored learning, motivation, emotion, intelligence, thought, and personality.

Though his writings were described by American psychologist G. Stanley Hall as "lusterless as lead, but just as solid," Wundt became widely read and acknowledged as the premier psychologist of his time. The work of Wundt and his students quickly became the most popularly accepted set of working premises employed by European university psychology departments, the only place psychology was an accepted part of the curriculum in the late nineteenth century. Wilhelm Wundt was a man of very strong opinions. He was eminently capable of expressing scorn for theories with which he disagreed. Child and educational psychology were particular targets for Wundt's derision, as were Oswald Kulpe and the other educators at the Würzburg University, where Wertheimer had studied.

Wundt's school of structuralism or elementalism held that each individual stimulus is experienced by the human mind separately from all other stimuli. It then produces within the brain a sensation that is remembered. When a stimulus is experienced again, the mind's perception of the event is based on that previous experience. Such perceptions are integrated within the brain following the experience of the stimulus. This would mean that the person's mind literally experiences what it sees, hears, smells, or touches, and nothing more. Wundt identified three facets of consciousness—sensations, images, and feelings. Even in those early days of Wundt's studies, there were many researchers and thinkers who saw flaws in this simplistic view of things. Wertheimer was one of them.

Example Wundt was already aware of the apparent movement that Wertheimer studied in 1910 and 1911, as were many other psychologists. Because Wundt believed that each stimulus created its own separate sensation, he postulated that apparent movement occurred when the movement of the eyes created a floating sensation illusion. Wertheimer invalidated this belief by having his research subjects look at lines set up so that two simultaneous motions occurred in opposite directions at the same time. Apparent movement, or "the phi phenomenon," was still observed. Since it was impossible for the eyes to move in two different directions at the same time, Wertheimer's experiment disproved Wundt's explanation.

Wertheimer's theory of perceptual grouping

As Wertheimer disciple Wolfgang Köhler explained in 1947, Gestalt, in the German language, can mean either the shape or form of an entity or the entity itself. Wertheimer had tried, many years earlier in 1924, to explain his theory by saying,

> The basic thesis of Gestalt theory might be formulated thus: there are contexts in which what is happening in the whole cannot be deduced from the characteristics of the separate pieces, but conversely, what happens to a part of the whole is, in clear-cut cases, determined by the laws of the inner structure of its whole.

Explanation Wertheimer's initial theories related to perception, or how people perceive the world around them and their relationship to that world. Gestalt theory relies upon a basic tenet that Wertheimer had proven with his early perceptual research in Frankfurt

in 1910 and 1911: that the human mind is not only capable of, but consistently, perceives things in other ways than was commonly believed at that time. These perceptions were nowhere near as simple, or "elemental," as Wundt and others had described. Nor are they mirror images of what the brain sees, hears, feels, or senses. What Wertheimer actually proved with his stroboscope and tachistoscope experiments was that the human mind consistently creates for itself the perception of motion from a rapid succession of non-moving and separate sensory stimuli. Human beings can see motion where there actually is none simply because, to the mind, it "makes better sense" that way.

Example As noted earlier, an example of Wertheimer's early research would be a set of Christmas tree lights strung around a tree that alternately light up and go dark, creating the illusion that the lights, though stationary, are in motion, and traveling around the tree. Wertheimer termed this mind-trick the phi phenomenon. This ability of the mind to create an illusion of movement is also the primary basis that made the invention of motion pictures possible.

This phenomenon could be dismissed as a simple illusion or hallucination. However, the phi phenomenon is so consistent to human beings' perception that it could not possibly be caused by brain pathology, as hallucinations are. This phenomenon could be categorized as an illusion. Putting a label on it does not answer the fundamental questions that Wertheimer was asking, however. An illusion is often thought of as an inaccurate assessment of a perception by the mind. For Wertheimer and other Gestaltists, seeing this illusion indicates that the mind is "doing its job"—interpreting perceptual input and trying to make rational sense out of it, rather than simply acting like a camera and passively recording what it has seen.

However, Wertheimer's hypothesis went far beyond observing illusions or helping to create movies. He demonstrated that human beings are innately able to experience both the entire event (the string of lights illuminating at set intervals) and the relationship to the whole of each of its individual components (each separate bulb as it lights up). Gestalt theory goes beyond stating that human beings have the ability to do this; it states that the mind has a compelling tendency toward this recognition, thus making the mind's capability a far more complex thing than the functions attributed to it by Wundt. In 1912 Wertheimer published his findings under the title "Experimental Studies of the Perception of Movement." This research into what has often been called "apparent movement" led to literally hundreds of research papers that further validated Wertheimer's work.

Principles of Gestalt psychology

Explanation Wertheimer did not immediately comprehend all the implications of his initial study. After the publication of his 1912 paper, Wertheimer became actively involved in the German war effort during World War 1. This meant that much of the time from 1914 to 1920 was devoted to research and development on subjects other than Gestalt theory. It was not until 1923 that Wertheimer published a tract further enlarging upon his ideas about perception and perceptual grouping. In reality, what he attempted to do was to look at what the human mind actually does as opposed to what it might be doing.

Wertheimer tried to illustrate his belief that people perceive all things in the world around them in the same manner that they see apparent motion as demonstrated in the phi phenomenon. They perceive things not as a group of separate sensations, but as one unified whole. He attempted to demonstrate this through the use of some elemental illustrations—clusters of dots, dashes, lines, figures, or musical notes—things that functioned as visual or auditory stimuli. He used them to show how the mind organizes perceptual information, whatever sense provides that perception. This ability to organize perceived information discounts the notion that the human mind reacts only to individual stimuli.

Pregnanz Pregnancy (*Pregnanz* in German), referring not to the word's literal definition but rather to being "pregnant with meaning," is the primary tenet of Wertheimer's Gestalt principles. He believed that this basic standard upheld all the rest. Gestalt theory espouses a fundamental belief that the human mind is innately meant to experience things in wholeness, to compose as complete a perception as possible. This can mean sensing things in an orderly, simple, consistent, and/or symmetrical manner as is feasible. From this primary principle of *Pregnanz*, all of the other principles emerge.

Example *Pregnanz* is exemplified by a line of bold-face print showing the capital letters "A B C." Each letter, not completely closed, is displayed above bold-face numbers "12 13 14." The demonstration reveals that the broken-line "B" is identical to the "13." However, the common perception is to see it as a "B" when it is placed with "A" and "C," and as a "13" when grouped with the "12" and "14."

Proximity Proximity is the premise that portions of an entire item which are physically close to each other will be seen as belonging together.

Example When "tap-tap, pause, tap-tap, pause, tap-tap" is heard, the listener will normally relate the two taps as belonging together rather than last tap of each section belonging with the first tap after the pause.

Symmetry Symmetry is the tendency to disregard proximity in favor of what the human mind observes to be a symmetrical relationship.

Example [ ] [ ] [ ]

In spite of the possibility that these should be grouped by closeness, or proximity, the mind quickly sees that the brackets are symmetrical and that the principle of symmetry overrules proximity.

Similarity Similarity is the concept that portions of the entire item that appear to be alike will be grouped together by the mind.

Example If dots of a certain shape or color are included in a larger pattern of dots, they will be distinguished as a separate portion of the larger pattern.

Closure Closure is the inclination of the mind to complete the stimulus, whether it is a visual illustration or something we hear. (Wertheimer also noted that there is anxiety until the stimulus is "closed.")

Examples If a person is given a picture to look at which has missing lines here or there, as some cartoons or caricatures are intentionally drawn, there is an inclination for the viewer to not consciously "see" the picture as incomplete. Instead the viewer will unconsciously fill in the missing features.

Wertheimer himself gave a more humorous example of closure that shows the anxiety preceding completion. It was one he often proved in restaurants after he and his guests had finished dining. It was found that the waiter without fail knew the exact amount of the dinner check if asked the amount prior to being paid. Yet if he was called back to the table a few moments after being paid and again asked the amount, the waiter would invariably be unable to remember how much had been owed.

Continuity Continuity is the tendency to see things as continuous, rather than stopping at certain points and then again going forward.

Example The simplest example of this principle is two intersecting lines that are viewed as intersecting with, and crossing, each other rather than perceiving this as two angular merging points.

Figure-ground   This principle was borrowed from the Danish phenomenologist Rubin, and is a classic in the psychology of perception. It involves being able to see two separate visions within the same picture. However, the human mind apparently is not geared to perceive both of them simultaneously. Perception, it was discovered, is selective. The perception portions of the brain tend to make one "picture" the foreground and the other the background.

Examples   The classic illustration of figure-ground is Rubin's "Vase." It is either a black Grecian urn, or two faces in profile looking at each other.

Another common example of this principle is the tendency of most people to focus upon the recognized face against a number of unknown people in a group picture, making that face the foreground and the unrecognized faces the background.

Many more of these Gestalt principles would be developed by Wertheimer's followers. They would involve not only perception, but also memory and learning. By 1933 it was estimated that there were 114 separate "laws" or principles.

Gestalt insight learning

The "insights" Wertheimer and the Gestaltists speak of are different from the almost miraculous, intuitional revelations of Freud and others in the field of mental health. Gestalt "insight" is rather a mode of problem-solving using a "Gestalt" or organizing principle. This idea presupposes what Wertheimer and his followers believed: that there is an order to the world around us. When we make that orderliness visible, "dis-cover" it, we are then able to use it to solve our problems. This has obvious repercussions involving multiple (if not all) fields of human endeavor, and most definitely includes both education and learning and mental health.

Example   Probably the most cited example of insight learning is found in the research that Wertheimer's associate Wolfgang Köhler did while stationed at Tenerife in the Canary Islands between 1913 and 1917. He worked with chimpanzees and used bananas as rewards. Köhler hid a stick in the ceiling of their cage while all the chimps were watching. The next day a bunch of bananas was placed outside the cage, out of their reach. One of the chimps immediately began looking for something with which to reach the bananas, and not finding it, climbed up to the ceiling, removed the hidden stick, and used it to get hold of

the bananas. Some chimpanzees carried out this procedure better than others, and their ability to succeed in obtaining the bananas was used as a measure of their intelligence. Köhler saw this as proving that the chimpanzees possessed the capacity for insight learning. They showed both continuity in being goal-directed, and closure by being able to solve the problem. (It is an interesting aside to this animal research that Koffka, Köhler, and other Gestaltists felt that the reason animals learned to negotiate mazes and other "tricks," developed as part of common psychological investigations of the time, was that the animals were not offered the chance to develop their own problem-solving techniques in these studies.)

Isomorphism   Based on his 1910 and 1911 research, Wertheimer had hypothesized that the actions of the brain that resulted in the phi phenomenon, or apparent movement, were identical to the mental processes that occur when real movement is perceived by the brain. This was based on painstaking studies that had repeatedly shown that the reaction of the mind to either real or apparent movement appears to be identical. From this, Wertheimer and his disciples inferred a further deduction: that there is a neurological correlation, a physiological patterning of the brain based on the psychological experience of the event. Put simply, Wertheimer and Gestaltists guessed that there was a correlation between the actual mental experience and the physical brain processes used to process it. Wertheimer guessed that there was a neurological "shortcut" utilized by the brain each time that motion is perceived, and that a tangible (physical) proof of his theory would eventually be found.

This revolutionary notion was an early step toward the mind-body connection, or holistic approach to the mind and body. Mind-body Gestalt, or wholeness, has always been a part of Eastern medicine, but has increasingly gained credence in Western medicine and psychiatry in recent years. Wolfgang Köhler took the mind-body notion further. Like Wertheimer, he believed that there is direct interaction between the perceived event and the brain process that perceived it. But Köhler theorized that these two functions were structured identically, and the perceived event was "mapped," as psychologist George Boeree puts it, within the brain. The Gestalt notion of isomorphism has not yet been proven to be unequivocal truth. However, neither has the mind-body connection of isomorphism been disproved.

Examples   Whether a person sees a comet actually race across the sky or a stationary neon light go on and off depicting motion, the person sees both events in

BIOGRAPHY:
Wolfgang Köhler

Though born in the Baltic state of Estonia, Wolfgang Köhler (1887–1967) was German. When he was six years old his family moved back to Germany, to a town named Wolfenbüttell. As a young man he attended the Universities of Tübingen, Bonn, and Berlin, and studied under both Carl Stumpf and physicist Max Planck. Having earned his Ph.D in 1909 for a paper on acoustics, Köhler moved to Frankfurt to join the Psychological Institute there. The next year, his fateful meeting with Max Wertheimer not only opened new doors, it changed his life. After becoming involved in Wertheimer's apparent motion studies, Köhler became convinced of the veracity of Wertheimer's Gestalt theory. He would spend the rest of his life deciphering and elaborating on that complex hypothesis.

In 1913, a new opportunity appeared for Köhler when he was offered the directorship of Anthropoid Station, a research center located on Tenerife, in the Canary Islands. He spent most of World War I there, doing research and beginning his first book, *The Mentality of Apes.*

Köhler returned to Germany in 1920, a time of great post-war chaos and political unrest. He was appointed Director of the Psychological Institute at the University of Berlin in 1922. Throughout the 1920s and '30s, Köhler became well known in psychological circles on both sides of the Atlantic. Together with Wertheimer and Koffka, in Germany he founded a psychological journal devoted to Gestalt psychology, *Psychologische Forschung.* He made several trips to the United States, and was a visiting professor at both Clark University in Worcester, Massachusetts, and the University of Chicago. He was also a William James

Lecturer at Harvard University. Additionally, in 1929 Köhler wrote the book that Wertheimer never did write: *Gestalt Psychology.* Though he certainly could have stayed in the United States, he opted to return to Germany about the time the Nazis took control of the German government in 1933.

This period of Hitler's rise to power became a time of great trial for Köhler. Seeing the beginnings of the persecution of Jews (and in fact all intellectuals) in Germany, Köhler courageously spoke out against this murderous and dangerously intolerant regime. Yet he managed to stay in Germany until 1935, when he published a letter denouncing Nazi policies in a Berlin newspaper. This resulted in Gestapo interference with his position as Director at the Berlin institute, and he shortly afterward immigrated to the United States. In 1938, he published *The Place of Value in a World of Facts*, a collection of his Harvard lectures that attempted to assess the value of things based upon

Wolfgang Köhler. (Archives *of the History of American Psychology.* Reproduced by permission.)

Gestalt theory. For the next 20 years, Köhler served as a professor of psychology at Swarthmore College. In 1956 he was elected President of the American Psychological Association. He then spent a brief time at Princeton University and finished out his career at Dartmouth College in New Hampshire. Köhler died at Enfield, New Hampshire, on June 11, 1967, at the age of 80.

the same way, using the identical brain processes, even though the comet actually moves, but the neon light does not.

HISTORICAL CONTEXT

The study of the mind is hardly a new endeavor. Eastern intellectuals, including Muslim (Sufi) thinkers

such as Afghanistan's Jalaludal Rumi and El Ghazali from Persia, and the writings of philosophers, physicians, and priests in Ancient Egypt and Greece, all refer to the study of what we would term psychology. But it was the thinkers of the nineteenth century, in Europe and specifically in Germany and Austria, who made strides to establish the field of psychology as we know it today. One of the earliest of these nineteenth-century intellectuals was the "father of modern psychology," Wilhelm Wundt, discussed above. Born in 1832, in a small village near Heidelberg, Germany, he studied medicine at Heidelberg, Tübingen, and Berlin. His major interest and earliest book concerned physiology, specifically the action of the muscles of the body and how they responded to specific stimulus.

Prior to and even during the early years of Wundt's professional career, philosophy was considered the preeminent discipline involved in the study of the mind, with psychology operating as a small facet of the larger field. The philosopher Goethe had examined the perception of color and other areas that we would consider psychological studies. As early as the late 1700s, philosopher Immanuel Kant had talked about "the unity of a perceptual act," meaning that though we view things as developing from bits and pieces, actually a formation by the mind has occurred, creating a "unitary experience." This idea is much more in line with the beliefs of the Gestaltists, and diametrically opposed to what Wundt would eventually propose. Despite this, it was Wilhelm Wundt who changed the relationship between psychology and philosophy. In 1867, he began giving a course at Heidelberg University entitled "physiological psychology," and established the first known psychological laboratory at the University of Leipzig in 1875. Wundt's work at Leipzig was notable for its insistence upon scientific research as opposed to the creation of abstract, unprovable theories. He praised the use of physical measuring equipment for these studies and greatly disdained anyone who tried to alter what he envisioned as pure, scientific psychology. His obsession with measurement would eventually be the basis for one important step in psychology: the development of the Binet Intelligence Scale.

If Wundt's groundbreaking work at Leipzig could be said to be one pole of the study of the mind, Sigmund Freud, operating in Vienna during those same years, might be described as the other pole. As Wundt demanded facts and physical proofs for his "introspective" manner of research, Freud postulated theories of psychoanalysis based upon little more than his own remembered (and therefore suspect) childhood experiences. Franz Clemens Brentano operated somewhere in between these two poles. Brentano was the grandson of an Italian merchant, an intellectual and former Catholic priest. He was born in 1838, and his ideas inspired most of the people who eventually influenced Wertheimer. Brentano publicly questioned the principle of papal infallibility and had wanted to marry. These actions made him the target of Rome's displeasure and eventually caused him to leave the Catholic Church. A highly charismatic teacher, he also very publicly disagreed with Wundt's ideas, considering

them to be rigid and artificial. Brentano promoted what he called "act psychology," encouraging the study of "acts" such as judging, recalling, expecting, inferring, doubting, hoping, and loving. Like Wundt, he called his approach to psychology "introspective," but his vision of this was in many ways closer to the later ideas of Wertheimer and the Gestaltists. He insisted on describing consciousness in the first person, and is considered by many to be the guiding force that led to both phenomenology and analytic philosophy.

Ernst Mach, who gave us the term "Mach 1 . . . Mach 2," looked at several areas of physics, including spatial patterns (such as geometric shapes) and temporal patterns (music). He theorized that these things retained their basic qualities even if the sensation changed. That is, our minds perceive a square as remaining a square whether it is lying flat on a piece of paper on a table or floating in the air in three dimensions; a melody is still recognized as the same piece of music whether hummed simply or played as part of a complex orchestral opus. (Mach used the German word "Gestalt," in its meaning of "shape" in his work, making him one of the early thinkers utilizing this concept.) One of Brentano's students at the University of Vienna was an eccentric but remarkable scholar, philosopher, musician, and composer named Christian von Ehrenfels. In addition to performing on the stage and promoting the legalization of polygamy, von Ehrenfels would take Mach's work further. In the 1890s he wrote a paper entitled "Gestalt Qualitaten," considered the beginning of the modern Gestalt movement. One of the attendees at von Ehrenfels's lectures at the University of Prague was a young law student named Max Wertheimer.

Another of Franz Brentano's students was a German youth from Bavaria named Carl Stumpf. Stumpf came from a musical background, but, like Mach and von Ehrenfels before him, he was also interested in space perception. This led him to research on the perception of both music and space. His belief was that the basic material of psychology is phenomena such as tones, colors, and images. He created a name for the study of these—"phenomenology"—and believed that psychology should be studied as "an unbiased experience," just as it occurs. Phenomenology has been described as "the discipline that helps people to stand aside from their usual way of thinking so that they can tell the difference between what is actually being perceived and felt in the current situation and what is residue from the past." His musical leanings led to studies of several auditory activities, including attention, analysis, and comparison of sounds. Equally, he was interested in speech development in children and the origins of childhood fears.

Most importantly, Stumpf was the first person since the ancient Greek philosophers who insisted that the whole of anything is different from its parts, the concept on which Gestalt psychology is based. Stumpf's beliefs earned him the ire of Wundt, and a bitter enmity existed between the two scholars for many years. Stumpf maintained that true experience could not be broken down into separate elements, but must be perceived in its entirety. If this does not happen, the perception loses its genuineness and becomes false and an abstraction. Clearly Stumpf's notion is the heart of Gestalt psychology, and this hypothesis was vehemently disputed by Wundt. G.E. Muller, who taught at the University of Berlin and together with Hermann Ebbinghaus and Friedrich Schumann developed the memory drum, had a primary interest in the study of memory. He wrote and lectured about what would eventually be called "proactive interference," old methods of learning that interfere with new ways of acquiring knowledge, a concept Wertheimer would use in his "Einstein Conversations" portion of *Productive Thinking*.

One of Muller's students was Oswald Kulpe, who went on to found the Würzburg School. Like Wundt, Kulpe was interested in the development of a scientific model of psychology. The difference between the two was that Kulpe wanted to study many of the things Brentano had spoken of—thinking, judging, remembering, and doubting—while Wundt saw these things as beyond the scope of psychology. Kulpe came up with the concept of "imageless thought," another idea that was anathema to Wilhelm Wundt. Wertheimer was one of Kulpe's students at Würzburg. It was Kulpe who supervised Wertheimer's dissertation on the use of word association techniques in identifying guilt or innocence in defendants in criminal proceedings.

Edmund Husserl became known as the "father of phenomenology" due to his extensive work on the perception of phenomena. Like Brentano, he was interested in the pure, subjective experience of things as they occur. Unlike Brentano, who believed that his "acts" only concerned things outside of the person, Husserl thought that the internal experience of phenomena was equally important. His phenomena were whole, unbroken, meaningful experiences instead of the fragments described by Wundt. Edgar Rubin was another phenomenologist from Denmark whose primary interest was in "ambiguous figures." It is to Rubin that the credit goes for the figure-ground concept borrowed by the Gestaltists.

Despite all the conflict between Wundt, the nominal founder of psychology, and other German psychologists, this time remained the "Golden Era" of German psychology, recognized around the world as on the cutting edge of all new psychological research and ideas. The ideas would be exported across the Atlantic to the United States and Canada through students who studied in Germany, then considered the perfect place for rounding out a good education. G. Stanley Hall, who had studied with Wundt, had been sufficiently impressed with the German model of a psychology laboratory to establish the first American one at Johns Hopkins Hospital in 1880. Hall would go on to Clark University in Worcester, Massachusetts, where he first introduced the German concept of graduate education. Later Hall would host Sigmund Freud and Carl Jung in Freud's only visit to the United States in 1909, when Freud and Jung lectured at Clark University. This visit would essentially introduce Americans to Freudian theory. The first psychological studies of learning, with rats negotiating mazes, occurred at Clark University under Hall's auspices. These studies clearly were more in line with Wundt's ideas than the Gestaltists. Yet Gestalt psychology, too, had made its way into the United States. Both Köhler and Koffka had made several trips to the United States throughout the 1920s and 1930s, lecturing at American universities and writing for American professional journals.

Adolph Hitler and the National Socialist Party (NAZI) that came to power in Germany in 1933 put an end to that German "golden age." Many of the original thinkers who had made Gestalt psychology possible did not survive to see that bitter day. Mach, Kulpe, and Brentano had all passed on by 1920, and von Ehrenfels, Stumpf, and Husserl did not see the beginning of World War II. Neither Kurt Koffka nor Wertheimer would live to see the Nazis defeated. Yet it is both remarkable and fortunate that so many of the great intellects of that time managed to survive those horrible years and to bring their most valuable possession, their brilliant ideas, across the Atlantic to America. Max Wertheimer, Wolfgang Köhler, Kurt Koffka, Erich Fromm, Albert Einstein, Karen Horney, and Erich von Hornbostel are only a few of the long list of these luminaries.

CRITICAL RESPONSE

Gestalt psychology in Europe
There was a remarkable volume of criticism between the Wundt's (elementalist or structuralist)

school of psychology and nearly every other psychologist of any note in Central Europe. But as noted, the era of structuralism had effectively come to an end with the widespread acceptance of Gestalt theories in Germany and across the rest of Europe in the 1920s. Despite Nazi Germany's devaluation of Gestalt psychology (and in fact all psychology) in the 1930s, the influence of Gestalt psychology remained across Europe even if it seemed watered down and rife with divergent groups with differing beliefs. Gestalt psychology could still be said to have successfully supplanted Wundt's assumptions for Europe, and indeed most of the world.

Early years of Gestalt psychology in the United States

The United States was the exception to that rule of Gestalt primacy. Though American psychologist William James had strongly disagreed with and debated structuralist ideas in Wundt's heyday, there were many American psychologists who very much supported his theories. Chief among these was probably E. B. Titchener. An English immigrant to the United States, Titchener had studied under Wundt at Leipzig and later returned to the United States to write *Titchener's Textbook of Psychology*, published in 1909. It is to Titchener that the credit can be given for developing the American version of Wundt's structuralism. (It is worth noting that in the United States, structuralism was the name usually used for this psychology, rather than elementalism.) A simple explanation of the difference between this theory and the "functionalist psychology" then prevalent in American universities was made by James Angell, an early American Psychological Association president in the early 1900s. Angell explained that "Structuralists ask, What is consciousness? (made of) while functionalists ask, What is consciousness for?" Neither Wundt nor his detractors in Europe had ever made the long-standing debate this easy to understand.

Whether Gestalt ideas would have thrived, declined, or "died a natural death," as so many theories of mental health have, across the rest of the world prior to World War II is unknown. (Gestalt ideas certainly have neither declined nor died a natural death as of today. It is still a popular and widely accepted concept in most areas of the world.) The rise of Adolph Hitler and the Nazis forced those responsible for Gestalt theory to escape to the United States in order to survive. This immigration essentially brought Wertheimer, Köhler, and Koffka's ideas to the forefront of American psychology. At first the difficulty of translating Gestalt's complicated context to English

slowed its acceptance in America, as did the suspicion that Gestalt was more philosophy than psychology. Yet another common criticism that found its way to Gestalt psychology's door was recurrent reports that further attempts at replicating Köhler's World War I research with primates in the Canary Islands had not shown the same results.

As in Europe, the psychological community in the United States had recently discarded Wundt's simplistic, coldly detached view of the mind. In America, other schools of thought quickly came into being and filled the vacuum created by the discrediting of structuralism. Thanks to both the positive message of their ideas and the prolific amount of writing publicizing their theories, the humanist school of psychological thought gained credence across the United States. Developed from the work of Abraham Maslow, Carl Rogers, and Wertheimer's fellow German émigré Karen Horney, humanist psychology's support rose as much from the American public as from the academic community. Classic Freudian theory, too, was well represented in the respected work of psychiatrists such as Karl Menninger, and an emerging behavioral school of psychology was beginning to gain credence. The most remarkable relationship among these various schools of psychology was the early and enduring kinship that came between the Gestaltists and the humanists. Because they shared positive beliefs regarding both the human condition and the human mind, Gestalt psychology soon found itself allied with the humanistic school of psychology. It would prove to be a mutually beneficial affiliation. Equally, in the growing behavioral movement in the United States, Gestaltists discovered the successors to Wundt's structuralism.

In the behaviorists, the carriers of Gestalt theory to the United States found an immediate and conveniently placed opponent. The behaviorist "S-R formula" (stimulus leading to response formula) seemed to Gestaltists appallingly similar to Wundt and Titchener's "brick and mortar," laboratory research response to all questions about human behavior. The entire concept of all activities of the mind being the result of reflexes and response to conditioning was pure heresy to Wertheimer and his disciples. "What is a stimulus?" Wertheimer is said to have asked when the S-R formula was explained to him, and "What is the relationship between the physical aspect of a stimulus and its perceptual aspect?" Despite this dispute, American psychology for the most part took a "take what you like and leave the rest" attitude regarding Gestalt psychology as well as behaviorism.

Other American criticisms of Gestalt theory

For Titchener and Wundt, perception had always been the result of the joining together sensations that had meaning derived from prior happenings. Wertheimer and the Gestaltists had always seen it differently. They were less interested in these supposed meanings, which they believed to be mostly false or unreliable. With seeming accuracy Gestalt psychology said that the human mind tends to organize sensory input in a manner that "makes sense" to that individual human mind, but is not necessarily an accurate depiction of the true physical qualities of that sensory input. The ambiguous figures and illusionary pictures discussed previously are examples of this. Another example is the classic differences noted between the descriptive statements about an event made by several different "witnesses" to that same event. By the 1930s, when Gestalt psychology truly became known in the United States, the study of psychology had moved far beyond these arguments about how things are perceived. Many American mental health professionals were bewildered by the ongoing attacks by Gestaltists on structuralism. Since Titchener's American brand of structuralism had long-since been eclipsed by humanist and behaviorist psychology, they saw these attacks as "beating a dead horse."

Harry Helson, an early follower of Wertheimer who came to the United States and modified many of his beliefs, was nonetheless highly supportive of Gestalt ideas. Yet even Helson had made note of a flaw that other American mental health professionals soon observed. Helson saw that Gestaltists had followed the advice of the philosopher Goethe regarding how to solve a problem: simply change the problem into a postulation. Wertheimer's followers, Helson noted, did not consider how the activities of the mind are organized as a issue to be studied and debated, but rather a "given," something obvious to them from their observation of the nature of the mind. Helson and Gestalt's American critics said the Gestalists solved the quandary regarding the organization of the mind by simply denying that there was a quandary. Also, it was unfortunate that when Gestalt psychology initially came to the United States in the 1920s and 1930s, many of those American psychologists who had heard Köhler and Koffka in their early lectures misunderstood the full scope of Gestalt psychology. They believed it to be nothing more than a new theory that addressed perception only. This was a misunderstanding that has persisted, according to R. I. Watson in *The Great Psychologists,* up until the present.

It is probable that Gestalt theory would have remained far more of an abstract notion with little application in everyday psychology had it been left to Max Wertheimer. Wertheimer possessed a restless, brilliant mind that was poorly suited to the day-to-day, more mundane task of making his ideas work in everyday life. In this way, he was far different from two of his contemporaries, Karen Horney and Carl Rogers. Both Horney and Rogers, throughout their careers, consistently saw patients and wrote books describing the application of their personality and therapy ideas. Wertheimer, on the other hand, threw out a brilliant theory to those around him, and then stood back and waited to see what they would do. Clearly the first two "catchers" of Wertheimer's ideas were his two laboratory assistants in Frankfurt in 1912, Wolfgang Köhler and Kurt Koffka.

Köhler's mind-body approach and Gestalt psychology

In 1913, Wolfgang Köhler left Frankfurt, Germany for primate research in Tenerife, in the Canary Islands. Many of the problem-solving studies that he did with chimpanzees there led directly to Gestalt therapy, the treatment of the mind using Gestalt principles. In 1917, he wrote of his experiences in his book, *The Mentality of Apes.* Increasingly, though, and especially after his return to Germany and appointment as director of the laboratory at the University of Berlin, Köhler concentrated on his belief that the physical body as well as the mind possesses Gestalt qualities. This belief, called isomorphism, would re-acquaint Western medicine with the mind-body connection that has always been accepted by many other societies. However, like his primate research, Köhler's isomorphism theory has not been well supported by research. Demonstrations of exactly how the physical brain works to interpret sensory stimuli were noticeably absent from Köhler's work. In reality, the scope of such research was probably far beyond the capabilities of Köhler's time.

Koffka and Growth of the Mind

Wertheimer's second laboratory assistant, Kurt Koffka, left Frankfurt soon after completing the original research and spent much of the next 16 years at the University of Giessen. Koffka also took several trips to the United States between 1911 and 1927, and was largely responsible for disseminating Gestaltist thought to America. His *Growth of the Mind,* originally published in German, was translated and printed in English in 1924. Using Gestalt theory as a background, the book was an introduction to child psychology with a special focus on childhood learning. Koffka agreed with William Stern's hypothesis that when learning takes place, there is a melding or "convergence" of outer conditions and inner (mental) capability. He was a strong opponent of rote learning, seeing it as the death of creativity. Equally, Koffka believed that neither a reward system nor trial-and-error were the reasons that humans learn, but rather that the mind has an innate desire to learn, to experience "good Gestalt." In these ways, Koffka applied Gestalt psychology to education, and the application of Gestalt ideas has spilled over into many educational concepts, including the Montessori method of education.

Research

Wertheimer's apparent movement study   Though the tachistoscope Wertheimer used at the Frankfurt Psychological Institute was more complex, the child's stroboscope he initially used in the hotel room demonstrates the same function. If one looks into a box that has two slits cut into it, and a source of light is placed so that it alternates shining behind each of the slits, the person looking into the box will perceive one moving light even though there are two lights and no movement. Whether the line between the two lights is vertical or horizontal, the effect is perceived the same way. The point of this, according to Wertheimer, is that we do not "put things together" to produce a certain stimulus. Apparent movement exists in our minds exactly as it is perceived.

Köhler's animal studies   The previously described experiments with chimpanzees on Tenerife in the Canary Islands were one of Köhler's research projects using animals. He also studied chickens. Grain was scattered on pieces of paper that were colored two different tones of gray. The hens were trained to take the grain from only one color of paper—the darker gray paper—by allowing them to eat freely from the dark gray paper and driving them away if they tried to eat the grain on the lighter gray paper. This process was repeated hundreds of times until the chickens "got it right" and only pecked at grain placed on the darker gray paper. Now a darker shade of gray paper was introduced into the experiment. The idea behind this research was that if the hens ate only from the same shade of gray paper (now the lighter shade), they would be responding to their training, to a specific color of paper. If they pecked at the darker tone of gray, it would indicate that they were making a judgment regarding the situation, using a concept that included a response as to which shade of gray was

darker. Köhler's chickens used the Gestalt method; they chose the darker shade.

Gestalt therapy   Easily the most impressive contribution to Gestalt psychology as a mode of treatment is the work of Fritz and Laura Perls and Gestalt therapy. "Fritz" Perls was born in 1893 in Berlin, and studied medicine and classic (Freudian) psychoanalysis. In 1926, Perls went to Frankfurt-am-Main to work with neurologist Kurt Goldstein at the Institute for Brain-Damaged Soldiers. There he met his future wife, Laura Posner, a psychologist quite influenced by the then-current Gestalt psychology. Perls, too, became interested in Wertheimer's theories. He was also interested in the humanist philosophies of Karen Horney, Wilhelm Reich, and others. Like other mental health professionals of the time, Perls chafed under the dogmatic tenets of Freudian psychiatry. Together with his wife, Perls began the development of a new type of therapy, which they called "Gestalt."

Like other schools of mental health treatment, Gestalt therapy developed its own personality theory, complete with its own vocabulary. Personality, Perls argued, is not put together by the addition of layer upon layer of conditioning, as behaviorists believe. Nor is it the result of the reaction to associative symbols as Freud believed. For Perls, the personality is seen as configured according to Gestalt principles. Gestalt therapy serves to help people reach awareness—not in amazing flashes of insight, but in small steps toward wholeness, or "Gestalt."

Some of the more common terms used in Gestalt therapy are listed below:

• Mental metabolism is the term Gestalt therapists use to describe the processes of the mind. The analogy is that human beings "bite off what they can chew"—whether it is food, ideas, or relationships. It is then "chewed" (assessed), and if it is nourishing (good for the person), it is kept. If it is toxic (bad for the person), it is spat out. Mental metabolism cannot occur unless the person trusts his or her own judgment, and his or her ability to sense stimuli outside of him or herself.

• Regulation of boundary relates to maintaining a permeable boundary between one's self and the external world. This boundary can be crossed when it is necessary or advisable, but remains in place to protect the person. (It is the basis of much of the discussion of "boundaries" so prevalent in mental health today.) Disturbances in this boundary—the inability to differentiate between self and others—is referred to as "confluence" (fusion). In "isolation," the boundary has become so impenetrable that it is impossible for the person to connect with others at all.

- Retroflection is dissention or splitting within the self, which can lead to mental health pathology or, at times, be the appropriate action. For example, if a person suppresses anger by "biting his tongue," it may be mentally unhealthy. However, if growing angry is going to make a problem worse, sometimes "biting one's tongue" is the better alternative to "biting the other person's head off."

- Introjection is the undiscriminating intake of external information without using any type of assessment or evaluation. An example might be how some people living in police states take in the propaganda that is fed to them, without evaluating it for truth, morality, or appropriateness.

- Projection is little different from the Freudian use of the word—the attributing to some external source of qualities that in reality belong to the person, i.e., "You made me do that." Typical of Gestalt and humanist psychology, "projection" is considered to be possibly good if used in relation to creating a work of art such as writing a novel, painting a picture, or acting in a drama.

- Deflection is the evasion of contact or perception. This can be done by not making eye contact, by talking about (rather than to) another person, or by not expressing or addressing a feeling. Like retroflection, deflection can be an appropriate response when it helps to avoid a severe argument.

- Organismic self-regulation is the process of learning and making choices holistically, and is markedly similar to Carl Rogers's "organismic trusting." Mind, body, thoughts, feelings, spontaneity, and deliberation are all integrated.

- Awareness is the only goal of Gestalt therapy. It is also one of the therapy's two primary tools. In the Gestalt lexicon, awareness is the ability to know and understand one's own existence. Awareness operates in a continuum that is forever in motion, with differing awarenesses coming to the forefront as their primacy becomes necessary.

- Dialogue is the other Gestalt tool. Gestalt therapists are free to "be themselves." They express how they are feeling as they help the patient reach awareness.

- Integration is the name given to the successful outcome of psychotherapy. It refers to the identification and acceptance of all of mind's functions—ideas, actions, and feelings.

The object of Gestalt therapy is not the modification of behavior. Its only goal is the above-mentioned awareness. There are no "shoulds" in this mode of treatment, and the most important thing to be achieved is the patient's autonomy and self-determination. (This achievement would be a "preference" rather than a "should.") The therapist's relationship to the patient is warm, honest, and supportive. It focuses on the present. In Gestalt therapy, it is considered appropriate to let the person know how she is perceived by others, or to mention how her awareness process is limited by the interactions between the patient and therapist. It is made clear to patients in Gestalt therapy that they are responsible for the choices they make. Though Gestalt therapy will work with any patient population, there are certain personality types who apparently can benefit more from Gestalt therapy than others. In the chapter on Gestalt therapy in *Current Psychotherapies*, Gary Yontef notes that Gestalt therapy is most effective for people "open to working on self-awareness and for those who want natural mastery over their awareness process." Yet it has been successfully used in situations as diverse as crisis intervention, with people in a ghetto poverty program, patients suffering from psychosomatic disorders, and with people who have difficulty dealing with authority. Gestalt therapists traditionally show very little interest in psychiatric diagnoses. Gestalt therapy can be done individually as psychotherapy or in group experiences or workshops. The average frequency of therapy sessions is once per week.

Case studies

The following case studies exemplify how Gestalt therapy works. They are citations from Gary Yontef's chapter on Gestalt therapy in *Current Psychotherapies*.

The patient is a 45-year-old married man named Tom. He is noted to be proud of his independence and self-sufficiency. This has caused his wife to feel unneeded and inferior. He is unaware of his own dependency needs and rage about having these unmet needs. He notes with pride to the therapist that when he was a kid he had to learn to rely upon himself because his mother was always so busy. The therapist replies, "I appreciate your strength, and when I think of you as such a self-reliant kid, I want to stroke you and give you some parenting." Tom looks tearful and replies that no one has ever been able to do that. The therapist observes that Tom looks sad, and the patient recounts more sad memories from his childhood. The end result of this therapy is Tom's awareness that he felt shame as a child toward his unavailable parents and in compensation, became

CHRONOLOGY

1880: Wertheimer born on April 15, 1880, in Prague.

1898: Begins studies at the University of Prague.

1902: Studies psychology at the University of Berlin.

1904: Receives his doctorate in philosophy at the University of Würzburg.

1910: Discovers the phi phenomenon on a train ride and published his groundbreaking paper "Experimental Studies of the Perception of Movement" two years later.

1923: Marries Anna Caro, one of his students.

1934: Arrives in New York and begins teaching at the "University in Exile" for the next 10 years.

1941: After Japan bombed Pearl Harbor, Wertheimer immediately volunteers himself to the War Department

1942: Begins work on his only book, *Productive Thinking*.

1943: Dies at his home after suffering a heart attack.

---

too-well able to take care of himself, to the exclusion of his wife and others.

This following case study was part of a film called "In the Now," a Gestalt therapy motion picture produced in 1969. A woman in her late thirties who lives in California and is called "Peg" was initially seen at a Gestalt workshop dealing with grief. At the workshop, she had been working on her grief and the rage she felt toward her late husband, who had committed suicide, leaving her with the care of their children. She had found it necessary to return to work after being a housewife for several years. In the film, as part of that workshop, she talks about a recurring dream that she has in which she is on a dirt road at Camp Pendleton, a nearby military base, watching several tanks roll by in a formation. She is holding a platter of cookies. She suddenly sees a pair of shiny black shoes within the line of tanks and discovers that the person in the shoes is her best friend's husband. She then wakes up, and finds that she is laughing, but states that the dream always becomes less funny once she awakens.

When she finishes recounting the dream, the therapist makes no response regarding the dream. Instead, Peg is immediately asked what she is doing now. She replies, "Trying to stop my teeth from chattering." The therapist asks her what her objection is. Peg speaks of not liking the feeling of anxiety and fear that she is experiencing at that moment. The discussion goes on to air Peg's feelings of low self-worth and fear of being ridiculed. The therapist asks several questions about what Peg is good at, and with prodding she is finally able to say that she is a good cook, housekeeper, and baker. The therapist notes that she would make someone "a good wife" and Peg replies, "I was a good wife." Ultimately she is able to talk about her belief that she doubts that she will ever "make anyone a good wife again." There is no analysis per se of her dream, simply a process of helping her to discover what it is that she is anxious about and getting her to talk about her imaginings of the ridicule that she fears. (An interesting aside regarding this case is that Peg, far from being ridiculous or worthy of her own low self-esteem, had shown the strength to start a crisis clinic in her home town. Despite her belief that she would not marry again, Peg also met a man at this Gestalt workshop whom she eventually married.)

The following conversation between a Gestalt therapist and patient gives some idea of what Gestalt "dialogue" can be like:

- Patient: "Right now I'm feeling tense."

- Therapist: "Who are you talking to?"

- Patient: "I was just thinking about this morning. I was feeling very hostile. I still think I am somewhat hostile."

- Therapist: "I am aware that you are avoiding looking at me."

- Patient: "Yes, because I feel that you are very arrogant."

- Therapist: "That's true."

- Patient: "And as if I might get into a struggle with you."

- Therapist: "You might."

- Patient: "So the avoidance of eye contact is sort of a put-off of the struggle. I don't know whether this can be resolved."

- Therapist: "Would you be willing to tell me what your objections are to my arrogance?"

- Patient: "Well, it's not very comforting. If I have a problem and I talk to you about it and you're arrogant, then that only makes me arrogant."

- Therapist: "You respond in kind is what you are saying. Your experience is that you respond that way."

- Patient: "Yes. Right on. Then at this university I feel that I must be arrogant and I must be defensive at all times. Because I am black, people react to me in different ways . . . different people. . . and I feel that I have to be on my toes most of the time."

BIBLIOGRAPHY

Sources

Boeree, C. George. *Gestalt Psychology.* 2000. http://www.ship.edu/~cgboeree/fromm.html.

Coleman, James. *Abnormal Psychology and Modern Life.* Chicago: Scott, Foresman and Co., 1956.

Does the Mind Always Represent the World Accurately and Unambiguously? 1998. http://www-rci.rutgers.edu.

Gestalt Psychology and Isomorphism. 2004. http://www.ipfw.edu/bordens/history/overhd4.htm.

Kallen, Horace. "Max Wertheimer: 1880–1943." *Social Research* 15 (1948):1–4.

Kaplan, Harold I., MD, and Benjamin J. Sadock, MD. *Synopsis of Psychiatry, Behavioral Sciences and Clinical Psychiatry.* Baltimore: William and Wilkins, 1991.

Newman, Edwin B. "Max Wertheimer:1880–1943." *American Journal of Psychology* 57 (July 1944): 3.

Watson, R. I., Sr. *The Great Psychologists,* 4th ed. New York: J.B. Lippincott Co., 1978.

Wertheimer, Max. "On Truth." *Social Research* 1 (1934): 135–46.

Wertheimer, Michael. "Max Wertheimer, Gestalt Prophet." *Gestalt Theory* 2 (1980).

Yontef, Gary, and James Simkin. *Current Psychotherapies, "Gestalt Therapy: An Introduction."* Itasca, IL: F.E. Peacock, Publishers, 1989.

Further readings

Henle, Mary. *"A Tribute to Max Wertheimer: Three Stories of Three Days,"* 1879 and All That: Essays in the Theory and History of Psychology. New York: Columbia University Press, 1986.

Wertheimer, Max. *Productive Thinking.* New York: Harper, 1945.

Wilhelm Max Wundt

BRIEF OVERVIEW

Wilhelm Max Wundt (1832–1920) opened an experimental laboratory that has been called the first of its kind in the history of psychology. By combining the methods of physiological examination with psychology theory, he created a whole new way to understand human behavior. Wundt has become known as the "founder of modern psychology," according to Thomas Hardy Leahey, author of the book *History of Psychology.* In 1987, Leahey wrote that Wundt "wedded physiology and psychology and made the resulting offspring independent." In 1875 Wundt was named a professor of physiology at the University of Leipzig, and he immediately established his innovative laboratory to empirically research his theories of psychology.

According to the 1997 *Biographical Dictionary of Psychology,* however, some of Wundt's colleagues disagreed with the designation of his laboratory's as the first of its kind. Two other experimental psychologists and contemporaries of Wundt, William James and G. Stanley Hall, both argued that they and others had employed similar experimentation methods in their labs. Yet Wundt did play a crucial role in the field as science was beginning to explore psychology in a new way. The dictionary comments that,

> the study of psychology had remained in the provinces of philosophy and the natural sciences. From philosophy had come (theories of) interaction-sim, empiricism and materialism, theories hypothesizing the nature of the mind, mind–body interaction and acquisition of knowledge.

1832–1920

GERMAN EXPERIMENTAL PSYCHOLOGIST, UNIVERSITY PROFESSOR

UNIVERSITY OF HEIDELBERG, PhD, MD, 1856

Wilhelm Wundt. (Corbis–Bettmann. Reproduced by permission.)

Wundt's early ideas were inspired by his colleague Johannes Müller's (1801–58) work in physiology. Müller used a system of specific procedures in his investigation of the human body that departed from the methods many others had used. Wundt had published his first book, *Grundzuge der physiologische Psychologie (Principles of Physiological Psychology),* in 1873–74, setting forth the premise on which all of his work would be based. The book contained six volumes and was republished in several later editions, both during his lifetime and following his death. Wundt believed that the core of an organism's movement and motivations was a psychosocial process. In other words, the nature of any response in any organism, including humans, was a product of both physiological and psychological stimuli. His notion that mental occurrences could be objectively knowable and measurable became a fundamental principle that would trigger generations of psychological study and experimentation. Wundt was able to utilize the knowledge both of the sense organs and the control they exerted over the brain and consequently over control of movement. He used introspection as a tool for unlocking the human psyche. Wundt believed that no matter how complicated mental processes might seem, they could be broken down into a series of simple elements.

Wundt's fourth edition of his *Physiological Psychology,* published in 1893, presented his "tridimensional theory of feeling." Wundt thought that feelings could be classified as pleasant or unpleasant, tense or relaxed, or excited or depressed. Furthermore, any feeling could contain feelings from each of the three categories. His approach eventually came to be known as structuralism, a theory described by his student, E. B. Titchener. Structuralism "sought to describe the structure of consciousness, its basic building blocks, by carefully observing conscious experience," through the use of introspection.

Wundt's research findings laid the groundwork for psychologists for many generations. He was best recognized as having established psychology as a discipline independent of philosophy, incorporating elements of anatomy and physiology. He provided the scientific method to investigate the mind, which had long been believed to be unknowable. But even Wundt did not think that the scientific method could uncover answers to all of the questions in human psychology. "With particular reference to language and its development," one Wundt biographer wrote, "he sought understanding through the study of history and culture rather than through experimental analysis." Wundt would write extensively on those matters during the last years of his life. "His greatest strength was . . . the systematization and synthesis of work that had preceded him, thus preparing the foundation for experimental psychology."

BIOGRAPHY

Wilhelm Max Wundt was born on August 16, 1832, in Neckarau, a suburb of Mannheim, Germany. His father, Maximillian (1787–1846) was a Lutheran pastor whom Wundt once described as a "jovial and generous person, but generous to a fault." Wundt's mother, Maria Friederike Arnold Wundt, (1797–1868) was from a modestly wealthy family whose governess had taught her French as a child. When Wundt was four, his father accepted a position in Heidelsheim, a small country village in stark contrast to the bustling port of Mannheim. Being transferred to such a place indicated that the senior Wundt was not an ambitious man, and he showed few signs of promise or dynamic behavior.

Although Wundt did have siblings, he grew up as an only child. One sibling died before he was born, another he did not remember, and his brother Ludwig was sent at the age of ten to live with an aunt in Heidelberg when Wundt was only two years old. Ludwig died in 1902. Though he had many cousins, Wundt spent his Heidelsheim childhood without many peers, except at school. He was usually surrounded by adults, including some who were kind enough to pay attention to him and guide his interests. A student of the village school for only two years, Wundt was prepared for a more disciplined academic career by his father's assistant pastor, Friedrich Müller, who tutored him until he was sent to boarding school at the age of 13. Müller's time spent in hours of study brought him closer to Wundt than the boy was to his own father and mother. As a child, Wundt's only real friend was a boy described as "mentally retarded with defective speech" who waited daily for him at the Wundt's cottage door. He became anxious when playing with other boys his own age, usually preferring to avoid the experience. Instead, he read voraciously from his father's library. Even before Wundt could write himself, he took on a literary project of compiling a history of what was common in all religions—aided in part not only through his experience of being the pastor's son, but by his experiences visiting a local Jewish merchant family and observing their prayer rituals in the synagogue and in their home. He was just 10 years old when he first read Shakespeare, and that pastime remained one of his pleasures throughout his life. With so much time spent alone, he also became a daydreamer whose studied introspection would lead him into the course of his professional life as a psychologist.

Wundt spoke little of his father or his paternal relatives. Wundt's daughter would later note that his paternal grandfather was pastor of a church at Wieblingen, a small town near Heidelberg where he had been also been a professor at the university, teaching about Baden's history and geography. Wundt's father had entered the life of the ministry not by choice, but because he was forced to replace the spot that had been originally held for his older brother, who had abandoned the study of theology. The family's long history in the pastoral life was important enough for Maximillian to take his place in it as well. A great-grandfather and two great uncles had also been members of the university faculty; these predecessors represented an honored status of academic and professional achievement which Wundt's father could never quite reach. Wundt recalled that his mother took the active role in managing the family's meager finances and attending to her son's education. He also remembered receiving loving consolation from his father after having been disciplined by his mother.

Wundt opened his autobiography with two exceptions to his fond memories about his father. "The first was a traumatic tumble down a flight of cellar stairs, and its recall was always accompanied by a vague feeling that this had happened while he was attempting to follow his father into the cellar," a Wundt biographer related. "In the other, Wundt was roused from

PRINCIPAL PUBLICATIONS

- *Principles of Physiological Psychology.* 1873–74. Reprint, Engleman, 1911.
- *Outlines of Psychology.* Translated by C.H. Judd., 1896. Reprint, Engleman, 1907.
- *Volkerpsychologie (Elements of Folk Psychology).* 10 vols, Engleman, 1900–1920.
- *Lectures on Human and Animal Psychology.* Translated by J.E. Crighton and E.B. Titchener. Macmillan, 1984.

a classroom reverie by a blow on the ear and looked up to see his father glowering over him." That particular day, his father's pastoral duties had included the role of school inspector—a person assigned to monitor the students in order to maintain discipline and to make sure that the classroom was being run properly—and the elder Wundt had observed his son misbehaving. The perception of his father as someone other than the loving person he thought he knew probably influenced Wundt negatively. Seeing his father as a source of pain might have led the young Wundt, who had identified so wholly with his father, to distrust himself.

Wundt also recalled two other public events that had had a great impact on him. The first memory was described by his biographer as follows,

> In Heidelsheim, on the afternoon of the final day of his first year's schooling, he watched from his doorstep as a crowd of peasants erected a "freedom tree" in the public square. Then he saw the burgo-master's house set ablaze by the demonstrators and later—while the local bailiff paced up and down inside the Wundt cottage—he saw them dispersed by a squadron of dragoons (soldiers armed with short muskets for the purpose of persecution).

When Wundt was not yet 17, three years after his father's death, the Republic of Baden was established. In June, Wundt witnessed the flashes of cannon fire in the distance, as Prussian army troops set out to suppress the young republic's independence. During the 1860s, Wundt became actively involved in the Workers' Educational League and served as a member of the Baden diet, or governing body, probably due to the influence of these experiences.

Upon his father's death, his maternal uncles assumed a prominent role in Wundt's education. His mother's two brothers, Johann Wilhelm and Philipp Friedrich, had both studied medicine at Heidelberg, and they had also begun to teach at the university. His uncle Friedrich had an especially illustrative career as an anatomy and physiology professor, and his influence secured Wundt a position at Heidelberg in 1858.

Formal schooling and the university

A year before he left for boarding school, Müller received his own pastorate in Münzesheim, not very far from Heidelsheim. Wundt was not happy with the situation, and eventually his parents let him move in with the younger pastor in order to continue his studies. When he entered the Bruchsal gymnasium (a college preparatory school), Wundt was sent to live with another Lutheran pastor's family there in what was a predominately Catholic town. That year turned out to be a disaster for him. He performed poorly at school, was homesick, and was unable to make friends. Once he even ran away back to his home. His mother took him back to school, however, as she was determined that he should get a proper education. At the end of the year, one of his teachers suggested to his parents that perhaps he could pursue a career in the postal service, since it was clear that he was probably not cut out for a profession that required any serious academic excellence.

His mother and her relatives ignored this advice and decided that young Wilhelm deserved a second chance. He was sent to his aunt's home in Heidelberg to join his brother Ludwig, who had become a very studious young man and a student at the university. His aunt enrolled Wundt in the Heidelberg gymnasium, where he experienced a whole new life of making friends and becoming active in extracurricular activities. His studies remained average rather than outstanding—a fact that one biographer suggested may have been due to his consuming interest in politics, especially the struggle for Baden's independence and the uprising of the Polish peasants in Heidelsheim. Following his father's death at the end of his first year in Heidelberg, some historians have suggested that his mother went to live in Heidelberg, too. If so, it is likely that Wundt moved in with his mother, and continued to live with her during the early years of his academic career. Once he became old enough attend college, Wundt was relieved that his mediocre grades were high enough to obtain financial aid from the state to attend the University of Heidelberg. As a young man who had been so close to his family, he was ready to venture out on his own, at least for a while. Because his mother's younger brother Friedrich was a professor at Tübingen,

Wundt was able to persuade his mother to allow him to attend that school. His uncle's influence transformed Wundt into a serious student who developed a passion for the study of cerebral anatomy. By that time, as well, Friedrich Arnold had accepted the position as the director of Heidelberg's Anatomical Institute, and the logical course for Wundt would have been to follow him back to Heidelberg, now that he had proven himself in his studies.

Wundt certainly was serious about his studies in a way he had not been before. But he needed to make up many courses in mathematics and science that he had neglected while a gymnasium student. As a result, he studied mathematics with a private tutor while completing lecture and laboratory courses in physics and chemistry. A newly arrived professor of chemistry, Robert Bunsen (after whom the Bunsen burner was named) had Wundt so enthused about the subject that for a brief time he considered changing his major to chemistry instead of working toward a medical degree. He stayed with medicine, however, and in 1855 Wundt successfully passed his state exams, becoming a licensed doctor. Even more remarkably, this once-marginal student earned the highest scores on every separate test: internal medicine, surgery, and obstetrics.

Professional career

Wundt had passed his medical examinations and received his medical degree. That feat alone far surpassed his and his family's expectations. Still, he was not completely convinced of his ability to sustain a regular medical practice. His inclination was to perform something of social consequence in his work. He did not become a doctor in order to serve only the wealthy people who could afford his professional services. Wundt had even considered becoming a military physician—an option that turned out to be unavailable during that period of peace when no such openings existed. When a friend who was working at a local city hospital needed to take six months away to study for his medical exams, he offfered Wundt the temporary post. Relieved to have such a post available to him, Wundt accepted. The hospital job presented many challenges. He was responsible for treating women in the public ward, and many of his patients were peasants, servants, and prostitutes. He was often on call for 24 hours at a time.

Two incidents during his tenure at the hospital helped Wundt decide that he was better suited for an academic career. Once, when he had been awakened from a deep sleep, Wundt mistakenly administered iodine to a patient in need of a narcotic for pain. Even after the alert patient spit the iodine out into his face,

Wundt did not fully awake. Thoughts about that near-catastrophe haunted him the rest of his life; in the short term, the error made him seriously question his medical abilities. The other problem was described by a biographer, who noted that the hospital often treated paralyzed patients who had suffered leg injuries and other accidents.

> In checking on the course of recovery, Wundt made fairly systematic observations on the impairment of localization of touch sensations, and he came to the conclusion that the results could not be harmonized with Weber's theory (E. H. Weber, 1846) that localization is based on a mosaic organization of the sensory innervation of the skin.

Wundt concluded that sensation alterations in these patients had not only physiological, but also psychological, implications. That experience marked his first foray into considering psychological issues, and he knew he would not be satisfied unless he pursued the matter. Without the support of his family, Wundt managed to gather enough money to attend a semester in Berlin where he studied simultaneously under Johannes Müller and Emil Du Bois-Reymond. Müller's *Handbook of Human Physiology,* published in 1833–1840, had already captured its place in history as the standard text that recognized physiology as a science. Du Bois-Reymond's 1848 book, *Researches on Animal Electricity,* had established him as the expert in electrophysiology.

Wundt returned to Heidelberg in the spring of 1857. He became an instructor there, teaching a general survey of experimental physiology in his first semester. Shortly into his teaching career, however, Wundt became seriously ill. Without warning, he began to hemorrhage violently. What the doctors thought about his potential for recovery had no influence on him. He himself believed he was near death. Wundt related the story by saying that it had brought him a "perfect tranquillity," giving him an entirely different perspective on his life. A biographer observed:

> Whether or not these attitudes were ultimately traceable to this traumatic experience, as Wundt implied, they were characteristic of much of Wundt's later work, and the reader must therefore be prepared to accept the fact that Wundt's empiricism, except in his earliest period, had mystical as well as experimental aspects.

Wundt stayed at Heidelberg until 1874. During his tenure there, he was promoted from the position of instructor to associate professor. In 1858, the noted physiologist, physicist, and psychologist Hermann von Helmholtz arrived at the university; shortly thereafter, Wundt began to serve as his assistant. His major projects at Heidelberg included the study of the neurological and chemical stimulation of muscles. Wundt's first writings, *Beiträge zur Theorie der Sinneswahrenehmungen,* were published in installments between 1858 and 1862, and also in a combined edition in 1862. This book contained much of his teaching, along with an overview of the work he would continue to pursue throughout his career. In the 1984 *Biographical Dictionary of Psychology,* the author stated, "In his work, Wundt made the point that psychology, before tackling metaphysical problems, should start by trying to understand the simplest experiences, and that this should be done using the methods of physiology." His most significant publication, *Grundzuge der physiologischen Psychologie, (The Principles of Physiological Psychology)* first appeared in 1873. The sixth, and last, revision of the work was completed in 1911.

At the age of 40, Wundt had still not received significant professional recognition; he remained an associate professor at Heidelberg. Although he had been recommended for an opening at Zurich University, possibly as early as 1872 when the chair of inductive philosophy was made vacant, he was not formally offered the position until the following year. Wundt delivered a memorable inaugural address when he arrived, offering himself as the philosopher who had come to fill the appropriate chair. He mentioned the names of other notable philosophers—including Aristotle, Gottfried Wilhelm von Leibniz, John Locke, Georg Wilhelm Hegel, and Immanuel Kant. Wundt had finally begun to gain some notoriety. The academic world of physiology and psychology was finally beginning to listen to him.

Leipzig

After a short tenure at Zurich, Wundt accepted the chair of philosophy at the University of Leipzig in 1875. He would stay in Leipzig for the rest of his life. In his inaugural message there in 1876, Wundt said that:

> The more we are inclined today, and rightly, to demand that experience shall have an influence on philosophy, so much the more is it in place to emphasize that precisely in our time philosophy must assert its old influence among the empirical sciences . . . Nothing can be more mistaken than the widespread opinion that these [empirical and materialistic] views emerged from the development of natural science itself. The standpoint of modern empiricism got its foundation from philosophers . . . Perhaps the time will not be far distant when the metaphysics which is now so scorned by empirical investigators will again be held in some measure of honor.

Soon after he was settled in Leipzig, Wundt set up his first room for demonstrations in the field of research that would come to be known as sensation and perception. An American psychologist named

BIOGRAPHY:

G. Stanley Hall

G. Stanley Hall (1844–1924) was a young teacher at Antioch College in Yellow Springs, Ohio, during the early 1870s when he first read Wundt's *Principles of Physiological Psychology*. As a student of both Wundt and Helmholtz, and later as a friend to William James, Hall received the first Ph.D. in psychology to be granted in the United States. Although he became known as much for his work in education as he was known for psychology, he remained devoted to both. He also followed in the footsteps on Wundt and James, establishing experimental labs at Johns Hopkins University in Maryland in 1883, which was second only to James' lab in America, and at Clark University in Massachusetts in 1889.

Granville Stanley Hall was born on February 1, 1844, in the small farming town of Ashfield, Massachusetts. He was the son of Granville Bascom and Abigail Beals Hall. When Hall graduated from Williams College in 1867, he went to the Union Theological Seminary in New York City. A grant of $500 the following year gave him the means to travel to Bonn and Berlin, where he studied theology and philosophy. From 1871 until 1876, he taught at Antioch before moving on to Harvard to complete his Ph.D. on the muscular perception of space. When he returned to Germany to study with the famous physiologists Wundt and Helmholtz, he gathered enough knowledge to pursue his own path in psychology.

Hall joined the faculty at Johns Hopkins, where in 1883 he established his own laboratory. His facility was regarded as the first working psychology lab in the United States—James's lab at Harvard was considered a teaching laboratory. In 1887 he began to publish the *American Journal of Psychology*. Hall founded other journals as well, including the *Pedagogical Seminary,* known currently as the *Journal of Genetic Psychology,* 1891; the *Journal of Applied Psychology,* 1915; and, the *Journal of Religious Psychology,* which he published between 1904 and 1914. One of his most impressive acts

was founding the American Psychological Association on July 8, 1892, when he invited 26 of the world's leading psychologists to attend a meeting. Only James and Dewey were unable to attend. By the end of the twentieth century, more than half of the world's psychologists belonged to the association.

As a pioneer in developmental psychology, also known as genetic psychology, Hall had been influenced by British naturalist Charles Darwin and his theory of evolution. Hall consequently began to reflect on childhood development, and he played a key role in the child study movement that grew for years in the United States. The movement did not last in that form, but it did provide the basis for the idea that studying children was beneficial and established the need for empirical work in that field. In 1909, Hall invited the famous psychologists Sigmund Freud and Carl Jung to lecture at the school. At the time of this conference, even the professional community regarded the field with suspicion. Hall was the pioneer who introduced psychoanalysis to America.

His interest in the psychology of religion led Hall to publish *Jesus, the Christ, in the Light of Psychology,* in 1917. His other major works included, *Adolescence: Its Psychology and its Relations to Physiology,*

G. Stanley Hall. (*Courtesy of the Library of Congress.*)

Anthropology, Sociology, Sex, Crime, Religion and Education, published in 1904; and *Life and Confessions of a Psychologist,* in 1923.

Hall was married to Cornelia Fisher in September 1879; and to Florence E. Smith, in July 1899. He had two children. He died on April 24, 1924, in Worcester, Massachusetts.

William James, who had also studied under Helmholtz and would remain at odds with Wundt's approach, set up a similar lab the same year at Harvard. By 1879, with his experimental laboratory fully established, Wundt would mentor his first American graduate

assistant, G. Stanley Hall, and a whole new era would begin in the study of psychology (see accompanying sidebar).

Students and psychologists from all over the world worked in Wundt's lab and eventually returned to their home countries to set up their own. A movement had begun that continues today. By the winter term of 1883–84, Wundt's laboratory had gained official status as an institute of the Department of Philosophy at Leipzig. Among his other contributions to his profession, Wundt founded the journal, *Philosophische Studien,* as a publication venue for the results of his experiments and those of his students. In 1903 the name of the journal was changed to *Psychologische Studien,* reflecting the new climate of acceptance for the serious scientific study of psychology.

In addition to his methodical research methods, Wundt was known for his quiet demeanor and diligence. When lecturing, for example, he could go on for more than two hours without using notes or pausing for questions. During the school year of 1889–90, he was elected to the post of vice-chancellor of the university, and in 1902 he was made an honorary citizen of Leipzig. In 1915 he was named a professor emeritus. Social and cultural psychology eventually occupied much of Wundt's time and study in his later years. He did not believe that his experimental methods were applicable to most areas of psychology. This shift in direction returned him to his first loves of literature, arts, and the ritualistic practices common among various ethnic and cultural groups that he believed revealed the true essence of cultural psychology. He published his 10-volume series, *Volkerpsychologie (Folk Psychology),* between 1900 and 1920.

Wundt married Sophie Mau in 1872. The couple had one daughter, Eleonore, who served as her father's personal secretary and assistant. She continued to preside over his work even after his death, and she also provided assistance to scholars who were studying her father's work. She was important enough, in fact, that when Chiba Tanenari, the first chair of psychology at Tokoku Imperial University, began to purchase the Wundt collection, he visited with Eleonore in Groábothen, the small town near Leipzig where the Wundts had made their home. Most of Wundt's personal collection remains in Japan today, due to the skillful negotiations and financing of Tanenari and his Japanese colleagues, who respected Wundt's work immensely and had elevated him to an enormous stature.

Wundt finished writing his autobiography, *Erlebtes and Erkanntes,* in 1920, not long before he died. In death as in life, Wundt would continue to have his disciples as well as his detractors. James had said that he was "only a rather ordinary man who has worked up certain things uncommonly well." Biographers Rieber and Robinson offered their own perspective on the importance of studying Wundt nearly a hundred years after his death.

The contributors to this collection do not pretend to cover every aspect of the vast work and complex influence of Wundt on psychology. We also do not speak with one voice. In fact, if you do not find argument and provocation in these pages, then we have failed in our task. Early experimental psychology was a complex enterprise, and the difficulties in interpreting and understanding it do not seem to lessen over time. So we agree on many things, disagree on quite a few things, and discuss all our ideas and readings in a spirit not only of mutual respect, but of outright enthusiasm and love for the productive argument.

THEORIES

The titles and headings that Wundt used in his work were as much a part of understanding his work as the theories themselves. In the case of his *Principles of Physiological Psychology,* (1902 edition) the categories he provided served as more than simply an outline. They provided a direction, resonating with the significance of organization that Wundt brought to psychology: Part I, "The Bodily Substrate of the Mental Life;" Chapter I, "The Organic Evolution of Mental Function;" and, Section 1, "The Criteria of Mind and the Range of the Mental Life." His first paragraph for that edition presented the guiding force, not only for this treatise, but for his entire, lifelong investigation. He wrote that:

> The mental functions form a part of the phenomena of life. Wherever we observe them, they are accompanied by the processes of nutrition and reproduction. On the other hand, the general phenomena of life may be manifested in cases where we have no reason for supposing the presence of mind. Hence the first question that arises, is an inquiry concerning the bodily substrate [defined here as the foundation, or core element upon which a force acts to cause change or motion] of mentality, is this: What are the characteristics that justify our attributing mental functions to a living body, an object in the domain of animate nature?

Wundt was not the first scientist to begin such an investigation, and he conducted his research at a time when the destination of such an inquiry remained unknown. He was like an engineer who tears down a building that he has analyzed from its pinnacle, examining each piece of the demolished structure to see how the whole had been created from the parts. In the case of human beings and the state of their mental life, Wundt began with the top of the pyramid—the human—and worked his way down to the smallest organism capable of sustaining life. His stated his mission this way:

> Here, upon the very threshold of physiological psychology, we are confronted with unusual difficulties. The distinguishing characteristics of mind are of

a subjective sort; we know them only from the contents of our own consciousness. But the question calls for objective criteria, from which we shall be able to argue to the presence of a consciousness. Now the only possible criteria of the kind consist in certain bodily movements, which carry with them an indication of their origin in psychical processes.

According to one biographical profile, Wundt's fame was "based principally on his having founded an experimental psychological science." Many critics and historians have suggested that his views and research were not as important as the methods he established for psychological investigation. Even Helmholtz declared that Wundt's experiments were "sloppy," and not up to his standards. The question remains whether Wundt has been represented fairly by observers and critics throughout history.

Wundt's basic tool of introspection became the guiding force for his research as well as for others' investigations. His ultimate goal was to understand human consciousness and the mental processes that composed the elements of it. His underlying approach to testing would later become known as structuralism, particularly under the American interpretation of Wundt's methods.

Main points

In theory, Wundt believed that the complexity of the human mental experience could be broken down into three main types: sensations, images, and feelings.

Sensations   As Wundt explained them, sensations were the basic forms of experience. They consisted of a direct relationship between an excitation, or stimulus, of the cerebral cortex (a center of intellectual functioning in the brain) and a sensory experience. These sensations could be placed into categories including modality, vision, or audition, in addition to describing such features as intensity and duration.

Images   Images were basically the same concept as sensations, though these were associated with a local stimulus in the cortex rather than an external stimulus outside the body.

Feelings   The category of feelings represented whatever did not come from the sense organs or a "revival of sensory experience." The "tridimensional theory of feeling" was Wundt's premise that all feelings could be categorized by three different sets of opposing emotions—pleasant or unpleasant, tense or relaxed, and excited or depressed. Any combination of one of each of the sets could describe any feeling.

General principles of the central functions

In the 1902 edition of Principles of Physiological Psychology, Wundt focused on the central functions, or the central nervous system. In discussing the research and experimentation that led to his conclusions, Wundt presented what he termed, "General principles of the central functions."

The five general principles that Wundt explained were:

- the principle of connection of elements
- the principle of original indifference of functions
- the principle of practice and adaptation
- the principle of vicarious function
- the principle of relative localization

Principle of connection of elements

Explanation   Wundt classified his approach to understanding the nervous system in three different ways: anatomical, physiological, and psychological. In terms of anatomy, the system was made up of many elements that were closely connected to one another. The nerve cells, or neurons, were controlled by the cell processes. The results of the cell processes often provided clues as to the directions in which the connections are made, Wundt noted. This principle also indicated that every physiological activity was also the sum of many functions, even if the researcher is unable to separate those functions from the whole and from the organism's complex behavior. Again, as with the other two perspectives, Wundt's described "physical" or psychological contents indicated that each of the complicated nerve processes can be broken down into its basic elements, all of which react in cooperation to create the whole. The indicators of this structure are found in the process of psychological observation itself, Wundt noted, and the fact that any psychical process imaginable—no matter how simple—must have arisen from a large group of interconnected pieces, or elements.

Examples   As an example of the anatomical sense of the connection element, Wundt offered that "the merit of the 'neurone theory' to have shown how this principle of the connection of elements is exhibited in the morphological relations of the central nervous system." The example that he used for the physiological aspect was that every sensation or muscular contraction are really complex processes that can be analyzed as the activities of a lot of different parts—the act of standing up out of a chair, for instance, is not one movement, but the result of many different steps that produce the result of standing. In the psychological view, Wundt noted that the "arousal of light or tone," is not simply the "action of stimulus upon the peripheral structures, but also and invariably the processes of nervous conduction, the excitations of central elements in the mesencephalic region, and finally certain processes in the cortical centers." As in the case of memory images, Wundt explained, it is the coordination center that is first involved in the activity, and subsequently the peripheral region.

Principle of original indifference of functions

Explanation Just as he theorized that the structure of functions could be broken down into their elements, Wundt outlined all of these five principles with the same understanding. Based on the "connection of elements," Wundt determined that the hypothesis of "wherever the physiological functions of the central elements have acquired a specific coloring (or peculiar quality) this unique character does not come from the elements themselves but rather from the connections." He offered evidence that this functional indifference had long been the norm by pointing out two phenomena existed to show that it was true. First, he stated that the function of the peripheral organs must represent a lengthy, continuous pattern in order for the sensations to appear in a person's consciousness. And, second, the disturbances of the function caused by central lesions could be "compensated [for] without disappearance of the lesions themselves."

Examples Wundt's premise in support of the first phenomena was that people born blind or deaf, or who have lost those senses in early childhood, did not have the sensations of light or sound. He concluded that the complex interaction and relation of the sensory aspects that are part of the "higher mental processes," meaning those more advanced, or complex, were a part of a central nervous system that was comprised, not of the origin of new specific qualities, but rather of the "indefinitely" complex interrelation of specific sensory elements of the mind.

Principle of practice and adaptation

Explanation Wundt used the word "practice" in the standard meaning of the term—as in the repeated performance of a function. With regard to the nervous system, practice indicated that every key element would get better as it went through the ongoing process of being fitted to perform or participate in a particular function. Adaptation would come with the practice and it would cause changes along the way until a different combination was born.

Examples When adaptation occurred with regard to nervous functions, the resulting adaptations that would become most important are those "newly practiced" elements which would take the place of the older ones.

Principle of vicarious function

Explanation Following directly from the previous principle, "vicarious function" was a special case of practice and adaptation: namely, one with a limited prospect. In other words, it involved a new structural extension that would be required to perform a function new to the involved elements. The structure has an inherent capability to perform the new task, even though it has never been expressed before. This idea can be broken down into two forms—a substitution by "extension of the area of function" and a substitution that happens by acquiring new functions. The first substitution was a gradual "compensation" of the disturbances. This occurred as a result of a significant partial impairment due to the increased activity in other areas that also shared in the function. Sometimes these compensations would come from the "higher" centers, and thus wipe out the trouble that was caused by the lesions of the "lower" centers.

Examples In the first form of substitution, Wundt used the example of what happened in certain cases of brain injury that are centered in the cerebellum or in the diencephalic and mesencephalic regions (part of the forward part and the middle part) of the brain—at least, as much as he knew in the latter part of the nineteenth century. He noted that the disturbances will gradually disappear in these cases of injury. The forms of vicarious function that involved spatial connection were different, according to Wundt. This difference could be understood by imagining that the speech centers of the brain just do not work. That they did not become atrophied could be a difficult concept to figure out, were it not for a simple explanation: If every complex function was based on the supposition that the central elements cooperate in a very detailed and complex manner, then the evidence suggested that more than just one area was involved in such a function. If aphasia—the loss of the ability to use or understand language that often accompanies an injury such as a stroke—occurred when the centers for speech in the left side of the brain were destroyed, the conclusion that these speech functions were solely based in that left side of the brain would be incorrect. Again, in this case, Wundt believed that speech was a cooperative function, with some language processing based in the right side of the brain, even if it was the smaller part of the function. Even though one side of the brain might be used more heavily in a certain task, that side was not the only method the brain used.

Because of that statement, substitution by using the functions of the other side was possible.

Principle of relative localization

Explanation   Wundt argued that even though the central functions and peripheral organs had their own distinct places, the central organ provided a way that those functions could join together. Titchener's translation of this text said that, "any absolute localization of function" was impossible. Yet, considering the fact that the central location of a system was not fixed, the movements of the various functions would have to be relative to environmental conditions, both internal and external. Concluding his discussion of this concept, Wundt explained that this principle included all of the preceding principles, and that therefore the idea of absolute localization contradicted all of them.

Examples   Wundt offered as an example of relative localization the understanding that a reference to the "visual center" was not restricted to the visual cortex; rather, nerve centers outside the brain also played an important role in the function of vision.

Summary of the central function principles

These five principles, Wundt noted, were not easily accepted with regard to the development of the central functions theory. Many other researchers had opposing views. Wundt's defense of his principles failed to dismiss that opposition. "Their progress was hindered, from the outset," Wundt wrote, "by the authority of scientific tradition; in some measure, more particularly in the domain of anatomical and physiological research." This body of the argument of Wundt's five principles offered a differing viewpoint, and in some cases, antagonistic, of previously held ideas about nerve physiology. Wundt did not intend for this theory, or any other of his theories, to be the final word, however. He simply wanted to foster continued experimentation and exploration that was based in sound scientific judgment.

Main points: Other key principles

Other theories grew out of Wundt's basic premise of critical introspection. These principles not only guided Wundt in his research, but they also provided Wundt's students and critics with numerous premises to examine. Five different key approaches emerged as the foundations of his thought.

Actuality principle

Wundt believed in the notion of consciousness as a natural reality. In order to track his system, the student of his work must also accept that premise—but methods of studying subjective experience were problematic. Wundt understood the immense challenge of such a task. As he reviewed the trials of his own personal life and growth, however, he believed it could be solved. One biographer noted:

> Wundt placed his subject matter in line to be another level following upwards in the series of sciences, *physics, chemistry, and biology.* Differences of considerable substance, however, separate this next level from the others. Physical sciences are about objects and energies conceptualized by physical scientists. Consciousness is not a thing–like physical concept. Rather, it is an immediate and transient *process,* the investigation of which amounts to no less than the study of *subjectivity.* Consciousness is a continuous flow, a constant unfolding of experience, which according to Wundt's findings cannot be separated into discrete "faculties" as had been done in ancient times.

This argument comprised Wundt's principle of actuality.

Explanation   Wundt and his researchers determined that consciousness worked in a unique way, and they believed that the elements of that operation could be observed and described. That belief alone provided motivation to push forward in defining the new science of psychology. Included in their discoveries were verifiable limitations of "mental capacities, on span, on the timing of the temporal flow, on the nature of selective attention and short-term memory," as a biographer stated. They found a limited number, usually six or seven, "attentional fixations" that resulted from each timing measure through which short-term memories were stored. Any differences among those experiences of sensation and emotion revealed a multidimensional aspect. Behaviors were thus motivated by the urges and tensions that had resulted from these combined experiences. The observation of these phenomena also revealed how these behaviors might fluctuate, which ones resulted from self-control, which took effort to manipulate, and which were automatically performed, similar to natural reflexes.

Examples   Emil Kraepelin, a student of Wundt's, proposed a theory of schizophrenia in 1917. It was based largely on what was beginning to emerge as Wundt's theoretical system. Kraepelin utilized Wundt's details of what has been described as "processes of central selective attention." Kraepelin's theory of schizophrenia held the premise that it was a result of the disintegration of attention, or the way that attention became skewed in the mind of the schizophrenic.

Principle of "creative synthesis" (Schöpferische Synthese)

This principle of creative synthesis would eventually become known as the principle of creative results. Wundt first referred to it in 1862, and it formed the core of his ideas even to his death. This concept states that such sensations as color, touches, musical tones, and words of speech are subjective reactions of the brain rather than either an interpretation of what has been put into the brain by stimulus or the taking in and storing of something brought into the brain from outside. Such reactions are what he called creative synthesis. One of Wundt's biographers noted:

> Sense organ and neural events may be described endlessly in terms of physics and chemistry, but such descriptions do not include (do not produce for us) the actual psychological qualities known as "sweet," "sour," "heavy," "dark blue," "dazzling crimson," "sharp," "painful," or "meaningful." To get those qualities you must have a living brain, one that is awake, conscious, and attentive, i.e., a brain that is reacting and having experiences.

Wundt continually expanded upon this principle throughout his life.

Explanation   In his autobiography, Wundt explained the thought process that led him to the notion of creative synthesis. He recalled that when he "first approached psychological problems," he "shared the general prejudice natural to physiologists that the formation of perceptions is merely the work of the physiological properties" of the sense organs. And he went on to say that:

> Then through the examination of visual phenomena I learned to conceive of perception as an act of *creative synthesis*. This gradually became my guide, at the hand of which I arrived at a psychological understanding of the development of the higher functions of imagination and intellect. The older psychology gave me no help in this.

Example   Wundt's theory of creative synthesis gradually evolved during his first years in Leipzig. He became more focused on emotions and motivation, as well as on volition, since these issues challenged his ideas of creative synthesis. He wrote in 1880 that "The course of both general and individual development shows that desires or urges (the German word, *Triebe*) are the fundamental psychological phenomena from which all mental processes derive." As Wundt was continually amending the principle to broaden its scope, eventually Wundt and his researchers reached their conclusion, which diverted from the conventional wisdom; namely, that consciousness was not simply the sum of its parts. Consciousness itself was seen a process that had two different stages: 1) a large-capacity short-term memory (at one time referred to as "the Blickfeld") and, 2) a narrow-capacity focus of selective attention, sometimes known as apperception, and manifested through effort. The latter travels through short-term memory.

Principles of psycholinguistics

Wundt's psychology found its greatest success and acceptance within the field of language. As a consequence, Wundt and his colleagues set forth a linguistic theory that was very detailed and comprehensive and resulted from their psychological principles. By the beginning of the twentieth century, many linguistics scholars and psychologists, especially in America, had adhered to Wundt's extensive writings on the subject. He first presented his ideas on the psychology of language in his initial lecture upon arriving in Leipzig in 1875. In 1883, in his *Logik,* he wrote extensively on language for the first time in publication. The first two books of his *Volkerpsychologie (Folk Psychology),* published in 1900, contained his treatise on linguistics and language performance. The section, entitled, "Die Sprache (Language)," was revised in 1904 and further revised and expanded in 1911–12.

Explanation   One biographer noted that the key to understanding Wundt's linguistic theories is the concept that "syntax, the sound systems, and all structures in language are seen as taking their particular form by virtue of the operating characteristics of underlying universal mental processes." According to Wundt, the mechanisms of attention, short-term memory, cognitive time limits, and self-control formed the foundation of language. Language's basic unit was the sentence, which served to identify a specific mental state. It represented the way in which the central focal attention process divides and subdivides mental impressions, with an understanding of the relationship between those divisions. No element of language— words or any other building block—could have any meaning except as it was connected to that relationship with the mental sentence that provided the reason for it.

Example   Based on his theory, Wundt and others studied language, particularly that of children. Before a child would begin to speak, the impact of emotional gestures and sounds would have begun to form language and the basis for it. As a child was able to increase the focus of attention on emotional urges, the mental activity providing for the creation of sentences would have begun to produce the elements necessary for language.

Wundt contributed to another popular twentieth-century focus of education, tree diagrams, which became a standard form of diagramming sentences. These diagrams formed a shape like a pyramid, starting at the top, in order to show the distinction between the subject and predicate of the sentence. Subject and predicate could be further divided and subdivided into other parts of speech. In his *Sprachpsychologie,* Wundt explained this by noting that the sentence was

> not an image running with precision through consciousness where each single word or single sound appears only momentarily while the preceding and following elements are lost from consciousness. Rather, it stands as a whole at the cognitive level while it is being spoken.

His idea was that a sentence was not a "chain of words or word concepts."

The emotion system

Wundt offered his studied beliefs regarding the emotions in contrast to other theorists of the day, all of whom worked in the traditions of either romanticism or rationalism. Wundt sided more with the principles of romanticism, meaning that human beings fall into the category of emotional beings rather than intellectual.

Explanation   Contemporaries such as William James, who were transforming such romantic tradition into a modern-day behaviorism, took exception to Wundt's approach. But Wundt noted,

> First, the definite outer symptoms of emotions do not appear until such time as the psychical nature of the emotion is already clearly established. The emotions, accordingly, precedes the innervation [a stimulation that results in movement] effects which are looked upon by these investigators as causes of emotion. Second, it is absolutely impossible to classify the rich variety of psychical emotional states in the comparatively simple scheme of innervation changes. The psychical processes are much more varied than are their accompanying forms of expression. Third, and finally, the physical concomitants stand in no constant relation to the psychical quality of the emotions. This holds especially for the effects on pulse and respiration, but is true also for the pantomimetic expressive movements. It may sometimes happen that emotions with very different, even opposite kinds of affective contents may belong to the same class so far as the accompanying physical phenomena are concerned.

When Wundt referred to "feelings," "moods," and "emotions," he was not specifying categories, only intensity levels. He would later present his ideas about sensory qualities, explaining affective and aesthetic qualities of experience.

Example   Wundt held to the idea that all mental states were transported through constant fluctuations of emotions, mood, or feeling. Sometimes these would become intense enough to precipitate action. Inherent in every mood, according to Wundt, was its opposite. Other psychologists moved out of the context of Wundt's ideas to provided their own generation of his tri-dimensional feelings. The three dimensions were ideas to which others basically adhered. The aspects of "pleasure versus displeasure," "high versus low arousal," and "concentrated versus relaxed attention" were explained further by the notions of the opposites of control, potency, and domination as opposed to submission. An example he used when discussing sensory qualities were a person's reactions to music and rhythms.

The volition system

Through the intensive reaction-time research program Wundt established at Leipzig, he and his fellow researchers were able to study what he called "decision and choice." Simply stated, they attempted to analyze volition, or self-control. Kurt Danziger published the first English account of the research in 1989, previously published only by the philosopher Theodore Mischel, who published in a philosophy journal and whose work was not known to psychologists.

Explanation   Wundt did not believe that emotions were sensations, or caused by external stimulus activity. He was convinced that they were internal products of the central nervous system with no other influences. Emotional forces were internal forces, ever-changing, and just features of consciousness. Wundt used the terms "volition" and "motivation" interchangeably with emotions. He thought that what might have been the controlled or voluntary efforts in primal beings could have become automatic mechanisms as humans evolved. Wundt did believe that in such highly evolved creatures as modern humans, "pure impulses or drives" could be contained by attentional control, and consequently become conscious volitions. A biographer noted:

> The automatization of actions, mental or otherwise is, however, a double-edged sword. Rapid articulate speech, for example, is a largely automatized process, but when we focus too intently on some motive or extraneous thought while speaking, we are in danger of losing control of the articulation process.

Human beings must continually refocus in order to keep control of the automatic control "wiring" that is inherent. If it is not "tuned up" lapses occur, just as short-term memory can fade without the appropriate mental exercises.

In discussing these automatic behaviors further, Wundt wrote that,

> It is not improbable that all the reflex movements of both animals and men originate in this way. As evidence of this we have, besides the above described reduction of volitional acts through practice to pure mechanical processes, also the *purposeful character of reflexes,* which points to the presence at some time of purposive ideas as motives.

Another biographer observed, "Like most of his other theories, Wundt's views on volition were subject to periodic revision. However, once he had developed the independent position of his mature years, these revisions did not affect his fundamental views."

Example   The automatic behaviors can be witnessed in considering the skills a person possesses when heading into the study of advanced math. Had the student not learned the basic rules of algebra so that its operations were automatic, the more complicated steps of higher mathematics would be virtually impossible. The same is true in writing and forming grammatical sentences. The mechanical aspect of language becomes so automatic that the writer can simply focus on content rather than the process—just as in conversations, when a person does not have to stop and focus on each step of the process, but rather only on what is being said. Still another example of this concept is the pianist who has developed the skill of playing well enough to talk or sing simultaneously, focusing on that behavior rather than the mechanics of playing. People experience such behavior daily even as they lock their houses when they leave, for instance, or do not stop to think how to open their garage doors, instead, simply pressing the opener automatically as they approach their house.

Apperception concept

Basically defined, apperception referred to the process of focusing on a particular content in consciousness. This term more specifically described the psychological processes that explained what was involved in patterns of deliberate, voluntary actions.

Explanation   Within Wundt's concept of the process of mental functions was included, as in his other theories, the polar opposite to the main focus. In other words, he described the point of focus as well as the rest of the field of consciousness. The polarization is the result of the process of apperception, which was a manifestation of volition. Apperception was the principle that motivated and provided experience to both direction and structure. It also indicated a "central" process that could operate in two directions, on sensory content that could result in more complex forms of

perception, and on the shaping of ideas. While that idea was not so revolutionary, Wundt's additional notion of the opposite, that apperception also operated on the motor apparatus, was more innovative. This idea meant that not only was the mind constructed with regard to focus and the field that surrounded it, but the actual movement of the body and the skeleton also functioned in the same way, by selectively controlling movements.

By the third edition of his *Principles of Physiological Psychology,* Wundt revised his concept of apperception even more. He offered the distinction between what he termed "impulsive" apperception, involving the motor direction of apperception; and "reproductive" apperception, indicating cognitive direction. Impulsive apperception, the controlling process, directly affects the motor apparatus. One of Wundt's biographers explained that during the process of development, "movement images are eventually formed by the differentiation and recombination of movement sensations." In reproductive apperception, those movements can be recalled. It involves only the memory of the movement, and not the movement process itself.

Examples   The sucking of an infant on the mother's breast would be just one such impulsive movement. Such "primitive" activities indicated that the central stimulus would immediately and directly result in particular patterns of motor behavior. The biographer noted, "But such motor activity leads necessarily to the formation of motor images (no matter how rudimentary) which can be recalled by reproductive apperception." With the way these activities can blend together, or fuse, and with the activities of analysis and consequent recombination, as Wundt saw it, new movements can be created.

Summary

In an 1894 autobiographical statement reflecting on his life's work, Wundt wrote that

> If I were asked what I thought the value for psychology of the experimental method was in the past and still is, I would answer that for me it created and continues to confirm a wholly new view of the nature and interrelations of mental processes. When I first approached psychological problems, I shared the general prejudice natural to physiologists that the formation of perceptions is merely the work of the physiological properties of our sense organs. Then through the examination of visual phenomena I learned to conceive of perception as an act of *creative synthesis.* This gradually became my guide, at the hand of which I arrived at a psychological understanding of the development of the higher functions of imagination and intellect. The older psychology gave me no help in this. When I then proceeded to

investigate the temporal relations in the flow of mental events, I gained a new insight into the development of volition . . . an insight likewise into the similarity of mental functions which are artificially distinguished by abstractions and name—such as "ideas," "feelings," or "will." In a word, I glimpsed the indivisibility of mental life, and saw its similarity on all its levels. The chronometric investigation of associative processes showed me the relation of perceptual processes to memory images. It also taught me to recognize that the concept of "reproduced" ideas is one of the many fictions that has become set in our language to create a picture of something that does not exist in reality. I learned to understand that "mental representation" is a process which is no less changing and transient than a feeling or an act of will. As a consequence of all this I saw the old theory of association is no longer tenable. It must be replaced by the notion of relational processes involving rudimentary feelings, a view that results in giving up the stable linkages and close connections of successive as well as simultaneous associations.

HISTORICAL CONTEXT

Wundt's life spanned 88 years. The world into which he was born in 1832 was certainly very different from the world in which he died—a post-World War I Germany. Europe was undergoing enormous political and physical changes. The landscape of what had been a continent of small kingdoms and tiny countries had evolved into a Europe of fewer countries and more deadly wars. Greece had become an independent state. Prince Otto of Wittlesbach became King of Bavaria before that nation joined a unified Germany. The medieval cannon-and-sword warfare had evolved into the airplanes, bombs, and the battles of a new century. Medical and scientific advances were slowly making the world a place with increasing life expectancy, wider opportunities for travel, and more accessible education to a class of people who could not have hoped for such intellectual adventures just decades earlier. The industrial revolution had swept through Europe first, and then the United States, bringing about technological capabilities that few had ever dreamed possible. The year Wundt was born, Michael Faraday's laws of electrolysis were made public. In 1839, when Wundt was only seven years old, Louis-Jacques-Mand Daguerre developed the first photographic images. By the time of Wundt's death, the average person could operate handheld cameras and view motion pictures. This period of significant social change caused a shift in in human consciousness as well—people began to view themselves as living within an ever-changing context.

Although Wundt spent a great deal of time alone throughout his childhood, he could not ignore the significance of what was going on in the world around him. Those events affected him and helped to shape the path he would follow into his profession. Just as his own personal life and development gave cause to his life of research and experiment, so did the changing world around him, especially in academia, medicine, and politics. While serving on the faculty at the university, Wundt also served as an elected representative from his district in Heidelberg, for the Baden diet (governing body), beginning on April 26, 1866. He would resign about 18 months later because he did not believe the life of his research would be compatible with the necessary demands of political life. He would become a champion for German unification. Wundt gave a speech to the Heidelberg branch of the Workers' Educational League in 1864, the text of which was found among his papers after his death. One of his biographers documented

Wundt stated that the goal of the entire working-class movement was the freedom and independence of the working class and its salvation from mechanization, but that this goal was indissolubly linked to German unity and freedom. German workers must therefore rise above their class interests, to fight with a sense of duty for the honor of the nation. Strength in warfare and soundness of character are independent of privilege, Wundt said, and they have more value than gold or possessions.

In his professional life, Wundt was first and foremost an innovator who followed no other trends. He was influenced by such great thinkers as Dutch philosopher Benedict de Spinoza—especially his idea of psychophysical parallelism that stated every physical event has a mental counterpart and vice versa—and his teachers and mentors such as Johannes Müller, Du Bois-Reymond, and Hermann von Helmholtz.

As Wundt was beginning his career at Heidelberg as an assistant to Helmholtz, an other great thinker, Gustav Theodor Fechner (1801–87) was finishing his work, *Elemente*. The Prussian-born scientist, who had studied medicine followed by mathematics and physics, was credited with presenting the formal beginning of experimental psychology. In *Serendip*, in a discussion entitled, "Mind, Brain, and the Experimental Psychology of Consciousness," the author stated that

While the philosophical message of the *Elemente* was largely ignored, its methodological and empirical contributions were not. Fechner may have set out to counter materialist metaphysics; but he was a well-trained, systematic experimentalist and a competent mathematician and the impact of his work on scientists such as Helmholtz, Ernst Mach, A.W. Volkmann, Delboeuf, and others was scientific rather than metaphysical. By combining methodological innovation in measurement with careful experimentation, Fechner moved beyond Herbart to answer Kant's second object regarding the possibility of scientific psychology. Mental events could, Fechner showed, not only be measured, but measured in terms of their relationship to physical events. In achieving this milestone, Fechner demonstrated the potential for quantitative, experimental exploration of the phenomenology of sensory experience and established psychophysics as one of the core methods of the newly emerging scientific psychology.

Wundt was ready to explore this changing climate. He agreed with Fechner, noted a biographer, that "the availability of measurable stimuli (and reactions) could make psychological events open to something like experimental methodology in a way earlier philosophers such as Kant thought impossible."

While he was assistant to Helmholtz, Wundt actually conducted most of his experiments at home, on his own time. Though psychology and psychiatry were both required medical school courses, Wundt first used the word psychology, in a course title in 1862. That would mark the true beginning for him of what would become a prolific writing career as well as that of experimental psychology. When he set up his first makeshift lab in 1875 for his demonstrations of sensation and perception, Wundt was sharing a stage only with William James at Harvard, who had embarked upon a similar path. On March 24, 1879, Wundt formally requested funds from the Royal Saxon Ministry of Education in order to set up and support a lab with psychophysical apparatus. Wundt was not granted the allocation. But two of his students, American G. Stanley Hall and fellow German Max Friedrich, nonetheless began their scientific investigations in a small classroom that had once been given to Wundt for storage. Until that time, psychology had no prominent place in the academic or scientific world. It had been relegated to either the philosophy or the natural sciences departments.

Wundt was influenced by German philosophical thought of the era. At the time, German philosophy held to the idea that sensations were psychological events, and thus internal to the mind. But sensation related to something that was external to the mind. With that disposition, Wundt's introspection was what modern-day philosophers or psychologists might call observation. A biographer wrote that Wundt's psychology was a "major occupant of that relatively brief period when the shape of modern psychology was still wide open." Contemporary to Wundt, and influencing his approach, were the British associationists and the German Herbartians (followers of philosopher Johann Friedrich Herbart). He concluded, along with them, that all psychology began in the conscious experience of individual human subjects. He gave the British the credit for being the first to develop a psychological system based on that premise. Yet, the same biographer noted that although Herbart had made some changes to the British system, "the very achievements of both these earlier forms of psychology had led to a new set of problems." He went to say "Their contributions had been indispensable in demolishing the legacy of faculty psychology, but the theoretical constructions with which they replaced the latter were base on fundamental errors and illusions."

In his psychology journal, *Philosophische Studien,* which he founded in 1881, Wundt again proved to be a pioneer. The journal was the first of its kind. If Wundt built on the foundation of what a few others had established, he also became the starting point for generations of other, world-famous psychologists, and many more people for whom experimental psychology would set the trends for a new century.

CRITICAL RESPONSE

The immediate critical response to Wundt's work, *Grundzuge der physiologischen Psychologie,* was strongly favorable. The reviews of the book appeared everywhere, and the discussions it prompted were dynamic. Students throughout the world who began to read it were immediately captivated—from Germany, from the United States, from England—and they all rushed to Wundt's classroom and the early versions of his laboratory. Following the initial fascination and praise, as time progressed the inevitable ideological battles arose. Cultural differences altered the unified voice of interest. Perhaps the most profound tribute would eventually be that so many branches of his theories spawned new fields of study—of both digression and support. In this way, Wundt played the vital role of beginning discussions that continued into the twenty-first century, debates that hinged on the understanding of valid scientific study.

Wundt was presenting a new science of psychology, ready to take its place among physics, chemistry, and biology. That reality often was lost, however, amidst the overwhelming number of his publications. A biographer noted,

> Certainly not the least reason for neglect of the whole Wundtian *corpus* is the challenge of sheer quantity. Wundt's academic career was huge—sixty years of productivity, 17,000 students, the all-time winner in the academic ritual of "publish-or-perish." Who could be surprised that the later recollections (Wundt memorial publications), appearing in several countries shortly

after his death, suggest the fable of the blind men feeling different parts of an elephant? One need mention only those dozens of American college boys who sailed off for a year or two at Leipzig in the late nineteenth century. They were armed merely with a semester of two of college German and an American small-college degree—hardly a match for the formidable academic preparation of German *Gymnasium* students.

Especially with some of these young Americans, as well as those other non-German speaking students, the debate over Wundt's work and what it was or was not grew particularly heated in the early years of World War I (1914–18).

Some of the criticism leveled at Wundt accused him as a representative of his nation's "evil" culture. Even American journalist H. L. Mencken (1880–1956) weighed in on the matter. He observed in the mid-1920s about the challenges of Americans translating German, and said that

> The average American professor is far too dull a fellow to undertake so difficult an enterprise. Even when he sports a German Ph.D. one usually finds out on examination that all he knows about modern German literature is that a *Mass* of Hofbrau in Munich used to cost 27 *Pfennig* downstairs and 32 *Pfenning* upstairs. The German universities were formerly very tolerant of foreigners. Many an American, in preparation for professoring at Harvard, spent a couple of years roaming from one to the other of them without picking up enough German to read the *Berliner Tageblatt.* Such frauds swarm in all our lesser universities, and many of them, during the war, became eminent authorities upon the crimes of [philosopher Friedrich] Nietzsche and the errors of [historian Heinrich von] Treitschke.

Any interpretation or criticism of Wundt must be mindful of this American attitude.

Also at the time of Wundt's first major publication of the *Physiological Psychology,* a review in the *Literarisches Centralblatt* in 1874 said that the book, "corresponds exactly to the need created by recent developments in physiology and psychology and the [consequent] lively demand for a *specialized* scientific treatment of the actual relations between body and consciousness." British psychologist James Sully in 1876, unlike William James, would write that he did accept the fact that Wundt had "defined the boundaries of a new department of research in Germany." He also complimented Wundt for "putting into systematic form the results of a number of more or less isolated inquiries." His colleague Friedrich Lange found Wundt's work so impressive that he recommended Wundt for the chair of inductive philosophy at Zurich University, even when Wundt's academic career had otherwise been undistinguished and lacked the fame that others in his field were enjoying.

One observer agreed with the perspective that provided an important clue in how to approach Wundt's critics, both contemporary and modern. He noted in 2000 that the world was beginning to notice Wundt again, and his work was beginning a new surge in popularity. Boeree reflected:

> Over 100 years after his work, we have finally caught up with him . . . Actually, he was massively misrepresented by poorly educated American students in Germany, and especially a rather ego-driven Englishman named Titchener. Wundt recognized that Titchener was misrepresenting him, and tried to make people aware of the problem. But Boring—the premier American historian of psychology for many decades—only knew Wundt through Titchener.

Much of the problem lay in the mistranslation, or the lack of translation of his works, especially for the English-speaking audience. The title itself of his *Principles of Physiological Psychology,* gave first witness to the issue. "Physiological" was a term that originally meant "experimental" but that used the methods of the physiology laboratory. Especially upon the advent of the behaviorists in the twentieth century, the confusion over the essence of Wundt's psychological theories would only increase before the real message of his work would be made clear.

This problem continued with various biographical profiles that inevitably list his greatest achievement as the establishment of experimental methods rather than his theories themselves. For instance, Zusne wrote in 1984 that Wundt's "systematic views are of lesser importance and constitute largely a descriptive system." Indeed, his work in establishing his lab alone was a significant achievement that would serve as a tribute to Wundt throughout the rest of history. Zusne was mistaken when he noted in his biographical profile of Wundt that "Wundt's elementism and the method of introspection did not survive the death of his truest disciple, E. B. Titchener." But even Zusne agreed that the path leading away from Wundt's laboratories into those of pioneering psychologists throughout the world found a basis in his theories. In establishing branches of applied psychology, others would use his theories to grow into branches from the seed Wundt planted, even though he did not believe in applied psychology himself.

Wundt's theory of emotions and creative synthesis would provide a cornerstone for the Gestalt school of psychology. His student Emil Kraepelin would use the basic tenets of Wundt's actuality principle and its descriptions of processes of central selective attention to form his own theory of schizophrenia in 1917.

Another biographer offered a different analysis of Wundt and the interpretations of his work. He wrote that:

But the difficulties of Wundt scholarship are not entirely a matter of translation. Some of them are intrinsic to the original texts. Wundt was virtually encyclopedic in his writings with the result that he would often discuss topics in different contexts and therefore arrive at somewhat different formulations. That can make it difficult to extract the definitive Wundt position on specific issues.

Wundt's long life and career complicated matters as well. Throughout the course of his work, some of his opinions changed due to the evolution of his own theories and experimentation methods. He was known to be sometimes reluctant to admit he had changed his mind, and the result was ongoing confusion about what he believed.

James, Hall, and the American school

As a group, the hundreds of young Americans who studied with Wundt were only part of the consideration of the impact he made in America. Certain Americans, professors and scholars such as William James and G. Stanley Hall, merited a closer study. These people were the movers of thought in the United States, and far more significant in the debate about Wundt. In his own review of Wundt's first work, James was very favorable. He welcomed it as a book "indispensable for study and reference," even if it did have many shortcomings, in his opinion. "But, they [the shortcomings] only prove how confused and rudimentary the science of psycho-physics still is," he added. Only later would James come to criticize Wundt for those shortcomings, as well as the different courses their philosophies took them (see accompanying sidebar).

Because James and Wundt were contemporaries who had studied with some of the same giants in the early years of physiological and psychological research, contrasting their views is essential to studying the arguments of Wundt. G. Stanley Hall's perspectives on Wundt are also useful, since not only had Hall studied with Wundt, but he also had taken what he knew back to America to begin a similar research path.

Often the focus of the debate between Wundt and James centers on the structuralist approach of Wundt compared to the functionalism of James. A writer noted that the two schools of thought were actually more similar to each other than to the rest of mainstream psychology. Both, he pointed out, were engaged in the principle of free will and opposed to the materialistic philosophy. Even their ideas of what made psychology worth studying, as well as the nature of its essence, did not differ much.

In comparing their ideas, it is helpful to consider the following points made by that writer. For Wundt:

> "Mind," "intellect," "reason," "understanding," etc. are concepts that existed before the advent of any scientific psychology. The fact that the naive consciousness always and everywhere points to internal experience as a special source of knowledge may, therefore, be accepted for the moment as sufficient testimony to the right of psychology as a science. "Mind" will accordingly be the subject to which we attribute all the separate facts of internal observation as predicates. The subject itself is determined wholly and exclusively by its predicates.

What James offered to make a similar point was that, "There is only one primal stuff or material in the world, a stuff of which everything is composed, and we call that stuff, 'pure experience.'"

Neither Wundt nor James were proponents of the Hegelian system of rationale, however, or other such philosophical ideas. They were similar, too, in the way they viewed materialism and reductionism. Wundt wrote:

> If we could see every wheel in the physical mechanism whose working the mental processes are accompanying, we should still find no more than a chain of movements showing no trace whatsoever of their significance for mind. All that is valuable in our mental life still falls to the psychical side.

The doctrine of materialism was equally distasteful to James, a follower of pragmatism, and a student of Charles Sanders Peirce, who had founded that philosophy. But James did not give credence to Wundt's introspection of consciousness. His own thoughts led him to focus on behavior in outer environments, though James would scarcely have believed that behaviorist psychology evolved from his own philosophy.

G. Stanley Hall commented in one paragraph about Wundt, in 1920, the year of Wundt's death, that

> Wundt has had for decades the prestige of a most advantageous academic chair. He founded the first laboratory for experimental psychology, which attracted many of the most gifted and mature students from all lands. By his development of the doctrine of apperception he took psychology forever beyond the old associationism which had ceased to be fruitful. He also established the independence of psychology from physiology, and by his encyclopaedic and always thronged lectures, to say nothing of his more or less esoteric seminary, he materially advanced every branch of natural sciences and extended its influence over the whole wide domain of folklore, mores, language, and primitive religion. His best texts will long constitute a thesaurus which every psychologist must know.

In the next paragraph, however, he went on to offer harsh criticism, saying that Wundt had suffered from a

BIOGRAPHY:

William James

As a contemporary of Wilhelm Wundt who studied physiology with many of the same people, including Helmholtz at the University of Heidelberg, William James (1842–1910) was considered the founder of American psychology. Even into the twenty-first century, he has retained his reputation as America's foremost psychologist. James was also known as a member of the pragmatist movement, which was founded by philosopher Charles Peirce. James held little respect for Wundt, however, and he challenged the claim that Wundt's experimental laboratory was the first of its kind. James established his lab at Harvard in 1875, although his research did not generate the intense interest that Wundt's did. Historical records have placed the opening of Wundt's famous Leipzig lab in 1879; he joined the Leipzig faculty in 1875, however, and began conducting his first experiments there.

William James was born a child of privilege on January 11, 1842, in New York City, the eldest son of Henry James, Sr. and Mary R. Walsh James. His grandfather, also named William James, had been a successful land speculator; he amassed a significant fortune, estimated at approximately 3 million dollars when he died in 1832. Henry, Sr. was well known for his salon for intellectuals and his somewhat renegade theology as a Swedenborgian, practitioners of Protestant Christianity who were very much caught up in religious mysticism. His brother Henry would eventually become famous in his own right as a novelist who chronicled the lives of wealthy Americans at home and abroad. James and his siblings enjoyed traveling to Europe, spoke both German and French, and were well-versed in artistic pursuits.

James enrolled at Harvard at the age of 19 as a chemistry student. He changed his major to medicine within a very short time, even though his real interest was science. When he was 21, in 1865, James had the opportunity to study along the Amazon River, traveling with the famous biologist Louis Agassiz, who was collecting samples of new species. In 1867 he traveled to Germany to study physiology. During his studies in Germany, he showed his first signs of serious depression, even harboring thoughts of suicide, as well as suffering from other health problems. He returned to the United States in 1869 to complete his medical degree. Reading a French philosopher named Renouvier helped James become a believer in the power of free will. As he adopted this belief to address his own problems, he thought his life and health might be improving.

James received his M.D. from Harvard in 1869; his Ph.D. and Litt.D., from Padua (Italy) in 1893; and an LL.D. from Princeton in 1896. His professional career was based at Harvard, where he began working in 1872 as an instructor in physiology. He taught physiology, psychology, and philosophy at Harvard—eventually becoming a professor—until 1907. He was a professor emeritus at Harvard from 1907 until his death in 1910. His major work was, *Principles of Psychology,* a book that James wrote over a 12-year period. A key theory he espoused therein would eventually become known as functionalism—his opposition to the structuralism of such psychologists as Wundt. Among his many other writings are *The Will to Believe,* published in 1897; *Varieties of Religious Experience,* 1902; *Pragmatisim,* 1907, which popularized the theory as a practical way to lead a useful life; and *The Meaning of Truth,* 1909. That same year he published, *Pluralistic Universe,* which contained some additional ideas of pragmatism. While recognized more for being a teacher and celebrity, rather than for the substance of his beliefs, James solidified his prominent reputation in American psychology.

James married Alice Gibbens in 1878, and the couple had five children. He died on August 26, 1910, at the family home in Chocorua, New Hampshire, after several years of suffering from heart problems.

---

narrow approach in his attempt to understand the human mind. In his discussion of what was on the horizon with Freud as compared to Wundt, Hall added that, "We cannot forebear to express the hope that Freud will not repeat Wundt's error in making too abrupt a break with his more advanced pupils like Adler or the Zurich group." Hall believed that, had Wundt spent more time studying biology and less time studying physics and physiology, he might have looked in greater depth at the theory of evolution or the role that genetics played in "psychic powers and activities." Hall's criticisms of Wundt came much later in his life, however; he had been very complimentary during most of his career.

The real breakdown between Wundt and his structuralism, and the Americans and their functionalism, was mostly due to the way Wundt's and others' theories were melded into the American culture. A 1969 book described the controversy by noting that:

> Functionalism *did* make its appearance as a psychology of protest. Its leaders *did* oppose the school that was then the establishment in American psychology: the classical experimentalists, essentially Wundtian in outlook, who saw as their basic and immediate scientific task the introspective analysis of conscious experiences under experimentally controlled conditions. These were its psychologists, who, during the ensuing controversy, came to be called structuralists. And the functionalists *did* place more emphasis on the study of behavior than the classical experimentation has accorded it. Without denying introspection a legitimate and useful role, the functionalists in their own researches drew heavily on behavioral data. Influenced as they were by Darwinian theory, they undertook investigations that required that most, and in some cases all of the empirical data be obtained from the study of behavior—researched in developmental psychology, in educational and other forms of applied psychology, and in animal psychology, to mention a few examples.

Another observer's view of the debate and antagonism between the Americans and Wundt was that it was "no confrontation at all in one aspect and a misfired polemic [argument] in another." Again, this writer criticized Titchener, among others, as a factor in the debate when he went on to say that:

> It [the functionalist/structuralist debate] was begun by a humanist, who found the Newtonian interpretations of science brought to this country by Wundt's students lacking in something vital to [man's] conceptualization. Titchener lost the totality (the one) in the constitutive total of basal elements (the many), and yet this self-organizing principle of mental life is most characteristic of the human experience. Rather than a full airing of the introspective-versus-extraspective *theoretical* slant implied, what developed was a temporary quibble over the rules of *methodological* procedure.

Other Americans who had once praised Wundt would eventually criticize him. These included James Mark Baldwin, who constantly referred to Wundt in his 1889 *Handbook of Psychology,* but barely mentioned him in his 1913 *History of Psychology,* except to criticize his "tendency to abstract classification and schematicism," in *Volkerpsychologie.*

Wundt's American loyalists One former student of Wundt, an American named Edward Wheeler Scripture,

would eventually Americanize some of Wundt's methods enough to use them for application with time-and-motion studies in industrial psychology and clinical applications for work with communication disorders. Scripture worked at the Yale Psychology Laboratory under the supervision of George T. Ladd. The two men were in continual conflict due to their philosophical conflicts. Scripture was to a great extent loyal to Wundt's teachings; Ladd apparently was not.

Charles Herbert Judd, one of the German psychology professor's American students, was named by one author as "by far the most loyal American student of Wundt." Judd took over control of the Yale lab when Scripture and Ladd were both fired for their conflict. But, again, with the Americanization process occurring in the form that application was taking in the United States, especially in the educational psychology—a field that with Hall's help was beginning to boom by the early years of the twentieth century—even a loyalist like Judd would eventually fall in line with the application theorists.

In 1912, Hall wrote about Wundt, again showing the conflicts that his former students had felt about the changes that experimental psychology had effected. Hall pondered:

> Perhaps what is now needed is another Wundt with another life . . . perhaps it is a bold synthetic genius who will show us the way out . . . It would seem as if laboratory psychology in this country was now sufficiently developed so that it should be less dependent upon the new departures made in Germany. The present impasse is the most challenging opportunity ever presented to psychologists. In this crisis our need is a new method, point of view, assortment of topics and problems. These, I believe, geneticism is very soon to supply. Meanwhile, we may have at least for a time to follow Wirth's call to go back to Wundt.

Wundt influenced many European contemporaries such as Belgian phenomenologist Albert Michotte (1881–1965). In much the same roles Wundt and James had played in their respective countries, Michotte was considered the founder of Belgian experimental psychology. He had studied with Wundt in Leipzig during the 1905–06 academic terms, inspired to pursue the issue of voluntary choice. Eventually he would become known especially for his research into the "perception of causality," and the direction he would provide to the later Gestalt psychologists. Michotte's work would also be an important stepping stone to the birth of the field of social psychology. Another Belgian, George Dwelshauvers (1866–1937) was a strong advocate of experimental psychology. He worked at Wundt's Institute in Leipzig after he received his doctorate in Brussels. He returned there in 1889, intending to open a psychological institute.

He wrote to Wundt, explaining that in doing so he would "let the true way of experimental psychology rescue his 'extremely unphilosophical country' from the 'ridiculous masquerades' of the 'spiritualists, positivists, and materialists'."

Wilhelm Wirth (1876–1952) took a position as an assistant to Wundt at Leipzig in 1900. He would eventually become known for his work in psychophysics. But after his arrival, he became one of Wundt's foremost defenders through his experimental work. The results he obtained supported Wundt when his critics were mounting the case against his methods and theories. That was also the time when his reaction-time studies had begun a resurgence. Following Wundt's retirement in 1917, however, Wirth left to pursue his own work in psychophysics. He would no longer carry much influence at Leipzig, especially in psychology, in the way his director once had.

Interest in Wundt experienced a serious revival in the 1970s, after his large contribution in psycholinguistics was rediscovered. A 1979 profile of Wundt for the American Psychological Association's *Contemporary Psychology,* series was entitled the "The founding father we never knew." The debate the review inspired led to the revised view of Wundt taken by twenty-first century psychology.

Scholars have continued to examine Wundt's work a century after his death. The intricacies of understanding he brought to the study of human consciousness might not ever be totally decipherable. But it is clear that his significance continued, as advancements in technology brought an entirely new direction in the study of the human brain and how it works.

THEORIES IN ACTION

Important beginning

The significance of Wundt's work and his place as a pioneer cannot be overstated. One observer wrote that, "The reaction-time studies conducted during the first few years of Wundt's laboratory constituted the first historical example of a coherent research program, explicitly directed toward psychological issues and involving a number of interlocking studies."

Another author stated:

One very important endeavor in Wundt's scientific work was to study the facts pertaining to the nature of the human organism, to isolate these facts by observation, and to measure them in terms of intensity and duration, that is to say, to study the psychic compounds formed by and revealed to us by our "introspective experience."

Wundt was an experimental psychologist. That meant that he was not sitting in a room listening to a client's problems, for instance, or helping direct a changed path in a client's life following some childhood trauma. It was Wundt's business to try to take apart the human psyche in the same way a mechanic might dismantle an automobile's engine and operating system. An explanation of Wundt's research and experiments serves as a necessary component to the observation of the theories that might have evolved from those experiments.

Research

Psychology historian Edwin G. Boring offered readers a description of what went on in Wundt's laboratory. Boring was able to classify 109 experimental articles from Wundt's journal, *Philosophische Studien,* into four categories.

The four categories, along with the percentage of the body of work they represented, were:

- Sensation and perception, over 50%.
- Reaction times (mostly before 1890), less than 20%.
- Attention and feeling (mostly in the 1890s), 10%.
- Association, less than 10%.

In the first category, the study of vision predominated the studies of sensation and perception, followed by auditory perception. Tactile sensation, although a crucial study area in the history of psychophysics, was the topic of only a few of the research studies. No articles were published on the sense of smell, and only a few on the sense of taste. Three researchers studied what Boring referred to as the "sixth sense" or the "time sense," in their experiments on the perception, or estimation of time intervals. Another historian explained that:

As a specialist in sensory perception, Boring strongly identified with the Wundtian experimental tradition. Although he suggested that reaction–time experiments were part of the core of the work of the early Institute, he concluded that this line of research ultimately failed when it proved impossible to measure separately the times required by discrete mental functions. The failure was by no means total, as Metge (1983) has argued [Anneros Metge, "The experimental psychological research conducted at Wundt's Institute and its significance in the history of psychology," in the book, *Advances in historiography of psychology*.] and Boring neglected to emphasize how important this "failed" program" was to the development of laboratory psychology.

In this case, the importance of Wundt's work was born of unexpected consequences, and it was not even his original intention. As the historian continued:

When Wundt came to Leipzig, studies of sensation and perception were primarily identified with physiology, and Wundt would change that identification only partially. Research on sensation and perception in the Leipzig Institute, in the large picture, was preliminary or ancillary to investigations of complex central-nervous processes. Reaction-time experiments sought to measure those processes directly. Leipzig researchers worked in hot pursuit of the parameters and laws of mental chronometry, and Wundt's theory of mental processes implied that reaction-time experiments could serve as the model for investigating many mental phenomena, including attention, will, association, feeling, and emotion.

But the so-called failure, however, led to an entirely new way of psychological experimentation, an outgrowth from the problems of these early experiments.

Wundt was not the first researcher to study reaction times. Early nineteenth-century astronomers, for instance, had continually encountered the phenomenon of the human factor in their quest to gain increasingly accurate simultaneous measurements of position and time for certain celestial events. This human factor would often cause variations of as much as a half-second. Wundt was curious about that difference—enough so that he wanted to explain why such differences existed and provide some standard measurement of reaction times. Thirteen years before he opened his laboratory at Leipzig in 1879, Wundt was credited for his discovery that the "observed time of a reaction was significantly greater than the time required for a nervous impulse to travel from sense organ to the brain plus that required to travel back to the reacting muscle," one biographer observed. That meant the central nervous processes were consuming a lot of the reaction time. Wundt still had to prove it with experimentation, however.

Wundt's instruments and reaction-time experiments

A Swiss precision mechanic named Mathias Hipp (1813–1901) developed a measuring instrument for Swiss astronomer Adolph Hirsch (1813–93) who wanted to measure, as one writer reported it, "the speed of thought." The chronoscope, which was a highly precise time clock, could register time intervals to the one–one-thousandth of a second. The instrument remained a laboratory standard for 50 years. In addition to Hirsch, a Dutch psychologist named Franciscus Cornelis Donders (1818–89) had devised the "subtraction method," which utilized the instrument to determine the difference in reaction times from a simple task to a more difficult task. Donders' experiments would help lead Wundt to measuring the focus of his own research—conscious mental actions. The foundation of his work would begin in the reaction-time experiments. American psychologist James McKeen Cattell, who worked in Leipzig on these experiments, helped to clarify the crucial distinction between psychometry and psychophysics in regard to these experiments. In 1888, he wrote that,

> We are naturally glad to find it possible to apply methods of measurement directly to consciousness; there is no doubt but that the mental processes take up time, and that this time can be determined. The measurements thus obtained are not psychophysical, as those which we have been recently considering, but purely psychological.

Throughout his research and experimentation, Wundt used a variety of instruments. Ten of those instruments, or similar copies, are housed in the Museum of Psychological Instrumentation at Montclair State University in New Jersey. Edward J. Haupt has copyrighted the captions that accompany their illustration; his basic descriptions are made available on the Web site *PsiCafe,* published by the University of Portland (Oregon) psychology department.

Those particular 10 instruments that are designated as Wundtian, and described in Haupt's words, are:

- Beat (making) apparatus—A drum rotated by weights, and turned in a complete circle in four seconds, with pins on the drum set in row at different distances so that placing the contact on the slider can select different time intervals and thus different intervals between contact closures.

- Eye-motion detector—Demonstrates the action of the extraocular muscles to move the eyeball.

- Pendulum apparatus—The tool of Wundt's "complication" experiment, with the subject required to visually track the pointer moving across a large dial; it was run with either a visual set or an auditory set, and was a response to an auditory signal; reaction time was longer with the visual set and demonstrated Wundt's "voluntary" action.

- Perimeter—Allowed the presentation of visual stimuli in all parts of the visual field and at a constant distance from the subject's eye; was used to examine visual field for defects and to plot visual acuity and color acuity; an instrument credited to have originated from Helmholtz.

- Rotary apparatus—The "improved" apparatus for the complication experiment, as described in 1902 in one of the last issues of *Philosophische Studien,* with Wundt observers puzzled by his emphasis of the voluntarist or anti-mechanistic conclusions due the fact that no other psychologist or scholar seemed to be interested in that at the time.

- Sound interpreter (pulse generator)—Produced pulse of a certain tone which came through a tube to a rotating disk with 15 precisely-sized holes that each could be filled with a stopper; the speed of the disk was calibrated through a rotation counter; it was a measure of the auditory system.

- Wundt-style tachistoscope—Presented visual stimulus for a very short adjustable exposure time by using a gravity-operated falling shutter; the onset of the shutter's drop was controlled by a solenoid, for vision experimentation.

- Wundt-style chronograph—Claimed time measurements to one–one-thousandth of a second.

- Wundt-style kymograph for experimental plethysmography (measurement to record bodily functions such as the velocity of heart rate, blood flow, and breathing with subsequent changes in the size of limbs and organs)—A soundless instrument up to 100 mm/second in order to determine plethysmographic signal.

- Wundt-style stroboscope—Suitable for exact psychological research, has eight image holders mounted by spring-held clips on eight radial pipes that can be place from 21 to 51 centimeters from the central axis around which the images revolve.

Case studies

As mentioned above, Wundt did use Donders' experiment with the subtraction method, but preferred to do it by means of the Hipp chronoscope rather than the chronograph when he set about his reaction-time studies at Leipzig. Not only did he employ a technical change, Wundt acted on a different concept as well. He believed that a stricter definition between choice and discrimination was vital.

Donders' experiment According to one historian, Donders' experiments relied on "the assumption that each part of the reaction (sensation, perception, discrimination, choice, reaction movement) took a specific amount of time." Speech sounds were the stimulus and the reactions, recorded on a chronograph that was made up of a kymograph, or moving drum, with a tuning fork that marked the drum with the regular vibrations. In this method the differences of the time measurements would be small. The first, or "a" reaction was the simple response to the stimulus; the "b" reaction was that involved with discrimination of the sensory functions, followed by motor selection in telling the researcher what choice had been made; and the "c" reaction held to the discriminatory function but not the motor.

Only five syllables— possible examples would be "ka, ke, ki, ko, ku,"—with particular choices of one of those syllables would comprise a particular reaction. In the case of the simple reaction, both the stimulus

and response was "ki;" for the "b" reaction, the stimulus was any of the five syllables with the respondent giving back that same syllable used in the stimulus; in the "c" reaction, the stimulus was any of the five syllables but the respondent was told only to react if hearing the sound of "ki." The last choice indicated that the response involved sensory discrimination but neither motor selection nor choice.

The average reaction time of the results were:

- "a" reaction: 197 milliseconds
- "b" reaction: 285 milliseconds
- "c" reaction: 243 milliseconds

Wundt liked such quantitative results when examining mental processes. Buthe decided that the Donders experiment needed an adjustment. He added a "d" reaction—discrimination without choice. What he was actually proposing here was a true psychological experiment. It was a thought experiment with no external measure as to when such a recognition would occur. Wundt would define a whole new way of experimental psychology with this. His techniques were those of self-observation, inner observation, and inner experience. Wundt held to a model for mental reaction that had five parts.

The five parts were:

- sensation, the movement of the nerve impulse from the sense organ into the brain

- perception, the entry of the signal into the field of consciousness (*Blickfeld des Bewuátseins*)

- apperception, the entry of the signal into the focus of attention (*Blickpunkt des Aufmerksamkeits*)

- act of will, in which the appropriate response signal is released in the brain

- response movement, or more precisely, the movement of the response signal from the brain to where it initiates muscular movement

Steps one and five, Wundt suggested, were purely psychological. The three middle steps were psychosocial because they had both a physiological and a psychic side. All five steps might be contained in a mental reaction. While the middle steps could not be measured, or timed separately, using the subtraction method would provide estimates of the times for apperception, and for an act of will, termed "discrimination time" and "choice time," respectively. For such experimentation, the subjects involved had to be trained in the self-observation that Wundt required so that they could properly report these psychic events.

Wundt's first doctoral students conducted experiments using this method. They followed the discrimination reaction time as it was laid out in his theory. One of the studies that used the visual stimuli had respondents press a key when they perceived a flash of light. Another reaction, the "d" reaction, provided two different images that were suddenly illuminated in front of the subject: either a white circle on black background, or a black circle on white background. As soon as the subject determined what was displayed, he would press a key. The first illumination triggered the Hip chronoscope to run, and pressing the key stopped the dial. The time that elapsed was given as the time of reaction. It is essential to note that Wundt carried out these experiments with his doctoral students Max Friedrich and Ernst Tischer. One acted as the subject, another initiated the reaction, and the third recorded the time. They took turns in different roles. Wundt utilized this model that was representative of the method he preferred to use: a subject, an experimenter, and an observer. The continued this particular experiment until they received an extremely short average time. It turned out to be similar to the result found by Donders: a range of 132 milliseconds (ms) to 226 ms. The "recognition" time added approximately 50 ms, which was Friedrich's average, to 79 ms, which was Wundt's. Using four different colors, the recognition time increased—Tischer's average was 73 ms and Friedrich's was 157 ms.

The results for the first experiment can be summarized as:

- simple reaction: 132–226 ms
- discrimination, two stimuli: 50–79 ms longer
- discrimination, four stimuli: 73–157 ms longer

The results for the second experiment can be summarized as:

- reaction with discrimination, but no choice: 185–303 ms
- simple choice—152–184 ms longer
- multiple choice—188–331 ms longer

Wundt's experimental lab hosted hundreds of experiments utilizing various methods. Even from the initial experiments of the first doctoral students, problems had already arisen with some of Wundt's early theories. Tischer's dissertation on the discrimination of sounds, for instance, posed the already recognized situation that auditory stimulus involved a much shorter reaction time than visual. At times, the discrimination time appeared to be zero, with the time necessary to react to a sound stimulus the same as the time necessary to react when the stimulus was "recognized." Kraepelin revealed in his article, also in the first volume of *Philosophische Studien,* that discrimination time was particularly unreliable when the

subject was influenced by drugs or alcohol. The American student Cattell, who had once been a devoted follower of Wundt, initially brought many improvements to the theory in his reaction-time experiments, only to abandon the pursuit later. His measurements lessened reaction times to such a degree that he was having a hard time keeping enough slack time to distinguish accurate discrimination time. Another student, Gustav Berger, shared the distrust of the "d" reaction, deciding that there was no definitive method for determining false reactions or to say with certainty that an apperception has occurred.

Wundt's reaction-time experiments were met with great interest in the first decade of his lab. By the end of the second decade, however, that interest had begun to wane and the experiments were rare. The new trends started focusing on emotions, and behavior theorists began to multiply. But by 1905, as was evident by the publications in his second journal (then known as the *Psychologische Studien*), the reaction-time studies had become prominent again. Some of them featured the sensory reaction that used the subtraction method and incorporated Wundt's theory of emotions. As previously noted, Wundt's assistant at Leipzig, Wilhelm Wirth played a key role in bringing reaction-time studies back into focus.

Relevance to modern readers

Due to the complexity of Wundt's work, and the sheer magnitude of it, the impact that it has on twenty-first century humans might not be as quantifiable has Wundt himself would have liked. Reaction-time studies will certainly continue to shed the light on research into human performance. Rather than as Wundt used them, to test for his theories, modern psychologists are more likely to continue using them as a tool to understand human capabilities, or the challenges that face human potential.

Wundt did lay the groundwork for what modern psychologists do and how they practice their science. He has provided at least six generations of investigators into the human psyche with the solid basis for their existence. The question remains whether Wundt contributed anything more than historical value with regard to relevance for the modern student. One historian attempted to answer that question by commenting:

> prejudging the value of what history has led to always results in bad history. It also results in redundant history; for if the past merely represent imperfect stages along the path to the achievements of the present, why bother with it? But if we suspend judgment on whether the path taken by the majority was the right one or the wrong one, or more likely something in between, then the work of those who, like Wundt, took

CHRONOLOGY

1832: Born in Neckarau, Baden, Germany, outside of Leipzig, on August 16.

1856: Receives a medical degree from the University of Heidelberg.

1857: Begins a seven-year position as lecturer in physiology at Heidelberg. During this time, serves as an assistant to renowned psychologist, physicist, and physiological psychologist Hermann von Helmholtz who arrived at Heidelberg in 1858.

1864: Appointed associate professor in physiology at University of Heidelberg.

1872: Marries Sophie Mau.

1873–74: Publishes first edition of *Principles of Psychology.*

1874: Appointed fellow professor of philosophy at Zurich University.

1875: Appointed one of two fellow professors at Leipzig University, focusing on practical-scientific theories.

1879: Establishes the laboratory for experimental psychology.

1883–84: Wundt's laboratory receives official status at Leipzig as an institution of its department of philosophy.

1896: Publishes *Outlines of Psychology.*

1900–20: Publishes *Volkerpsychologie (Folk Psychology).* 10 volumes.

1920: Publishes autobiography entitled *Erlebtes und Erkanntes.*

1896: Dies in Groábothen, German, near Leipzig, August 31.

---

another path becomes much more interesting. For it is possible that it may open up perspectives that have been closed off by the biases of the present.

In fact, Wundt has provided all humans with a method by which to continue to examine themselves, and the state of their consciousness. In the early twenty-first century, the issue of dementia—usually appearing in the form of Alzheimer's disease—haunts medical and psychological research. Americans and other members of modern cultures throughout the world have a lifespan longer than any in the history of humankind; thus, the incidence of Alzheimer's disease is increasing rapidly. As researchers work furiously to uncover the mystery of a genetic link, those who work daily with those who have the disease face another issue: What sort of communication is possible as the patient retreats further into a vacant memory? Some research has begun to show that the sensations such as sound and touch, as well as visual stimuli of lights, can often spark some memory. A response such as the squeeze of a hand could give recognition to someone outside the patient's own confused mental state. Wundtian psychology represents the underlying strength than can motivate research in such areas as Alzheimer's, or even in studying the recovery from strokes or other "accidents" of the brain as well as other forms of mental illness.

Understanding Wundt's premise for glimpsing the human mind serves as a vital lesson. Opportunities for scientific discoveries must continually expand. No matter what the cause or reason, human sensations remain as relevant in the modern world as they did for Wundt in the laboratory. Wundt offers the experience that what *is* known about humans provides enough of a mystery for several lifetimes of research.

BIBLIOGRAPHY

Sources

Allen, Gay Wilson. *William James.* New York: Viking Press, 1967.

American Psychological Society. *American Psychological Society* Web site. [cited April 2004.] http://www.psychologicalscience.org.

Boeree, C. George. *Wilhelm Wundt and William James.* Shippensburg, Pennsylvania: Shippensburg University, 1999, 2000. http://www.ship.edu/~cgboeree/wundtjames.html.

Feinstein, Howard M. *Becoming William James.* Ithaca and London: Cornell University Press, 1984.

"G. Stanley Hall." *PSI Cafe.* Psychology resource site, 2001. [cited April 2004] http://www.psy.pdx.edu/PsiCafe/KeyTheorists/Hall.htm.

James, William. *The Principles of Psychology.* Chicago: Encyclopedia Britannica, 1952.

James, William. "Psychology: Briefer Course." *Goethe, William James, Spinoza.* Set Five, Vol. 4. Chicago: Great Books Foundation, 1951; 1966; 1958; 2000.

James, William. *The Will to Believe, and Other Essays in Popular Philosophy.* Dover Publications, 1956.

James, William. *Writings 1902–1910, (The Varieties of Religious Experience, Pragmatism, A Pluralistic Universe, The Meaning of Truth, Some Problems of Philosophy, Essay).* New York: Literary Classics of the United States, 1987.

Meyers, Gerald. *William James, His Life and Thought.* New Haven and London: Yale University Press, 1986.

"Mind, Brain, and the Experimental Psychology of Consciousness." *Serendip.* Bryn Mawr College. September 3, 1996 [cited April 2004]. http://serendip.brynmawr.edu/exhibitions/Mind/Consciousness.html.

Ohles, John F., ed. *Biographical Dictionary of American Educators.* Vol. 2. Westport, CT: Greenwood Press, 1978.

Rieber, Robert W. and David K. Robinson, eds. *Wilhelm Wundt in History, The Making of a Scientific Psychology.* New York: Kluwer Academic/Plenum Publishers, 2001.

"Wilhelm Wundt." *Indiana University.* Dec. 11, 2003. http://www.indiana.edu/~intell/wundt.shtml.

"Wilhelm Wundt." *University of Leipzig (Germany).* [cited April 2004.] http://www.uni-leipzig.de/~psy/eng/Wundt-e.html.

"Wilhelm Wundt." *Lifschitz Psychology Museum.* Virtual Museum Web site. [cited April 2004.] http://www.netaxs.com/people/aca3/lpm-info.htm.

"Wilhelm Wundt." *McGraw-Hill/Dushkin.* 2004. http://www.dushkin.com/connectext/psy/ch01/wundt.html.

"Wilhelm Wundt." *PSI Cafe.* Psychology resource site, 2001. [cited April 2004.] http://www.psy.pdx.edu/PsiCafe/KeyTheorists/Wundt.htm.

Sheehy, Noel, Antony J. Chapman, and Wendy A Conroy, eds. *Biographical Dictionary of Psychology.* London and New York: Routledge, 1997.

Washington, Peter. *Madame Blavatsky's Baboon: A History of the Mystics, Mediums, and Misfits Who Brought Spiritualism to America.* New York: Schocken Books, 1995.

Who Was Who in America. Vol. 1, 1897–1942, Chicago: A. N. Marquis Company, 1942.

Wundt, Wilhelm. *Principles of Physiological Psychology.* 1902. Translated by Edward Bradford Titchener, 1904.

Zusne, Leonard. *Biographical Dictionary of Psychology.* Westport, CT: Greenwood Press, 1984.

Robert Mearns Yerkes

BRIEF OVERVIEW

Robert Mearns Yerkes was a leading figure in comparative psychology, a branch of psychology that studies animal behavior and often makes comparisons from species to species. The ultimate goal is to find general principles that may sometimes shed light on human behavior. Yerkes published several books on the subject. Among them was *The Great Apes: A Study of Anthropoid Life*, an influential book he coauthored with his wife, Ada Watterson Yerkes. He also started the first U.S. scientific journal devoted solely to the study of animal behavior. In 1929, Yerkes founded the Yale Laboratories of Primate Biology, the first laboratory for nonhuman primate research in the United States. The laboratory was later renamed the Yerkes National Primate Research Center.

Early in his career as an animal researcher, Yerkes also worked with John Dodson to develop the Yerkes-Dodson law. This law originally related the strength of a stimulus to the speed of avoidance learning in mice. It has since been used, however, to explain the effect of arousal on human performance. The basic idea is that there is an optimal level of arousal for the best performance on any task, and this level depends upon the task's difficulty.

In addition, Yerkes played a major role in the rise of human intelligence testing. During World War I, he headed a committee that developed the first group intelligence tests, which were used to assess Army recruits. These tests, known as the Army Alpha and

1876–1956

AMERICAN COMPARATIVE PSYCHOLOGIST, RESEARCHER

HARVARD UNIVERSITY, Ph.D., 1902

Robert Yerkes. (*Courtesy of the Library of Congress.*)

Beta tests, captured the public's interest. After the war, when Yerkes and others promoted the use of group tests in the general population, they found a ready market. Their tests became the forerunners of standardized tests such as the SAT.

The Alpha and Beta tests had been given to some 1,750,000 Army recruits during the war. Afterward, this huge trove of data was studied intensely. Yerkes's own analyses led him to controversial conclusions about apparent racial and ethnic differences in intelligence. They also raised alarms about a supposed decline in the nation's brainpower. These conclusions have since been refuted on several grounds; at the time, however, they fueled much social debate and helped lead to laws limiting immigration.

BIOGRAPHY

In an autobiographical essay written in middle age, Yerkes recalled that he had been a "moody, strong-willed, unsuggestible child, difficult to control." Throughout Yerkes's career, a stubborn streak in his personality sometimes led to conflicts with other scientists. Yet it also gave him the tenacity to hold onto his

dream of building a primate research center, where both his name and his scientific legacy live on to this day.

Early life

Yerkes was born on May 26, 1876, in Breadysville, Pennsylvania. He was the oldest child of Silas Marshall Yerkes and Susanna Addis Carrell Yerkes. Growing up on a farm, he developed a lasting interest in the domesticated and wild animals that were all around him: cows, horses, mules, sheep, hogs, chickens, turkeys, ducks, pigeons, rabbits, dogs, cats, rats, mice, snakes. The bond Yerkes probably felt such a strong bond with these creatures in part because of his lack of human playmates. His sister, born four years after Yerkes, had died at the age of three from scarlet fever. His other sister and two brothers were even younger, so Yerkes spent much of his time playing alone.

Yerkes, stricken with scarlet fever at the same time as his sister, only narrowly escaped her fate. The family's doctor was an older cousin, whose caretaking of Yerkes during the crisis made a deep impression on him. As he later wrote in an autobiographical essay, "Ever since, in my daydreams, I have imagined myself as physician, surgeon, or, in other guise, alleviator of human suffering." Yerkes set his sights on becoming a doctor.

In the essay, Yerkes described his mother as "a woman of rare sweetness of disposition and unusual ability" as well as the most important influence in his early life. His father was a different matter, however. Yerkes later recalled that he and his father "had little in common intellectually, and more often than not we disagreed in practical matters." This tension was just heightened by the fact that the father wanted his sons to stay on the farm, while Yerkes had big dreams of a medical education.

Nevertheless, Yerkes's formal education got off to a slow start. When he first began attending the local country school at the age of eight, he was unable to read well and too shy to make friends easily. Yerkes soon adapted, however, and even found that he enjoyed the lessons. He particularly liked "arithmetic and algebra, because I found them stimulating, interesting, game-like . . . and physiology and hygiene, because their objectives, information, and principles impressed me as particularly important."

Yerkes attended the ungraded local school for seven years. At age 15, he and a cousin were sent to the West Chester State Normal School, a school for training teachers. This was Yerkes's first experience with living away from home and his introduction to higher education. He planned to study at the normal school, then transfer to the Jefferson Medical College of Philadelphia. After only a few months, however, Yerkes found himself back home. The family was having trouble paying for his education. There were heavy debts on the farm and three younger children to feed and clothe.

College years

At this point, a kindly uncle came to his rescue. The uncle was a homeopathic physician in Collegeville, Pennsylvania, home of Ursinus College. He offered Yerkes a chance to earn his way through college by doing chores around the uncle's house and stable. Yerkes jumped at the opportunity. In 1892, he entered Ursinus Academy, a preparatory school where he studied ancient languages. A year later, he was admitted to the college program.

At Ursinus College, Yerkes majored in chemistry and biology. He also took pre-med classes in human anatomy and physiology. In addition, he performed the chores at his uncle's house. Despite the busy schedule, however, Yerkes later remembered this as a happy time. He also never forgot the generosity of his uncle, describing him as "a wise, broad-minded, generous gentleman, a beloved physician, and a staunch, dependable friend."

In 1897, Yerkes graduated from Ursinus College. His plan all along had been to go straight to medical school after graduation. Once again, however, fate intervened. Yerkes was unexpectedly offered a loan of $1,000 to do graduate work in psychology, biology, and philosophy at Harvard University. At age 21, he made a decision that shaped his whole future when he chose to attend graduate school at Harvard instead of medical school in Philadelphia. As he recalled,

> Readily I convinced myself that I was young to enter medical school and might better devote at least a year to special work in Harvard before completing my medical training. It was my earnest desire to work with pre-eminently able investigators and teachers.

That fall, Yerkes entered Harvard, although not as a graduate student. Instead, he first had to take some undergraduate classes and prove his fitness for graduate study. In 1898, he was awarded the A.B. degree and granted graduate status. Yerkes by this point already knew that he was keenly interested in both psychology and zoology. He decided to combine these interests by studying the new field of comparative psychology. Encouraged by his teachers, he set his sights on a psychology degree rather than a medical one.

At least two professors, who became Yerkes's colleagues and friends, had a lasting influence on him during his student days. One was Hugo Münsterberg, a

PRINCIPAL PUBLICATIONS

- *The Dancing Mouse: A Study in Animal Behavior.* New York: Macmillan, 1907.

- With J.W. Bridges and R.S. Hardwick. *A Point Scale for Measuring Mental Ability.* Baltimore: Warwick and York, 1915.

- "The Mental Life of Monkeys and Apes: A Study of Ideational Behavior." *Behavioral Monographs* 3 (1916) 1–145.

- "Provision for the Study of Monkeys and Apes." *Science* 43 (1916) 231–4.

- (Editor). "Psychological Examining in the United States Army." *Memoirs of the National Academy of Sciences* 15 (1921) 1–890.

- *Almost Human.* New York: Century, 1925.

- With B.W. Learned. *Chimpanzee Intelligence and Its Vocal Expressions.* Baltimore: Williams and Wilkins, 1925.

- "The Mind of a Gorilla." *Genetic Psychology Monographs* 2 (1927) 1–193, 375–551.

- With Ada W. Yerkes. *The Great Apes: A Study of Anthropoid Life.* New Haven, CT: Yale University Press, 1929.

- *Chimpanzees: A Laboratory Colony.* New Haven, CT: Yale University Press, 1943.

leader in applied psychology, which looks for practical uses for psychology in settings such as business, industry, health care, education, and government. Applied psychology later became an interest for Yerkes, too, when he set out to solve practical problems with intelligence tests. Another professor was biologist Charles Davenport, a leader in the eugenics movement, which held that the human race could be improved through selective breeding. Like Davenport, Yerkes later became an outspoken supporter of eugenics.

Harvard University

In 1902, Yerkes received his Ph.D. in psychology, along with an offer to stay on at Harvard as an instructor. There was just one catch: The job, which involved both teaching comparative psychology and doing research, did not pay well. Yerkes had borrowed heavily to finance his education, so taking the job would be a hardship. When asked by Münsterberg whether he could afford to accept the position, Yerkes later recalled that his response was, "No, but I shall, nevertheless." Yerkes taught at Harvard for the next 15 years, first as an instructor, and then as an assistant professor.

While at Harvard, Yerkes married botanist Ada Watterson. Their two children, Roberta and David, were born during this period as well. Years later, Ada teamed up with her husband to write *The Great Apes,* which proved to be one of Yerkes's most important books. In an autobiographical essay penned around the same time as the book, Yerkes noted that his marriage to Ada had "perfectly blended our lives and incalculably increased our professional and social usefulness."

Yerkes's early animal research addressed such topics as sensory function, instinctive behavior, learning, and problem solving. In 1907, Yerkes published a classic book titled *The Dancing Mouse: A Study in Animal Behavior,* in which he explored the genetics and behavior of mutant house mice. The next year, Yerkes and Dodson coauthored a paper that presented what became known as the Yerkes-Dodson law. In 1911, Yerkes founded the *Journal of Animal Behavior,* the first U.S. journal devoted specifically to animal behavior research.

That same year, Yerkes bought a farm in Franklin, New Hampshire, which he planned to use as both a summer home and a location for studying primates. During 1914–15, he also studied primate behavior on an estate in Montecito, California. In 1916, he published an article in the journal *Science,* in which he made the case for establishing a laboratory especially for this type of research.

Yet, despite these successes, he faced several challenges. Research in comparative psychology was seen as a low priority at Harvard. Yerkes was advised to switch to educational psychology if he wanted to get ahead. Although he later claimed that he had disregarded the advice, he did begin to venture into areas outside animal behavior. Among other things, he wrote a psychology textbook and coauthored a book about self-psychology.

In 1913, Yerkes started working half-time as a psychologist in the Psychopathic Department at Boston State Hospital. While at the hospital, Yerkes became aware of the urgent need for practical tests that could be used to assess the mental abilities of patients. Here was a problem that combined aspects of both educational and applied psychology.

The Binet-Simon scale, the first useful test of intelligence, had recently been imported to the United States from France. In its original form, the test assessed intelligence in terms of age levels. Other researchers had suggested that the results could be turned into a score called an intelligence quotient (IQ), which involved dividing mental age by chronological age. Yerkes and his colleagues at the hospital devised their own method for converting the test into a point scale. Using this method, the test could now be scored simply by tabulating the number of points earned on a wide range of items. Their method removed the need to link results to the subject's age.

By 1917, Yerkes had built a reputation solid enough to get himself elected as president of the American Psychological Association (APA). Still, Harvard declined to promote him to a position as full professor. When the University of Minnesota asked him to head up the psychology department there, Yerkes accepted. As soon as Yerkes made plans to move to Minnesota, however, he got sidetracked by America's entry into World War I.

World War I

When the United States entered the war, Yerkes was 40 years old. He was eager both to serve his country and to advance his career. Beyond that, however, he also wanted to show the nation just how valuable the young science of psychology could be. As APA president, he convinced the association's council to form 12 committees that would explore possible military applications for psychology. Yerkes named himself head of the committee that was charged with studying possible applications of intelligence testing.

To form his committee, Yerkes called on all the top U.S. intelligence testers of the day. They included Henry Goddard, who had introduced the Binet-Simon scale to the United States, and Lewis Terman, who had just developed an Americanized version of the scale called the Stanford-Binet. From the outset, Yerkes had big ambitions. He aimed to greatly expand intelligence test methods within a very short period of time.

The first version of the Binet-Simon scale had been published by French psychologist Alfred Binet and his associate, Théodore Simon, in 1905. Binet's original goal for the scale was relatively modest and very practical: He wanted to identify mentally retarded schoolchildren who might benefit from special education programs. The test was designed specifically for children, and it was meant to be given on an individual basis.

Any test Yerkes devised for the military would have to differ from this model in several key ways.

First, it would have to be designed for adults rather than children. Second, given the huge number of recruits, it would need to be given in a group rather than individually. Third, Yerkes was not satisfied with the idea of a test that would merely weed out mentally unfit recruits. Instead, he wanted to develop a test that could also identify those recruits with superior ability who might make good officers.

Yerkes managed to convince the U.S. Army to give his idea a try. His committee quickly put together two prototype tests: one for recruits who could read English, and another for those who could not. Results from a trial on 80,000 men were promising enough that the Army authorized testing of all new recruits by the beginning of 1918. Yerkes told the newspapers that psychology was now in a position to help win the war.

The tests were promptly revised and renamed Army Alpha, for literate recruits, and Army Beta, for illiterate ones. Soon, the tests were being given at a rate of 200,000 per month. By the war's end in November 1918, about 1,750,000 men had taken one of the tests—an incredible logistical feat. Many corners had been cut to accomplish this feat, however, rendering the data of questionable value. In addition, the trial period had been too brief to draw any firm conclusions about the usefulness of the test. Army commanders themselves were divided in their opinions. Nevertheless, Yerkes had succeeded in placing group intelligence testing on the map.

National Research Council

Yerkes had been elected to membership in the National Research Council in 1917. After the war, he had to choose between working with the council in Washington, DC, or belatedly assuming his post at the University of Minnesota. Yerkes chose the National Research Council, in part because he wanted to oversee publication of a lengthy report about the wartime testing program. Beyond that, however, he hoped that taking this job would help him to find financial support for a long-time dream: to establish a laboratory for studying nonhuman primates. No such lab existed in the United States at the time, yet Yerkes was determined to see his dream become a reality.

First, though, he would have to attend to several other projects for the council. Yerkes founded and chaired the Committee on Scientific Problems of Human Migration. At the same time, he chaired the Committee for Research in Problems of Sex. In 1921, Yerkes also served as editor for a massive report titled "Psychological Examining in the United States Army," which detailed findings from the Army Alpha and Beta tests.

Yerkes never lost sight of his goal of doing primate research, however. In 1923, he began raising two apes in his home. Chim was later recognized as a bonobo, which resembles a chimpanzee but is more slender, while Panzee was a common chimpanzee. Yerkes described his research on the pair in a book titled *Chimpanzee Intelligence and Its Vocal Expressions.* The following year, Yerkes spent the summer in Havana, Cuba, where he was able to observe a large primate colony. This work led to yet another book, titled *Almost Human.*

Yale Laboratories of Primate Biology

In 1924, Yerkes returned to the academic world. He joined the faculty at Yale University as a professor of psychobiology, the study of mental functions and behavior in relation to other biological processes. In 1925, he received funding for four years of primate research in New Haven, Connecticut, the home of Yale. While this was certainly a step in the right direction, Yerkes continued to push for a primate research center located in a warmer clime. Finally, in 1929, the Rockefeller Foundation provided the funds he needed to set up the Yale Laboratories of Primate Biology in Orange Park, Florida, not far from Jacksonville.

Yerkes had been waiting for such an opportunity all of his professional life. Building and running the facility would prove to be huge undertakings, however. These duties kept Yerkes so busy, in fact, that he had relatively little time to do research of his own. According to Donald Dewsbury, a comparative psychologist who has studied the history of the field, Yerkes's most fundamental accomplishment during this time may have been "the demonstration that chimpanzees could be kept successfully, bred, and studied in captivity. Much later progress was possible only because Yerkes invested heavily in housekeeping and developing methods of keeping and caring for chimpanzees."

Yerkes served as director of the laboratory until 1941. Although he was often preoccupied with administrative tasks, other researchers made good use of the facility. Nearly 200 articles from research conducted at the laboratory were published while Yerkes was director there. The most notable studies covered topics such as the role of the brain's frontal lobe, by Carlyle Jacobsen; learning, by Kenneth Spence; morphine addiction, by Shirley Spragg; and mating behavior in chimpanzees, by Yerkes and James Elder.

Yerkes's time at the laboratory was not without controversy, however. As 1939, the renewal date for the Rockefeller Foundation grant approached, the foundation asked several leading scientists to review

Robert Yerkes with young chimps. *(Archives of the History of American Psychology—The University of Akron. Reproduced by permission.)*

the laboratory's progress. The reviewers issued a report that criticized many of the laboratory's policies and practices. First, the foundation had wanted to make sure that researchers from around the country had ready access to the facility. Yerkes preferred to rely on permanent staff, however; many of the reviewers saw this as a sign that he wanted to control the research done there. Second, the scientists took issue with Yerkes's insistence on using the facility to study chimpanzees, which are classified as apes. Chimpanzees are closer relatives of humans than monkeys, but they are also rather difficult to study in captivity. The reviewers felt that monkeys would have been less expensive to raise and equally appropriate for many research purposes. Third, they cited Yerkes's style of observational research, which was out of vogue at the time. In addition, some reviewers were offended by Yerkes's personal style, especially what they interpreted as his need to dominate others.

Eventually, the Rockefeller Foundation did renew its funding, but with a decreasing budget each year. Just when it looked as though the laboratory's days might be numbered, the dean of the Yale Medical School worked out a deal to save the facility. Part of the deal, however, was that Yerkes would retire. Yerkes, who was in his sixties, realized that he had no choice but to comply. Upon his retirement in 1941,

Yale renamed the facility the Yerkes Laboratory of Primate Biology in his honor.

After Yerkes's death, Yale officials decided that the long distance between the university and the Florida laboratory did not allow for the best use of the facility. Emory University, located in Atlanta, took over ownership of the lab. In 1965, the facility was moved to the Emory campus. In 2002, the facility was renamed once again as the Yerkes National Primate Research Center. Today, it is one of eight national primate research centers funded, in part, by the National Center for Research Resources of the National Institutes of Health.

Life after Yale

In 1944, Yerkes also retired from his position as professor at Yale University. The next several years were spent working on an autobiographical book, which he called "The Scientific Way." Unfortunately, the 425-page manuscript was rejected by several publishers, including Yale University Press, where his daughter Roberta was an editor. The book was never published.

Despite this final setback, Yerkes was able to look back over a long and highly productive career. He had received numerous honors, including honorary degrees from Ursinus College and Wesleyan

University and the Gold Medal of the New York Zoological Society. He had also been elected to the National Academy of Sciences, and he had served as president of the American Society of Naturalists. Yerkes died of a heart attack on February 3, 1956, at the age of 79.

THEORIES

In a 1996 article, Dewsbury wrote that Yerkes was "arguably the most important comparative psychologist and psychobiologist of the [twentieth] century." Yerkes is, first and foremost, remembered for his success in establishing the study of nonhuman primates as a field of scientific research. He also made other important contributions to psychology, however, two of which are the Yerkes-Dodson law and major advances in intelligence testing.

Yerkes-Dodson law

Main points   The Yerkes-Dodson law, as originally stated, relates the strength of a stimulus to the speed of avoidance learning. In their research with mice, Yerkes and Dodson used three levels of task difficulty: easy, medium, and hard. They also used three levels of stimulus strength: weak, intermediate, or strong. They found that, if the task was easy, it was learned most quickly when the stimulus was strong. If the task was difficult, however, it was learned most readily when the stimulus was weak.

Specifically, the mice in Yerkes and Dodson's experiment were placed in specially designed boxes. Soon, the mice became cornered; in order to escape, they had to choose between entering either a black passageway or a white one. If they chose the white passageway, they were always allowed to pass through, and they would return to a roomier nest box. If they attempted to enter the black passageway, however, they would always receive an unpleasant electric shock. In this case, then, the stimulus varied with the strength of the shock, and the task difficulty varied depending on how much the two passageways differed from one another in brightness. Each mouse was tested a number of times. The researchers then measured how quickly the mice learned to pick the white passageway every time.

If it was easy to tell the difference between the two passageways, the mice learned to avoid the shock most quickly when the shock was strong. If it was hard to tell the difference, however, they learned fastest when the shock was weak. Yerkes and Dodson concluded that "the relation of the strength of electrical stimulus to

rapidity of learning or habit-formation depends upon the difficultness of the habit, or, in the case of our experiments, upon the conditions of visual discrimination."

Explanation   Yerkes and Dodson's findings languished in relative obscurity for several decades. In the 1950s, however, psychologists introduced the concept of general arousal. They noted that the relationship between arousal and performance tends to take the shape of an upside-down U. A certain amount of arousal is thought to produce the best performance; too much or too little arousal, on the other hand, is detrimental.

Proponents held that the optimal level of arousal varies depending on the difficulty of the task at hand. The level tends to be relatively high for easy tasks and low for difficult ones. Some researchers pointed to Yerkes and Dodson's research as an early demonstration of this principle. It is certainly possible to see getting an electric shock as something that might lead to general arousal. Yerkes and Dodson, however, never used the term arousal in their writings; psychologists applied it to their findings many years later.

Researchers have since tried to study arousal theory in a wide variety of ways. "Arousal" has been correlated with the level of electric shock, threats, incentives, and even as the amount of caffeine in someone's system. Not surprisingly, these diverse studies have yielded mixed results. Some have found the predicted effect on performance, but others have not. Many psychologists now believe that the concept of general arousal is overly broad, since it fails to distinguish between such states as stress, anxiety, fear, motivation, and attention. This limitation does not necessarily reflect poorly on the Yerkes-Dodson law, however. The law can still be taken the way Yerkes and Dodson intended: simply as a description of the relationship between the strength of a stimulus and the speed of avoidance learning.

Examples   Over the years, researchers have tried to use arousal theory to predict people's performance on many kinds of tasks. One example is eyewitness memory. Using the modern restatement of the Yerkes-Dodson law, many researchers have predicted that an increase in emotional arousal from low to moderate levels should improve memory. If arousal increases even more, however, going from moderate to high, memory should start to decline again. This prediction raises an interesting question: Does arousal theory mean that eyewitness testimony is unreliable in situations where emotions run high, such as when someone is the victim of a violent crime or involved in a terrifying car crash?

It might seem logical that high emotion would interfere with memory, but research has shown that this is not necessarily the case. In fact, studies have found that people often remember the details of very emotionally-charged events quite well. While there may indeed be some differences in how emotional events are remembered, the relationship between emotion and memory seems to be more complex than previously thought. It appears to depend on a host of factors, including the nature of the event, the type of details being recalled, the amount of time that has passed, and whether or not there are any cues to jog the person's memory. Overall, there is little reason to believe that emotional arousal automatically impairs the ability to store a memory.

Intelligence testing

Main points   Most of Yerkes's research was done in animals. A detour from this path, however, led to a lasting achievement: the development of the first tests of mental ability designed to be given to large groups of people. This accomplishment paved the way for the mass intelligence testing that is still a very common practice in American schools.

America's entry into World War I was a turning point, not only for the nation, but also for psychology. In *The Mismeasure of Man,* American paleontologist and author Stephen Jay Gould noted that Yerkes

> was a superb organizer, and an eloquent promotor of his profession. Yet psychology still wallowed in its reputation as a "soft" science, if a science at all. Some colleges did not acknowledge its existence; others ranked it among the humanities and placed psychologists in departments of philosophy.

Yerkes wanted to show that psychology could be not only practical, but also as rigorous as chemistry or physics. The new field of intelligence testing seemed to be a fast track to both of these goals.

Yerkes had some background in the field. He and his colleagues had just devised a method for converting the Binet-Simon test into a point scale. He also benefited from the assistance of several leading experts on intelligence testing. Nevertheless, the task he took on was Herculean. In very short order, he and his committee devised two new tests for use with Army recruits. Unlike previous intelligence tests, these assessments would be given to large groups of men at one time, rather than to each person individually.

The Alpha test was designed for men who could read and write. It included arithmetic problems, word pairs to be rated as synonyms or antonyms, number sequences to be completed, scrambled sentences to be unscrambled, analogies, and multiple-choice questions that drew on general knowledge or "common sense."

The Beta test, in contrast, was intended for men who could not read and write English. This group included not only recruits with learning problems, but also recent immigrants and those with a limited education. Men who took the Beta test were asked to trace the path through mazes, find the missing element in pictures, imagine how pictured shapes might be fitted together, and substitute symbols for numbers in a code. Each test took less than an hour to complete and could be given to a large group all at once.

Test scores were reported using letter grades from A to E, including pluses and minuses. The grade of A was said to indicate "a high officer type when backed up by other necessary qualities." B indicated "splendid sergeant material," and C indicated a "good private type." On the other hand, men who scored D, while usually fair soldiers, were thought to be unsuited for tasks requiring much skill, planning, or alertness. Those whose scored E were deemed unfit for regular Army service.

The tests had been cobbled together very quickly, with little time for refining the tasks and procedures. The rushed development may well have reduced the tests' accuracy and reliability. Aware of this problem, Yerkes and his colleagues said that men who received low scores on the Alpha test should be retested on the Beta. Those who got low scores on the Beta should be retested using an individual intelligence test. When this policy was followed, test scores tended to rise on each retesting. Given the realities of wartime mobilization, however, the policy was ignored more often than not. Most men were hurried through a single testing session, the results of which stayed with them for the rest of their military careers.

It is unclear just how much the Army actually relied on Yerkes's tests. There seems to have been some skepticism about the results. There also was some resentment of the testing program, which took up valuable space and time. According to Gould, "Yerkes's corps encountered hostility in some camps; in others, they suffered a penalty in many ways more painful: they were treated politely, given appropriate facilities, and then ignored." In addition, a second Army testing program headed by psychologist Walter Dill Scott divided the available resources. Some observers claimed that Scott's program was more useful.

Explanation   In the decades since the war, Yerkes's testing methods have continued to draw criticism. For one thing, several items on his tests seemed to be biased toward members of the majority American culture. Men taking the Alpha test were expected to know that Overland cars were made in Toledo, Crisco was a food product, and Christy Mathewson was a famous baseball player. Those taking the Beta test were asked to notice the missing details in pictures of a tennis court, a person bowling, and a phonograph. Clearly, anyone from outside mainstream, middle-class America might have been at an unfair disadvantage on such items.

Another problem was the difference in the way directions were given for the Alpha and Beta tests. Men taking the Alpha test were given a clear verbal explanation about the purpose of the testing. Relatively complete written directions were also printed on the Alpha test forms. In contrast, men taking the Beta test were told nothing about test's purpose. The directions for various tasks were barked out in very brief commands. The intent was to overcome the language barrier for recent immigrants. The real effect, however, was probably that many recruits felt totally bewildered.

The instruction manual for the tests was quite detailed. As a result, it is possible to very closely reconstruct the suggested test procedures. The clipped commands and gestures used when giving the Beta test sometimes seem to border on slapstick. For example, Gould has cited these instructions given for a picture completion task: " 'This is test 6 here. Look. A lot of pictures.' After everyone has found the place, 'Now watch.' Examiner points to hand and says to demonstrator, 'Fix it.' Demonstrator does nothing, but looks puzzled. Examiner points to the picture of the hand, and then to the place where the finger is missing and says to the demonstrator, 'Fix it; fix it.' Demonstrator then draws in finger. Examiner says, 'That's right . . .' " After a few more demonstrations, the examiner says, " 'All right. Go ahead. Hurry up!' During the course of this test the orderlies walk around the room and locate individuals who are doing nothing, point to their pages and say, 'Fix it. Fix them.' " After three minutes, the examiner announces that time is up.

While the Beta test did not require reading, it did require the ability to use a pencil and a knowledge of numbers. For people with no formal education, these requirements were often a big hurdle. In addition, different Army camps seemed to use different criteria for deciding which men would take the Alpha test and which would take the Beta. Finally, although the Army was supposed to provide an adequate building at each camp for the testing, this was not always realistic. Often, the tests wound up being given in cramped rooms in which the men sitting in the back had difficulty seeing or hearing the examiner.

It seems likely that many recruits did not perform their best under such stressful conditions. To demonstrate this point, Gould tried giving the Beta test to a modern group of 53 students at Harvard University. He stuck to Yerkes's procedure as closely as possible. These students had a couple of advantages over the World War I recruits, however: They knew what was happening, and they did not have the pressure of real-life consequences riding on their results. Nevertheless, more than 10% of students from one of the world's leading universities scored just a C, meaning they would have been seen as mentally fit for no higher a rank than private.

For actual World War I soldiers, scores on both the Alpha and Beta tests did tend to agree overall with officers' ratings of their men's intelligence. There was also a lower but still moderate association between test scores and actual military performance. What is true for a whole group of men, however, is not necessarily so for any particular individual. The tests probably underrated the intelligence of many men who simply did not understand what was expected of them. In general, the tests seem to have been most accurate for literate, native-born Americans.

The end of the war brought Yerkes's testing program to an abrupt halt. Yerkes claimed that his test had helped to win the war, but not everyone agreed. Some critics argued that there were too many flaws in the tests for the results to be meaningful. But while the tests may not have won the war, they certainly helped Yerkes score a victory. If nothing else, he had introduced the idea of intelligence testing on a large scale.

Examples After the war, Yerkes began to sort through the mountain of data that had been collected. He soon reached some questionable conclusions that led to much public debate. The first dealt with the average mental age for Army recruits; Yerkes claimed it was shockingly low: just over age 13. This mental age was thought to be barely above the cutoff for mild mental retardation. The supposed decline in national intelligence became a rallying cry for eugenicists. They argued that the nation's declining intelligence was due to unfettered breeding by the poor, the feeble-minded, non-whites, and immigrants. It became all too easy to twist such "science" into bigotry.

Of course, Yerkes himself might have helped to set the record straight. He could have pointed out that problems with the hastily thrown-together tests could have led to faulty data. In fact, there were clear signs that this was true. For example, an unusually large number of men scored zero on parts of the Army intelligence tests, indicating that they simply did not understand the instructions.

Instead, Yerkes adopted the eugenicist view. Gould quotes Yerkes as saying that an average mental

Konrad Lorenz followed by a row of young geese. *(Photo Researchers, Inc. Reproduced by permission.)*

age of 13 only confirmed "that the average man can manage his affairs with only a moderate degree of prudence, can earn only a very modest living, and is vastly better off when following directions than when trying to plan for himself." Furthermore, Yerkes believed that this low level of intelligence was due to genetics and therefore unchangeable. Trying to help the average man improve his lot in life was just a wasted effort. As Yerkes put it, "much of our effort to change conditions is unintelligent because we have not understood the nature of the average man."

Yerkes reached two other controversial conclusions. He noted that blacks and recent immigrants tended to score lower on the Army intelligence tests than native-born whites did. Once again, it might have been sensible to conclude that the tests were biased toward members of the majority culture. In fact, there were strong hints that group differences in test scores reflected differences in life experiences. For example, there were many more black recruits than white ones who had not attended school. Looking back, it seems logical that social conditions—such as racial discrimination and poor conditions in black schools—may have led to fewer educational opportunities for blacks. Less education, in turn, probably hurt black recruits' performance on the tests.

Yet Yerkes chose to put a eugenicist spin on the numbers. He believed that less schooling among

blacks simply meant that they were not as inclined toward education as whites. Critics such as Gould have since noted that Yerkes ignored his own data on this point. There were regional differences in schooling, with evidence of wider educational opportunities for blacks in the northern states than in the southern ones. In turn, black recruits from some northern states tended to score higher on the Army tests than either southern blacks or southern whites.

Some of Yerkes's conclusions about the test scores of recent immigrants now seem equally dubious. When Yerkes broke down the test results by country of origin, he found that recruits whose ancestors came from the "Nordic" countries of northern Europe tended to score higher than those of "Slavic" or "Latin" ancestry. This finding suited the views of racial supremacists quite well, since they believed in the superiority of Nordic peoples. But Yerkes glossed over one key fact: Most immigrants from the Slavic and Latin countries of eastern and southern Europe had arrived in the United States only recently. Many, therefore, did not speak English well. In contrast, the main wave of immigration from northern Europe had passed years before. Most recruits from those countries were already fluent in English, an obvious advantage when taking the tests.

Yerkes also found that the average test scores for foreign-born recruits rose the longer they had lived in the United States. This result held true regardless of

BIOGRAPHY:
Konrad Lorenz

Konrad Lorenz (1903–89), an Austrian naturalist, was one of the founders of ethology. This field, which has sometimes been described as the biological study of behavior, sprang up in Europe in the first half of the twentieth century. Its emphasis was on observing animals in natural surroundings, although Lorenz worked largely with captive animals.

Lorenz's father was a physician who wanted his son to follow in his footsteps. While young Lorenz obediently earned a medical degree, he soon realized that his true love was animals. He returned to school, and in 1933, he received a Ph.D. in zoology from the University of Vienna.

Soon thereafter, Lorenz began the work for which he is best known. At his family's home in Altenberg, Austria, he spent summers studying the behavior of greylag geese. Lorenz observed that the geese lived a family existence that was in many ways similar to human family life. Lorenz also identified the process of imprinting, in which a young animal that is exposed to a foster "mother" in place of its real mother during a critical period in development will become attached to the substitute. Lorenz raised goslings that, removed from their real mother, accepted him as their mother figure. The scientist was often seen walking down a path or rowing a boat with a line of goslings following behind. Lorenz also found that mallard ducklings would imprint on him, but only if he squatted down and quacked.

Lorenz theorized that animals have fixed-action patterns, genetically programmed behavior patterns that remain dormant until a specific stimulus triggers them. In birds, fish, and insects, such critical behaviors as courtship, nesting, and caring for the young are, to a large extent, fixed-action patterns. In mammals, and especially in humans, behavior is more modifiable and dependent on learning. Nevertheless, Lorenz believed that fixed-action patterns still play a role. In 1973, Lorenz received the Nobel Prize in Physiology or Medicine. He shared the prize with two other founders of ethology: Nikolaas Tinbergen, a Dutch-born zoologist who helped develop the theory of fixed-action patterns; and Karl von Frisch, an Austrian zoologist who studied the communication system of bees.

---

their country of origin. In hindsight, this seems to be a clear sign that test scores were tied to people's knowledge of the English language and familiarity with American culture. In other words, it was strong evidence for an environmental influence on intelligence test scores. Yerkes himself acknowledged the possibility when he wrote, "At best we can but leave for future decision the question as to whether the differences [in scores] represent a real difference in intelligence or an artifact of the method of examination."

Yet many eugenicists chose to see the same data as evidence for a genetic difference in intelligence among groups of people. They used this viewpoint to argue for restrictions on immigration. Gould is one of many later critics who have decried the eugenicists' misuse of scientific data. In *The Mismeasure of Man,* he wrote:

> The army mental tests could have provided an impetus for social reform . . . Again and again, the data pointed to strong correlations between test scores and the environment. Again and again, those who wrote and administered the tests invented tortuous, ad hoc explanations to preserve their hereditarian prejudices.

Comparative psychology
Main points Yerkes's work on the Army intelligence tests had considerable impact on society at large. In the context of Yerkes's career, however, this work was really a sidelight. His main area of interest was always comparative psychology. In this area, Yerkes made his most important contributions to science. Today, he is remembered mainly for his research on nonhuman primates. Early in his career, though, he also studied learning in mice, turtles, green crabs, frogs, and crawfish.

Comparative psychology is a branch of psychology that studies animal behavior and frequently makes comparisons among species. Beyond that, however, there have never been clear-cut boundary lines between comparative psychology and other kinds of animal research. In common practice, the study of learning, motivation, and memory in animals—especially rats, monkeys, and pigeons—is now often categorized as experimental psychology. The study of physiological aspects of behavior in humans and other animals is often categorized as physiological psychol-ogy. Other kinds of psychological research on animal behavior have traditionally fallen under the heading of comparative psychology.

In the 1930s and 40s, ethology sprang up as another new discipline. This closely related field also studied animal behavior, but from a more biologically oriented point of view. Ethologists tended to be trained in zoology and based in Europe (see accompa-nying sidebar). Their research—focused mainly on birds, fish, and insects—was conducted in the field, where they could observe animals in their natural environment. Ethologists were typically focused on studying instinctive behavior and the evolution of behavioral patterns. Comparative psychologists, on the other hand, tended to be trained in psychology and based in North America. Their research—focused mainly on mammals—was done in laboratories or research centers, where the psychologists could control experimental variables and gather data for statistical analysis. Comparative psychologists were often interested in developing general theories of behavior and learning.

Yerkes played a big role in shaping the prevailing view of what comparative psychology should be. He always believed strongly in the importance of doing experiments under controlled laboratory conditions. He also believed however, that it was critical to under-stand an animal's natural habits and instincts. Therefore, when ethology began to emerge as a new field, Yerkes welcomed it enthusiastically.

For Yerkes, the study of animal behavior was only a means to the end of understanding human psychology. Over the years, he became fond of some of the chim-panzees he studied. Yet for him, animals were always just stand-ins for humans. He believed that any knowl-edge gained from studying animals should be used to serve humanity through better education and breeding—a policy he referred to as "human engineering."

Explanation   Early in his career, Yerkes helped break new ground in comparative and experimental psychology. For example, his book *The Dancing Mouse: A Study in Animal Behavior* was one of the earliest studies of behavioral genetics. Yerkes also studied sensory function, learning, and problem solving in several species. In addition, he collaborated with John B. Watson, the father of behaviorism, to develop new methods for the study of color vision. Later, he studied sexual, social, and maternal behavior in primates. Beyond that, Yerkes was an extraordinary organizer, administrator, and promoter of large-scale research projects. In a book titled *Comparative*

Psychology in the Twentieth Century, Dewsbury concluded that "no one made a more substantial or more sustained contribution to comparative psychol-ogy than Robert Mearns Yerkes."

Yet Yerkes also had significant failings as a scien-tist. His later research with chimpanzees, in particular, was often colored by his personal biases—especially his research on family groups and gender roles. For example, Yerkes interpreted the social groups formed by captive chimpanzees at the Yale research facility as evidence of unchanging family bonds. Later researchers studying chimps in the wild, however, such as noted English zoologist Jane Goodall, have found a different pattern. Under natural conditions, chimpanzee clusters tend to break apart and then regroup on a regular basis. This fact was not known until after Yerkes's time, however. Working without benefit of such knowledge, Yerkes seems to have imposed his own sense of family values onto what he observed among the chimpanzees.

Yerkes's opinions about gender roles also seem to have affected his research. In experiments with chim-panzees, Yerkes concluded that males were normally dominant over their female partners. Males granted special privilege to females during estrus, however, the phase of the chimpanzee menstrual cycle when females are most receptive to mating. Thus male dominance was seen as natural, and any special privilege that a female might gain was bestowed on her by the male only in return for sex.

Examples   The studies that Yerkes conducted to find this supposed effect have not held up well to scientific scrutiny. In a so-called food chute test, Yerkes put male-female chimpanzee pairs into a cage. He then dropped pieces of banana into the cage through a chute. The experimenter recorded which chimpanzee got the food and observed how the animals interacted. Yerkes reported that the males usually got the food. When the females were in estrus, however, the males allowed the females to have the food. As Yerkes explained in his book *Chimpanzees: A Laboratory Colony*:

> The behavioral picture is clear-cut. A male who previ-ously has completely controlled the situation and taken the food time after time as if it were a matter of course yields without protest, although possibly somewhat reluctantly, to the female when, at the beginning of genital swelling and willingness to mate, she claims the food. Thereafter as long as she is sexu-ally receptive and also acceptable to her mate, she may if she so desires continue to control the food-getting situation without competition or conflict. But

the very day detumescence [the subsiding of genital swelling] begins, the behavior of the males changes . . .

Despite Yerkes's claim, however, the results do not seem to be clear-cut at all. Critics have pointed out several weaknesses in the design and analysis of the food-chute study. For one thing, Yerkes chose to use menstrual cycles rather than pairs of chimpanzees as his unit of statistical analysis. From a statistical point of view, this choice was problematic. From a theoretical point of view, it showed a tendency to see the animals as interchangeable parts rather than distinct individuals.

An even bigger problem may have been the way Yerkes tended to ignore any results that did not confirm his ideas. Although Yerkes used several chimpanzee pairs in his study, he focused mainly on the results from one pair, Jack and Josie, who showed the expected pattern in their relationship. Yerkes found reasons to discount the findings from other pairs that showed the relationship less definitely and completely.

Such selective use of data—using those results that support the researcher's hypothesis and throwing out the rest—goes against the basic principles of science. In a 1998 article, Dewsbury noted that some modern primate researchers have come to refer to the practice jokingly as the "Yerkes transformation." Yet there is no evidence that Yerkes himself thought he was doing anything wrong. To the contrary, he presented a full account of his results as well as his reasoning for ignoring most of them. Given the similar problems with Yerkes's intelligence test work, it seems possible that he simply failed to keep pace with new developments in statistical analysis. It is also possible that his personal biases were so strong that he deluded himself about the appropriateness of his methods.

Later scientists still have not settled some of the issues raised by Yerkes. For example, Goodall observed that females were indeed groomed more often and were more successful at begging food during the estrus phase. Other scientists, however, have found no difference in male-female food sharing during estrus compared to other times. Dewsbury concluded that "recent data do not resolve either the issue of dominance reversals [during estrus] or the replicability of the effect described by Yerkes."

HISTORICAL CONTEXT

The informal observation of animal behavior is as old as humanity. Animals have been the subjects of systematic study since at least the time of the ancient Greeks. During the early years of the twentieth century, however, the study of animal behavior became more experimental in nature. Rather than just observing animals in the field, psychologists were now researching their behavior in laboratories, where conditions could be precisely controlled. It was a heady time for comparative and experimental psychology. Yerkes was one of the pioneers who helped map out this new direction.

Birth of a new discipline

Yerkes was a college student during the 1890s, the same decade in which comparative psychology first emerged as a separate discipline. In 1894, German philosopher-psychologist Wilhelm Wundt published his *Lectures on Human and Animal Psychology,* which helped establish animal research as a respectable field of study. That same year, British psychologist C. Lloyd Morgan published *An Introduction to Comparative Psychology,* which helped to set the agenda for animal studies to come. Among other topics, Morgan discussed habit formation and instinctive behavior.

In the late 1890s, at Clark University, Linus Kline and William S. Small began work that led to the first psychological studies of rats navigating mazes. Around the same time, at Harvard University, Edward L. Thorndike produced his classic thesis, "Animal Intelligence: An Experimental Study of the Associative Processes in Animals." Most of Thorndike's thesis dealt with learning in dogs, cats, and chicks. During this decade, then, the groundwork was laid for the kind of research on animal learning that would become so important in future decades.

By 1899, courses in comparative psychology were being taught at the University of Chicago and Clark University. Both Clark and Harvard University also had laboratories devoted to the field. The stage had been set for a period of rapid growth and progress, and Yerkes was poised to help lead the charge into the twentieth century.

The first years of the new century were a golden age in comparative psychology. In an article in *American Psychologist,* Dewsbury outlined three core issues that were explored during this period: the evolution of instinctive behaviors, the relationship between behavior and development, and the nature of intelligence and other higher mental processes. These issues are still at the heart of comparative psychology today. In fact, according to Dewsbury, "one might argue that all of 20th-century comparative psychology is but a footnote to this period and a series of attempts to resolve issues that were brought into focus at this time."

By the early 1900s, a whole generation of comparative psychologists was being trained at universities around the country. Early on, comparative psychology appeared to be headed for a central role in the still-young science of psychology. The leading psychologists of the day were eager to show that psychology was every bit as scientific as chemistry or physics. Comparative psychology, with its close ties to biology, seemed to be custom-made for this purpose. Soon, however, the tide began to turn. Psychologists started to focus on proving their usefulness by finding practical applications for their work. As Yerkes himself found during his tenure at Harvard, applied psychology became the surest path to job advancement. Comparative psychology suddenly seemed much less appealing to ambitious young psychologists.

Comparative psychology survived the crisis. For several decades, it served as a training ground for psychologists who went on to work in other fields. By the 1930s, comparative psychology had re-established itself as a separate discipline, although it never recovered the brief prominence it had enjoyed at the turn of the century. Today, it remains a relatively small specialty; it does overlap considerably with other fields, however, such as experimental psychology, physiological psychology, neuroscience, and ethology.

Key issues in comparative psychology

In the field's infancy, comparative psychologists needed to choose their ultimate goal. Should they study animal behavior for its own sake? Or should the overriding goal always be to shed light on human behavior? Early comparative psychologists quickly took sides on this issue, and some even kept one foot in both camps. For example, in the late 1890s, Kline designed a laboratory course at Clark University where the students studied animal instincts and habits, regardless of any relevance to humans. At the same time, however, Kline studied other animal behaviors from a decidedly human point of view. For example, he studied "the migratory impulse vs. love of home" in both humans and nonhuman animals.

Yerkes came down on the side of using animal research to reach insights into human psychology. This approach has sometimes come under attack, however. Some critics have argued that it blinds scientists to the true nature of other species, encouraging them to see animals merely as convenient stand-ins for humans. Others have argued that it may obscure the true essence of humanity, since it makes it harder to see which behaviors humans really do share with other animals and which are uniquely or primarily human.

Another critical issue in the early days of comparative psychology was deciding which species to study. Early comparative psychologists tended to study a wide range of animals. For example, Kline's course covered amebae, earthworms, slugs, fish, chicks, rats, and cats. By the 1920s, however, laboratory rats had become by far the most popular subjects. Fairly or not, comparative psychology earned a reputation as rat psychology. This reputation has proved hard to shake, despite the efforts of psychologists, including Yerkes, who extended their research to other species.

Yet another issue that needed to be settled was whether comparative psychology would be conducted in a laboratory or in the field. Laboratory studies had the advantage of offering greater control, although it was hard to say how the artificial setting might affect the results. Field studies offered a glimpse at more natural behavior, but the uncontrolled circumstances made it hard to sort out causes and effects. Laboratory research has largely won out in psychology. The laboratory studies of comparative psychologists have been complemented over the years, however, by the field observations of zoologists.

Evolution of instinctive behaviors

At the dawn of the twentieth century, the new field of comparative psychology was being heavily influenced by British naturalist Charles Darwin's theory of evolution. In 1872, Darwin had published a book titled *The Expression of the Emotions in Man and Animals* that was a forerunner of later writings on comparative psychology. In this book, Darwin suggested that many expressions of emotion are genetically based rather than learned. As such, they are the product of evolution, and their roots can be traced back to humankind's shared past with other animals. Therefore, neither emotions nor their expression are uniquely human. Darwin believed that other animals may experience some of the same emotions as humans. These animals also may display those emotions in ways that resemble the facial expressions and gestures of people.

Today, scientists are divided on whether Darwin was right about this matter. Some prefer to consider the expressions of animals strictly as communication signals. Others have no qualms about attributing emotions to animals. Even among the latter group of scientists, however, there is no clear agreement about which emotions animals feel, and whether the animals experience those feelings in the same way as humans do.

Whatever the final verdict on emotions in animals, Darwin's ideas raised a crucial question: Should humans be seen as just one species among many? Or should they be seen as unique and distinct from other animals? Many comparative psychologists, who wanted to draw parallels from animal to human behavior, took the first position. Wundt, for instance, wrote that "the mental life of animals shows itself to be throughout, in all its elements and in the general laws governing the combination of the elements, the same as the mental life of man." Others, however, cautioned against anthropomorphism—ascribing human thoughts and feelings to nonhuman animals.

Darwin also wrote about the process of natural selection, in which the fittest members of a species tended to survive longer and produce more offspring than other members. In the post-Darwin era, scientists began to look for genetically programmed behavior patterns that might aid survival. Such patterns, which develop without the need for learning, are known as instinctive behaviors. For example, Morgan studied newborn chicks and ducklings hatched in an incubator. He found that pecking, walking, scratching, preening, stretching up and clapping the wings, scattering and crouching when alarmed, and making a danger sound were all inborn behavior patterns. Chicks and ducklings arrived in the world already programmed to display such behaviors, although they sometimes needed practice to reach a high level of skill.

The evolution of behavior remains a core concept in comparative psychology to this day. While most psychologists now accept that some behaviors are instinctive, they also stress that the way these behaviors are expressed can be affected by development and experiences.

Animal learning as lab science

Morgan also studied the way animals learned brand-new behavior patterns that, like instinctive behaviors, became automatic and unconscious. He called this process habit formation. Morgan was mainly interested in answering two questions: how a new behavior pattern was learned in the first place and how it became automatic afterward. He broached a number of topics that later became central to comparative psychology. These topics included the role, if any, of consciousness in guiding animal behavior, the effect of imitation on learning, and the process of learning by trial and error.

Inspired by Morgan, turn-of-the-century scientists such as Thorndike, Small, and Kline began transferring the study of animal learning into the laboratory. In his groundbreaking thesis on animal intelligence, Thorndike defined intelligence in terms of an animal's

ability to form new mental associations. He also described ingenious devices for studying animal learning and showed how they could be used in controlled research. For example, he constructed puzzle boxes for cats and then studied their behavior as they attempted to escape.

Earlier psychologists, writing about human thought and learning, had also focused on associations. For them, however, this meant the association of ideas or mental processes with one another. In contrast, Thorndike viewed associations as links between the situation in which an organism found itself and the organism's impulse to act. This view was an important step toward the behaviorists' concept of learning as the association between a stimulus and a response.

Around the same time, Russian physiologist Ivan Pavlov was studying the digestive systems of dogs. He noticed that dogs would salivate when they saw their keeper, apparently in anticipation of being fed. This observation led him to perform a classic series of experiments. Pavlov showed that, by repeated association, a previously neutral stimulus (such as a bell) could be substituted for a natural stimulus (such as food) to produce a natural response (such as salivation). This process became known as classical conditioning. Pavlov's work was first published in his native Russian. In 1909, Yerkes and Sergius Morgulis coauthored a paper that brought Pavlov's ideas to an English-speaking audience.

Thorndike's and Pavlov's theories laid the groundwork for the behaviorist revolution, led by Watson starting in 1913. Watson wanted to remove consciousness from the realm of psychology. Instead, he believed that psychology should focus strictly on behavior. Watson held that most behavior was the direct result of stimuli in the environment. In a nutshell, behavior that led to positive consequences was rewarded and continued, while behavior that led to negative responses was eliminated.

Later in his career, Watson began to focus more on the implications of behaviorism for humans. In the early years, however, he was concerned mainly with animal behavior, including behavior that was instinctive as well as learned. With Yerkes, Watson developed new methods for the study of color vision in animals. With psychologist Karl Lashley, he collaborated on studying terns, a type of sea bird, found on a cluster of islands off the coast of Florida.

As behaviorism took a more extreme turn in the coming decades, it branched off from comparative psychology. Eventually, the radical behaviorism of B.F. Skinner became so popular that behaviorist-based experimental psychology eclipsed its comparative cousin. It is worth noting, though, that the two disciplines grew up side by side in the first decades of the twentieth century. In fact, when the *Journal of Animal Behavior* was founded in 1911, Yerkes became the journal's editor, and Watson became the editor of an associated monograph series. Watson himself championed Yerkes for the editor's position, saying "there is no one else to do it who has the courage, the orderliness, and the persistence."

CRITICAL RESPONSE

Yerkes won many accolades over the years. He also received his share of criticism, however. The most serious charge was that he let his personal beliefs and feelings override his objectivity. In work on group intelligence testing during World War I, Yerkes was criticized for the racial and ethnic bias that seemed to distort his analysis. In research on primate behavior, he was taken to task for the gender stereotypes that seemed to sway his findings.

Group differences in intelligence

Yerkes reached three controversial conclusions based on data gathered with the Army intelligence tests. First, he claimed that the average mental age in the United States was a mere 13 years. Second, he said there were genetically based racial differences in intelligence, with whites outperforming blacks. Third, he said there were also genetically based ethnic differences in intelligence within the white population, with individuals whose ancestors came from northern Europe surpassing those from southern or eastern Europe. In an article quoted by Dewsbury, Yerkes wrote:

> If we may safely judge by the army measurements of intelligence, races are quite as significantly different as individuals . . . Almost as great as the intellectual difference between Negro and white in the army are the differences between white racial groups.

Yerkes published his massive report on these findings in 1921. Two years later, Carl Brigham, a young psychologist who had been one of Yerkes's assistants, published his own book on the subject. Titled *A Study of American Intelligence,* Brigham's book repeated many of the same claims made by Yerkes. Brigham also noted that immigration from southern and eastern Europe had been increasing in recent years. Based on the eugenicist views that he and Yerkes shared, and that were common at the time, Brigham warned that growing numbers of presumably inferior immigrants would further taint the gene pool

in the United States. He urged that immigration restrictions be imposed before it was too late.

The next year, Congress passed the Immigration Act of 1924, which limited the number of immigrants who could enter the country. Strict quotas were set for each national group. Since the quotas were based on the makeup of the U.S. population in 1890, before the recent wave of immigration from southern and eastern Europe, the quotas for those areas were quite low. Public sentiment against immigration was strong enough that the bill probably would have passed in any case. Nevertheless, the support of respected psychologists such as Yerkes and Brigham certainly bolstered the cause.

Even at the time, however, their conclusions did not go completely unchallenged. Walter Lippman, a columnist for *New Republic* magazine, wrote a series of articles in which he ridiculed Yerkes's claim that the average intelligence of recruits was on par with that of a typical 13-year-old. At the same time, several reviews published in psychology journals commented on Brigham's tendency to neglect or dismiss data that did not agree with his interpretations. They also noted statistical oddities that called into question the validity of the data.

The strongest challenge, however, came from psychologists who embraced the views of Franz Boas, the leading American anthropologist of the time. Boas argued that many racial and ethnic characteristics were passed down from generation to generation not by heredity, but by culture, through shared values, language, and childrearing customs. One of the first researchers to apply this culture concept to group differences in intelligence test scores was Otto Klineberg, a graduate student in psychology who happened to study anthropology with Boas.

In 1926, Klineberg began working on his dissertation. While giving intelligence test items to Yakima Native American children in the state of Washington, Klineberg noticed that the children were almost completely unaware of time. Even when urged to hurry, they still took their time, but they also made relatively few mistakes. Here was a clear example of a cultural, rather than genetic, difference that would put the Yakima children at a disadvantage on any timed intelligence test. Yet it was unrelated to any real difference in mental ability. Instead, it was rooted in cultural values that equated speed with carelessness.

This experience attuned Klineberg to cultural factors affecting intelligence test scores. Soon, he followed up on his dissertation with studies of the psychological characteristics of African Americans and

Native Americans. His 1935 book *Negro Intelligence and Selective Migration* argued that it was superior cultural and environmental advantages that caused northern blacks to score higher on intelligence tests than their southern black counterparts. He found that, when black students moved from racially segregated schools in the South, which usually were poorly funded, to integrated schools in the North, their intelligence test scores tended to improve. In fact, their scores rose to the level of northern-born blacks once they were in the integrated schools.

By the 1930s, most psychologists had conceded that culture and environment played a major role in causing group differences in intelligence test scores. Brigham even admitted that he had overstated the case for genetic differences. He acknowledged that the tests of the day assessed not only pure intelligence, but also knowledge of language and culture. In Brigham's own words (as quoted by Gould): "Comparative studies of various national and racial groups may not be made with existing tests. . .One of the most pretentious of these comparative racial studies—the writer's own—was without foundation."

Gender roles

Yerkes also had firmly traditional views on gender roles. In his unpublished autobiographical book, quoted by Dewsbury, Yerkes wrote that "women are more deeply concerned with the perpetuation of the species than are men; more wrapped up in the problems and chores, privileges and satisfactions of housekeeping." He also believed that, because of innate differences between women and men, "from birth educational practices should be adapted to sex as well as to individual characteristics."

Yerkes's views seem to have influenced the way he ran the Yale Laboratories of Primate Biology. There were no female scientists or students at the facility during his entire time as its director. In the 1930s, a female graduate student named Eleanor Gibson approached Yerkes about working with his chimpanzee colony. Yerkes told her that he did not allow women in his laboratory. This response was undoubtedly his loss, since Gibson went on to do important research on perceptual learning and development.

Critics have charged that Yerkes's ideas about gender roles also may have affected the way he interpreted the results of his chimpanzee studies. In studies of chimpanzee pairs where food was dropped into the cage through a chute, Yerkes claimed that males ordinarily controlled access to the food due to dominance. Females only got to take control when the males

granted them that privilege in return for sex. In *Chimpanzees: A Laboratory Colony*, Yerkes wrote that "the patterns of dominance and privilege differ notably. In the former, action tends to be prompt, clear-cut, decisive, commanding or demanding, while in the latter it more often is delayed, tentative, questioning, or suggestive of inhibition." Yerkes saw the males as naturally more active, and the females as more passive.

In Yerkes's anthropomorphic descriptions of the animals' behavior, the females often sound rather silly, while the males come across as patronizing. Consider this description of Jack and Josie, in which both chimpanzees are trying to gain access to the food chute:

> Presently he came to the chute ready for the experiment. She came also and attempted to take control, but he gently shouldered her to one side . . . Jack did not seem irritated by Josie's assumption of right to take control; instead, by playful, gentle, and good-natured tactics he managed to dominate and have his own way.

Several feminist authors have taken Yerkes to task for his choice of language. They have also objected to the implied message that his findings reveal a broader truth about primate (including human) relationships; namely, that males are naturally dominant and females naturally submissive. For example, in her 1948 book *Adam's Rib,* Ruth Herschberger wrote satirically:

> On March 15, 1939, as Josie stood resolutely beside the food chute, she little realized that she had become representative of all womanhood, a model upon which personnel directors and police captains could in the future base their decisions and argue their case. Nor did her cage-mate, Jack, as he elbowed her gently aside, realize that he was from that moment the incarnation of the dominant male, an inspiration to all humans who sought "friendly masculine ascendancy" over their womenfolk.

THEORIES IN ACTION

Yerkes helped establish comparative psychology as a scientific discipline in its own right. Beyond that, the Army intelligence tests that his committee developed during World War I became the model for future group tests of mental ability. In addition, his studies of chimpanzee behavior laid the groundwork for modern research at nonhuman primate laboratories.

Group tests of mental ability
Research The Army Alpha and Beta tests opened the floodgates to a host of other group tests of mental ability. Today, most U.S. students are assessed with at least one of these tests at some point while in school.

The SAT is just one familiar example. This sort of test is typically given to a whole class of students or group of individuals at once. The test often consists of numerous multiple-choice questions, which are answered on a special answer sheet that can be scored by a machine.

One of the big advantages to such tests is that they are standardized. This means that the tests themselves have undergone extensive testing before ever being used in an actual classroom or other real-life situation. During the development phase, a test is given to a representative sample of individuals under clearly spelled-out conditions, and the results are scored and interpreted according to set criteria. The goal is to establish a standardized method of giving, scoring, and interpreting the test in the future. This helps ensure that as much as possible of the variance in scores will be caused by true differences in ability, and not by differences in the testing procedure.

Norms are also provided to help with the interpretation process. These are the test results gathered from a particular group of test takers during the development phase. The norms can then be used as benchmarks for interpreting individual test scores in the future. Depending on the test, different kinds of norms may be provided. For example, age norms and grade norms indicate the average scores of a group of test takers who are of a certain age or in a particular grade.

The other major advantage to group tests is their efficiency. It might take hundreds of hours for a skilled examiner to administer 100 individual intelligence tests. In contrast, it might take just a few hours to give a group test to an entire roomful of people. Clearly, group testing is much less expensive and time-consuming. In fact, without the development of group tests, intelligence testing would never have become the large-scale industry that it is today.

Group tests also have some disadvantages, however. The group setting makes it impossible to take into account individual factors—such as being sleepy, sick, uncooperative, or anxious—that might affect a person's score, but that have nothing to do with his or her intelligence. The group format also does not allow an examiner to note why a particular answer was chosen or question was skipped. It simply scores how many correct answers were chosen. No distinction is made between questions that were missed because the person simply did not know the answer and those that were missed because the person could not read them, did not understand them, or simply was taking his or her time in an effort to avoid careless mistakes.

Another drawback relates to the multiple-choice format that these tests favor. Multiple-choice questions may call for the use of different psychological strategies than the open-ended questions often found on individual tests. For one thing, multiple-choice questions, which are based on the assumption that there is one right answer, may penalize creative thinkers, who often see the same problem from many different angles. Nevertheless, research has shown that scores on the best group tests are generally highly correlated with those on individual tests. In other words, a person who gets a certain score on a group intelligence test is likely to also get a similar score on an individual intelligence test.

The mass testing of mental abilities remains controversial. Yet many organizations have concluded that the pros outweigh the cons. Group tests assessing various mental abilities have become a fixture in American society. These are just a few common examples:

- Multidimensional Aptitude Battery. This is a test of general thinking ability, designed to be given to groups of adolescents or adults. It is an adaptation of the Wechsler Adult Intelligence Scale–Revised (WAIS–R), the most widely used individual test of adult intelligence.

- Cognitive abilities tests. These are two distinct group tests designed to assess the general mental ability of schoolchildren.

- SAT. This is a test of general scholastic ability that is used to help colleges make decisions about which students to admit.

- Graduate Record Examinations (GRE). These scholastic ability tests are used to make graduate school admission and placement decisions.

- Armed Services Vocational Aptitude Battery. This is an example of a test that attempts to measure several specific aptitudes. It is used to screen military recruits and help place them in appropriate jobs.

- General Aptitude Test Battery. This test also assesses several aptitudes. It was developed by the U.S. Department of Labor and is currently used by the U.S. Employment Service to help guide job placements.

Certainly, a huge amount of data has been amassed over the years on the validity and reliability of various group intelligence tests. In addition, great strides have been made in the way such tests are standardized and normalized. Nevertheless, the underlying philosophy and basic procedures for most group tests still bear a strong family resemblance to their ancestor: Yerkes's World War I Army tests.

The SAT   While all group intelligence tests owe a debt to Yerkes, one test has a more direct link to him.

The original version of the modern SAT was developed by Brigham, Yerkes's junior colleague in the Army testing program. Soon after the war, Brigham began adapting the Army Alpha test for use in screening college applicants. In the 1920s, Brigham first tried out his new test on freshman at Princeton University and applicants to the Cooper Union, an all-scholarship college in New York City.

Several years earlier, in 1900, the College Entrance Examination Board had been founded. The board was set up by the presidents of a dozen leading universities, who sought to simplify the application process for the benefit of both prospective students and admissions officers. In order to do that, the board wanted to devise a common entrance exam that could be used by all the universities. That way, an applicant would have to take only one entrance exam, rather than a separate test for each school to which he or she applied. At first, the exam consisted of essay tests in specific subject areas. When the board heard about Brigham's research, however, they put him in charge of a committee, which was asked to develop a test that could be used by a broad range of colleges as an objective measure of academic potential. The test also needed to streamline the admissions process and level the playing field for students from a wide variety of backgrounds.

In 1926, Brigham's test, which later came to be known as the SAT, was given to high-school students for the first time. Then, in 1933, officials of Harvard University set out to find a way of evaluating candidates for a new scholarship program. The program was intended to help academically gifted young men who had not graduated from the elite Eastern boarding college preparatory schools that supplied most of Harvard's students. The officials settled on Brigham's test, because they thought it measured pure intelligence rather than the quality of a student's high-school education. By the late 1930s, the SAT was being used as a scholarship test by all of the prestigious Ivy League schools.

Use of the SAT soon spread beyond its Ivy League roots, and the test remains very widely used today. In fact, in 2003, a record 1.4 million high school seniors took it. Yet, in spite of—or perhaps because of—the SAT's popularity, the test has been a lightning rod for controversy over the decades. Critics have charged that the test systemically underestimates the academic ability of females, applicants over age 25, and those whose first language is not English. In addition, some studies have shown that the SAT does not predict college performance—such as freshman grades, undergraduate class rank, college graduation rates, or attainment of a graduate degree—as well for black students as it does for white ones.

In general, studies have shown that high school grades are better predictors of college grades than SAT scores are. The SAT still does a fair job of predicting how well a college freshman will perform, however. When SAT scores and high school grades are both used, their combined predictive ability is slightly better than that of grades alone. One problem with using grades alone is that they are less comparable, since they may reflect not only a student's ability, but also the difficulty of the courses the student has taken and the standards of the school. On the other hand, SAT scores alone can not reveal anything about a student's motivation or work habits. Therefore, most psychologists currently recommend that, if SAT scores are used at all, they should be combined with grades, portfolios, or other evidence of academic potential.

As an interesting aside, it is worth noting that a version of the SAT introduced in 2005 includes a new essay-writing section. In part, then, the test has come full circle. Yerkes and his followers introduced the idea that large groups of people could be tested and compared quickly using objective methods. Many people still believe that group tests can be quite useful as an efficient screening tool. Even advocates of this approach recognize that it has its limits, however. To fully assess any individual's capabilities, it is necessary to look at other dimensions besides a test score.

Case studies   Several colleges and universities have studied the validity of the SAT. The aim of such studies is to measure the predictive power of SAT scores for that particular college's student body. The College Board (the current name for the College Entrance Examination Board) encourages such research through its Validity Study Service. The service itself has come under fire in recent years however. Critics claim that it encourages the use of flawed research methods that overstate the SAT's benefits.

Nevertheless, validity research at individual institutions has generally found that the SAT has relatively weak predictive ability. The National Center for Fair and Open Testing (nicknamed FairTest), an organization that opposes the misuse of standardized testing, has documented some of the less encouraging results. For example, researchers at the University of Pennsylvania looked at high-school class rank, scores on the SAT I (the main test), and scores on the SAT II (optional subject area tests). They compared all these factors to students' cumulative grade point average (GPA) in college. The researchers found that the SAT I was the poorest predictor of all, explaining a mere 4% of the

CHRONOLOGY

1876: Born on May 26 in Breadysville, Pennsylvania.

1897: Graduates from Ursinus College in Pennsylvania.

1898: Earns an A.B. degree from Harvard University.

1902: Receives a Ph.D. in psychology from Harvard.

1902–1917: Teaches comparative psychology at Harvard.

1908: Publishes the Yerkes-Dodson law, developed with John Dodson, which related the strength of a stimulus to the speed of avoidance learning.

1911: Founds the *Journal of Animal Behavior*, the first U.S. scientific journal devoted solely to animal behavior research.

1913–1917: Works half-time as a psychologist in the Psychopathic Department at Boston State Hospital.

1915: Introduces a point scale for measuring intelligence, developed with J.W. Bridges.

1917: Elected president of the American Psychological Association. Became a member of the National Research Council.

1917–1918: Chairs a committee that developed the Army Alpha and Beta intelligence tests during World War I.

1919–1924: Works for the National Research Council.

1923–1924: Raises a bonobo and a chimpanzee in his home.

1924–1944: Holds a post as professor of psychobiology at Yale University.

1929: Publishes *The Great Apes: A Study of Anthropoid Life*, coauthored with his wife, Ada Watterson Yerkes.

1929–1941: Founds and directs the Yale Laboratories of Primate Biology, the first laboratory for nonhuman primate research in the United States.

1956: Dies on February 3.

variation in college grades. The best predictor was high-school class rank, but it still explained just 9% of changes in cumulative GPA. Even when SAT scores and class rank were combined, they accounted for only 11% of the variation, failing to explain almost 90% of the variation in college grades.

Relevance to modern readers High-stakes tests are tests that are used to make major decisions about a student, such as promotion to the next grade, graduation from high school, or admission to college. The use of standardized tests for such purposes started with Brigham's SAT, and it has grown to massive proportions over the decades. The No Child Left Behind Act of 2001 promised to spur even more growth in the mass testing movement. The act required that each state give standardized tests of language arts and mathematics to all third- and eighth-graders by 2005. In 2007, standardized tests of science were to be added to the mix.

Some psychologists and educators oppose such mass testing on principle. Others, however, believe the tests could be beneficial, but only if they are well designed and fairly used. According to the APA's Code of Fair Testing Practices in Education, professionals are obliged

> to provide and use tests that are fair to all test takers regardless of age, gender, disability, race, ethnicity, national origin, religion, sexual orientation, linguistic background, and other personal characteristics . . . Fairness implies that every test taker has the opportunity to prepare for the test and is informed about the general nature and content of the test, as appropriate to the purpose of the test. Fairness also extends to the accurate reporting of individual and group test results.

Such issues are obviously very important to students, whose lives may be negatively affected by unfair or misleading test scores. Another concern for students is the possibility that high-stakes group testing may produce "teaching to the test." In other words, schools and teachers may start focusing on the narrow range of skills assessed by the test in order to raise scores, while neglecting other equally important areas of study. When this happens, it is students who are the ultimate losers, since they may miss out on the benefits of a well-rounded education.

The flip side of this issue is the question of whether students who take test preparation classes can substantially raise their test scores. Experts differ in their estimation of how much such classes really help. FairTest claims, however, that a good coaching program can raise an individual student's scores by 100 points or more. Since many such programs offered by private companies are quite expensive, FairTest believes that this adds an element of income bias to the SAT. It also implies, however, that use of a test preparation service—whether it is a pricey class or a free tutoring program—may give students an edge on the test.

Primate research

Research   While group intelligence testing was an important sidelight in Yerkes's career, animal research was really his central focus. In particular, Yerkes broke new ground by establishing the first U.S. laboratory exclusively for the study of nonhuman primates. This accomplishment opened the door to future psychological and medical research in apes and monkeys.

Today, the Yerkes laboratory is one of eight National Primate Research Centers funded by the National Institutes of Health. The goal of these centers is to establish nonhuman primate models of human health and disease for biomedical research. All of the current centers are affiliated with academic institutions. They are devoted to primate research related to major human diseases, such as AIDS, cancer, Alzheimer's disease, Parkinson's disease, and cardiovascular disease. At the Yerkes National Primate Research Center, current research interests include aging, AIDS, drug addiction, malaria, Parkinson's disease, transplantation, and vision disorders. They also include primate evolution and social behavior—two subjects that have long been at the core of comparative psychology.

The evolutionary studies currently being done at the Yerkes center make use of the latest tools and techniques to compare humans with chimpanzees. Some studies use modern technologies that would astonish Yerkes, including sophisticated brain imaging techniques and computer-based tests of learning and memory. The center also makes use of genomic mapping to identify differences in DNA among primate species. It turns out that human nuclear DNA is 98.4% identical to that of chimpanzees.

Some studies of social behavior use advanced neuroscientific techniques to study behavior at the molecular and cellular level. The goal is to learn more about the nerve cell mechanisms underlying social behaviors. Conversely, the researchers also hope to understand how social experience may affect the anatomy and physiology of the developing brain.

As valuable as these techniques are, however, they will never replace careful observations of animals under more natural circumstances. Observational studies are still a cornerstone of comparative research. Yerkes's scientists are also conducting studies of the complex social structure of ape society. It appears that apes and humans have a lot in common when it comes

to their social psychology, including their tendency toward both aggression and social cohesiveness. Chimpanzees even have their own version of "you scratch my back, and I'll scratch yours." Scientists have noted that one chimpanzee will sometimes do a favor for another in exchange for favors received, a process known by researchers as reciprocal exchange.

Case studies   Among the most fascinating published case reports are studies of apes born at the Yerkes Field Station. For example, American psychologist Sue Savage-Rumbaugh has studied language ability in bonobos. She is best known for her work with Kanzi, the first ape to learn language in the same manner as human children.

Kanzi was born in 1980. He was raised by a female bonobo named Matata. The pair came to the Georgia State University Language Research Center when Kanzi was six months old. For the next two years, researchers worked every day with Matata, trying to teach her to communicate with lexigrams, symbols that were composed of shapes and lines presented on a keyboard. Kanzi was always with his mother, but he did not seem particularly interested in the lessons. Meanwhile, Matata was making very slow progress, and the researchers were becoming discouraged.

When Kanzi was two-and-a-half years old, the Yerkes center requested that he be weaned from his mother so that Matata could be returned to the field station for a brief visit. While his mother was gone, Kanzi unexpectedly began using the lexigrams on her keyboard. Although he had never before shown any sign of interest in the lexigrams, he had apparently learned to connect them with both the objects in his world and the spoken English words that the symbols represented. This was the first time that an ape had ever been shown to match specific words spoken by a trainer to corresponding symbols. The fact that Kanzi had accomplished this without specific training was quite remarkable.

Kanzi's keyboard originally had just 10 lexigrams. Gradually, however, the researchers began adding new symbols and using them in conversations with Kanzi. Gestures, pictures, videotapes, and activities were all used to help the animal learn to associate the right words with the lexigrams. The researchers claim that Kanzi eventually learned to understand 500 words and use more than 200 lexigrams on his keyboard. These claims are backed up by studies done under controlled conditions.

Yerkes would undoubtedly have been very gratified by such innovative primate research. His own contribution has by no means been forgotten. In a tribute to the

FURTHER ANALYSIS:

Harlow's monkey infant experiment

Harry Harlow (1905–81) was an American comparative psychologist who made his mark by studying mother love in monkeys. In 1930, Harlow joined the faculty at the University of Wisconsin, where he established the Psychology Primate Laboratory. At the time, it was widely believed that humans and other social animals lived in organized groups mainly for the purpose of regular sexual contact. Harlow had a different idea: that mother love and social ties might also be important.

In 1957, Harlow began working with rhesus monkeys, which are more mature at birth than human infants, but which nonetheless are similar in development. In a series of landmark studies, Harlow separated young rhesus monkeys from their natural mothers, giving them instead two artificial substitutes: one made of wire, and the other made of cloth. Even when the wire "mother" was outfitted with a bottle for feeding, the infant monkeys showed a clear preference for cuddling with the softer cloth "mother," especially when they were scared. In related studies, Harlow showed that monkeys who were deprived of maternal contact and comfort as infants grew up to be poor mothers themselves.

Harlow also showed that young monkeys who were raised with real mothers and young peers naturally learned to play and get along with other monkeys. Those that were raised with real mothers but no young playmates were often fearful or inappropriately aggressive, while those raised without either real mothers or peers were socially inept and often unsuccessful at mating as adults. Taken as a whole, Harlow concluded that his studies showed that society was not based on sex alone. He also found that mother love by itself was not enough to help a youngster grow up to be socially competent. Instead, normal parenting and mating behavior as adults depended on both healthy maternal and peer contacts early in life.

Harry Harlow holding a rhesus monkey. (UW Harlow Primate Laboratory—The University of Wisconsin. Reproduced by permission.)

center that bears his name, Savage-Rumbaugh and her colleagues have dubbed the lexigram language "Yerkish."

Relevance to modern readers   Nonhuman primates are humans' closest relatives in the animal world. As a result, they share many characteristics with humans, including complex communication systems, long-lasting social relationships, and the use of tools. Studying the psychology of nonhuman primates can teach people about their own psychological nature (see accompanying sidebar).

Humans and nonhuman primates also share a similar physiology. By studying the brains of monkeys and apes, researchers have gained insight into how the human brain works. In addition, primate research has been crucial to understanding biological processes, such as reproduction, and medical conditions, such as AIDS and addiction. Over the years, primates have also been used in Nobel Prize-winning research; some of these studies have resulted in a yellow fever vaccine (1951), a polio vaccine (1954), and key discoveries about visual processing in the brain (1981).

One continuing concern is the ethical treatment of animals used for research purposes. Several safeguards have been put in place to help prevent abuses, however. Four federal government agencies—the U.S. Department of Agriculture, the U.S. Public Health Service, the National Research Council, and the Food and Drug Administration—regulate different aspects of animal research. In addition, the APA has issued its own Guidelines for Ethical Conduct in the Care and Use of Animals. According to these guidelines, "psychologists should conduct their teaching and research in a manner consonant with relevant laws and regulations. In addition, ethical concerns mandate that psychologists should consider the costs and benefits of procedures involving animals before proceeding with the research."

When these high standards are met, primate research can be of great benefit to both psychology and society at large. No single individual has had a greater impact on primate research in the United States than Yerkes. It is fitting that his namesake laboratory continues to carry on the work that was dearest to his heart. In an autobiographical essay written around the same time that his primate lab opened, Yerkes wrote:

> It is as if I am now on the threshold of a great undertaking which from the first was dimly envisaged and later planned for with increasing definiteness and assurance . . . It promises the fulfillment of my persistent dream for the progress of comparative psychology and the enhancement of its values to

mankind through the wise utilization of anthropoid apes and other primates as subjects of experimental inquiry.

BIBLIOGRAPHY

Sources

American Psychological Association Committee on Animal Research and Ethics. *Guidelines for Ethical Conduct in the Care and Use of Animals.* 2004 [cited May 18, 2004]. http://www.apa.org/science/anguide.html.

American Psychological Association Joint Committee on Testing Practices. *Code of Fair Testing Practices in Education.* 2004 [cited May 18, 2004]. http://www.apa.org/science/fairtestcode.html.

Burkhardt, Richard W. Jr. "The *Journal of Animal Behavior* and the Early History of Animal Behavior Studies in America." *Journal of Comparative Psychology* 101 (1987) 223–30.

Christianson, Sven-Åke. "Emotional Stress and Eyewitness Memory: A Critical Review." *Psychological Bulletin* 112 (1992) 284–309.

Dewsbury, Donald A. "Comparative Psychology and Ethology: A Reassessment." *American Psychologist* 47 (1992) 208–15.

Dewsbury, Donald A. *Comparative Psychology in the Twentieth Century.* Stroudsburg, PA: Hutchinson Ross Publishing Company, 1984.

Dewsbury, Donald A. "Issues in Comparative Psychology at the Dawn of the 20th Century." *American Psychologist* 55 (2000) 750–53.

Dewsbury, Donald A. "Robert M. Yerkes: A Psychobiologist With a Plan." In Gregory A. Kimble, C. Alan Boneau, and Michael Wertheimer, eds. *Portraits of Pioneers in Psychology, Volume 2.* Washington, DC: American Psychological Association, 1996.

Dewsbury, Donald A. "Robert Yerkes, Sex Research, and the Problem of Data Simplification." *History of Psychology* 1 (1998) 116–29.

Fancher, Raymond E. *The Intelligence Men: Makers of the IQ Controversy.* New York: W. W. Norton, 1985.

Gould, Stephen Jay. *The Mismeasure of Man.* Rev. ed. New York: W. W. Norton, 1996.

Herschberger, Ruth. *Adam's Rib.* New York: Harper and Row, 1948.

Plucker, Jonathan. *Robert Mearns Yerkes.* Indiana University. 2003 [cited May 18, 2004]. http://www.indiana.edu/~intell/yerkes.shtml.

Winton, Ward M. "Do Introductory Textbooks Present the Yerkes-Dodson Law Correctly?" *American Psychologist* 42 (1987) 202–3.

Yerkes, Robert Mearns. "Autobiography of Robert Mearns Yerkes." In Carl Murchison, ed. *History of Psychology in Autobiography, Volume 2.* Worcester, MA: Clark University Press, 1930, 381–407.

Yerkes, Robert Mearns. *Chimpanzees: A Laboratory Colony.* New Haven, CT: Yale University Press, 1943.

Yerkes, Robert Mearns and John D. Dodson. "The Relation of Strength of Stimulus to Rapidity of Habit-Formation." *Journal of Comparative Neurology and Psychology* 18 (1908) 459–82.

Yerkes, Robert Mearns and Sergius Morgulis. "The Method of Pavlov in Animal Psychology." *Psychological Bulletin* 6 (1909) 257–73.

Further readings

American Society of Primatologists. 2004 [cited May 18, 2004]. http://www.asp.org.

CARE: APA Board of Scientific Affairs, Committee on Animal Research and Ethics. American Psychological Association. 2004 [cited May 18, 2004]. http://www.apa.org/science/resethicsCARE.html.

College Board. 2004 [cited May 18, 2004]. http://collegeboard.com.

Georgia State University Language Research Center. 2004 [cited May 18, 2004]. http://www.gsu.edu/~wwwlrc.

Green, Christopher D., ed. *Classics in the History of Psychology.* York University [cited May 18, 2004]. http://psychclassics.yorku.ca.

Goodall, Jane. *Through a Window: My Thirty Years With the Chimpanzees of Gombe.* Reissue. Boston: Houghton Mifflin, 2000.

Jane Goodall Institute. 2004 [cited May 18, 2004]. http://www.janegoodall.com.

Murphy, Kevin R., and Charles O. Davidshofer. *Psychological Testing: Principles and Applications,* 5th ed. Upper Saddle River, NJ: Prentice-Hall, 2000.

National Center for Fair and Open Testing. 2004 [cited May 18, 2004]. http://fairtest.org.

National Primate Research Centers. National Institutes of Health. 2004 [cited May 18, 2004]. http://www.ncrr.nih.gov/compmed/cm_nprc.asp.

Primate Info Net. Wisconsin Primate Research Center, University of Wisconsin-Madison. 2004 [cited May 18, 2004]. http://www.primate.wisc.edu/pin.

Savage-Rumbaugh, Sue and Roger Lewin. *Kanzi: The Ape at the Brink of the Human Mind.* New York: John Wiley and Sons, 1994.

Secrets of the SAT. PBS Frontline. 1999 [cited May 18, 2004]. http://www.pbs.org/wgbh/pages/frontline/shows/sats.

Testing and Assessment. American Psychological Association. 2004 [cited May 18, 2004]. http://www.apa.org/science/testing.html.

Yerkes National Primate Research Center. Emory University. 2002 [cited May 18, 2004]. http://www.emory.edu/WHSC/YERKES.

Glossary
and Index

Glossary

A

accommodation: one of Piaget's two poles (with assimilation) of an adaptive interaction between the organism and the environment to incorporate new knowledge. Accommodation is the action that bends the organism to the successive constraints of the environment, modifying existing schemes to fit new experiences.

active imagination: a method used in Jungian analysis to help patients integrate material from the personal and collective unconscious through art, writing, or similar forms of self-expression.

actualizing tendency: in Rogerian theory, a life-force common among all living things to do good things. Also called "core tendency."

adaptation: one of the two (with organization) basic invariants of biological and intellectual functioning. Adaptation has two interrelated parts, assimilation and accommodation. Adaptation occurs whenever an organism-environment interchange modifies the organism in a way favorable to its preservation.

anal stage: the second stage in Sigmund Freud's theory of psychosexual development characterized by concerns over elimination, usually taking place around two years of age.

analytical psychology: Jung's name for his clinical approach to psychotherapy, which focuses on achieving psychological wholeness by coming to terms with the personal and collective unconscious.

anima/animus: the contrasexual part of a person's psyche, personified as a woman in a man's psyche or a man in a woman's psyche.

animism: attributing notions of life, will and consciousness to inanimate things. Characteristic of the preoperational child, according to Piaget.

archetypes: fundamental patterns or templates arising from the collective unconscious that organize human experience into images or mythic expressions. In classical Jungian analysis, the archetypes are personified as heroes, magicians, gods or goddesses, and other universal images.

artificialism: notion that human beings have made the natural world of mountains, lakes, trees, the moon and the sun, etc.

assimilation: process of changing elements in the environment in such a way that they can be incorporated into the existing biological or intellectual structure or scheme. It is one of Piaget's two poles (with accommodation) of an adaptive interaction between the organism and the environment.

associationism: the view that mental processes can be explained in terms of the association of ideas.

attachment: the bond between an infant in the first year of life and the mother, or other primary caregiver.

attribution theory: a term used to describe how people explain the causes of behavior, both their own and those of others.

authoritarian personality: a personality pattern characterized by rigidity, dependence on authority, conformity to group values, and intolerance of ambiguity.

autohypnosis: the ability to hypnotize oneself without the aid of another person.

avoidance learning: an individual's response to avoid an unpleasant or stressful situation; also known as escape learning.

B

behavior modification: a treatment approach, based on the principles of operant conditioning, that replaces undesirable behaviors with more desirable ones through reinforcements.

behavior therapy: a goal-oriented, therapeutic approach that treats disorders as maladaptive learned responses that can be replaced by healthier ones.

behaviorism: a theory of human development initiated by Edward Thorndike and developed by John Watson and B.F. Skinner, emphasizing the study of measurable and observable behavior.

Bender-Gestalt test: diagnostic assessment test to identify learning disability, neurological disorders, and developmental delay.

Binet-Simon test: intelligence test created by Alfred Binet and Theodore Simon, for European subjects.

C

castration anxiety: the fear of losing one's penis. In Freudian terms, this fear causes the boy to abandon his incestuous attachment to his mother and begin to identify with his father.

catharsis: the release of repressed psychic energy.

centering: the way a child views an object only in relation to its particular function, and focuses only on one aspect at a time. Characteristic of Piaget's preoperational stage.

circular reactions: the repetitive mechanism by which a scheme is developed. The child performs an action, is interested in the result, and repeats the same action again. Characteristic of Piaget's sensorimotor stage.

classical conditioning: the process of closely associating a neutral stimulus with one that evokes a reflexive response so that eventually the neutral stimulus alone will evoke the same response.

client-centered therapy: Rogerian method of psychotherapy in which the client, not the therapist, controls the direction of therapy. Also called people-centered therapy.

clinical psychology: the application of psychological principles to diagnosing and treating persons with emotional and behavioral problems.

cognition: a general term for the higher mental processes by which people acquire knowledge, solve problems, and plan for the future.

cognitive behavior therapy: a therapeutic approach based on the principle that maladaptive moods and behavior can be changed by replacing distorted or inappropriate ways of thinking with thought patterns that are healthier and more realistic.

cognitive dissonance: inconsistency between attitude (or belief) and behavior.

cognitive psychology: an approach to psychology that focuses on the relationship between cognitive or mental processes and behavior.

cognitive therapy: beck's approach to psychotherapy that focuses on helping individuals understand the relationships between their thoughts and and subsequent behavior.

collaborative empiricism: underlying fundamental of Beck's method of psychotherapy in which the therapist works together with the patient to uncover the specific underlying assumptions that trigger the patient's emotional pain and motivational difficulties.

collective unconscious: Jung's term for an unconscious common to all human beings underlying the personal unconscious. The collective unconscious is the source of archetypes and common mythologies.

combat neurosis: mental disturbances related to the stress of military combat. Today called post-traumatic stress disorder.

comparative psychology: a subfield of experimental psychology that focuses on the study of animals for the purpose of comparing the behavior of different species.

compensation: a defense mechanism in which an individual unconsciously develops or overdevelops one area of personality as substitutive behavior to make up for a deficiency or inferiority in another area.

concept formation: learning process by which items are categorized and related to each other.

concrete operational stage: third stage of Jean Piaget's theory of cognitive development. At this stage, children begin to develop clearer methods of thinking, although they have difficulty conceiving abstract thought.

conditioned response: behavior that is learned in response to a particular stimulus.

conditioned stimulus: stimulus that leads to a learned response.

consciousness: awareness of external stimuli and of one's own mental activity.

conservation: the understanding that certain objects or quantities will remain the same even when there is a change in physical appearance. Conservation of number, length, liquid, area, weight, and volume develop sequentially throughout the concrete operations stage, according to Piaget.

construct: in Kelly's theory, the mental patterns that people build as a way of understanding their world. We live, work, and interpret new information through these constructs, building on them as new information is gained.

constructive alternativism: Kelly's theory that there is no objectivity, or absolute truth, in determining the reality of a situation. The meaning of all that happens in a person's life emerges from the way in which that person interprets it.

continuity hypothesis: Beck's theory that human behaviors can be placed at various points along a continuum instead of being divided sharply into "normal" and "pathological" behaviors.

counterconditioning: weakening or eliminating an undesired response by introducing and strengthening a second response that is incompatible with it.

covert conditioning: a method for changing behavior that involves the client using imagination to target unwanted behavior.

cross-cultural psychology: a subfield of psychology concerned with observing human behavior in contrasting cultures.

cross-sectional study: research that collects data simultaneously from people of different ages.

D

defense mechanisms: unconscious strategies for avoiding or reducing threatening feelings such as fear and anxiety.

dependent variable: variable measured in an experiment or study; what the experimenter measures.

derealization: type of dissociation in which a person perceives reality in a grossly distorted way.

desensitization: behavioral modification technique in which undesired behavior, such as anxiety, is paired with another response that is incompatible with it, such as relaxation.

developmental psychology: the study of the ways in which people develop physically, emotionally, intellectually, and socially over the course of their lives.

Diagnostic and Statistical Manual of Mental Disorders (DSM-IV): a reference work developed by the American Psychiatric Association and designed to provide guidelines for the diagnosis and classification of mental disorders.

diencephalon: located above the brainstem, the site of the thalamus and hypothalamus.

differential psychology: the area of psychology concerned with measuring and comparing differences in individual and group behavior.

displacement: a defense mechanism in which an unacceptable impulse, such as aggression, is redirected to something more acceptable, such as participating in a boxing match.

E

ego: in psychoanalytic theory, the part of human personality that combines innate biological impulses (id) or drives with reality to produce appropriate behavior. The ego includes psychological processes concerned with one's self-image.

egocentrism: a cognitive limitation wherein people (usually children) fail to understand how someone else's point of view might be different form their own, or a failure to coordinate one's point of view with another's perspective.

emotional intelligence: the ability to perceive and constructively act on both one's own emotions and the feelings of others.

empiricism: type of research that is based on direct observation.

equilibration: as used by Piaget, self-regulatory developmental process in which new environmental events are assimilated into existing cognitive structures, and existing structures are transformed to fit new environmental situations to restore cognitive balance.

ethology: the study of animal behavior as observed in the natural environment and in the context of evolutionary adaptation.

eugenics: the systematic attempt to increase desirable genetic traits and to decrease undesirable ones in a population.

experimental design: careful and detailed plan of an experiment.

experimenter bias: the subtle and unintentional influence of the experimenter on the subjects in an experiment.

exposure-response prevention: a behavioral treatment technique in which a person is exposed to an anxiety-producing event and kept from responding in an undesirable manner.

extinction: the elimination of a conditioned response by withholding reinforcement.

F

field theory: as defined by Lewin, a way of looking at the human mind as a complex energy field containing tension systems in various states of equilibrium, or balance. Human behavior represents a change in the state of this energy field.

figure-ground perception: the ability to visually differentiate between a sensory stimulation and its background.

formal operations stage: the fourth stage in Piaget's theory of cognitive development characterized by a person's ability to reason about abstract concepts.

free association: first used in psychoanalysis, a way to retrieve unconscious thoughts from patients by having them respond to a list of words by freely say with what they associate that word.

frequency distribution: systematic representation of data, arranged so that the observed frequency of occurrence of data falling within certain ranges, classes, or categories is shown.

fully functioning person: in Rogerian theory, a mentally healthy person.

G

genetic epistemology: psychological study of species behavior pioneered by Jean Piaget that attempts to explain knowledge, and in particular scientific knowledge, on the basis of its history, its sociogenesis, and especially the psychological origins of the notions and mental operations on which it is based.

genital stage: the fifth and last stage in Sigmund Freud's theory of psychosexual development in which a person's sexual drives are increased and parental attachments are dissolved.

Gestalt psychology: a field of psychology that emphasizes the study of experience and behavior as wholes rather than independently functioning, disparate parts.

H

hierarchy of needs: theory of human motivation developed by Abraham Maslow that emphasizes developing one's full potential. The hierarchy is depicted as a pyramid with five levels, ranging from the most basic needs at the bottom to the most complex and sophisticated at the top.

human potential movement: a movement that focuses on helping people achieve their full potential through an eclectic combination of therapeutic methods and discipline.

humanistic psychology: a theoretical and therapeutic approach that emphasizes people's uniqueness and their power to control their own destinies.

hypnosis: a temporary narrowing of conscious awareness.

I

id: in psychoanalytic theory, the most primitive, unconscious element of human personality.

identification: a type of defense mechanism in which a person takes on the characteristics of someone else.

individual psychology: today called differential psychology, Alfred Adler's theory that emphasizes individual differences in behavior.

individuation: the process by which a person becomes a single integrated being; self-realization. Individuation is the goal of Jungian psychotherapy.

imprinting: a type of learning characteristic of fowls that occurs only during a critical period of development soon after birth.

intellectualization: a type of defense mechanism in which a person detaches himself from a painful or anxiety-producing situation by dealing with it solely in intellectual, abstract terms and ignoring its emotional components.

intelligence: active, organized process of assimilating the new to the old and accommodating the old to the new through which one's mental mode of understanding, or the schemes one has constructed, are changed to make room for the new information.

IQ: a single number for expressing overall result of an intelligence test.

J

just community: Kohlberg's method of encouraging moral development by letting members of a community to collectively decide their own moral norms.

L

latency stage: the fourth stage in Freud's theory of psychosexual development, in which a person's sexuality is dormant and his or her attentions are focused outside the family.

learned helplessness: an apathetic attitude stemming from the conviction that one's actions do not have the power to affect one's situation.

learning theory: theory about how people learn and modify pre-existing thoughts and behavior.

locomotions: in Lewin's terms, the psychological movements people tend to make toward entities in their life space that have a strong positive valence, and away from those with a negative valence.

longitudinal study: research method used to study changes over time.

M

mandala: a circular painting or symbol, typically divided into four sections or quadrants, that represents the center or the self. Jung encouraged his patients to paint mandalas as part of the process of active imagination.

metapsychology: general term used to describe the attempt to establish principles to explain all psychological phenomena. Also called meta-analysis.

midbrain: also called mesencephalon, the small area near the lower middle of the brain that controls smooth and reflexive movements and regulates attention, sleep, and arousal.

moral development: the process of how people come to incorporate society's ideas of right and wrong into their own mental patterns. Kohlberg postulated six stages of moral development.

multiple intelligences: Howard Gardner's theory that people may have eight different types of intelligence.

N

narcissism: excessive preoccupation with self and lack of empathy for others.

neurosis: term used to describe conditions involving anxiety or psychological distress.

neurotic need: Horney's theory that people with neurosis have 10 unrealistic psychological needs that they use extreme measures to fulfill.

O

object constancy: a cognitive skill where the infant perceives that the same object will continue to be the same no matter what its position or the perspective from which she may view the object.

object permanence: a cognitive skill where the child perceives an object or other's continued existence even when it is removed from the perceptual field. Object permanency is a developmental task of the preoperational child, in Piaget's stages.

Oedipus complex: theory set forth by Sigmund Freud that children are torn between feelings of love for one parent while feeling a sense of competition with the other.

ontogenesis: the sequence of developmental events in the history of an individual organism as it moves from simplicity to higher complexity.

operant conditioning: approach to human learning based on the premise that human intelligence and will operate on the environment rather than merely respond to the environment's stimuli.

operations: the actions that take place in the mind rather than in the physical environment, as used by Piaget.

oral stage: the first stage in Sigmund Freud's theory of psychosexual development in which a child is primarily concerned with gratification through sucking.

P

parallel play: type of play in which young children play together, but each child is involved in her own world of play, with its own rules. Characteristic of Piaget's preoperational stage of development.

penis envy: according to Freud, a girl's wish for a penis; she blames her mother for depriving her of a penis and desires her father because he possesses one.

perception: area of psychology associated with the functioning of sensory systems and how information from the external world is interpreted.

perceptual distortion: in Rogerian theory, a defense mechanism in which a person re-interprets reality to reduce their psychological stress.

persona: a person's outward social "face," or manner of dealing with the world.

personal construct psychology: Kelly's psychology, in which a psychological test, known as the repertory grid , provides people with different ways of examining their unconscious mind, and along with that the typical human behaviors such as anxiety, guilt, creativity, aggression, and depression, among others. In this way, patients could evaluate themselves and reveal their own cognitive processes.

phallic stage: the third stage in Freud's theory of psychosexual development in which a child experiences and resolves the Oedipal crisis and assumes his or her sexual identity.

phenomenological therapy: also called humanistic therapy, an approach emphasizing a close, supportive relationship between the client and the therapist. Two well-known forms of phenomenological therapy are client-centered therapy and Gestalt therapy.

phylogeny: the history of genealogical development of a species.

post-traumatic stress disorder (PTSD): a psychological disorder that develops in response to an extremely traumatic event that threatens a person's safety or life.

preconscious: according to Sigmund Freud, that part of the human mind that lies between the conscious and the unconscious, which can be accessed and brought into consciousness without the use of special techniques.

preoperational stage: the second stage in Jean Piaget's theory of cognitive development characterized by egocentrism, centration, and irreversibility in thought.

psyche: Greek word meaning the mind. A person's mental self.

psychoanalysis: a method of treatment developed by Sigmund Freud that emphasizes thorough examination of a person's unconscious motivations, feelings, and relationships.

psychometrics: the design and analysis of research, resulting in the measurement of human characteristics (psychological testing).

psychosexual stages: stages of development described by Sigmund Freud that focuses on the location of sexual impulses at different ages.

psychosis: a symptom of mental illness characterized by a radical change in personality and a distorted or diminished sense of objective reality.

psychotherapy the treatment of mental or emotional disorders through the use of psychological techniques rather than through physical or biological means.

R

rational-emotive behavior therapy: a mode of treatment developed by Albert Ellis in which a client is challenged to examine his or her irrational beliefs and taught to think more rationally with the goal of reducing emotional problems.

rationalization: a type of defense mechanism in which a person gives an intellectual reason or rationale for an emotionally motivated action in order to assign socially acceptable motives to one's behavior or to mask disappointment.

reaction formation: a type of defense mechanism in which a person deals with unacceptable feelings by adopting diametrically opposite ones.

reflection of feelings: method used in Rogerian therapy in which the therapist encourages the client to interpret thoughts or events by various methods, as the phrase "How do you feel about that?"

regression: a type of defense mechanism in which a person reverts to behavior characteristic of an earlier period of life in order to gain access to the sources of gratification experienced during that period.

reinforcement: a stimulus that increases the probability that a particular behavior will occur.

repression: a principal defense mechanism in which a person selectively forgets disturbing material.

Rorschach technique: popularly known as the "Inkblot Test," a widely used projective psychological test used to assess personality structure and identify emotional problems.

S

scheme: a term defined by Piaget as the basic unit of knowledge that a person uses to organize past experiences and to understand new ones. A cognitive map of organized action. Sometimes called "schema." In Beck's theory, schemes are stable patterns of thinking, of which there are five types.

Scholastic Assessment Test: series of tests used to measure verbal and mathematical abilities and achievement in specific subject areas.

self-actualization: the final and most complex step in Abraham Maslow's hierarchy of human motives, encompassing the basic need for self-fulfillment.

self-conscious emotions: emotions such as guilt, pride, shame, and hubris.

sensorimotor stage: the first stage in Jean Piaget's theory of cognitive development characterized by a child's ability to grasp properties of objects and the concept of object constancy.

sensory deprivation: an experimental procedure involving prolonged reduction of sensory stimuli.

shadow: the "dark" side of the personality; elements that have been shut out of the conscious ego because of the patient's fear of parental or social disapproval. In Jungian thought, the shadow appears in dreams as a member of one's own sex.

shaping: a gradual behavior modification technique in which successive approximations to the desired behavior is rewarded.

significance level: a method to describe the reliability of test results.

Skinner box: a specially used cage with levers for releasing food used to condition animals.

social learning theory: a theory that posits that people learn behavior by copying "models" and receiving reinforcements.

social referencing: the process by which infants seek out and interpret the emotional responses of their parents to form their own emotional understanding of unfamiliar events, objects, or persons.

Stanford-Binet intelligence scales: test developed by Binet and modified for an American audience by Lewis Terman at Stanford University. It is still widely used.

strange situation: a research technique developed by Mary Ainsworth and used in the assessment of attachments.

stranger anxiety: fear of people with whom a child is not familiar.

structuralism: Wundt's approach to experimental psychological testing, in which each stimulus is experienced by the mind as separate from all others. Also called elementalism.

sublimations: a type of defense mechanism in which unacceptable impulse is diverted to a more appropriate or socially acceptable form. It differs from displacement in that sublimations are generally associated with the conversion of impulses to scientific, artistic, and other creative or intellectual activities.

superego: in psychoanalytic theory, the part of the human personality that represents a person's inner values and morals; also known as conscience.

symbolic imitation: child's play that incorporates a pretend or symbolic object in imitative play.

synchronicity: Jung's term for meaningful coincidences that have no apparent causal relationship.

T

temperament: an individual's characteristic emotional nature, including energy level, prevailing mood, and sensitivity to stimuli.

transference: the tendency of clients to transfer to the therapist their emotional responses to significant people in their lives.

U

unconditioned response: response that is natural and not learned, such as jerking the hand from a hot stove.

unconditioned stimulus: stimulus that naturally elicits behavior, such as food.

unconscious: the part of the mind whose contents people resist bringing into awareness.

V

valence: in Lewin's terms, the psychological value of something or someone. A positive valence satisfies a need and is sought after. A negative valence is avoided.

validity (in testing): term used in testing to describe tests that measure what they are intended to measure.

W

Wechsler intelligence scales: developed by David Wechsler, a series of intelligence tests encompassing both verbal and nonverbal abilities.

Index

The volume number is the number to the left of the colon. Page numbers are to the right of the colon. Page numbers in boldface refer to the primary article about a subject. Italicized page numbers indicate an illustration on the page. Display materials such as graphs, charts, figures or tables are indicated by the letters g, f, t or c.

synchronicity, 1:215–216
  see also Jung, Carl Gustaf
systematic desensitization, 2:341, 424
Szeminsa, Alina, 2:350

T

T groups, 2:290–291
tachistoscope, 2:430, 442
Takahashi, K., 1:13
Takooshian, Harold, 1:18, 26
talk therapy. *See* cognitive therapy
"talking cure" or "talking therapy",
  1:162, 171
  see also psychoanalytic theory
Tanenari, Chiba, 2:453
tape-recording, 2:382, 393
taste aversion therapy, 2:341
TAT (thematic apperception test), 1:3,
  204, 2:396
Tavistock Clinic, 1:4, 9
Taylor, Jeremy, 1:227
teaching machines, 2:406–407, 421
team-building programs, 2:301
technical action research, 2:296, 301
  see also Lewin, Kurt
The Technology of Teaching (Skinner),
  2:406–407
telepathy, 1:215
television violence, 1, 61–62
  see also aggression
temperament types. *See* Pavlov, Ivan
  Petrovich; personality types
tension systems, 2:285–287
Terman, Lewis, 1:94, 106–107,
  108–110, 116, 2:476
Terry, W.S., 1:34
Testing Problems in Perspective
  (Anastasi), 1:19
Thanatos (death instinct), 1:155
Thandeka, 1:139
thematic apperception test (TAT), 1:3,
  204, 2:396
Theoretische Biologie (von Uexküll),
  1:244
"A Theory of Human Motivation"
  (Maslow), 2:315
A Theory of Justice (Rawls), 1:271
Theory X, 2:321
therapist qualities and role, 1:188, 213,
  2:382–383
thinking *vs.* feeling, 1:212
Thomas, Hobart "Red", 2:380, 381
Thomas J. Watson Research Center,
  1:276
Thompson, Clara, 1:182, 183, 196
Thorndike, Edward L., 1:306, 2:389,
  392–393, 414, 485
"A Threat in the Air: How Stereotypes
  Shape the Intellectual Identities
  and Performance of Women and
  African Americans" (Steele),
  1:140

Three Essays on the Theory of Sexuality
  (Freud), 1:146
Thurstone, Louis L., 1:27–28, 31,
  111–112
time-and-motion-studies, 2:465
Titchener, E.B., 2:390, 440, 448, 462,
  465
Titchener's Textbook of Psychology
  (Titchener), 2:390, 440
Tolman, Edward, 2:279, 294–295, 339,
  360, 415
topological psychology, 2:284, 293
  see also Lewin, Kurt
Toward a Psychology of Being
  (Maslow), 1:317, 2:307
*Toward Neutral Principles of
  Constitutional Law* (H.
  Wechsler), 1:134
toys, 2:367
training groups, 2, 290–291
transference, 1:167–168, 171–172, 188
trauma, 1:248, 2:329
*Treatment Choice in Psychological
  Therapies and Counselling*
  (British National Health
  Service), 1:80
tree diagrams, 2:458
"On Truth" (Wertheimer), 2:425
Tryon, R.C., 1:22
Tsion, Ilya Fadeevich, 2:327
Turiel, Elliott, 1:269, 272
Turkle, Sherry, 2:367
Twelve Step groups, 1:80
twin studies, 1:23–24
"two-factor" theory of intelligence, 1:17
"A Two-Year-Old Goes to Hospital"
  (Bowlby, Robertson film), 1:9
Tyrell, Mark, 1:198

U

"Über Coca" Freud), 1:152
Uexküll, Jakob von, 1:244
Uganda field studies (attachment
  theory), 1:2, 12–13
Uncommon Knowledge, Ltd (Tyrell),
  1:198
unconditioned reflexes, 2:331
unconscious (as component of the
  mind), 1:155, 156, 162, 165
Understanding Psychology (Kelly),
  1:233
"Understanding Psychotics' Speech"
  (Wertheimer), 2:433
UNESCO (United Nations Educational,
  Scientific and Cultural
  Organization), 2:350, 351
"Unfinished Business: Toll of Psychic
  Violence" (Clark), 1:132
universities for psychology research.
  See research institutions
University of Berlin, 2:281, 286,
  428, 430

University of California at Berkeley,
  1:12, 245
University of California at Los Angeles,
  1:137
University of Chicago, 1:50, 255, 268,
  2:364, 390, 485
University of Chicago Counseling
  Center, 2:394–396
University of Geneva, 2:349, 350–351
University of Illinois, 1:244
University of Iowa, 1:41, 51–52, 52, 232
*University of Iowa Studies in Child
  Welfare* (Lewin, Dembo, Barker),
  2:299, 301
University of Minnesota, 1:12, 50,
  115–116, 2:395
University of Paris, 1:96–98
University of Pennsylvania, 1:28, 69,
  70, 86, 138
University of Regensburg, 1:12
University of Toronto, 1:3, 3–4, 8
University of Vienna, 1:191
University of Virginia, 1:4–5
University of Wisconsin, 1:7, 2:303,
  305–306, 494
Upham, Thomas, 1:288–289

V

v-chip, 1:61–62
Vaihinger, Hans, 1:231, 241
valence, 2:284
Varela, Francisco, 1:244
Varieties of Religious Experience
  (James), 2:464
vicarious function (in structuralism),
  2:455–456
vicarious learning, 1:39
  see also observational learning
Viennese Psychological Society, 1:154
violation of expectation (VOE) tasks,
  2:363
violence, 1:49–50
  see also aggression
virtual reality therapy (VRT), 2:342
virtue, 1:259–260
visual psychology, 2:428, 430
VOE (violation of expectation) tasks,
  2:363
volition system (in structuralism), 2:458
Volkerpsychologie (Folk Psychology)
  (Wundt), 2:453, 457
Voneche, Jacques, 2:360–361
VRT (virual reality therapy), 2:342
Vygotsky, Lev, 2:340, 360, 361–363

W

Wahba, Mahmoud, 2:318–319
WAIS (Wechsler Adult Intelligence
  Scale), 1:113